KU-107-302

GLOBALIZATION

The Making of World Society

Frank J. Lechner

WILEY-BLACKWELL

A John Wiley & Sons, Ltd., Publication

This edition first published 2009
© 2009 by Frank J. Lechner

Blackwell Publishing was acquired by John Wiley & Sons in February 2007. Blackwell's publishing program has been merged with Wiley's global Scientific, Technical, and Medical business to form Wiley-Blackwell.

Registered Office
John Wiley & Sons Ltd, The Atrium, Southern Gate, Chichester, West Sussex, PO19 8SQ, United Kingdom

Editorial Offices
350 Main Street, Malden, MA 02148-5020, USA
9600 Garsington Road, Oxford, OX4 2DQ, UK
The Atrium, Southern Gate, Chichester, West Sussex, PO19 8SQ, UK

For details of our global editorial offices, for customer services, and for information about how to apply for permission to reuse the copyright material in this book please see our website at www.wiley.com/wiley-blackwell.

The right of Frank J. Lechner to be identified as the author of this work has been asserted in accordance with the Copyright, Designs and Patents Act 1988.

All rights reserved. No part of this publication may be reproduced, stored in a retrieval system, or transmitted, in any form or by any means, electronic, mechanical, photocopying, recording or otherwise, except as permitted by the UK Copyright, Designs and Patents Act 1988, without the prior permission of the publisher.

Wiley also publishes its books in a variety of electronic formats. Some content that appears in print may not be available in electronic books.

Designations used by companies to distinguish their products are often claimed as trademarks. All brand names and product names used in this book are trade names, service marks, trademarks or registered trademarks of their respective owners. The publisher is not associated with any product or vendor mentioned in this book. This publication is designed to provide accurate and authoritative information in regard to the subject matter covered. It is sold on the understanding that the publisher is not engaged in rendering professional services. If professional advice or other expert assistance is required, the services of a competent professional should be sought.

Library of Congress Cataloging-in-Publication Data
Lechner, Frank J.
    Globalization : the making of world society / Frank J. Lechner.
        p. cm.
    Includes bibliographical references and index.
    ISBN 978-1-4051-6906-6 (hardcover : alk. paper) – ISBN 978-1-4051-6905-9 (pbk. : alk. paper)   1. Globalization.   I. Title.

JZ1318.L436 2009
303.48'2–dc22

                                                          2008045564

A catalogue record for this book is available from the British Library.

Set in 10.5 on 13pt Minion by SNP Best-set Typesetter Ltd., Hong Kong
Printed in Singapore by C.O.S. Printers Pte Ltd

2   2010

Demelza Jones

GLOBALIZATION

To my children,
Suzanne and Philip

CONTENTS

PLATES

FIGURES

TABLES

BOXES

PREFACE AND ACKNOWLEDGMENTS

For many years, I have taught courses on global change at Emory University in Atlanta. It was and is a pleasure: the subject is rich and fascinating, and most students are eager to learn more about it. Since the topic is complex, even a bit unwieldy, explaining concisely "what globalization is all about" is a challenge. This book tries to meet that challenge. My goal was to write a clear and stimulating text for the students I have taught and hope to teach – and for their peers elsewhere.

Along the way, I also offer colleagues in the field my take on the subject. Some shop talk here and there is part of a virtual conversation with fellow scholars. But there are no academic prerequisites for reading the book. I hope "general" readers who pick it up will find it a trustworthy source on globalization that strikes a middle ground between breezily popular and densely academic work.

I use "globalization" to refer to the ways in which, as more people become more connected across larger distances, they create a new world society in which they do more similar things, affect each other's lives more deeply, follow more of the same norms, and grow more aware of what they share. The book first shows how globalization shapes everyday experience through what we eat, how we play, and what we watch. It then examines how various globalizing institutions, from economic to religious, help to build world society. That world society faces distinct problems, for example in dealing with inequality and the environment, which I discuss in the concluding chapters.

Each chapter introduces an aspect of globalization with an extended example, to show how globalization affects a particular place, issue, or group of people. I put the examples in context by examining major trends and discuss how we can best make sense of those trends, often focusing on a specific question or debate. For convenience, each chapter begins with a list of its main subtopics and ends with questions for further reflection and suggestions for further reading, including both accessible and more scholarly items. A glossary offers definitions of selected terms.

To avoid overloading the text itself with extraneous features, I have revised The Globalization Website (www.wiley.com/go/globalization) – an online resource I put together in the early 2000s – specifically in order to complement the book, including further illustrations, a more elaborate glossary, some technical discussion, additional data, and useful links.

Among the many people who contributed to this book directly or indirectly, I would like to thank a number of Emory students, especially Kali-Ahset Amen, Selina Gallo-Cruz, Jinwon Chung, Gianluca De Fazio, Matt Mathias, Lesley Watson, and several students in the summer 2008 section of Global Change, for their helpful comments on draft chapters. I also thank Roland Robertson for leading the way; John Boli for fruitful collaboration; Amy Benson Brown for stylistic advice; a reviewer for great comments; Ben Thatcher and Justin Vaughan for moving the project along; Claire Creffield, Claire Cameron, and Dave Nash for excellent editing and picture research; my late colleague Harold Berman for being a source of inspiration; and my wife, Jennifer, for her unstinting support.

My children, Suzanne and Philip, did more than anyone to help and distract me. I dedicate this book to them, with all my love.

ACRONYMS

AFL-CIO	American Federation of Labor–Congress of Industrial Organizations
ATTAC	Association pour la Taxation des Transactions financières pour l'Aide aux Citoyennes et Citoyens (Association for the Taxation of Financial Transactions for the Aid of Citizens)
BBC	British Broadcasting Corporation
CCW	Convention on [Prohibitions or Restrictions on the Use of] Certain Conventional Weapons
CEDAW	Convention on the Elimination of All Forms of Discrimination against Women
CFC	Chlorofluorocarbon(s)
CIA	Central Intelligence Agency
CITES	Convention on International Trade in Endangered Species of Wild Fauna and Flora
CNN	Cable News Network
CP	Confédération Paysanne
CPI	Consumer Price Index
CSD	Commission on Sustainable Development
DAWN	Development Alternative with Women for a New Era
DD	Doordarshan
ECOSOC	Economic and Social Council

EU	European Union
FA	Football Association
FAO	Food and Agriculture Organization
FDI	Foreign Direct Investment
FGC	Female Genital Cutting
FIBA	Fédération Internationale de Basketball (originally: Amateur)
FIFA	Fédération Internationale de Football Association
FMLN	Frente Farabundo Martí para la Liberación Nacional (Farabundo Martí National Liberation Front)
FOE	Friends of the Earth
GATT	General Agreement on Tariffs and Trade
GDP	Gross Domestic Product
GHG	Greenhouse Gas
GJM	Global Justice Movement
IAW	International Alliance of Women
ICBL	International Campaign to Ban Landmines
ICC	International Cricket Council
ICC	International Criminal Court
ICJ	International Court of Justice
ICRC	International Committee of the Red Cross
ICTY	International Criminal Tribunal for the former Yugoslavia
ICW	International Council of Women
IGO	Intergovernmental Organization
ILO	International Labour Organization
IMF	International Monetary Fund
INGO	International Nongovernmental Organization
IOC	International Olympic Committee
IPCC	Intergovernmental Panel on Climate Change

ITTO	International Tropical Timber Organization
MDG	Millennium Development Goals
MLB	Major League Baseball
MTV	Music Television
NASCAR	National Association for Stock Car Auto Racing
NATO	North Atlantic Treaty Organization
NBA	National Basketball Association
NGO	Nongovernmental Organization
OECD	Organization for Economic Cooperation and Development
OPEC	Organization of the Petroleum Exporting Countries
PCA	Permanent Court of Arbitration
PCIJ	Permanent Court of International Justice
PPP	Purchasing Power Parity
PT	Partido dos Trabalhadores (Workers' Party)
RINGO	Religious International Nongovernmental Organization
RMB	Renminbi
TRIPs	(Agreement on) Trade-Related Aspects of Intellectual Property Rights
TYSA	Tucker Youth Soccer Association
UAE	United Arab Emirates
UK	United Kingdom
UN	United Nations
UNEP	United Nations Environment Programme
UNESCO	United Nations Educational, Scientific, and Cultural Organization
UNFF	United Nations Forum on Forests
UNPROFOR	United Nations Protection Force
US	United States (of America)
USSR	Union of Soviet Socialist Republics

VOC   Vereenigde Oost-Indische Compagnie (United East India Company)

WAO   Wet op de Arbeidsongeschiktheid (Labor Disability Insurance Act)

WEDO   Women's Environment and Development Organization

WHO   World Health Organization

WIDE   Women in Development in Europe

WINGO   Women's International Nongovernmental Organization

WIPO   World Intellectual Property Organization

WLUML   Women Living Under Muslim Laws

WSF   World Social Forum

WTO   World Trade Organization

WWF(N)   World Wildlife Fund/Worldwide Fund for Nature

YMCA   Young Men's Christian Association

1

INTRODUCTION

As more people become more connected across larger distances in different ways, they are creating a new world society in which they do more similar things, affect each other's lives more deeply, follow more of the same norms, and grow more aware of what they share. "Globalization" is one name for that process. With many examples, this book describes how and why it happens. As a preview, this introduction summarizes my main themes and the thrust of the chapters to come. Readers who prefer to plunge in can skip straight to the next chapter.

Themes

Globalization refers to the growth of ties that span space. Since people can link up across wider spaces in many ways, that definition is quite generic. Businesses that sell their wares abroad, or missionaries eager to save souls, or migrants leaving home in search of opportunity are all globalizers. Globalization occurs in many fields, world society has many dimensions. The definition therefore takes a broad and inclusive view: globalization is not a single thing or force but rather a set of human actions that share a similar quality and point in the same direction. In Chapter 2, I break the definition into four components, implicit in the opening paragraph, as a convenient tool for further analysis. "Ties that span space" minimally involve spreading or diffusing things or information, greater interdependence among more people, new forms of organization, and a wider awareness of commonalities. Applied to a great variety of social practices, from economic to legal to religious, this conveys the inherent diversity of globalization. To capture some underlying patterns that help to build world society, I still prefer to use the singular, globalization, but the plural, *globalizations*, does at least equal justice to what is happening.

Since globalization is still unfolding, describing it is a bit like charting the course or gauging the flow of a river from midstream. Yet while we cannot see exactly where we are going, the shape of world society is becoming clearer. For all the diversity described in later chapters, it has its own features, its own institutions, its own problems. In an earlier book, *World Culture: Origins and Consequences*, John Boli and I examined world culture as part of world society, arguing that this culture increasingly informs how we think and shapes much of what we do (Lechner and Boli 2005). Here I expand our argument to show how globalization creates a new framework for social life around the globe. My subtitle deliberately hedges a little: this book is about "the making" of world society – still incomplete, still in process. As later chapters will show, it involves many brakes and barriers that limit globaliza- tion in some way. At the risk of disappointing global enthusiasts, my point is not that everything or everyone is "going global," that world society somehow will sweep all before it. Rather, I want to show how new kinds of social organization intertwine with older ways of doing things.

The very term world society sounds ambitious. It captures something big and implicitly makes a grand claim. One reason it sounds ambitious is that most of us identify "society" with the state or country we live in. "Society" means Japanese society, American society, and so on. This kind of society is a package deal, con- taining a state that organizes a people, controls a territory, and fosters a culture. If the world consists of societies in this sense, how could there be room for "world" society? It is an interesting global fact that we often equate society and nation-state, but we are free to decline the package deal offered by world culture and instead think of world society in a different way. It will not be, and cannot be, a nation- state on a global scale. But we do need a name for the ways in which relations- across-spaces are crystallizing and congealing, for new ways of organizing and interpreting distant-but-common activities and experiences, and I use "world society" simply as a convenient name for that complex social reality. (Among scholars, the term is sometimes used as a label for one way of thinking about glo- balization (Meyer, Boli, et al. 1997), which has in fact influenced my own perspec- tive; to avoid confusion I will describe this way of thinking by its older name, "world polity theory.")

If some kind of "world society" is emerging, it is also tempting to think that this will leave nation-states behind as hopelessly old-fashioned. If we have more in common with distant peoples, what we have in common with those nearby should matter less. This makes intuitive sense but we should resist the intellectual tempta- tion. Nation-states are not going away; neither will national identities. Globalization will have to work in and through nation-states. At the same time, what nation-states do, and how people identify with them, will change. That was the topic of my book *The Netherlands: Globalization and National Identity*, which focused on the way the Dutch have dealt with their national identity in response to globalization (Lechner 2008). If anything, the problem for world society is not how to overcome nation- states but how to build them where they do not exist. After all, many so-called nation-states are neither – they are countries that have neither competent states nor coherent nations. Yet a reasonably stable world society will need responsive and competent states that manage the affairs of particular areas and carry the hopes of particular peoples.

Globalization is a big enough theme for one book, but I also view it as part of a still-greater transformation, both technical and social. In just a few centuries, human beings have learned how to put nature to work for us more effectively, how to move things and people more easily, and how to share information more quickly. "Human beings" is vague and misleading, of course: some groups in some places have done all this, and the benefits have not spread to everyone. Yet the massive technical transformation, from electricity to engines to telephones to the Internet, does affect everyone. World society would be impossible without it. Along with new ways of doing things, we have devised new ways of organizing social affairs. Again, the "we" did not include everyone – a caveat that applies elsewhere in the book though I sometimes leave it unstated – but a particular kind of social change nonetheless ripples around the world. Modern societies do not all follow a single path to a single destination, but typically they do work differently than those that came before: they have more specialized institutions, they grant more leeway to individuals as consumers and citizens, and they over-turn all sorts of hierarchies based on naked power, traditional privilege, or old beliefs. For centuries, these technical and social revolutions have spilled across the borders of states. Globalization follows from, complements, and reinforces them.

The idea that a social transformation upsets old hierarchies would hearten enthu-siasts who think globalization creates a "flat" world, in which more people have more equal access to more opportunities (Friedman 2007). Critics would counter, of course, that the world is hardly flat, since quite apart from the abject poverty of billions not everyone can partake equally of all its opportunities. Globalization may just create a new hierarchy in place of the old. A stronger version of this criticism suggests that globalization has always done this, imposing a particular view of how to organize society while slotting the world's regions in a rank order that favors the West (or in current parlance, the North). Allied with this critique is the idea, preva-lent among scholars and activists, that globalization is a poor word choice to capture the expansion of a free market, capitalist, or "neoliberal" system, a mainly economic process driven by powerful groups to serve their interests. From this perspective, globalization is all one-way, from North to South or from West to East: under the guise of globalization a new "empire" takes over the world. The argument often focuses on the role of the United States as a "hegemonic" power, one that is able to use its special strength to create a world in which all will abide by rules that work to its advantage. This critical view of globalization has a sharper but also more limited focus than my own. I see it as an argument not about globalization as such but about one form of globalization and the way this form became more prominent at the end of the twentieth century. Since the argument is important, I come back to it repeatedly along the way. Perhaps not surprisingly, given my choice of topic, I think it is more fruitful to view current trends in terms of globalization rather than a world empire. Broadly speaking, the term empire and the reasoning behind it – not shared by all who adopt an overtly critical perspective on globalization – do not do justice to what is happening in the twenty-first century. About the United States my verdict will be more mixed: it obviously has had great influence in globalization, especially at key junctures, but its role is also variable and increasingly constrained.

The critical view of globalization owes much to Karl Marx (1818–1883), often credited with predicting its current sweep in the *Communist Manifesto* of 1848 (written with Friedrich Engels, 1820–1895), while my inclusive one owes more to Max Weber (1864–1920), the German sociologist who was less confident than Marx about our ability to predict the sweep of any big historical process or explain it in terms of one grand theory. Along with their colleagues, they investigated a great transformation that took place during the second wave of globalization. Just as the third wave is in fact shaped by the legacies of the second, so the analysis of the current period inherits ideas from that earlier era. How far they can take us is an open question. Part of our intellectual inheritance is a certain amount of disagreement about how best to understand society and how best to explain its recent transformation. We have no single "theory of society," and there is no all-encompassing account of globalization either. Trying to devise one would be premature, perhaps impossible. Playing different accounts off against each other, partly to see how some might work together, is an option I have explored before (see Lechner and Boli 2005: ch. 2, which summarizes four theoretical perspectives). In this book I take a slightly different tack by turning a spotlight on various aspects of globalization in order to assess explanations of globalizations rather than offer a theory to surpass all theories.

Together, those explanations have to help clarify what it means to live in a world that works and feels like a "single place," to quote Roland Robertson (1992: 6), a pioneer in studying globalization. If they do not add up to one theory, they can still serve as platforms from which to look at the world. "Globalization" is not just a process occurring out in the world, or a term with which to capture its direction, but also a vantage point from which to think about that world (Velho 1997). Thinking globally carries its own risks. Once you start, it is hard not to think of anything in global terms, linking it to one overarching process. Because globalization seems to be part of, or at least to accompany, many things people care and puzzle about, it is an easy step from simply trying to "think globally" to crediting or blaming globalization for just about anything – wealth or poverty, better or worse music, growing or disappearing forests. But the old truism that correlation is not causation often applies, since globalization does not cause many things commonly attributed to it. Much as this book makes a case for globalization, it also cautions against committing that globalization fallacy.

By making a case I do not mean that I come to cheer globalization. My goal is to give a clear-eyed, hard-nosed account of what is happening, based on a wide range of scholarly work. Yet by comparison with other accounts, mine is likely to sound more cheerful. While popular writers occasionally sing globalization's praises, among academics a more somber tone prevails, reflecting what one scholar calls "globophobia" (Ritzer 2007: 1) – globalization is "predatory" (Falk 1999), it takes place in "hard times" (McGrew 2007). My approach is different, partly because I disagree with some of the reasons for the widely shared academic aversion, partly because I try to steer clear of pleading a political cause. This does not mean I am sanguine about globalization's prospects. The technical transformation referred to above made world society possible, and technology has helped to raise the globe's carrying capacity, thus enabling more people to live longer and in greater comfort, yet in using nature we have also changed it, at times destroying what was there. Most of the resources we have mined cannot be renewed, raising the question how we will cope in the future, and if worst-case scenarios about global warming come to pass, that may threaten the very viability of world society. I address the issue as a global problem in a later chapter but do not presume to offer a definite answer and therefore remain ecologically agnostic for the purposes of this book. The view from midstream runs the risk of ignoring the precipice up ahead. But perhaps a clear grasp of globalization will give us a better sense of the resources we have that may help keep us afloat.

For more than ecological reasons, globalization is controversial. People argue about it in the streets, in the halls of power, and in seminar rooms. Globalization generates heat. Of course, as will become apparent, I am not neutral on many of the controversies, and I will explain where I stand in many of the debates. But more than anything I would like to shed light on the disputes themselves by delving into actual research to show what we know and do not know. In some cases, that will go a long way. For example, the opening paragraph claimed that world society witnessed "more" of several things, and historical evidence can help to defend or qualify the point. In other cases, my approach can only go so far. Deciding whether globalization is "predatory," or times are "hard," or technology spells future doom, involves different sorts of judgment, some normative. The best way to analyze globalization is itself a matter of dispute, and on that score I will argue only by example, since the proof of the pudding is not in any recipe. In fact, I doubt there is a "best" way; rather, several good ways serve different purposes.

My purpose is to offer a persuasive argument about globalization as a process creating a new world society, describe in some detail how it is unfolding across many places and in many institutions, and serve as a guide into the diverse literatures that make sense of it. Since those literatures are enormous, this guide can only sketch a partial map. The combined size of the literatures dealing with globalization makes it impossible to cover it all. It goes without saying that about any subject I discuss there is more to be said – for example, the chapter on states (Chapter 6) has much on social spending but nothing on defense, the religion chapter (Chapter 9) focuses on Catholicism rather than Buddhism, and the environment chapter (Chapter 12) picks three issues out of many on the global agenda – and I will therefore not belabor the obvious by saying it again after saying it here.

Structure

Each of the chapters to come is about a global something – global food, global law, global religion, and so on. I use each topic, illustrated with many examples, to make a point about globalization, enter a debate about its direction, or sketch a problem in world society. The chapters stand on their own and can be read in any order – for example, readers who first want to delve into the substance of global institutional change might want to focus on chapters 5 through 9 rather than start with food or sports. Each chapter draws on a distinct literature and concisely summarizes the state of the art as best I can. Yet I have also grouped the chapters for a reason. The first part illustrates how globalization changes everyday experience, the second focuses on the new institutions that may be the backbone of world society, and the third zeroes in on issues widely viewed as problems world society will have to confront.

In a way, it all started with food. Europeans' quest to add flavor to their food motivated them to seek ways to reach Asia. As Chapter 2 explains, this helped to set off what we may call the first "wave" of globalization. In that wave, Jamaica became a "sugar island" at the center of a global network. In the nineteenth century, a second wave followed, which rolled across newly cultivated American wheat fields, tied to world markets via train and telegraph. Both Tokyo's large fish market, a hub in the global fishing industry, and McDonald's in East Asia, an exemplary American multinational serving a quintessential global food, embody key features of the third wave that is still going on. Together the waves, a metaphor suggested by Robbie Robertson (2003), convey how globalization is nothing new yet also very different now. Each new wave relies on a distinct technical infrastructure and alters the global environment. Global food thus gives us a glimpse of the continuity and breaks in globalization history.

From the second wave we inherit many of the games people now play around the world – most games have become "global games," a process Chapter 3 describes. The global triumph of soccer is obviously familiar, and that very familiarity shows how people around the world have been drawn into the same story, the same sort of experience, the same organized activities. Partly thanks to the Olympic Games, many other sports also have become globally standardized, played by the same rules and with international organizations ultimately in charge. Global sports, and the global "sporting system" in which they are all embedded, thus illustrate how many common activities have become globally organized. The fact that America has long stood "offside" in the soccer world tells us that America is not the dominant player across all fields, one instance among others of the way in which globalization also constrains the presumed hyperpower.

Sports spread partly through mass media, especially television, in the third wave. Though still very much tied to domestic markets and shaped by state policies, global television has also served to expose more audiences to more similar shows, characters, music, and advertising. At times, it creates common occasions witnessed by billions simultaneously, one way of fostering global awareness. Reflecting on changes in India's media market, Chapter 4 reviews how media globalization is happening and asks whether the flow of shows and the rise of commercial formats reduce the variety in what we watch. At the risk of equivocating, I invoke the term "glocalization" to answer yes – and no. Through cultural encounters critical audiences actively sift and sort increasingly globalized "content," while preserving a sense of distinction. India's popular Bollywood film tradition further supports this way of thinking about media globalization, which runs counter to claims about the persistence of "cultural imperialism." The flow of cultural products, though certainly dominated by US producers in both movies and TV programming, is not one-way, which sustains global variety even as the contrasts across media markets diminish.

For many people globalization simply means that international trade and investment are knitting together a vastly larger world economy. China, of course, plays a crucial role in this part of the story, as Chapter 5 explains. Its shift to a "market economy with socialist characteristics" tied it much more closely to the world economy, and many of its domestic reforms mirror broader global trends. For China, it has paid off. The world economy, too, has performed much better in the third wave, as more places have become more intricately connected in production, through trade, and via the financial markets, although the global pay-off has been much more uneven. Reviewing the history of economic reconstruction after World War II and a new global thrust from about 1980, the chapter describes just how intricate the connections have become. More than any other feature of globalization, these economic trends have also provoked critics who argue that the singular "neoliberal" global expansion of recent decades is both unjust and unsustainable. The chapter concludes with a brief discussion of this diagnosis of globalization as the virulent spread of "market fundamentalism."

Even if it is an exaggeration to say that markets rule the world, the economic expansion after World War II has made states much more dependent on forces they cannot control. Are they bound to retreat? Chapter 6 argues that the fear is premature. Already in the second wave, some states started using their new-found powers to build a safety net that sheltered some groups from the impact of globalization. In the third, it is more difficult to keep that net in good repair but its basic role has not changed. Welfare states that put their economic house in order may well be a linchpin rather than a liability in the globalization process. The larger point, a paradox only if we think of markets and states in opposition to each other, is that globalization also enhances state authority in some ways – states cannot do just "their own thing," they are also charged with global tasks. This applies not just to welfare but also to other such tasks, including education. Globalization, then, certainly challenges states but also operates in and through them. The problem is not with competent states at risk of retreating but with those that have little to retreat from in the first place.

While world society still relies on state authority, it is also building institutions that organize its affairs in a different way, trying to "run the world," or bits and pieces of it, in the absence of a world state. Slowly but surely, "global governance" is taking shape, as Chapter 7 explains with a focus on law. For example, as the "legal capital of the world," The Hague is home to several legal bodies with international responsibilities, including the International Court of Justice and the International Criminal Tribunal for the former Yugoslavia (which announced its closing as I completed this book). Contrary to its founders' intent, the United Nations has become a law-making body at the center of a web of governance. Farther outside the orbit of states, many private groups have devised ways of regulating their cross-border activities, notably in business. In some respects, at least, "international" law is turning into "world law," though the actual structure of governance is still quite messy. To make sense of the trend, which leaves a world of states behind but has yet to crystallize into a world society with a common legal culture, I draw on the work of Hugo Grotius, the seventeenth-century Dutch scholar who was a pioneer in thinking about international law.

Among the people who connect across state borders are groups committed to particular causes that seek allies abroad and form networks to take on a wide range of issues. By linking up, voluntary associations thus create a global civil society, again in the absence of a global state. Chapter 8 begins with the movement against female genital cutting (or mutilation), a practice widely denounced as a cruel violation of women's human rights, and shows how groups coalesced around the issue to bring it to global attention, mobilize support, and put pressure on relevant states. Exactly how global civic action gets organized varies from case to case – the Red Cross differs from the International Campaign to Ban Landmines, for example. Thanks to the enormous growth in international nongovernmental organizations or INGOs, ranging from professional associations to the International Olympic Committee (IOC) to Greenpeace, global civil society basks in the glow of a new kind of authority, yet it also faces many constraints. I critically review the argument that it represents a "power shift" in world society.

Perhaps the largest, and oldest, "civic" organization in the world is the Roman Catholic Church. It has always had a universal vision and mission, but after the Second Vatican Council in the 1960s, it changed its relation to the world at large, accepting the fact that Catholicism was just one religion among others and committing itself to human rights and freedom of religion. Not coincidentally, the Church's center of gravity also moved South: more new adherents came from developing countries. As Chapter 9 describes, the Church thus went through a globalization phase of its own during the tenure of Pope John Paul II, whose unprecedented travels expanded the Church's reach. One reason for the trips was religious competition: in many countries, Pentecostal groups made inroads, turning that branch of evangelical Christianity into one of the fastest-growing religious communities, with its own global impact. While Catholics and Pentecostals differ in many ways, they roughly converge in viewing religion as distinct from worldly institutions and embedded in a diverse culture. For many Muslims, that religious relation to world society is more problematic – its institutions are not rooted in Islamic tradition, its practices make adherence to traditional rules of conduct more difficult, and its dominant powers call into question the superiority of Islam. A militant minority has turned Islam into a kind of ideology, centered on building an Islamic state under Islamic law, that differs from non-Islamic forms of religiosity, but the chapter argues that this politicization of religion is likely to fail and increasingly will give way to distinctly Islamic accommodations to world society. Again using Catholic examples, it concludes by suggesting that religion viewed as part of civil society, enlivened by the faith of millions of believers, does not become impotent but instead addresses global problems in distinctive fashion.

Religions move to new places because believers do. In fact, some 3 percent of the world population or about 200 million people do not live in their country of origin – a big number, certainly, but also a reminder that even in the global age most people stay put. Migration has many benefits, for migrants and host countries alike, but those who move change the places where they arrive and this often creates tension, perceived as a problem especially by people who feel their way of life changing. Starting in my home territory – DeKalb County, Georgia – Chapter 10 describes who moves where and why, reviews some of the responses to migration, and throws cold water on one pessimistic American diagnosis of its impact. Again arguing against overly global views of globalization, I also suggest that true "transnationalism" still only involves a small number of people, another indication that globalization has its limits.

One force that drives migration is inequality: many poor people move to get ahead. Using the experience of Malawi as an example, Chapter 11 emphasizes just how deep global inequality is. Referring to South Korea, it also suggests that in some respects global gaps are shrinking. The chapter tries to answer the larger questions about what is happening to inequality worldwide but also explains why it is difficult to gauge inequality accurately. Overall, it takes issue with the common lament that globalization makes the rich richer and the poor poorer – among other reasons, because it is a fallacy to attribute many of the existing gaps to the process of globalization. Globalization has made some of the poor richer but also leaves the excluded poor relatively worse off. How to make Malawians full participants in world society remains one of its biggest challenges, and the chapter offers no easy answers in that regard.

As the common label, "developing countries," indicates, recipes intended to help Malawi and similar places do better necessarily include one ingredient: development. But under current global norms, some kinds of development are better than others: development must be "sustainable." Chapter 12 recounts how that norm developed as the centerpiece of a global environmental "regime," a common set of assumptions, rules, and procedures applied to a problem recognized as intrinsically global. Starting with a controversy over an Indian dam project, intended as a spur to development there, the chapter describes how since the 1960s environmental awareness and concern has spread, in part thanks to a global movement led by environmental INGOs. World society has taken some action in dealing with some environmental problems, as illustrated in the cases of ozone depletion, deforestation, and climate change, but the institutional means for addressing them still leave much to be desired. The shortcomings of the global regime(s) give some environmentalists reason to advocate more drastic changes in the relation between humans and nature, which also leads them to devalue development.

Both global inequality and environmental damage have helped to inspire a movement critical of globalization and its impact, the topic of Chapter 13. Once called the "antiglobalization" movement, a more common label is the "global justice movement." Composed mainly of groups on the political left, it flexed its collective muscle in opposition to the World Trade Organization (WTO) in Seattle in 1999 and at many subsequent gatherings of international economic organizations. Since 2001, when it was first staged in Porto Alegre, Brazil, the World Social Forum has also provided an ideological home for globalization critics. While it is internally diverse, with different groups choosing different targets and tactics, the movement has propagated the common view that globalization really is an unjust and unsustainable neoliberal project. As part of the "counterculture" of world society, it challenges many rules of the current global game. How to do better is less clear: the critics' proposals range from drastic "deglobalization" to more gradual reform in the direction of "global social democracy." However vital the global justice movement has been, such proposals have not yet attracted a major global following or had a great impact on world society. Yet the future direction of globalization depends on the way world society deals with its critics.

Further Reading

David Held, Anthony McGrew, David Goldblatt, and Jonathan Perraton, *Global Transformations: Politics, Economics, and Culture* (Stanford University Press, 1999)

Frank J. Lechner and John Boli, *World Culture: Origins and Consequences* (Blackwell, 2005)

Frank J. Lechner and John Boli (eds.), *The Globalization Reader* (Blackwell, 2008)

George Ritzer (ed.), *The Blackwell Companion to Globalization* (Blackwell, 2007)

Robbie Robertson, *The Three Waves of Globalization: A History of a Developing Global Consciousness* (Zed Books, 2003)

Roland Robertson, *Globalization: Social Theory and Global Culture* (Sage, 1992)

— PART I —
GLOBAL EXPERIENCE

2

GLOBAL FOOD AND THE HISTORY OF GLOBALIZATION

- Sushi and Globalization
- Setting the Stage: Definition and History
- The First Wave of Globalization: Jamaica
- Some Patterns in the First Wave
- The Second Wave of Globalization: North Dakota
- Some Patterns in the Second Wave
- The Third Wave of Globalization: McDonald's in East Asia
- Some Patterns in the Three Waves
- Summary and Conclusion

Sushi and Globalization

The Tsukiji fish market in Tokyo is the largest in the world. Six days a week, traders buy thousands of pounds of fish at dockside auctions in order to resell it to chefs and retailers – 50,000 people working to satisfy the needs of the region's more than 20 million residents (Bestor 2004: 9). Tsukiji is a very Japanese place, with its own Japanese trading customs, linked to distinctively Japanese businesses, and catering to Japanese tastes in seafood. At the same time, it serves as the central hub of the global fishing industry (Issenberg 2007). Thanks to modern shipping technology – the more valuable fish flies in via Narita International Airport – it enjoys a global supply, ranging from Canadian salmon and Maine sea urchin roe to Okhotsk crab and Thai shrimp. For Tsukiji, the world's oceans are a single source, and it in turn has become "fishmonger for the seven seas" (Bestor 2004: 35). As the trend-setting market, Tsukiji sends signals via fax or the Internet to ports around the world, where its prices serve as daily benchmarks. Everyone in the trade must be constantly aware of what is going on in Tokyo. The flow of fish through Tsukiji shows globalization in action. The scale and scope of the industry convey what is new in contemporary globalization.

Among Tsukiji's suppliers are fishermen from Maine. When they bring bluefin tuna ashore in New England, Japanese buyers waiting to purchase the catch inspect the quality of the fish and get on their cell phones to check the latest prices back home (Bestor 2000). Deals at dockside depend on information instantaneously available halfway around the world: Tokyo traders determine the fishers' livelihood. The best tuna may continue its journey via jet plane from New York to Japan, to be assessed and auctioned by the world's experts there before flying back to New York's restaurants. In those restaurants, and of course in many other places, a particular kind of Japanese cuisine has made inroads: sushi has "gone global" (ibid.). Whereas raw fish, prepared just so, was once an exotic taste outside of Japan, it has enticed more and more consumers elsewhere. Surrounded by Japanese rituals, "authentically" presented by Japanese chefs, it promises a vicarious taste of Japan. Stripped of pretension, it has become a standard item on global middle-class menus, available prepackaged in supermarkets. Yet however mundane "sushi" has become in this form, it remains identified with Japan, which set the standard in the first place. By eating sushi, consumers also connect with Japan.

Because the Japanese themselves eat so much fish, they are also involved in many international efforts to increase production. Off the coast of Spain, for example, they help to finance tuna farms, run by Spanish workers and supplied with Dutch-caught herring filled with vitamins from European pharmaceutical companies (Bestor 2000). Near Australia, too, tuna ranching has become big business (Issenberg 2007). Rather than harvesting whatever the seas produce, fishing there becomes a kind of transnational industry, in which the farms operate as links in a "commodity chain" that Tsukiji ultimately ties to plates in Tokyo homes. One reason for the joint venture near Spain, or the ranches off the Australian coast, or the dealings with Maine fishers, is that the Japanese cannot go it alone. Global rules set 200-mile fishing limits, reserving the oceans near each country's coast as a zone for exclusive use by its own fishermen. Other rules limit, at least in principle, what fishers can catch in the open ocean. As the "command and control center" of the global fishing trade (Bestor 2004: 34), Tsukiji experiences the impact of such international regulations intended to safeguard ocean habitats. How well the rules really work to protect the fish is another matter.

Food brings the world home in Japan. In the comfort of their sushi shops, Japanese consumers can take in the world's bounty. By the same token, outside Japan more people enjoy similar seafood in Japanese style. Their diets still differ, but they have much more in common. At a minimum, globalization means that people become connected across large distances by doing the same sorts of things or having the same sorts of experiences. When it comes to eating fish, it matters ever less where you are. In the fishing industry – the term itself is revealing – more people also are connected in the chain that links fisher to transporter to auctioneer to trader to retailer to consumer. Decisions by Tokyo shoppers affect the fortunes of Maine fishermen, and in a way vice versa. As global supply meets global demand, all parties become interdependent. That fishing has become an industry tells us that it is ever more organized – how to refrigerate or freeze fish, how to transport it quickly, how to handle transactions are all highly standardized. Countries have made some common rules to constrain who can fish where and how much, at least tentatively instituting a global framework to govern the industry. For the professionals involved, the global scope of the industry is obvious. As consumers partake of its products, they take in a bit of global culture as well.

Setting the Stage: Definition and History

The fishy example suggests a definition of globalization as the process in which more and more people become connected in more different ways across larger distances. Space becomes less of a constraint on social life; more of the things we do become "deterritorialized," more social relations become "supraterritorial" (Waters 2001; Scholte 2005). As the example shows, connections can take different forms. Diffusion, the simple spreading of things or information, ties people through common practices or shared experience. Interdependence means that actions in one place meaningfully affect others in a distant place. Increasingly, such links become organized, subject to common rules or dealt with by specific institutions. More connected people also grow conscious of those connections, developing a shared culture that gives meaning to their common world. Globalization has at least these four elements: diffusion, interdependence, organization, and culture or consciousness. In this book, I use this generic definition of globalization and refer repeatedly to its core elements as a way to make sense of its complexity.

Claiming that more people "think globally," leaving aside for the moment how many think so and how deeply, captures the notion that the world as a whole, as a "single place," enters into our experience in many ways (Robertson 1992: 6). It is a key element in one well-known definition of globalization as "the compression of the world and the intensification of consciousness of the world as a whole . . . the increasing acceleration in both concrete interdependence and consciousness of the global whole" (8). When one plate contains fish from several oceans, caught only shortly before, that compression becomes palpable. For producers and consumers alike, the world's oceans are now one body of water, almost universally accessible. As we take what we desire, we obviously affect the global waters in turn. Small individual actions, like buying a particular kind of fish, may have large consequences for a species or even a whole ocean habitat. As a global industry, fishing also has global effects, evident in the fivefold increase in fishing capacity since the 1970s that has resulted in lower yields and ever-declining stocks, which has put whole species at risk in spite of rules instituted to protect ocean habitats (Gelchu and Pauly 2007). In this way, it harms what we have come to call, a bit misleadingly, "the environment." More and more people have become aware of that harm, one instance of a new global consciousness that views the quality of the world's "environment" as a problem in its own right, the main topic of Chapter 12. What to do about it is in dispute, not least because different parties have different interests. But the disputes about how to conserve fisheries, or how to protect the oceans from human harm, or whether to turn away from "global" toward "local" food,

Box 2.1 Globalization: definitions and dimensions

Definitions

Ritzer 2007, p. 1: "Globalization is an accelerating set of processes involving flows that encompass ever-greater numbers of the world's spaces and that lead to increasing integration and interconnectivity among those spaces."

Robertson 1992, p. 8: "Globalization as a concept refers both to the compression of the world and the intensification of consciousness of the world as a whole."

Scholte 2005, p. 59: [Globalization refers to] "the spread of transplanetary – and in recent times also more particularly supraterritorial – connections between people. A global [relation] . . . can link persons situated at any inhabitable point on the earth. Globalization involves reductions of barriers to such transworld social contacts."

Waters 2001 [first edition 1995, p. 3]: "A social process in which the constraints of geography on social and cultural arrangements recede and in which people become increasingly aware that they are receding."

Lechner, this book: Globalization refers to the process in which more people become more connected in more different ways across larger distances.

Dimensions

1 *Diffusion:* Active dissemination of practices, values, and products throughout the globe (Albrow 1997). Example: "Japanese cultural motifs and material have increasingly saturated the entire world's consumption and popular culture. Against all odds, so has sushi" (Bestor 2000).

2 *Interdependence:* Reciprocal effects of actions by different groups across borders and spaces, specifically involving integration of markets and technologies. Example: "Now, a Massachusetts fisher's livelihood can be transformed in a matter of hours by a spike in market prices halfway around the globe or by a disaster at a fish farm across the Atlantic" (Bestor 2000).

3 *Organization:* More activities and institutions governed by global norms, shaped by global models, linked to transnational organizations (Meyer, Boli, et al. 1997). Example: "[I]nternational environmental campaigns forced many countries, Japan among them, to scale back their distant fleets" (Bestor 2000).

4 *Culture/Consciousness:* Increased awareness of the unity of the world as a whole, taking the globe as a focus for human activities (Robertson 1992, Albrow 1997). Example: "In the newly rewired circuitry of global cultural and economic affairs [involving fish], Japan is the core and the Atlantic seaboard, the Adriatic, and the Australian coast are all distant peripheries" (Bestor 2000).

themselves display a global awareness. "The world" enters into what we eat and do and argue about.

The global fishing industry is part of a global food industry. To invoke a watery metaphor, it exemplifies a new "wave" of globalization that follows at least two earlier waves (Robertson 2003). The metaphor serves to capture some distinctions between periods in the form of a simple historical model. As this chapter shows, the quest for better food and the production of new staples were very much a part of the first wave of globalization from roughly 1500 to 1800. In the second wave, roughly from 1800 to World War I, the mechanization of agriculture and the cultivation of new regions created world markets for food. The third wave builds on the first two, but it also brings something new: more people now enjoy more food from more places than ever before, a larger portion of producers serve distant customers, rules and institutions with global reach manage much food production, and as the world becomes a single market more consumers can taste nearly anything from nearly anywhere. Since World War II, global connections of all sorts, not just those we make through food, have deepened and widened. This has tempted some scholars to declare, more emphatically than this book, that a new "global age" has arrived in which people lose a sense that their surrounding community or nation-state mainly shapes their lives and identities and instead become enmeshed in far-flung webs (Albrow 1997).

Japan's prominence in the global fishing industry illustrates one thrust in the history of globalization. In the first wave, initiated by European expansion in the 1500s, Japan initially engaged, then closed itself off. In the second, it was forced to open up, then pursued an independent development strategy. After World War II, the country quickly rejoined the most developed industrial countries. In some ways, this makes Japan an outlier – always guarded, never colonized, highly successful in at least two waves. But the Japanese experience also hints at one of the great reversals in globalization: European-led globalization challenged Asia at the outset; in the second wave, European powers gained partial dominance in the region; in the third, Asia is reasserting itself as economic power and cultural trendsetter. If the story of the first and especially the second wave could once be told as the "rise of the West" (McNeill 1963), the third wave plot features the "rise of the rest" (Amsden 2001).

On the whole, globalization has served Japan well. Within Asia, not everyone globalizes or benefits from globalization, of course. Japan itself has been a selective globalizer, for example by limiting immigration; North Korea, Bhutan, and Nepal have more clearly stood apart for various reasons. As Asia's own rocky globalization record shows, globalization works differently for different regions, and some people gain much more than others. Even the winners cannot be entirely secure, since globalization makes them vulnerable in new ways. But the occasional pain of higher food prices experienced in places like Japan pales compared to the perils of globalization for the "bottom billion" (Collier 2007), the poorest of the poor who are still likely to suffer hunger pangs. For example, after Haiti started lowering tariffs on rice in the 1980s, the former luxury turned into a staple food when cheaper "Miami" rice from the US largely displaced that of less productive Haitian farmers, who as a result often had to leave their land; but when formerly stable rice prices doubled in 2007–8, they caused a "food crisis" among poor Haitians who, as they stood in line waiting for meager handouts, were all too aware of their dependence on foreign supplies (Williams 2008). As Haiti's plight reminds us, even as more people enjoy more food in greater variety, not everyone has easy access to food from anywhere. Globalization has unequal effects, and each wave runs up against limits. Food not only displays the sheer scale of globalization in the third wave, it also represents one of world society's main challenges.

Much of this book focuses on the contemporary third wave of globalization, to show the varied and uneven ways more people and places become involved. To highlight both what it inherits from the past and how it fosters new connections, I briefly describe the first two waves in the following sections, focusing on food once again, before drawing some lessons about the history of globalization.

The First Wave of Globalization: Jamaica

In 1670, one Francis Price, a former British officer, filed a patent on a piece of land in central Jamaica he named Worthy Park, which was to become a large sugar plantation that survived into the twentieth century (Craton and Walvin 1970). Fifteen years before, British troops had expelled the Spanish from the island; with the government's encouragement, would-be planters like Price now moved into the countryside to make the victory pay off. That proved difficult. As in other parts of the New World, the island's native inhabitants had been decimated by European germs, leaving no indigenous labor force. In spite of modest Spanish efforts to grow sugar in the West Indies, Jamaica had no viable economy, which meant that the British had to start nearly from scratch. The island lacked the infrastructure that would make plantations immediately profitable. To purchase land, prepare it for production, and buy provisions, entrepreneurs needed capital, which they had to borrow on stiff terms from financiers back home. From the outset, they were in debt to bankers and merchants, for whom risky loans at high interest were good business. While the home country provided capital, it offered few willing or even indentured workers. Soon after, slaves solved the labor shortage: in 1670 Jamaica already had nearly 8,000 out of a total population of about 13,700, within half a century they would outnumber whites ten to one (21–2). In the 1700s some 600,000 entered Jamaica altogether (Mintz 1986: 53), with several hundred laboring at Worthy Park itself in any one year. As sugar production there shifted into high gear after 1700, under the direction of Francis Price's son Charles, Worthy Park became a major node in a transatlantic network.

Worthy Park kept some cattle for fertilizer, had some small vegetable plots, and set aside land for a house, offices, and slave quarters, but most of it was devoted to one thing only: growing sugar cane. In an annual cycle, slaves supervised by an overseer would tend to the fields and cut the cane, to be processed in the on-site factory run by more skilled slaves who squeezed the juice from the cane and then boiled it to crystallize the sugar, using the by-product for rum. All metal equipment came from Britain. Because Worthy Park did not grow its own food, that had to be imported as well: some supplies came from the American mainland colonies, salted herring for the slaves from the Dutch. Since few slave infants survived to working age, planters like the Prices constantly had to buy new arrivals from Africa. They rarely had ready cash to pay for all this and borrowed money instead, pledging part of their land or crops as collateral. Capital flowed through their hands to food suppliers and slave traders and African slave sellers – and often right back to other home-country financiers. Sugar made the network work: as the British public developed its sweet tooth, sugar imports exceeded all other colonial crops in volume and value, reaching 100,000 "hogsheads" by 1730, most of which the British consumed themselves (Mintz 1986: 39). Worthy Park produced several hundred of these hogsheads, earning up to about £10,000 a year.

Many parties, on all sides of the Atlantic, had a piece of the sugar action. They were actors in a globalizing market, at the crest of the first wave of globalization. In this wave, a taste for sweetened food spread in Europe, which consumed more than 240,000 tons a year by 1800 (Mintz 1986: 73). In England alone, consumption increased by more than 400 percent, from four to eighteen pounds per person, in the eighteenth century (67). Everyone involved in the Britain-Africa-New World triangle depended on the others, seeking riches through commerce, producing commodities for distant markets, and financially tied to a few sources of capital. Rules of production and finance were gradually worked out, turning the slave-sugar trade into a new economic system. At the heart of it all, the sugar plantation was a "pioneer institution of capitalist development" (Tomich 1990: 2). While the Atlantic triangle was not strictly global, many participants expanded their horizons, literally and figuratively. Jamaica itself was in a sense a product of this early globalization, a "sugar island" in the "West Indies," defined by Europeans in terms of its function for the emerging system but also a "creole" community resulting from cultural exchange (Gunn 2003: 281–2) in which slaves had an important role.

The wave had started not with a desire for sugar but with a search for spices (though sugar itself was long considered a "spice"). Seeking access to the Asian spice trade by sailing west to evade Mongol blockage, circumvent Islamic lands, and outrace the Portuguese, Christopher Columbus had landed on a nearby island, thinking he had reached India. Others followed, lured not by spices but by the prospect of finding silver and gold. Besides precious metals they brought new foods home: potatoes and tomatoes entered the European diet. In the early part of the wave, far-flung regions for the first time exchanged foods globally (Robertson 2003: 94). When the Portuguese reached China, for example, they introduced maize, sweet potatoes, and peanuts, crops that later would help to sustain China's population boom (Gunn 2003: 68–9). They brought back sugar cane from Asia for planting on São Tomé and other islands. On his second voyage, Columbus himself took sugar cane from the Canary Islands to the New World, where in the 1500s it proved a suitable crop first on Santo Domingo, then in Brazil (Mintz 1986: 32). From

CUTTING CANES.

Plate 2.1   Slaves working in a Jamaican sugar cane plantation (date unknown, location possibly Worthy Park)
Source: © National Library of Jamaica

modest beginnings, it grew into a major crop. On the other side of the globe, meanwhile, Europeans gained a foothold in Asia, using their superior power to enforce positive terms of trade in spices, tea, and other goods. The fruits of global ventures in both hemispheres mixed in British cups in the form of sweetened tea, its combination of exotic ingredients eventually defined as typically British. European trade thus linked the hemispheres in an entirely new way. Aware of the connections, at least the elite began to see the world whole, a global consciousness evident in geographical treatises and in maps and globes made for European seafarers and power brokers that for the first time included most regions of the world (Gunn 2003: 32–3, ch. 5).

Some Patterns in the First Wave

Commerce and Christian fervor, the lust for money and the urge to save souls, channeled the first wave. But states were deeply involved from the beginning, starting with Iberian monarchs Ferdinand and Isabella sponsoring Columbus's journey.

Sugar, too, reflected state power. After all, British force claimed Caribbean islands for British planters. Sugar production there resulted from a power struggle with Spain. Having seized control of Jamaica, the British government stimulated sugar production via land grants. It controlled the trade by requiring planters to sell in the home market while at the same time protecting them against foreign competition – a hallmark of the "mercantile" system. As an interest group, the plantocracy gained influence in Parliament, which passed favorable laws. In Jamaica itself, they dominated the Assembly, using public power to serve their interests. British naval forces patrolled shipping lanes and British power long backed the slave trade as well. By charging duties, the Crown more than made up for its expenses. If the colonial trade worked to the disadvantage of the British public, since freer trade might have lowered prices and stimulated innovation, both special interest groups and the government itself profited handsomely (Mintz 1986: 56). In part due to sugar's appeal, the Caribbean became one focus in the struggle for global dominance between Britain and France. Immediately after Britain prevailed in 1763, depressing French production, Jamaican sugar experienced its golden age. Throughout the first wave, the process of making and selling sugar thus unfolded "under the wing of the state" (41). Not just the sugar trade flourished. With "the full weight of the state behind them," English traders did well in many parts of the world (Robertson 2003: 92), as Britain turned from plain old conquest to building a commercial empire.

In the first wave of globalization, more people became more globally connected in more ways than ever before (Robertson 2003: 78). They could taste the links in the tea drunk in Britain, the tobacco smoked in France, the peanuts in Chinese dishes, or the herring given to Jamaican slaves. Global connections thus changed the daily lives of millions. The links grew along with new crops in new places – potatoes in the Netherlands, maize in China, sugar in the Caribbean. Globalization thus also changed the world in a very physical sense, especially through New World crops in China and India (Mazumdar 1999). The new links benefited some and harmed many others. British planters and traders were among the winners, Native Americans and African slaves among the losers. Early globalization thus began to create a global hierarchy. The links were mostly the work of Europeans, with Britain gaining a leading role. British power served as a driving force in and was much enhanced by globalization. Though there were still few "international rules of engagement" (Robertson 2003: 88), Britain began to make some. The case of Jamaica illustrates the legacy of the first wave, when in more parts of the globe economic activity focused on producing commodities for the world market, whites came to view themselves as superior to other races, and English began to serve as the lingua franca.

Caught up in several long-distance flows of people, money, and goods, Worthy Park was part and parcel of this globalization. But we cannot make too much of the example. Though over time more Europeans used more sugar, it remained a luxury product through the 1600s and even by 1800 was still a small part of their overall diet. Most people got most of their food from places nearby, and foreign trade overall comprised only a few percent of the British economy. For all the brutal drama of the slave trade, only a small minority of Africans moved across the ocean; relatively few white Europeans made similar treks as migrants or sailors. Information and goods moved slowly – it took a Jamaican shipment of sugar several weeks to reach London, and by modern standards the speed did not increase greatly for centuries – effectively separating regions and societies in spite of the growing links. Britain came to dominate the "Euro-American world system" that included Jamaica but in the 1700s it had yet to make its mark on the very different "China-centered East Asian world system" (Marks 2002: 68).

The continents were connected, to be sure, partly because Europeans used New World resources to gain advantage in Asia, which has tempted some to argue that the start of direct shipments of silver from South America to the Philippines makes 1571 the year globalization was "born" (Flynn and Giráldez 2006). But the link was still fairly loose, and since European powers had further carved up the world into imperial zones, the world market was weakly integrated at best (Tomich 1990: 14–5). So was world culture: "Western" religion and practices took hold in the New World, but the encounters of civilizations in Asia left regional cultures there mostly intact (Gunn 2003: ch. 7). Westerners learned much about others but many others did not reciprocate this interest: "[o]utside Europe, interest in foreign lands remained relatively small" (Osterhammel and Petterson 2005: 52). In spite of the new maps and globes available to a Western reading public, this was still "a world that did not understand itself" (Robertson 2003: 78) – the maps and globes themselves contained many blank spots. Its web of connection was still small, thin, and fragile.

None of this detracts from the significance of the first wave. Its legacy set the stage for the next one, in which industrializing Western countries dramatically diverged from others. Early globalization concentrated greater power and resources in the hands of Europeans, helping to create the conditions for further advances. "[T]he remarkable innovations of the Industrial Revolution would not have had the deep and sustained consequences that they did if British industry had not operated within the [previously developed] global framework of sources of raw materials and markets for finished products" (Findlay and O'Rourke 2007: 39). To embellish the point slightly, "[g]lobalization made the Industrial Revolution," not least by giving British textile makers a powerful incentive to compete with more efficient Indian exporters (Robertson 2003: 116). The prime, though unintended, British creation of the first wave, the newly independent United States, would also come to play a global role.

The Second Wave of Globalization: North Dakota

In 1875, the Amenia and Sharon Land Company, a group of American investors, bought 28,000 acres from the Northern Pacific Railroad in Cass County, North

Dakota (Drache 1964). In return for the right to sell large tracts along new lines – 25,600 acres for each mile of railroad – the company had built track from Minnesota into the Dakota Territory in the early 1870s, crossing the Red River of the North in 1872 and reaching Bismarck by June 1873. Where the railroad went, settlers quickly followed: in 1870, the Dakota side of the river valley counted only 2,405 residents, by 1890 the population of the new state of North Dakota had grown to over 190,000. They came not only from more crowded states to the east but also from Britain, Germany, and Scandinavia, where the railroad company advertised its good land. As an agent for the railroad company put it, the settlers "rapidly converted the raw prairie into a great field of waving grain" (26). Wheat proved a hardy and bountiful crop in the relatively arid and flat North Central region. By the end of the century, the area produced over 440 million bushels or about two-thirds of America's wheat crop (13). In North Dakota alone, over 4 million acres were devoted to wheat, increasing to over 8 million by 1910 (10). When the railroad company ran into financial difficulty, investors like those who made up the Amenia and Sharon exchanged their bonds for portions of its land grants, joining the Great Dakota Boom and eventually accumulating some 58,000 acres (74). The boom was really a global one, just one instance of how new means of transportation and communication helped new people settle distant places in ways that would link them far more tightly to the world at large.

Rather than divide its holdings into traditional family farms – a tenant system did develop in the 1890s – the Amenia and Sharon created a new kind of business, the large-scale, professionally managed, for-profit "bonanza" farm. Most of the absentee owners in Connecticut knew and cared little about farming but one of the company directors, E. W. Chaffee, went west to make a go of farming the land it had acquired. Though instructed simply to prepare the property for profitable sale, Chaffee was seized by a vision of the land's potential. He hired a professional sod buster to get started. He built lodging for the workers he hired as needed, season by season. To make optimal use of the workers and increase the return on capital, he bought new machinery – ploughs, binders, and threshers, some steam-powered. Given the scale of the operation, with dozens of horses and more than a hundred men in the fields during busy periods, he had to institute clear procedures. Strict accounting by a full-time bookkeeper was essential to keep track of costs and revenues; any activity that was not profitable would have to be changed. Chaffee branched out into elevators, creating an agricultural company that encompassed many phases of food production. In the 1890s, his son added an experimental plot designed to test new varieties of grain to be supplied to tenants. In everything they did, the Chaffees aimed for optimal efficiency, applying the latest techniques. They thus built one of the first "factory farms" (Drache 1964: 91), demonstrating the benefits of agriculture run as a rational business.

The bonanza farms did not last in their original form, partly due to their sheer scale, but they show how the second wave of globalization rolled across the

American prairies in the late nineteenth century. Even before the arrival of railroads, still hampered by distance, American farmers had already ventured into the "Great West," but trains that "broke much more radically with geography" (Cronon 1991: 74) helped them conquer that huge space. They could bring their produce to market more cheaply, save time by avoiding muddy roads, and obtain supplies more reliably. Going from New York City to the Fargo area might have taken about three weeks as late as 1857, two decades later it would take less than a week (77). Information also moved more quickly: telegraph and later telephone lines were built along with the railroad tracks, enabling people like the Chaffees to communicate across their far-flung holdings, keep in touch with company directors, and stay abreast of wheat prices. News from New York, or from London or Argentina for that matter, could reach Fargo in mere minutes.

The Amenia and Sharon operation was unusually large, but even smaller ones required much capital. Individual settlers from Europe might have enough to start on their own but, like their predecessors in Jamaica, many needed credit. Laying track cost even more, requiring huge infusions of capital from domestic and foreign lenders. The Dakota Boom was also a Capitalist Boom, connecting lenders, companies, farmers, and all sorts of middlemen across America and across the Atlantic. Most Dakota grain went to Chicago, the key node in the network where from the 1850s onward revolutionary new ways to store, move, and sell grain were invented (Cronon 1991: 120). Though family-run farms by no means disappeared, the Amenia and Sharon pointed to a new form of enterprise, relying on wage labor rather than household or slave labor. On an even larger scale than the bonanza farms, the railroads ran their business in a new way, using very precise accounting to set rates and manage costs, if only to hold bankruptcy at bay. This wave of globalization involved millions of people moving millions of miles. Many were native-born, but in America immigrants helped to settle the prairies, build the railroads, and enlarge the cities. They followed the tracks of trains and capital.

Just as Jamaica was shaped by its special role in the first wave of globalization, the Dakotas, and the whole North-Central US, developed thanks to their role in the second wave. Domestic investors, settlers, and consumers provided the key impetus, to be sure, but foreign money, immigrants, and markets pushed the second wave as well. North Dakota became bread basket to the world. Still on the very periphery of world affairs in 1850, it was fully involved by 1900. The same goes for large swaths of Canada, Argentina, and Australia: places linked by new technology, occupied by people from afar, and brought into cultivation to become a source of food and profit; by 1913 they produced more wheat than all of Europe and held more people than all of France (Frieden 2006: 71). In a truly global market, each country could specialize. In fact, they had to specialize: whatever the exact form of their operations, farms turned into businesses competing in the global market. By practicing monoculture, as on the Dakota farms, they also altered the land. The waving grain that marked this wave of globalization physically changed the world.

Some Patterns in the Second Wave

The story of America's western expansion involves more than hardy pioneers, greedy speculators, and innovative businessmen, all looking for the main chance in a growing market opened up by new technology. As British power did in Jamaica, the American state played a key role behind the scenes, at times much more overtly. By granting land to railroads and selling public land cheaply to settlers, most notably with the Homestead Act of 1862, the federal government encouraged the expansion. In various ways, the state used its military power of persuasion to clear lands that were inconveniently occupied by Native Americans, losers in this round of globalizing ventures as slaves had been previously. Property rights guaranteed by the state, enforceable in court, provided the incentive for development, whether by farmers or railroads. Expansion happened in part because Congress wanted it to happen. Conquering people, space, and nature itself was a matter of deliberate effort. Bringing new people, new practices, and new principles, backed by new power, to new lands created an empire of sorts. Though not exactly comparable, this had much in common with the scramble for empire by the European powers in Africa and Asia. The "developmental states" of this phase of globalization, America included, were committed both to industrialization and to territorial control in a global quest for wealth and power. At a critical time in globalization, when new kinds of connections quickly sprouted, America had advantages of scale and structure that helped it sow the seeds of future dominance.

The entry of the Amenia and Sharon Company into Dakota Territory in 1875 was but one small step in the very large process of unifying the world that had already unfolded by that time, the "drawing together of all parts of the globe into a single world" (Hobsbawm 1975: 65). In the preceding 35 years, British trade with the other continents had increased sixfold, and in the 1870s the leading nations annually exchanged some 88 million tons of seaborne goods, by comparison with 20 million in 1840 (48ff.). Thanks to the work of explorers, most blank spots on the maps of 1848 had been filled in, so that in 1875 educated people knew their world much better (ibid.). In 1848 a journey around the world would have taken 11 months – the American prairies were one obstacle – but by 1872, with the benefit of steamships and railroads nearly everywhere, Jules Verne's Phileas Fogg might indeed have done it in 80 days.

The very food people ate, perhaps the most tangible object of diffusion, illustrates most plainly the drawing together. At least in the industrializing countries, globalization meant more food for more people and, in spite of tariffs, at lower prices. A global food system emerged, tying all participants into a network of interdependence. Specialized farms and regions, using the latest machines and fertilizers, fed their products into an elaborate system for processing and distribution, creating a "social division of labor [that] has taken on a truly global dimension" (Mazoyer and Roudart 2006: 395). Its new "market geography" depended less on local soils and climate, more on "prices and information flows of the economy as a whole" (Cronon 1991: 121). Global economic integration "reinforced itself" – as more countries developed more ties, more wanted to join in more ways (Frieden 2006: 49). Judged by the convergence of prices for global staples such as wheat, this integration or "big bang" of globalization had unfolded only since the 1820s (O'Rourke and Williamson 2002: 23). The network operated according to some common rules, or at least Britain tried to impose some, with support from others – for example, that trade ought to be free and currencies backed by gold (Frieden 2006: 45ff.). Its infrastructure, too, needed common rules, developed by organizations like the International Telegraph Union (1865). To coordinate their services, railroads in the US (1883) and elsewhere set their clocks to the same time in the same zones, standards that would soon be extended to the world as a whole. By the late nineteenth century, then, the web of connectivity had become stronger, wider, and more intricate. Exposed to news from abroad, aware of those who left for distant parts, enjoying new foods from new places, more people knew they were connected in a single global space where the rhythm of daily life depended on globally set times.

The second wave crashed and dissipated in the early twentieth century. Many factors and events led up to the Great War that marks its end, a conflict later renamed World War I in recognition of its global import. Debate about its causes continues, but behind all of them lie the weaknesses of global organization as it evolved by 1900. The world market created enormous wealth but new interdependence brought new uncertainty, only partly met by new forms of state protection. Though tied together through free trade, leading nations still strove to safeguard their power by extending their imperial reach – "empires of disadvantage" for most of their subjects (Robertson 2003: 147). Britain was no longer and the US not yet strong enough to dictate terms to others. The world economy was thus "incapable of avoiding . . . what came after it" (Frieden 2006: 123). Global integration fostered global tension, which broke the nineteenth-century web during the long crisis of 1914–45.

The Third Wave of Globalization: McDonald's in East Asia

In 1971, when Japanese airline officials were still exploring ways to transport North Atlantic tuna back home, Tokyo university student Den Fujita introduced McDonald's restaurants in Japan. They were a hit: by the mid-1980s, one Japanese outlet set the global one-day sales record, Fujita's multi-million dollar empire imported 12,000 tons of American beef and 15,000 tons of Idaho potatoes, and there soon would be more than 1,000 restaurants in the country (Ohnuki-Tierney 1997: 162). Creative adaptation was part of the corporate recipe, which added items like teriyaki burger to the standard menu. But while McDonald's appealed to a younger generation, it could not quite shake the perception that it just offered snack food. At least at first, the golden arches fit in awkwardly.

Trying to follow in Fujita's footsteps in 1975, Daniel Ng faced a similar challenge in Hong Kong, but initially decided not to offer Chinese items and to focus on standard fare instead (Watson 1997a: 82–3). The restaurant setting had to be just as "American," and so in Hong Kong McDonald's has the same bright arches, clean toilets, brisk service, and crispy fries, giving an American visitor the "uncanny sensation" that it is "just like home" (Watson 1997b: 22). Unsmiling workers, or individually dispensed napkins, or hovering customers waiting for a table, will quickly remind her that she is not in Kansas anymore, and in that sense McDonald's has acquired a Chinese flavor. But Hong Kong has adapted to McDonald's as well. It took some effort to teach people how to order their food McDonald's-style and to market the new culinary brand as something a modern person should aspire to consume. As in Japan, the bun/burger combination, without the all-important rice, at first seemed a mere snack to most customers, but a younger generation, enjoying outings and birthday parties at the cool American place, gradually treated it as a proper meal. At McDonald's, kids set the tone by choosing what they want, making it an entirely normal part of their culinary repertoire. Turned into common consumer items, the hamburger and Coke retain only a faint American aura.

As emblems of the third wave of globalization McDonald's outlets, to be sure, do not exactly parallel Jamaican plantations or Dakota farms. For one thing, McDonald's franchises do not really "produce" the food they serve. Rather, they stand at the apex of an intricate food industry, converting patties of mass-produced beef, slices of specially grown potatoes, and chemically flavored carbonated sugar water into "fast food." McDonald's adds a final touch, of course, and uses some techniques that would surprise food professionals of an earlier era, but its ingredients are a legacy of the second wave. Food was a commodity produced by industrial means in globally specialized regions – "industrial food" derived from staples to be marketed internationally (Goody 1982: ch. 5) – long before Ray Kroc served his first brand-name hamburger. Nor is the Americanized food experience of Tokyo or Hong Kong consumers all that unprecedented. In the first-wave Columbian exchange, after all, Asia massively imported New World crops, which over the centuries became entirely indigenous (Crosby 1972). The McDonald's bun may come in an unfamiliar shape, but bread had already made inroads in Japan since the late nineteenth century, changing the "typical" Japanese breakfast (Ohnuki-Tierney 1997: 167–8). Asians obviously had been very active in the previous waves, China in the first, Japan in the second. McDonald's established its beachhead in Tokyo not just because Japanese consumers had more money to spend but also because Japan had resumed the deliberate borrowing-to-outperform strategy it applied in the late nineteenth century (Westney 1987). Economic p[...] something to do with it: McDonald's provided a small boost t[...] transition" in growing countries, already underway in the secon[...] tinuing in the third, that added fat, sugar, and above all variety t[...] Japan did more rapidly what Europe and North America had don[...] in the rapid rise in its per capita meat consumption from 7.3 to [...] year in the four decades after 1955 (Drewnowski 1999: 200).

In a way, then, McDonald's shows that the third wave does more of the same, shipping more industrialized food across larger distances to more different places to be processed in standard ways and boost a common global diet. But as the site where many elements of the modern global food industry come together, McDonald's restaurants also exemplify distinctive features of the third wave. The intricacy of the industry, enabling standard items to appear fast on customer's trays, is itself a mark of deeper integration, a step beyond what was possible in the second wave. McDonald's actively promoted the integration by changing the way famers grow potatoes and ranchers raise beef to its specifications, and by managing the much longer supply chain (Paterson 2000: 136). As dispersed contributors to a growing market, Jamaica and the Dakotas lacked the corporate framework that turned McDonald's into a global powerhouse, a framework that came to structure even the business of agriculture itself, which went through a process of "agro-industrialization" (McMichael 2007: 228). While those production sites paid little attention to consumers, McDonald's in fact produces a particular consumer experience along with the food itself, instilling one model for how to eat and how to think about eating. Without implying that its Asian customers think deep global thoughts as they dig into their fries, McDonald's sells a certain minimal global awareness.

What to make of "the" McDonald's experience is still in dispute. Certainly, just as sushi has turned from an exotic taste into a regular consumer item, McDonald's in East Asia has become an equally routine fixture in the region's culinary landscape. In globalization, nothing stays exotic very long. In one way, this means that globalization standardizes experience through organized diffusion: from Topeka, Kansas, to Hong Kong or Tokyo, more people eat and do more of the same sorts of things. In fact, McDonald's has been turned into a metaphor itself, a source of the predictably regimenting, sameness-imposing "McDonaldization" that first swept through institutions in the West and now has gone global (Ritzer 2004). From this perspective, any McDonald's restaurant could be anywhere. McDonald's is, so to say, everywhere at once yet nowhere in particular. It helps to "deterritorialize" eating itself – another step beyond the second wave.

But, as Fujita and Ng were well aware, place still has power as well. As McDonald's in East Asia shows, globalization must involve some localization, and localization is a "two-way street," implying "changes in the local culture as well as modifications in the company's standard operating procedures" (Watson 1997b: 37). The Asian consumer enjoying her hamburger, with or without teriyaki, does not simply take what the company gives but also gives the company a message it must take seriously about what experience she expects. Making McDonald's part of her culinary repertoire, thus making McDonald's part of a varied culinary scene, she helps to create a new kind of "glocalized" mixture, in her own life and in the place where she lives. To many students of globalization, led by Robertson (1992, 1995), this sort of "glocalization," the more or less deliberate filtering or adaptation of global models and practices within particular local contexts that in turn reshapes those models and practices, is one of the key features of globalization. We will see many instances of it.

If Jamaican slaves and Dakota farmers were some of the quintessential figures of previous waves, Asian consumers are key players in the third. Some of what they do is different from what any predecessors did in the second wave, indicating how the third wave has rolled on. In some of what they do they differentiate themselves as distinct participants in globalization, indicating that preserving difference is one of the sensitive issues in globalization. But it is easy to overstate differences as well. As McDonald's in Asia illustrates, the third wave also carries on much of what the second, or even the first, wave started.

Some Patterns in the Three Waves

To one group of scholars, the continuities across the waves seem deeper than I have suggested. The arrival of McDonald's in Tokyo and Hong Kong, they think, signals the full incorporation of those places into a world system that has its origins in the sixteenth century and has not fundamentally changed since then. Spreading out across the globe, Europeans in the wealthy "core" created a world-spanning division of labor in which they controlled the essential capital and the biggest guns while other, poorer "peripheral" regions supplied labor and raw materials. With the aid of strong states, they strove to increase their wealth by exploiting the unequal relationship with those regions. In the process, they turned life-sustaining goods into commodities to be sold for profit in a world market. Because many states competed, this emerging world economy was no empire in which one center took all the spoils – one reason for its long-term success – though after a short period of Dutch dominance Britain gained nearly unrivaled power. To justify their new-found advantage, the Europeans also created ideas that served their interests, defining their inherent superiority and universal mission. By the late 1600s, according to "world-system theory," a new capitalist world economy was in place, a hierarchically organized, geographic division of labor within a world market, complemented by a system of states in the "core" and an ideology to match (Wallerstein 1974, 2004). The first wave of globalization, in this picture, permanently altered the way the world worked. Subsequent globalization merely expanded the system.

Even though the world system stayed the same, some things changed, of course. New technologies, like train and telegraph, gave the core new ways to bring goods to market and run the system itself, at least temporarily increasing the rate of capital accumulation. British hegemony effectively ended around 1900, and the US took over the leading role, its superior military power anchoring the post-war restoration of the old order. Only parts of the major continents were truly involved in the division of labor at the outset, but expansion meant pulling in more and more areas – nearly always to the advantage of the core – to the point where the capitalist world system spanned the globe by the early twenty-first century. While the basic inequality in the system persists, individual countries or regions may change position – former leader Spain fell back into the "semipe-riphery," formerly closed-off Japan made it into the core. Exploitation, too, is inherent in the system, as is the relentless pursuit of more capital, but how this is done changes over time, especially as slavery makes way for wage labor. The earlier examples from the first two waves illustrate some of these points: both Jamaica and the Dakotas operated within a capitalist world economy. So does McDonald's, as it brings a new phase of corporate capitalism to new regions, turning not just food itself but the very experience of consuming it into a com-modity. In the larger capitalist scheme, however, things that appear to be new also reinforce a very old structure.

Some global historians would question the claims of world-system proponents. In the sixteenth and seventeenth centuries, the two sides of the globe worked in rather different ways, and Europeans were clearly dominant on only one side, making the "world system" of that era at best a weak and partial one, by contrast with that of the late twentieth century. In the early phase Britain's naval strength did not greatly exceed that of its rivals, by contrast with its dominance in the late nineteenth century or later US superiority, so that "hegemony" may not have meant the same thing across the centuries. Both the rules governing state interaction and the rules for managing business and trade changed rather drastically, away from overt imperialism toward a world of independent states and away from mercantil-ism toward free trade, making it difficult for global historians to view waves of globalization as building a single system. Only by abstracting from many historical details for the sake of identifying one underlying pattern could one see such five-century consistency – too much to ask of scholars who reject the "narrow confines" the world-system model imposes (Osterhammel and Petterson 2005). Within those confines, globalization appears as always the same sort of process, to be explained in the same sort of way, emphasizing the demands of the world economy as the driving force. Outside of them, the world economy turns out to be only one force among others (Lechner and Boli 2005), not all connection equals hegemony (Grew 1999), and the elements of globalization relate in complex ways (Held et al. 1999). If the different waves of globalization have their own distinct features, not neces-sarily derived from the requirements of the world economy, then a less constrained, more inclusive analysis of patterns in the waves might better grasp the making of world society.

Tsukiji and McDonald's offer evidence that the third wave is not just *déjà vu* all over again, to invoke an American baseball cliché. If food helps us take the measure of society (Grew 1999), it tells us something about the way world society is now congealing, as a system in which parts are more intricately connected and a community in which people have more in common. The sheer scale of integra-tion is different, evident in fish flying across the globe or a multinational corpora-tion supplying standard food in widely dispersed places. More food travels longer distances to more people than ever before – "widespread" globalization is rela-tively recent (Grew 1999; Sobal 1999: 173). The impact is greater as well, evident in the ability of the new global infrastructure to support more than 6 billion people, a population about four times that of the second wave, in which many now live longer than any of their ancestors – in this regard, the Japanese lead a global trend.

Globalization did not by itself cause this break with the past but it played a critical role. The impact seeps into daily life as more people, global consumers all (Sklair 1995), gravitate toward a "global diet" (Drewnowski 1999) and develop a "global palate" (Pilcher 2005), of which a taste for sushi or hamburger are only small examples. The structure of world society shifts as new places take on new roles – the Asian resurgence, again led by Japan, being a major case in point. This is not a world made in America, or even in the West. The third wave also causes distinct problems, for example through the sheer pressure tuna fishing puts on ocean habitats or beef production on arable land. Such distinct problems provoke dissent, evident in the way both overfishing and McDonald's have become targets of globalization critics. More than before, world society itself turns into a subject of debate and an object of action.

Just as the grand world-system idea of a pattern of continuity across five centuries calls for a scheme that tries to make sense of globalization in one theoretical swoop, accentuating what is new in the current phase suggests that we may need different ideas to make sense of different patterns in it. Due to the twisting and turning of the third wave, the different elements – diffusion, interdependence, organization, culture/consciousness – may not change at the same rate or in the same direction: organization may not keep pace with interdependence, or culture with organization. Globalization comes in different kinds – as noted in the first chapter, globalizations, plural, might be a better catch-all concept. Nor do the elements globalize for the same reasons or in the same way: explaining diffusion may involve different ideas than accounting for a new global awareness. Just as social science has yet to come up with a single theory of society or social change, aiming for one general theory of globalization may therefore be overly ambitious.

At least at this stage of our knowledge, it makes little sense to attribute globalization to one cause or one set of factors or the effects of one "logic" within one system; instead, we are likely to learn more from exploring how different causes intertwine. People developed Jamaican plantations, Dakota wheat fields, Asian McDonald's franchises, or Japanese fishing techniques because they wanted to make money. In that sense, the lust for riches "causes" globalization. At each stage, technology made certain kinds of links possible but beckoning opportunity also spurred innovations that led to new links. In that sense, technology "causes" globalization. Pursuing opportunity and capturing profits, in Jamaica or Dakota or elsewhere, required not just money but also the strong hand of government. In that sense, power shapes the course of globalization. How and where people pursue opportunity depends on problems they face at the time – the "discovery" of the New World was itself the response to a distinct set of problems, and the Industrial Revolution that fueled the second wave dealt with problems created by the first. In that sense, contingent combinations of circumstances "cause" globalization. Rather than advocate a particular theory, stressing any one of these ways of looking at globalization, this book presents a more synthetic picture that combines elements of several perspectives to capture the mix of patterns that makes up globalization.

Summary and Conclusion

From any point of view, using my definition of globalization as a yardstick, we can see that over the past 500 years more people have become more connected in more different ways across larger distances. In three "waves," illustrated by the food-related examples drawn from Jamaica, the US and East Asia, we have been moving toward a world that works as a single society. Thinking about globalization in terms of waves accentuates what is new in each period, and therefore is a way of questioning grand claims about continuity across centuries, but of course that need not lead us to ignore any links to the past. Old versus new is not a matter of either-or. Much of this book reflects on what might be distinct in the current wave, but even if there is no single path we can trace back five centuries, the "making" of world society was well underway by the late nineteenth century, when most people's fates clearly depended on their counterparts in a nearly "universal human community" (Osterhammel and Petterson 2005). Since then, the links have become more intricate, our collective awareness of them more intense. "Globalization" captures the thrust of the long-term process.

How does it work and where does it lead? Unfortunately, there is no single answer to those questions. But partial answers, supported by good evidence, can tell us much. The next chapter takes the first step, focusing on the globalization of sports to outline a direction in globalization.

Questions

1   The sushi example helps to make the four dimensions of globalization more concrete. How could another commodity serve to make the same point?
2   The distinction between the waves assumes that technological advances made new connections possible. If new technology is that important, could one make a case that a fourth wave started in the late twentieth century?
3   How might McDonald's employees differ from Jamaican slaves and Dakota farm workers, and what does this tell us about the changing role of labor in the global economy? Do McDonald's owners/investors similarly differ from their counterparts on Jamaican plantations or American bonanza farms?
4   The chapter argues that McDonald's in East Asia represents something new in the third wave but one could counter that English coffeehouses in the 1600s were also "global" establishments of a sort. How might they exemplify features of globalization in the first wave?

Further Reading

Theodore C. Bestor, *Tsukiji: The Fish Market at the Center of the World* (University of California Press, 2004)

Geoffrey C. Gunn, *First Globalization: The Eurasian Exchange, 1500–1800* (Rowman & Littlefield, 2003)

Robert B. Marks, *The Origins of the Modern World: A Global and Ecological Narrative* (Rowman & Littlefield, 2002)

Sidney W. Mintz, *Sweetness and Power: The Place of Sugar in Modern History* (Penguin, 1986)

Jan Aart Scholte, *Globalization: A Critical Introduction* (St Martin's Press, 2005)

Immanuel Wallerstein, *The Modern World-System: Capitalist Agriculture and the Origins of the European World-Economy in the Sixteenth Century* (Academic Press, 1974)

3

GLOBAL SPORTS AND THE DIRECTION OF GLOBALIZATION

- Soccer: Local to Global
- Soccer and the Globalization of Sports
- Soccer in the Third Wave
- The Global Sporting System
- America in Global Sports
- Summary and Conclusion

Soccer: Local to Global

Only in recent decades did soccer become popular in the Atlanta area, long a bastion of baseball and American football. While doing participant observation as a volunteer soccer coach, I watched the globalization of soccer unfold there. From the start, my teams were quite diverse – several players had parents from places like Colombia, Costa Rica, Ethiopia, and the UK. Among the many immigrants in DeKalb County, one of the most rapidly diversifying on the East Coast of the US (see Chapter 10), soccer was the favorite game, and this slowly added a new dimension to our league. Starting at an early age on small fields, in 3-on-3 games without a goalkeeper but with coaches moving among the players, the budding athletes would graduate at about age six to a more sophisticated 4-on-4 game, still without a goalie but with coaches retreating to the sideline. Any dreams of introducing Dutch "total soccer" to the fields of DeKalb County usually came to naught but this did not diminish the occasional bliss of seeing a run into open space or tough defense stopping a talented opponent. After we graduated to a more intricate 8-on-8 format, now with a goalie, one memorable game was saved by a brave dive toward the ball that earned my Indian-Korean-American goalie a bloody nose; in another tough contest, my Dutch-American son did his coach proud with a lovely pass from the right wing to our streaking Somali-Lebanese-American forward, who finished the play with an unstoppable kick to the upper right-hand corner.

Such experiences create a virtual solidarity among coaches everywhere, all trying to teach the "beautiful game," the prime example of globally organized leisure activities this chapter describes. Unlike some of their coaches, DeKalb players did not think much about their counterparts abroad while trying not to miss in front of an open goal or clearing the ball when opponents threatened to score. And yet, in their own way, they did think globally as they learned and enjoyed the same game in roughly the same way as millions of other kids around the world. By comparison with their peers in Europe or Latin America, they knew less about the stars of the game or the intricacies of international competition. When one kid wore a Beckham jersey, prior to that player's transfer to the Los Angeles Galaxy, it sparked no recognition from his peers; when I joked with another about following the example of Zidane, the name on his shirt, the joke fell flat because he did not know what I meant – he had just picked up the jersey at a sale. My players had yet to become fully immersed in the culture of global soccer but, more than friends focused on American football or baseball, they had taken their first steps. Some, in fact, became quite sophisticated over time, following foreign teams and top players on TV and via the Internet.

They belonged to the Tucker Youth Soccer Association (TYSA), in most years comprising more than 1,500 active players and more than 100 coaches. In addition to recruiting amateurs, TYSA hired professional coaches for its more advanced teams, including former pros from the UK and South Africa. In the summer, some of those teams might go on trips abroad to sharpen their skills against foreign opponents. Notwithstanding our slightly deviant games for the younger age groups, including roll-ins rather than throw-ins, TYSA was committed to playing by the rules set by FIFA, the world soccer federation. Via its affiliation with the Georgia Youth Soccer Association, which in turn was affiliated with a similar national organization and the United States Soccer Federation, TYSA was in fact connected to FIFA. Together with other organizations, TYSA helped to train coaches as well so that even those who did not grow up playing could teach the game the right way. With somewhat less fervor and success, TYSA also promoted local professional teams. Soccer flourished in Atlanta as a recreational sport but it did not yet compete with baseball, basketball, or football as a fan spectacle, and the region long failed to attract a first-rate Major League Soccer professional team. Only the World Cup tournament aroused real fan interest in our area.

Soccer came to Atlanta at the tail end of a globalization process that has its roots in the nineteenth-century second wave. Of course, football, as most non-Americans called it long before Atlantans got involved, has become *the* global game. It is unique in its popularity, in the attention it gets, the money it generates, and the passion it stirs among fans worldwide. Yet its path to global popularity parallels that of many other sports. This chapter first describes that path, showing through the example of soccer, if non-Americans will excuse the term, how all sports spread from a few places to many others, creating new forms of competition and organization as well as a common sports consciousness. It then makes the point that most games in the world today are global games to some extent, part of a global "sporting system" and therefore subject to global norms and expectations. To be a proper sport, taken seriously around the world, a game has to fit these rules. That tells us something about the direction of globalization, as global practices seep into daily life and become ever more organized.

In that sporting system, characteristic of third-wave globalization, America plays a peculiar role. Just as many people consider it an imperial power in business or politics, many would also say it is a dominant force in sports, for example because games invented in the US, like basketball and volleyball, are now popular everywhere and because America's commercial approach to professional sports has had an impact all over the world. But the issue is more complex. The fact that Atlanta trailed in soccer already suggests that America is follower as well as leader, a distinct sports culture as well as a global model, a country changed by global sports even as it changes the global sports scene. The globalization of baseball, once America's "national pastime," has faltered, partly due to America's dominance, while the originally similar game of cricket has spread widely, as Britain's former dominions took it up with gusto to challenge its imperial dominance. A closer look at America's role in sports thus helps us to assess the broader argument that each phase of globalization is strongly shaped by the influence of a single dominant power or "hegemon."

Soccer and the Globalization of Sports

Soccer arrived in DeKalb County from the UK via a circuitous route. According to an old cliché, it is Britain's most enduring export (Murray 1996: 22; Missiroli 2002: 3). After a group of British college students agreed in 1848 on rules that would enable them to play against each other, the game quickly spread (Guttmann 1994: 42–3). Within a few years, now-legendary clubs such as Sheffield United and Aston Villa were founded. Though some would trace the modern game's origins farther back (Goldblatt 2008: 31), in 1863 the game's pioneers formed the Football Association (FA), whose officers formulated the code of "association football" at a famous meeting in the Freemason's Tavern in London in October of that year. Bolton Wanderers won the first FA "Challenge Cup" in 1872, but the Cup Final only began to draw sizable crowds in the 1880s, reaching over 100,000 spectators in 1901. The first "international" between England and Scotland, reported in the press, also took place in 1872. Originally a middle-class leisure activity – still a minor pastime in the 1870s (Goldblatt 2008: 32) – soccer soon attracted workers as well, turning the soccer grounds of England, according to yet another cliché in the stock history of the game, into the Labour Party at prayer. The best clubs went professional, which the FA, long reluctant to shed genteel amateurism, approved in 1888; Scotland followed suit in 1893. Within a few decades, soccer thus acquired most of the trappings of the modern game – a simple set of standard rules, broad appeal across classes to amateurs and professionals alike, organized nationwide competition with a Cup Final as dramatic apex, a network of clubs under the canopy of a national organization, and growing public interest in soccer as spectacle and entertainment. That package became a model. In sports, and beyond, such models set the direction for globalization.

Many were eager to export the package. After discovering the game in England, the Dutch teenager Pim Mulier took it back home, founding the first Dutch club in Haarlem and helping to set up a national federation (Murray 1996: 23). Most exporters, of course, were British – sailors who brought the game to Italian port cities, for example, or traders who introduced the game in Milan and Turin, all mixing business and pleasure (Guttmann 1994: 53). In Argentina, British teachers played a leading role, introducing the game to their students in the Buenos Aires area, after which the game quickly took off, stimulated by massive immigration from Europe (Murray 1996: 32–3). A British college also took the initiative in Uruguay, which, as an early adopter, became a soccer power despite its small size (Giulianotti 2000). Soldiers in the British army and Indians working in the public services played the game, resulting in a memorable victory by Mohan Bagan over the best British colonial teams in 1911 (Murray 1996: 18). Soccer aficionados like to think that the game's simple rules and inherent interest account for much of its success, and no sensible sociologist would risk their ire by denying it. Yet more mundane reasons also account for soccer's diffusion. With the power and allure of Britain backing them, many of its representatives carried it from the imperial center to peripheral areas. Their example and instruction took hold. The center's cachet helped to make soccer cool.

In retrospect, soccer's success may seem obvious, assured by the pleasures of the game, the wide range of eager exporters, and the status benefits to early adopters. That still gives a bit too much credit to its British creators. Most of the early adopters lived in countries going through similar changes, as cities grew, industry took off, and both middle and lower classes had a little more disposable income. More people demanded diversion, had time to attend, and could pay for the privilege. Modernization and globalization moved in tandem; what appeared as diffusion was also due to independent domestic development. Even so, in the first phase of diffusion only small numbers actually played, and not all countries were equally enamored of the game; its rise was quite "resistible" (Goldblatt 2008: ch. 4). Ireland resisted perhaps most emphatically, trying to avoid the humiliating taint of the colonial master's game and turning instead to more "authentic" Gaelic ones (86–7). More favorably disposed toward the mother country, Canada nevertheless took up ice hockey as a favorite pastime more suited to brutal winters – and one in which Canadians happened to excel (89). Despite some early soccer success, cricket became the quintessential colonial sport in India, in part because the native Indian elite preferred it and some "entrepreneurs" then promoted it among the people at large (Kaufman and Patterson 2005). In Japan, baseball gained greater popularity, as sports entrepreneurs there found it a better fit with Japanese traditions (Guttmann and Thompson 2001). In Asia, overall, the spread of soccer was "patchy" (Murray 1996: 59). Americans, as we will see, certainly tried soccer – a "hidden part of its sporting universe" before World War II (Goldblatt 2008: 88) – and cities like St Louis developed a soccer tradition long before Atlanta, but for many reasons soccer did not take hold across the US. Soccer diffusion was strikingly global but also uneven. Imperial domination did not translate into universal emulation.

In spite of such differences, soccer-playing countries began to form a community of sorts. As railways and the telephone connected people more easily across larger distances, domestic competitions soon developed in many places. International competition grew rapidly as well. In the first international game outside the UK, Uruguay beat Argentina, 3-2, in 1901; three years, later France first played Belgium; in 1905, the Dutch defeated the Belgians, 4-1, in a game that started a long rivalry (Murray 1996: 31). Soccer became part of the Olympic Games in 1908. Though only a few European teams showed up to play, to the dismay of the victorious hosts, the first World Cup in Uruguay in 1930 marked the beginning of what became a quintessential global event. Club teams also developed connections abroad, as Southampton did on its first tour of South America in 1905 (39). Celtic's 2-1 defeat by a Copenhagen team in 1907, the first British team loss on the continent, showed that its inventors already were encountering tougher opposition (38). Many clubs began to play such international matches, creating new ties and a common soccer culture.

Across the wealthier countries, soccer became well organized: "Within the first decade of the twentieth century soccer teams and controlling bodies were to be found in every country in Europe" (Murray 1996: 31). In the Netherlands, for example, the Koninklijke Nederlandse Voetbalbond (KNVB) – "Koninklijke" ("Royal") added to its name in 1929 conveying elite approval – was founded in 1889 and subsequently channeled all official soccer activity in the country, scheduling competitions, setting rules, licensing coaches and referees, and overseeing the national team. In a country with some 1 million active players (out of a current population slightly over 16 million), that is a huge task. Though France hardly joined the international soccer rage, Frenchmen did take the initiative to found a global organization, the Fédération Internationale de Football Association (FIFA), in 1904 (Guttmann 1994: 55–6). At first a body of and for Europeans, it gradually realized its "internationalist" ambition to "control every type of association foot-ball," foster friendly relations among members, and thereby bring everyone involved in soccer together in one "family" (Sugden and Tomlinson 1998: 5–6, 49). For more than a century, under FIFA's aegis, soccer has been a deliberately global game. As TYSA officials would be proud to acknowledge, DeKalb athletes are now part of that "family."

Soccer in the Third Wave

No one knows exactly how many people around the world played by, say, the 1930s, but soccer had gained both players and fans on most continents. Each country crowned its own champions. The World Cup, now a regular event, determined the world's best national team. Anyone at all involved in soccer knew it as a game played by millions according to the same rules everywhere. Even before World War II, then, soccer had globalized, as a beneficiary of the late-nineteenth-century wave of globalization. Its path was firmly in place. Yet it hardly had the modern game's global presence. World Cups did not involve many countries. Few players earned a living at their game. Among those who did, only Latin American players tended to go abroad. Even across Europe, there was no standard annual tournament. In the absence of TV broadcasting, public interest was limited. Soccer was not yet a big deal, and it only turned into one after World War II.

In the post-war years, nearly everybody everywhere, to exaggerate slightly, enjoyed a chance to play. With government support, a generation of Hungarian players formed a dream team in the 1950s. Brazil soon followed with its own cohort of special players, who proceeded to win three Cups. For all its isolation, North Korea competed in the 1966 World Cup, surprisingly reaching the quarterfinals. In newly independent African countries such as Ghana and Cameroon, soccer became the national sport. In Middle Eastern countries, international soccer stirred national passions from about the 1970s. When South Korea and Japan vied to organize the 2002 World Cup, this symbolized the game's bigger profile in Asia. "Everybody" came to include millions of women. In this respect, at least, America was a leader in world soccer, thanks to the relative success of its women's movement and the growing role of colleges in fostering women's sports (Markovits and Hellerman 2003). The American women won the first women's World Cup in 1991 and the first Olympic soccer finals in 1996, the fruit of many years' work starting in leagues like TYSA.

While the women's game still lacks commercial success, at the professional level in the men's game everybody was part of one soccer market. By the end of the twentieth century, for example, when the best Dutch players decamped to top foreign teams, Dutch clubs in turn recruited Korean and American players and also began scouting small clubs and sandlots in Africa in search of fresh talent. Some years later, when the Dutch club PSV faced Arsenal in a Champions League contest, no English and only a few Dutch players took the field. Though globalized, the market was still patchy, divided by region: Europe attracted most high-priced talent, and within Europe the Italian, Spanish, and English leagues dominated. Across the market, Brazil supplied the most and some of the best talent, causing FIFA chief Sepp Blatter to worry in 2008 that naturalized expatriate Brazilians might claim too many spots on too many national teams, which might turn the World Cup into an intramural contest. In the eyes of such officials Brazil, long a major soccer power, threatened to turn into a hegemon displacing the former core countries.

Everybody, both national teams and top clubs, faced increasingly intense international competition. The European and World Cup championships, now broadcast live, drew enormous audiences. In Europe, international club competition, consisting of several parallel tournaments since the official start of a club championship in 1955–6, became a regular feature of public life and a mainstay on television, with cumulative viewership of several billions (Sugden and Tomlinson

1994: 74). Everybody is also more organized. Latin America already formed a regional organization in 1916, but other continents followed from 1954 onward (6). Their clout is evident in FIFA, to which nearly every country now belongs. Non-Western countries have come to the fore, as illustrated by the election of Brazilian Joao Havelange as president in 1974 against European opposition. Everybody is also more aware of what everybody else is doing. Coaches must keep tabs on foreign competition, switching to more defensive strategies when others find answers to offensive maneuvers that had once been successful. Countries know where they stand by virtue of continuous international competition and a FIFA ranking system. A large menu of televised soccer, now supplemented by the Internet, keeps fans completely informed about developments around the soccer world. Peak "mega events" (Roche 2000) like the World Cup have become elaborately staged rituals that command passionate interest from many millions. They have become a near-global public attuned to regular country and club competitions, making soccer the first game to succeed in this kind of profitable consciousness-raising (Leifer 1995).

Soccer is more than a game. Soccer experts describe it as a "Network" (Sugden 2002), in which professional clubs, operating as businesses, compete for the best players. Those with the biggest home market tend to win out. The overall market is shaped in part by media providers that seek content to carry their advertising. That advertising comes from businesses treating the game as a marketing tool. Teams and corporations seek larger audiences, both by increasing quality and by offering more "product." As demand increases, so do incentives for everyone who is involved in the business of soccer. Fan interest spurs teams to improve, which has implications for the player market, which leads to a new competitive situation, which influences media and corporate strategies, which in turn affects fans and teams. The Network is big business, with revenue estimated at some $250 billion in the early 2000s (Giulianotti and Robertson 2004).

Allowing again for a little hyperbole, everybody now operates within this Network. But it does not stifle national differences entirely. As a minor example, Italy claimed its own role in soccer history, by changing the name of its federation to refer to the traditional game of *calcio* (Guttman 1994: 54). At various times, the country's national teams contributed new soccer styles, most notably the tough and opportunistic defensive approach known as *catenaccio*. For many countries, in fact, the idea of a distinctive style reinforces a sense of national identity, as happened to the Dutch when "their" team went to the World Cup Final in 1974 thanks to its special brand of "total soccer," featuring players in constant motion, taking each other's roles, always pressing to attack (Winner 2000). Brazil is even better known for a playful and offensive approach based on superior ball control that helped to make soccer the "symbol" of the nation there (Bellos 2002). Some would argue that in the modern game the belief in distinct styles is a bit of a myth, if only because many of the best players work in countries other than their own and because coaches learn from each other to blend styles as needed (Lechner 2007). Yet diversity persists, partly along national lines. In fact, it is expected: a self-respecting nation defines itself as a particular variation on a global theme, as a "glocal" version of the global game (Giulianotti and Robertson 2004). To use another metaphor, soccer cultures are tributaries to the common stream of the global game.

The Global Sporting System

Drafting part of this chapter during the 2006 Winter Olympics in Turino, Italy, put soccer in perspective. It is, of course, only one of many sports people play and enjoy. A die-hard soccer fan might question whether hurtling down an icy path on a little sled or sliding a rock across ice while sweeping with brooms should properly be considered sports. The Olympics nevertheless puts a global stamp of approval on such activities. The summer and winter games together encompass about 36 different sports, some old, like running, some new, like snowboarding (Etter 2006). In a little over a century, many traditional leisure activities have thus been transformed into, and new ones invented as, global games. Around the world, people now practice and watch the same sorts of things in the same sort of way. As a result of this "sportization" of leisure (Maguire 1999), we are part of a global "sporting system" (Van Bottenburg 2001).

The history of soccer is only part of a larger "extraordinary story of cultural diffusion," mostly from Europe and the US (Mangan 2001: 2). Britain moved first in organizing a number of games and exerted special influence abroad. The very idea of sports as a good and healthy thing, rooted in its public school culture (Mangan and Hickey 2001), is a British export. Particular sports like soccer, tennis, rugby, cricket, and golf are British inventions. Tennis may have been the "first global sport" (Smart 2007: 115; Gillmeister 1998), with a first international tournament, forerunner of the Davis Cup, held in Newport in 1878, other events soon attracting players from many countries, an international federation established by 1913, and the "Grand Slam" championships inaugurated by 1923. But Britain was only one source. Volleyball and basketball, mainstays of the Summer Olympics, were products of the American Young Men's Christian Association (YMCA), invented to occupy Christian youngsters during the winter and spread by missionaries who believed in "muscular Christianity." Gymnastics started as a nationalist effort to lift the health and spirits of Germans, partly to protect German youth against the poison of British competitive team sports (Guttmann 1994: ch. 10). Cycling, practiced wherever people rode bicycles, got a boost not just from the Olympics but also from its most challenging event, the Tour de France. Nordic and alpine countries contributed skiing and skating, in which the UK has had little success, as illustrated by British ski jumper Eddy the Eagle's failure to live up to his nickname, while Korean short-track speed skaters and Chinese figure skaters have shown what it takes to become competitive. After first importing American sports like baseball more eagerly than their British rivals (Guttmann and Thompson 2001), the Japanese later adapted martial arts tradition to the new sports culture by developing judo, only to watch a Dutch athlete take the heavyweight gold on its home turf in 1964. Though first played in modern form in the UK, a middle-class pastime turned into a real sport (Guttmann 1994), table tennis over time became a favorite activity in Asia, with Chinese or sometimes Korean players usually victorious in international competition. In this story of diffusion, the memory of origins blurs as more and more people participate. Sports no longer flow from a single source in a single direction, if they ever did.

Few sports can match the intensity of international soccer competition but even on a smaller scale all have "Networks" of their own – regular and intense international competition, followed by the media, supported by commercial sponsors, promoted by governments, and, taken together, "truly worldwide" in their scope and appeal (Smart 2007: 114). The competition started early: already in the nineteenth century, many were eager to be the "best in the world," and controversies about who really was "world champion" spurred events and organizations to settle the issue (Van Bottenburg 2001: 7). Today, of course, every sport has its international championships, with Olympic gold often the premier prize. To be successful at the top level, everyone has to keep up with strategies, training methods, and, let's not forget, drugs used by competitors. In high-level team sports, players are temporary nomads who move where opportunity calls, part of a transnational labor market. Within the Network of Networks of global sports, every sport is vying for attention, money, and participants – basketball versus soccer, beach volleyball versus "regular" volleyball, snowboarding versus skiing, and so on. The global sports system regulates competition worldwide and is itself intrinsically competitive.

FIFA was one of 16 international sports organizations founded before World War I (Van Bottenburg 2001). Today there are more than 70, and among them volleyball appears to have the most national branches (8, 10). Even in the early phase, often in what we now call international nongovernmental organizations (INGOs), sports pioneers were busy standardizing their games and setting up bureaucracies to manage them, a feature of all modern sports (Guttmann 1984). Like TYSA's players, participants became embedded in a layer cake of organizations linking local fields and courts to national and international bodies. They do not fully control their sports, if only because governments usually still set and enforce rules on issues such as doping, gambling, broadcasting, and the business of sports. Yet they are a tangible dimension of "world society." Though they vary in size and power, these bodies do the same sorts of things. Since sports organizations have been around a long time, newer ones copy what established predecessors do, partly for simplicity, partly to gain status. As in many other areas, early models have taken hold across a variety of organizations. Many of them are also quite deliberate about adopting such models, especially when they try to live up to the expectations set by the International Olympic Committee (IOC) as a condition for inclusion in the Games. To qualify as an "International Olympic Federation," a sports organization must comply with the Olympic Charter, follow the IOC anti-doping code, arrange regular competitions, and so

Plate 3.1 Baron Pierre de Coubertin (1863–1937), founder of the modern Olympic Games
Source: © Bettmann/Corbis

on. Each worldwide body in turn contains national organizations that must follow its general rules. The IOC is at the center of a web in which all the nodes are increasingly alike.

Especially for the more "minor" sports, the chance to take part in the Olympics of course offers a strong incentive to follow IOC dictates. Sharing in the bounty of commercial endorsements and television contracts adds to their appeal. For advocates of minor sports, following the beaten path is only rational. But concrete benefits are not the whole story. The sports path becomes beaten as many organizations move in a certain direction, following an implicit map of how to "do sports." As a nongovernmental organization, the IOC also exercises a strange sort of authority in serving as a guide along this path. Its clout partly derives from its claim to represent common values in a common sporting culture. Its script helps to articulate what is, or is not, legitimate in the world of sports. In this way, the IOC and the wider world of sports illustrate a "neoinstitutionalist" or "world polity theory" argument (Meyer, Boli, et al. 1997; see Chapter 6) about how world society becomes organized not simply through the pressure of political power or

Box 3.1   Features of the global sporting system

Top sports by number of national organizations
(Van Bottenburg 2001)

1   Volleyball
2   Track and field
3   Soccer
4   Basketball
5   Tennis

FIFA/Coca-Cola ranking of national soccer teams (fifa.com, July 2008)

1   Spain
2   Italy
3   Germany
4   Brazil
5   The Netherlands

Selected dates in the development of the global sporting system

1872   First international soccer game, Scotland–England, Glasgow
1877   First cricket Test match, Australia–England, Melbourne
1896   First modern Olympic Games, Athens
1900   First Davis Cup tennis tournament
1903   First Tour de France
1930   First World Cup, Uruguay
1991   First women's World Cup, China

Selected sports mega events

2004   Olympic Games, Athens
2006   World Cup, Germany
2006   Winter Olympic Games, Torino
2008   Olympic Games, Beijing
2010   World Cup, South Africa
2010   Winter Olympic Games, Vancouver
2012   Olympic Games, London

the deals of profit-seeking businesses but also through the mutual modeling of voluntary organizations with global aspirations. This modeling, or "script enactment" as it is sometimes called, occurs in many other areas of global life, from education to the environment, typically making different places work in similar ways. Sports are only one instance out of many.

In the culture of modern sports we can still detect traces of British influence, such as the belief in the importance of physical achievement and proving one's worth through playful competition, but in many ways that culture is now far removed from the playing fields of British public schools. The very fact of the removal is important: sports create a sense of commonality and connection not just within a local elite but also among millions across large distances. They share an entirely taken-for-granted global culture of common knowledge and interests guided by common rules. Not everyone knows the fine points of judging in gymnastics or figure skating, or how to stay upright on skates to begin with, or even what ice or snow feel like, but, overall, sports are an integral part of the global cultural repertoire. They are therefore "symptomatic" of an emerging transnational culture (Maguire 1999: 41), an integral part of globalization's third wave. Since some professional sports have become an entertainment spectacle, sports culture is also entwined with the culture of consumerism. Though few can match the intense public following fostered by the top domestic leagues, sports create global connections among couch potatoes as well.

For more and more people, the global sports repertoire on display at the Olympics offers increasing local variety – more structured, pleasurable activities to choose from or to watch – while at the same time it diminishes the contrasts across places – over time, the Dutch play more like the Japanese who play more like us in the American South (Maguire 1999: 47–8, 80, 207ff.). The mix of choices still sets communities or countries apart, as demonstrated by Norwegian alpine sports success in Turino. As in the case of soccer, nations still can try to define themselves by creating a "style" in one sport or another. The global Olympic ritual offers further opportunities for self-presentation, as illustrated by Barcelona mixing Catalan themes into its ceremonies in 1992 (Hargreaves 2002) and Turino emphasizing its "passion" as a theme throughout its events. Corporate sponsors, such as Nike using Japanese cooking and sports clubs in its Japanese advertising, appeal to specific audiences by speaking the "languages of the local" (Andrews and Ritzer 2007: 141). But this straining for diversity and marketing of identity occur within the confines of a single system. A system it is: everyone knows what a "real" sport is supposed to be, how it should be organized, and what it means to practice one. Everyone knows what the Olympics are and how they are to be staged. Particular sports can, and do, carve their own path within the system, but, like countries and participants, they also operate under its overall constraints. No one group controls it.

Perhaps more than most countries, the US has made its own choices and carved its own path in a sporting system that envelops it as much as it does others. At the same time, America's sporting record illustrates some of the ways the country has made its mark on globalization, a recurring theme in later chapters.

America in Global Sports

For children in DeKalb, soccer is only one of many options. In spring, TYSA might lose players to baseball; in winter, many switch to basketball; and in the hot Georgia summer, swimming is the obvious alternative. For older children, high schools organize numerous sports activities. As in other parts of the US, Friday night high school football is a big attraction for spectators. So are college sports, especially the men's football and basketball teams at local universities. Like any self-respecting metropolitan area, Atlanta has the requisite professional teams in football, baseball, basketball, and hockey. Throughout the region, some stock-car races organized by NASCAR draw crowds larger than many of those games. This enormous range of activities for casual athletes and fans, supplemented by intense national sports coverage on television, draws people into a distinctly American sports culture. For most, international soccer, let alone other global sports, is not on their mental horizon. Major broadcast events like the Olympics, the World Cup, or Wimbledon might draw some interest but much of the time America is a sports "island" (Eriksen 2007: 157). Not surprisingly, winners in American professional leagues are declared "world" champions. Grating as it may be to the rest of the world, the boast is not entirely unreasonable, since, even if they only compete on their island, the quality of American pro teams is typically unmatched.

Not in soccer, of course. In the global game, America still plays a modest role, notwithstanding the victories of its women's team and the occasional success of its men. America's sports culture is exceptional partly because interest in soccer is still so anemic. This American exception has deep historical roots (Markovits and Hellerman 2001). In the late nineteenth century, some Americans tried soccer, and it flourished in many immigrant communities, but the game did not take hold as a common pastime or spectator favorite. At elite colleges that set the tone among the upper strata, sports fanatics developed a distinctly American version of a running and kicking game much like rugby that became American football. Others pioneered a new variation of an old stick and ball game, deliberately distinguishing it from an earlier British version. The fact that immigrants enjoyed soccer did not raise its stature in the eyes of Americans. When sports inventors at the YMCA added basketball and volleyball to the American menu, there was even less room for soccer in America's "crowded" sports space (ibid.). Even so, soccer enthusiasts had chances to increase interest in the game, but they largely failed to do so except in a few places. An upsurge in interest in the 1920s and American participation in the 1930 World Cup, indicative of a "hidden" soccer culture, left no lasting imprint (Goldblatt 2008). When in the second half of the twentieth century America developed its distinct seasonal rhythm of sports to play and watch – baseball in summer, football in fall, then basketball and hockey – soccer did not fit in. The briefly successful efforts of Pelé and other stars in a professional league in the 1970s could not sway American fan interest for long. Far from shaping the global game, America has stood "offside."

The sheer size of the US helped to make it a sports island. It had the critical mass of athletes and fans to make several sports viable on a national scale. It was wealthy enough to make those games lucrative. It developed a distinctive system for developing talent, centered on colleges whose own sporting traditions and local support limited foreign experiments. For sports fans as well as for young aspiring athletes, the variety available within the US also made looking across the oceans unnecessary. Because the most prominent sports were regarded as "typically American," practiced best by Americans as a matter of course, they did not foster national interest in international competition. Only the Olympics, or occasional events in niche sports like tennis or golf, sparked such interest. The distinctive mix of games, pursued at different levels, in a distinctive sequence through the year, followed by an inward-looking audience of fans, on America's sports island has prevented the US from being a model for other sports cultures. Sports around the world do not work like sports in the US. Since no one actually emulates the US, strictly speaking, sports are not becoming "Americanized."

Baseball is a case in point. Much of the world has remained outside the diamond (Kelly 2007). In the mid-nineteenth century, Americans marked their national distinction by developing their own bat-and-ball game rather than following British cricket fashion. Playing baseball was a way of not being British, which later limited its appeal in the British Empire. By the end of the century, after many fits and starts, professional teams in organized leagues played in regular, fairly balanced competitions intended to appeal to the domestic market, creating an American public for America's pastime (Leifer 1995) in a way that would later hinder its reach abroad. Baseball's rules developed in the Major Leagues and came to be controlled by the commissioner of Major League Baseball (MLB), but the very fact that America was at the center of the baseball world kept the game from flourishing globally (Kelly 2007: 188). Missionaries were able to convert athletes abroad to baseball, in Central America and East Asia above all, but even though these areas fell under American influence the sports export lacked the strong British imperial impulse. In Japan, Taiwan, Korea, the Dominican Republic, and several Latin American countries baseball became very popular indeed, and by the end of the twentieth century they had begun to supply many outstanding players to the US leagues, where teams such as the Dodgers (Klein 2006) made concerted efforts to recruit and train them. But the success of Dominican and Japanese stars also confirmed that baseball still revolved around the Major Leagues. International competition and organization were an afterthought. By the early 2000s, baseball was not yet fully part of the global sporting system. America's own prowess had limited its impact.

To the consternation of baseball fans, the IOC brought home the point by deciding in 2006 to eliminate baseball (and women's softball) as an Olympic sport, one
of the few games ever to suffer that fate. In spite of Asian fervor and Cuban
excellence at previous Games, the IOC concluded that baseball was just not global
enough. The presumed superpower in sports had not been able to export its own
national pastime very effectively. That baseball might not be less "global," in terms
of individual participation or the competitiveness of countries, than luge or curling
or pentathlon did not sway the IOC. America's prime role in financing the
Olympics, both through corporate sponsors such as Coca-Cola and through rich
TV broadcasting contracts, did not earn it respect either. To add insult to injury,
the US also failed to retain a representative on the IOC executive committee in
2006. In sports, being a superpower had lost some of its luster. The sporting system,
Americans learned, operated by its own rules, beyond the control of any single
group or country.

The IOC decision seemed harsh in part because even baseball had shown unmistakable signs of globalizing. By 2008, according to MLB statistics, 28 percent of
players were born abroad, and foreigners made up an even larger percentage of
minor leaguers (SI.com, April 1, 2008). Some were among the most celebrated –
Sammy Sosa from the Dominican Republic chased the single-season homerun
record, Ichiro Suzuki from Japan became a superstar playing for the Seattle Mari-
ners, and the Boston Red Sox paid $50 million just for the right to negotiate with
Japanese pitching ace Daisuke Matsuzaka, who quickly became known to American
fans as "Dice K." Thanks to the influx of such top Asian and Latin American talent
into America's Major Leagues, the balance of power shifted. In the 2006 World
Baseball Classic, an ad hoc international tournament staged by MLB, the US stood
little chance against several competitors. In a final some American commentators
recognized as a sign that "the world is shrinking" (Stark 2006), Japan beat Cuba.
Notwithstanding the IOC's put-down, baseball was becoming ever more global. In
the end, however, international competition still did little to move baseball beyond
the diffusion it had attained to become a truly integrated, globally organized game.
The 2006 Classic tournament was "planned as an American event to be supported
by the rest of the world" – a case of "internationalism in service of an MLB event"
(Klein 2006: 247). For a "real" world series to become meaningful, MLB would have
to "decenter somewhat" (251), and it took a small step in that direction by opening
the 2008 season in Japan. Whether it can succeed in creating a more global baseball
public by applying the lessons it learned in creating its own leagues remains an open
question (Leifer 1995).

By contrast with baseball, basketball is well on its way. Until a few decades ago,
it suffered from the same global limitations as baseball. Invented and cultivated in
the US, it had remained a niche sport elsewhere. At the professional level, the
National Basketball Association (NBA) ruled and few other countries could muster
similar leagues. Among amateurs, American college players were also at the top,
on a par with even the "amateurs" from communist countries that had decided
to challenge America's supremacy on the court and thereby infused international

competition with a little Cold War passion. But when the all-star professional "dream team" made its appearance at the 1992 Olympics, after FIBA (the international basketball federation) finally allowed pro participation, the quality gap with the rest of the world proved large. Yet that display of dominance also contained the seeds of change. The team's performance served as a public relations show, part of a campaign by the NBA to advertise its game abroad. The players also hawked their wares – several notoriously refused to put on the attire of the official team sponsor and insisted on loyalty to their own instead. Though the Americans still won quite easily, among the hundreds of millions of Olympic TV viewers were athletes watching and learning, inspired by the feats of American stars to take up the game in earnest. The very fact that basketball players had become global stars, making a splash at the Games simply by showing up, indicated that awareness of the game was steadily increasing. In global sports, basketball was becoming a big deal.

That did not happen by chance. After professional basketball ran into trouble in the US, the NBA made a concerted effort to improve its image in the 1980s. The play of a new generation of great athletes and intense competition between the Los Angeles Lakers and Boston Celtics greatly increased domestic fan interest. But NBA commissioner David Stern, appointed in 1984, had bigger plans to turn basketball into a prime entertainment product. His vision was global: NBA basketball could and should become popular everywhere. Under his leadership, the NBA packaged games as TV spectacles. It sold broadcasting rights in several countries, enabling more fans elsewhere to follow American basketball. It also worked with companies to promote the stars themselves, first "Magic" Johnson and Larry Bird, then Michael Jordan, as global pitchmen and icons. Playing basketball well helped to sell shoes, as Michael Jordan proved in teaming up with the Nike athletic shoe company. Nike's own global ambitions perfectly matched Stern's plans. Blending competition and commerce by turning sports into a commodity and making the most of global media became the NBA model.

In many ways, it worked. Jordan enjoyed unique global fame in his heyday and sold untold numbers of shoes. In Europe, Latin America, and China fans started following NBA games, slowly crystallizing into a global basketball public. By contrast with soccer and baseball, America appeared on top of the world in basketball, for at least this corner of the global sporting system seemed made in America. Critics lamented this apparent success. To them, the NBA model stood for a distinctly American approach to globalization – a way to make the world safe for capitalism in every sphere in every country by subjecting even games to the demands of markets and corporations (LaFeber 1999). Basketball was just one more vehicle of hegemony. Even in basketball, this hegemony faced limits – in the UK, for example, the NBA had little success in penetrating the domestic sports market, already crowded with competing games more suited to local tastes (Maguire and Falcous 2005). Nor did America invent the model it appeared to push. Though the NBA came to symbolize America's role in recent sports globalization, it hardly started from scratch. Americans may have been especially good at turning sports into business and sports events into media spectacles, but they are not the only ones. In Britain, the Slazenger brothers started making tennis equipment as far back as 1881 and began sponsoring Wimbledon in 1902. British soccer players turned professional in the nineteenth century without any encouragement from Americans, and their successors across Europe and Latin America developed a professional culture of their own. Within FIFA, the German shoe company Adidas has long been the most important corporate sponsor with close ties to the leadership (Sugden and Tomlinson 1998). The economic benefits of soccer on TV have long been as obvious to European clubs as to any Americans.

The liberalization of the European market for soccer players by a European court ruling that disallowed so-called transfer fees and limits on the number of foreign players per team, a seemingly "American" move to treat players as mere high-priced labor, was likewise an indigenous initiative, carried out by a European institution applying European law in a lawsuit brought by a European player. Treating sports as a commodity, an entertainment product and a vehicle for advertising, is no longer a peculiarly American approach to sports, if it ever was. Treating sports as a business, with team owners seeking profits and athletes commanding very high salaries, is also common. In both instances, certainly, America helped to lead the way. In the 1980s, for example, the National Football League's expansion into Europe showed how to make well-presented, "skilfully packaged" games pay off (Maguire and Falcous 2005: 40). But inferring from this influence that sports are being "Americanized," or that America causes the "neoliberal" transformation of games into markets, only puts a convenient label on global trends.

To fans, American hegemony looked even more fragile. Like MLB, the NBA changed rapidly by the 1990s, attracting more and more foreign players. In the early 2000s, some 15 percent of the league's players came from places like Georgia (the country) and Argentina, Spain and China, France and Germany, and even the Netherlands. At that time, a team with Yao Ming, Dirk Nowitzki, Manu Ginóbili, Pau Gasol, and Steve Nash would have given any "purely" American team trouble. While the NBA was still at the center of the basketball world, international competition intensified as well. The US finished only sixth at the 2002 FIBA world championships, third in the 2004 Olympics, and again third in the 2006 FIBA tournament, contests won by Yugoslavia, Argentina, and Spain, respectively. In team play, in the "fundamentals" of shooting and passing, and in knowledge of the international game the best non-Americans had more than caught up. Though both its men's and women's teams dominated at the 2008 Olympics, on the court, America was no longer assured of success.

America's experience in baseball and basketball resembles England's travails in cricket. Long before soccer, cricket had been the favorite game of its upper classes. In the nineteenth century, the agents of empire took it overseas, especially to the Caribbean, South Asia, and Australia. The rules were still set in England, more specifically at Lord's, a famous club. When international five-day Test matches started in 1877, English teams prevailed. But even before the dominions attained independence, they took to the game with a passion – at first certain elite groups, soon followed by a broader swath of the population at large (Kaufman and Patterson 2005). Playing the game was a way to absorb the best of British culture. At the same time, it offered an irresistible opportunity to challenge the English at their own game. Both in India and the West Indies, cricket became the national sport, indeed an emblem of nationhood (Appadurai 1996). One oft-quoted enthusiast went so far as to claim that "Cricket is an Indian game accidentally discovered by the English" (Nandy 2000: 1). The former subjects gradually caught up with their colonial masters – the game turned into "liberation cricket" (Beckles and Stoddart 1995). In 1928, the West Indies were granted Test status, the right to participate in formal international competition (Beckles 1998: 47). For the West Indies, a 1950 Test match victory over England by no less than 326 runs was an especially dramatic occasion (xv). In the 1970s and 1980s, their team, led by outstanding black stars, would in fact dominate world cricket, inspiring national pride and striking a blow for racial equality.

The balance of power between England and its political offspring shifted beyond the boundary of the cricket grounds as well (Rumford 2007). In 1976, the Australian entrepreneur Kerry Packer introduced one-day internationals or ODIs, a new, more media-friendly format for international contests that challenged the staid old multi-day Test format and quickly gained popularity even as regular Tests also increased. More and more countries joined the International Cricket Council (ICC) as affiliates, though less than a dozen hold full-fledged "Test" status. In 2005, the ICC (founded as the Imperial Cricket Council in 1907) moved its headquarters from London to Dubai, closer to its chief Asian public, on a self-professed mission to become a "leading global sport." Partly to tap into Asian passion, the ICC aggressively pursued commercial opportunities and introduced a more regular schedule of international competition in the 1990s. Cricket fostered a global labor market as well – as in other sports, professional players increasingly moved to teams that offered the best terms, and both Asian and West Indian players were among the game's biggest stars. Thanks to this "post-Westernization," cricket now "operates within a global frame" (Rumford 2007: 213). Even for the winners this poses new problems: the more commercially oriented global game and the more professional attitude of its players undermines some of the national fervor and allegiance that marked liberation cricket, contributing to what some fans view as a crisis of West Indian cricket (Beckles 1998).

The increased competition Americans face in "their" sports may lack the drama of West Indian or Indian victories over the former colonial power. Yet their experience confirms that sports also serves as an arena of conflict, an opportunity to challenge power and shift old hierarchies. To take an old cliché perhaps too literally, globalization levels the playing fields. The sheer financial clout of the MLB and the NBA keeps America the center of baseball and basketball more than England was able to stay on top in cricket – or soccer, for that matter. But whatever the advantages globalization gives the great powers, and whatever the resistance by centers of power such as MLB, the process also "decenters" many activities and institutions.

The sports record thus sheds light on a prominent argument about globalization. America's distinct place in world sports puts in perspective the common view that stresses America's undue influence in the process. In men's soccer, the US has been on the B-team. Its sports culture actually does not serve as a model to emulate. The more diffuse influence of American corporations and popular tastes mostly reinforces trends already underway elsewhere. Across the sports landscape, American influence varies – still great in games like basketball, possibly growing in soccer, diminished in the Olympic arena. That influence also varies by region and period; in Europe, for example, American sports like volleyball and basketball only gained popularity after World War II but even then they could not dislodge long-time favorites (Van Bottenburg 2001: 143–4). Clearly, America's unrivaled economic power does not directly translate into cultural influence (Guttmann 1994), in sports as in other forms of globalization. Global sports are not "made in USA" and globalization does not equal Americanization: the process is more complex. In sports, the US is at most a hamstrung hegemon. But the lessons we can draw from America's sports record do not automatically carry over to other facets of globalization. As an economic superpower, the US might have much more leverage to push economic integration along the lines it prefers. It set the tone in science, at least for some decades after World War II. In law and religion, as we will see, it plays yet different roles. The fact that the sports pattern does not carry over so easily is instructive in itself. It confirms a point made in the previous chapter and illustrated again in later ones, namely that different activities and institutions globalize in different ways.

Summary and Conclusion

Soccer is serious business, not just in monetary terms (Giulianotti and Robertson 2004). As this chapter has shown, it tells us much about globalization. Since the nineteenth century, more and more people have become involved in similar leisure activities that follow globally common rules, are managed by organizations with global authority, and draw athletes and fans into networks of competition. More people have become more connected through standardized play. The world has become, so to speak, a single playing field. The process shows all the elements of globalization: diffusion, interdependence, organization, and shared consciousness in a global sports culture.

Because a global way of "doing" sports is already set, new entrants onto the field tend to copy the behavior of established participants. That copying is not entirely voluntary, since being taken seriously, for example as a potential Olympic sport, requires it. For promoters of any new sport, going global is now an entirely natural thing to do. And once a sport has gone global, reversing globalization by returning to just doing different things in unconnected places – "deglobalization" – becomes harder to imagine. The global sporting system tends to reinforce itself.

Organization leads to more organization, and that is one direction in overall globalization.

By going into some details of soccer's origins, this chapter has also made the point that the current shape of the sporting system, as well as other global institutions, depends on its early history. Britain had a leading role in the nineteenth century and left its mark; so did the US and several other countries. The sports most people play today, their rules and organizations, originate in just a few places. On playing fields and courts, power conferred privilege. Talking about this "path dependence" of global sports is a fancy way of saying that its history matters. Yet the constraints of history leave room for change. The very extent of soccer's globalization dramatically illustrates the point. Baseball's diffusion to Japan and Central America offers another example. East Asians' dominance in the British parlor game of table tennis is a third. Perhaps if some of TYSA's more talented players help the US to break through in international soccer they will cut a new path in America's sports culture. As globalization unfolds, in soccer as in other sports, the effect of origins continues to blur. Both the origins in the second wave and their blurring represent another feature of globalization's overall direction.

We should not take the main lessons of this chapter too far. Though the sporting system fosters similarity, different sports still follow their own paths to some extent. Even when Swiss or Eastern European players consistently beat British or Australian competitors, Wimbledon and the Australian Open remained key Grand Slam tournaments. The "majors" in golf are similarly entrenched. In soccer, team success in the European Champions League matters greatly whereas in other sports it is the regional or world championships that have priority. Convergence in the way sports are run, viewed, and marketed does not eliminate all those differences. The same applies to countries. As noted, they typically keep their own mix of favored sports even if the menu expands thanks to globalization. Local circumstances obviously make some paths more plausible – Norway might produce some good long-distance runners, but Ethiopia will not supply many great skiers. Such local differences also create vested interests, for example on the part of media companies that wish to hold on to audiences for certain profitable sports – one reason for the persistence of America's different sports culture. In globalization, difference itself comes to matter more as well. Particular groups and countries quite deliberately want to set themselves apart even in the global game. To say that national difference "repudiates the global" (Rowe 2003) overstates the point, but globalization does not imply that everyone simply becomes a global player.

Globalization builds bridges to and from America's sports island. The traffic is two-way. From the US flow new games and ways to market them, among other things. To the US flow a variety of games as well as talented professional athletes. The world "Americanizes" to some extent, but direct US influence is limited, not least because the sporting system sets its own rules and its paths are well trodden. The US itself also globalizes as its fans and athletes become more connected and globally aware. For players in DeKalb County, as for their counterparts in other wealthy countries, globalization means having more options. Some of the ones they choose make them more similar to their peers. But the overall distinctiveness of the local sports culture, in our case marked by the popularity of American football, is hardly at risk.

As our experience in the Atlanta area shows, globalization does not mean that global rules, organizations, or models just take over. The global connections of world society do not substitute for local ties. These can move in tandem. The enormous volunteer effort that keeps TYSA running strengthens our local connections even as we become more tightly linked to the global game. It therefore goes too far to say that globalization completely changes social life, moving us away from things we do "inside" nation-states toward things that go on "outside," across borders (Albrow 1997). In sports we see that globalization also occurs in and through local and national settings. It does not replace one kind of society with another but adds a layer of connections and a new kind of shared awareness.

In sports, globalization lessens the contrasts across places while also producing new variety in the way people choose and play games. The influence of hegemons is limited. Countries and athletes carve out distinct niches. Each place still moves along its own path. But the story of global sports nevertheless reveals the oft-felt fear that in linking people globalization makes them more similar, that the pleasures of shared games also suppress the vitality of different sporting traditions. The next chapter takes up that issue explicitly.

Questions

1   In late-nineteenth-century Britain cricket was very popular, yet in the competition for global attention it lost out to soccer. But why not cricket? What would cricket aficionados have had to do, what could they have done, to prevail in that competition?

2   The chapter emphasizes the role of the International Olympic Committee in setting rules for the global sporting system. How did it get and how does it maintain that role? The IOC itself vaunts its commitment to the global vision of "Olympism," rooted in the idealistic notion of its founder, Pierre de Coubertin, that sports could bring the world together. In what way have the Games made that vision a reality, and in what way do they deviate from it?

3   The neoinstitutionalist or "world polity" argument about sports emphasizes the way common models, promoted by international organizations, through normative pressure lead different groups to adopt similar sorts of practices. Yet the chapter also alludes to the way sports offer opportunities for groups and nations to distinguish themselves. Is this a contradiction?

4   What would it take for baseball to become more truly "global"?

Further Reading

Richard Giulianotti, *Football: A Sociology of the Global Game* (Polity Press, 1999)
Richard Giulianotti and Roland Robertson, *Globalization and Sport* (Blackwell, 2007)
David Goldblatt, *The Ball Is Round: A Global History of Soccer* (Riverhead Books, 2008)
Joseph Maguire, *Global Sport: Identities, Societies, Civilizations* (Polity Press, 1999)
Andrei S. Markovits and Steven L. Hellerman, *Offside: Soccer and American Exceptionalism* (Princeton University Press, 2001)
Maarten Van Bottenburg, *Global Games* (University of Illinois Press, 2001)

4

GLOBAL MEDIA AND THE VARIETIES OF GLOBALIZATION

- Indian Television and Globalization
- Patterns in Global Television
- Interpreting Global Television
- Cultural Imperialism and Beyond
- From Bollywood to Bollyworld
- Summary and Conclusion

Indian Television and Globalization

Before 1991, watching television was not a favorite pastime for many Indians. Only a minority of households owned sets in the first place. Viewing options were limited to a single, government-operated channel, called Doordarshan (DD). Broadcasting mostly in Hindi, it did not entice the many Indians who spoke other languages. In the 1980s, it had made a modest effort to become more entertaining, adding a popular family drama and some Hindu epics to its schedule (Kumar 2006) and experimenting with a second channel. Prodded by sports fans eager to watch the Asian Games of 1982, it had finally started broadcasting in color. Although it ran commercials, it did not feel compelled to seek the highest ratings. In the minds of state officials, its prime task still was to edify the viewing public, in the interest of promoting development in a unified nation. Of course, state control also happened to be in the political interest of the ruling elite – DD's function, said one candid politician, was to "give the views of the government" (cited in Butcher 2003: 54). Since independence, that elite had pursued a particular vision of national progress, relying on domestic production for the domestic market rather than seeking access to foreign markets. India, they thought, could chart its own path. In practice, socialism with Indian characteristics erected high barriers around many sectors of Indian society, including its media. As late as 1979, for example, the government sharply raised the tariff on imported electronics and commissioned a domestic company to produce picture tubes – which it did at higher cost (Kumar 2006: 68–9). No other broadcaster could challenge DD's "notoriously monotonous and unimaginative" state monopoly (Thussu 2007a: 594). At least when it came to TV, India's media landscape remained rather barren.

A decade later, that mediascape had changed nearly beyond recognition, illustrating, as this chapter explains in greater detail, how media globalization unfolds in the context of and intertwined with a distinct culture, as a "glocal" process rather than an alien imposition. DD was still in business but now offered many different channels, including several that catered to India's multilingual regions. It presented more entertaining fare as well, a change it had not made by choice but rather in response to the challenge of commercial broadcasters. In the early 1990s, private companies had used newly developed cable and satellite technology to gain access to Indian homes, circumventing a rule against private broadcasting. Even though only a small minority of well-to-do Indians were connected in this way – barely more than a million in 1992 (Thussu 2007a: 594) – the commercial providers soon proved popular. A home-grown company, named Zee, made inroads, along with a foreign competitor, Star Plus, which was part of a larger Asian network owned by Rupert Murdoch's News Corp. Regional providers added even more diversity. As the technological possibilities expanded and competition intensified, government policy also changed. Already tentatively liberalizing in the late 1980s, the Indian government decided to open up its economy in 1991. The subsequent wave of liberalization helped media competition to flourish and foreign imports to spice up the Indian viewing diet. By 2005, India's 400 million viewers could choose from a menu of many public channels and some 200 digital channels, offering programs of all kinds, from comedy to news to talk shows to children's programs (ibid.). In the Indian mediascape, a larger audience now enjoyed more variety than ever before.

Some of that variety came from abroad. For example, Murdoch's Star TV introduced the first music television channel, the first full-time news network, the first reality TV series, and, most strikingly, the first successful adaptation of an international game show (Thussu 2007a). The initial Indian version of the British show *Who Wants to Be A Millionaire?* entitled *Kaun Banega Crorepati?* featured a Bollywood film star, Amitabh Bachchan, as host – later replaced by Shah Rukh Khan, heartthrob of the next generation – and included questions about Hindu tradition that would have stumped Western guests. But the lighting, the drama, and the half-desperate telephone calls by contestants seeking answers to tough questions all followed standard procedure, as required by the production company that sold the show to Star. The content mix reflected a lesson Star had learned. Even if executives initially had visions of offering the same sort of material across Asia, they quickly discovered that that would not work. They had to adapt to local tastes, popular shows had to use the main local language, and images had to be familiar to viewers more attuned to Bollywood, India's own popular movie style, than Hollywood. Sports coverage had to focus on cricket as much as any other game. And of course new channels had to respect old sensibilities. For example, when a 1995 talk show hosted by self-described "glocal girl" Nikki Bedi (Kumar 2006: 176) featured an outspoken gay guest who called Mahatma Gandhi a "bastard *bania*," or miser, the ensuing protests got the show cancelled (ch. 5). When "Gandhi" meets "prime-time," to paraphrase the title of one study, Gandhi prevails. Even if some of the local adjustments do not quite succeed – *Baywatch* star Pamela Anderson apparently lost some of her luster when dubbed in Hindi (Butcher 2003: 70) – in India, as in many other places, global diffusion necessarily involves a lot of "indigenization."

Indians joined the global market for television content, buying show formats from foreign producers, American television serials, or the rights to broadcast Hollywood movies. Though appealing to small audiences, English-language channels such as CNN and MTV gained a foothold in the Indian market. Apart from Star, other international broadcasters, such as Sony, also competed for Indian viewers. For advertisers the market proved to be a great lure. Television enabled them to reach hundreds of millions of middle-class viewers in a rapidly growing country. Broadcasters – to apply the old term to all TV "content providers" – were all too happy to give them a platform to hawk their wares. Among those wares were the staples of global consumption like Pepsi and Coke, newly allowed into the country as part of its overall liberalization. Indian television turned into a marketplace, a regional niche within the global media market that connected Indian viewers to distant people and places. Greater dependence on foreign products carried advantages beyond the rich menu of viewing options: gone was the overpriced domestic equipment once mandated by the government.

The Indian government had changed course. Though it did not entirely privatize broadcasting, it deregulated the sector. A 1995 Supreme Court decision required the government to step down from its commanding heights, handing control to an independent public broadcasting corporation. It would have had trouble maintaining the status quo even if it had tried: with new technology, public expectations of television content quickly changed in the early 1990s, and in a democratic country the state ignores such expectations at its peril. Both domestic and international broadcasters proved a formidable force, at times allied with local cable operators, a force that could not be easily contained. Partly by choice, partly by necessity, state media policy liberalized – but only up to a point. For all the dramatic changes in the Indian media landscape, the state still set the terms of competition and retained the ultimate power (Thomas 2005: 209). For example, when Murdoch's Star network wanted to start a Hindi news channel in 2003, the state imposed a stringent local ownership requirement, forcing Star to seek domestic partners (Chang 2007). The governing elite also had not given up on its nationalizing vision – the idea that TV could bring Indians together as Indians. The more competitive reality may have tempered that ambition but the state was hardly ready to "retreat" (see Chapter 6). After 1991, the organization of Indian broadcasting became much more complex, but among the many players the state still stood out, as the "player" that could also referee the game.

Through the 1980s, most Indians rarely watched TV. Those who did were stuck with the uninspiring state channel, showing Indian productions. Limited in its reach, TV contributed a little to national awareness, not much to any global awareness. With the proliferation of channels and shows, that changed. Among the harbingers of change were two televised global beauty contests of the mid-1990s, Miss World and Miss Universe, that were won by Indian women, and the 1996 Miss World broadcast from Bangalore, which showed how India had joined one global television ritual (Kumar 2006). The shift encountered some resistance: the swimsuit portion of the competition had to take place in the Seychelles to avoid offending traditionalist critics. But the direction of change was clear. As a result, the larger audience of the early 2000s, with access to far more channels, viewed the world differently. More than before, they shared television experiences with others around the world. Even if the shows they watched had a distinct Indian twist, they also knew what played elsewhere. As consumers zapping across channels, choosing what they liked, they acted much like their fellow couch potatoes abroad. The many channels provided much more information about the world at large, from more different viewpoints. In many ways, then, Indian leisure activity became "deterritorialized," no longer strictly tied to locality or nation, more similar to that in other countries, recognizable to foreign viewers – thus instilling a "new awareness of connection to the global" (Butcher 2003: 14). Yet both region and nation were very much present on the screen. In language and imagery, Indian television was still distinctly Indian. For DD in its several incarnations that was no surprise. Only slightly more surprising were the efforts of the new players to ingratiate themselves with audiences by "indigenizing." Competition spurred some organizations to "go local" even more literally, catering to specific groups in specific regions rather than maximizing national exposure. As it globalized, India's television culture also nationalized and regionalized in a new way. Global media culture, as the Indian example illustrates, thus comes in many varieties.

India's experience of radical transformation in its media landscape is dramatic but not unique. As the next section shows, still focusing on television, many places went through similar changes. Together, these transformed the global media system. Apart from describing the changes, that section addresses one of the common worries about globalization, namely that it makes people and places more alike. The evidence from India already hints that the issue may be more complex – after all, even their still quite limited forays into media globalization have also brought Indians a richer broadcast menu. As we look at the global media system more broadly, we find other reasons to think that in globalization many forces add variety to offset some unmistakable trends toward similarity. This way of thinking, now common among many scholars in the field, goes against the previously dominant view that describes media trends as a form of "cultural imperialism." But while the scholarly influence of the cultural imperialism perspective has frayed, some of its arguments may still be relevant. As some of its current advocates might argue, in India a capitalist-inspired commercial media model now prevails, media treat viewers as consumers, their shows celebrate the pleasures of consumption in standard capitalist fashion, and foreign powers have intruded into the landscape to uproot domestic culture and state control for the benefit of outside investors. Though I side with scholars who think such complaints are overstated, I also suggest that simply being for or against "cultural imperialism" is not productive anymore in trying to understand global media.

Patterns in Global Television

Indians were not the only ones to enjoy *Millionaire*. By 2002, the format had been sold to 80 countries. For all the local variations – including questions on the Quran in the Arab version hosted in Cairo by a Christian from Lebanon – its common features helped to make it a global hit (Bielby and Harrington 2004: 84–5). Other formats did equally well. *Pop Idols*, a show that enabled audiences to vote on contestants in a singing competition, traveled from New Zealand to many places, including the US (ibid.). In each case, of course, the talent, such as it was, hailed from the country where the program would be shown. By following the travails of the participants and encouraging the audience to discuss them, the format gave a game show the feel of "reality" unfolding. An even more emblematic "reality show" was *Survivor*, adapted in many countries from an originally Swedish concept. Marooned in isolated places, contestants had to meet far-fetched challenges to prove their worth to fellow contestants and a voting audience in order to prevail as the ultimate survivor. A "genre hybrid," the reality show format popular in the early 2000s covered the drama of an improvised soap opera played by amateurs in quasi-documentary fashion (Mathijs and Jones 2004: 3; Bignell 2005: 14–8).

The quintessential reality show of the period was *Big Brother*, developed by a Dutch producer and exported to more than a hundred countries. Contestants agreed to live together in a house for an extended period, following rules set by the unseen Big Brother while under the constant gaze of cameras, trying to outlast fellow residents by winning the favor of the voting audience. As usual, local flavor changed the common format. Whereas in an American version contestants just talked sex, their Dutch counterparts took action (Bignell 2005: 49). In Italy the show turned into a form of soft porn while in Africa even more modest couplings provoked charges of immorality (Mathijs and Jones 2004). By contrast with the tense, dog-eat-dog atmosphere of most Big Brother set-ups, the Australian version was more laid back, with an outdoorsy cast living in a real Aussie house complete with barbecue grill (Roscoe 2004). For them, Big Brother was a Great Mate. Even there, however, production crews had to follow a common "bible" of instructions laid out by Endemol, the original Dutch producers. In all the different versions, the show also "filtered across multiple media," including the Internet (Mathijs and Jones 2004: 4). In most places, the show helped to draw a young audience attractive to advertisers. Though we do not have solid studies of their reactions, most viewers seemed to judge contestants by how well they stayed true to themselves (Carter 2004). By giving the audience some control, the format also gained control of their attention (ibid.) – critical in a crowded media market. The format promised high returns at low cost, an irresistible combination for commercial channels everywhere. Though viewers did not mind becoming voyeurs, critics had greater misgivings about the "globalization of privacy publicized" inherent in the format (Bignell 2005: 38–9).

While adapted formats were the favored fad of the early 2000s, canned shows held their own. Many staples came from the US. In the early days of television, they included comedies like *I Love Lucy* and western soaps like *Bonanza*. Later, prime-time soaps like *Dallas* turned into international hits. American-produced drama, including crime shows like *CSI* or hospital shows like *ER*, stayed popular into the 2000s. But the US was not the only source of such programming. Britain's ITV sent its melancholy, down-to-earth *Inspector Morse* into the world to become a "global icon," watched by at least a sixth of the world's population spread across 200 countries (*Independent* 2007). Morse was one of many such characters, many of them British, who achieved global fame. For a time, *telenovelas* from Latin America, limited-run melodramatic serials, drew large audiences from Poland to China to Italy and, of course, across Latin America itself. Whether in the "weepy" Mexican variety or the more "realistic" Brazilian versions, *telenovelas* typically feature a battle between good and evil, in which good prevails to allow love to flourish (Barker 1997: 86–90). Modeled only partly on American soaps, *telenovelas* have long since gone their own way, incorporating both universal and Latin American themes to achieve a distinct blend. They add variety and sameness to global TV menus: they expose "cracks in the hegemony of the United States" while at the same time dissolving some cultural differences among audiences (Martín-Barbero 1995: 284). Still popular in their "home" markets, they have lost some ground abroad as audience tastes shift, yet another indication of how any kind of TV content is at the mercy of the viewer.

Adapting foreign drama makes canned shows taste fresh. Watching the hit soap *Goede Tijden, Slechte Tijden* (Good Times, Bad Times), few of its Dutch fans thought about its foreign roots, even though the plot of many episodes was translated quite straightforwardly from a predecessor show in Australia (Moran 1998: 123–33). The Dutch show had a Dutch feel, down to details like characters slicing their cheese in a particular way, and thus erased any awareness of its origins. Translation can be tricky, of course. For a French version of the American show *Law and Order*, for example, writers had to make stories fit the Napoleonic legal code; they also took out references to the mob – in France, one said jokingly, "we are all nice people" (Barnes 2007). But typically adapters are still expected to follow the production "bible," which in the case of *Law and Order* specified such details as the proper spelling of the noise used to signal shifts in storytelling – "Ca-ching." Adapting cartoons is a bit easier   in principle, the animated material will work anywhere, provided some decent dubbing replaces the original voice talent. Unbeknownst to Americans, Fred Flintstone speaks many languages, and in Italy Yogi Bear became an "up-market character" representing all kinds of causes (Hubka 2002: 245–6).

This diffusion of shows and formats has turned television into a global medium. Viewers everywhere take in content from anywhere – Dutch reality shows, British detective series, American comedy and drama, Latin American soaps, Japanese documentaries, reality and lifestyle and children's programming of all sorts. But the flow of content is not a current that erodes any local culture it reaches. While many audiences have some common tastes, most also require significant concessions of broadcasters, as even "bible"-believing reality show producers realize. Seemingly common content also does not come across in exactly the same way everywhere. Viewers vary in how likely they are to be exposed to foreign content in the first place, how likely they are to retain anything about it, and if they do, how likely they are to be affected by what they have watched (Elasmar 2003). Classic studies have shown how viewers in the Netherlands treated the old American soap *Dallas* with humor and irony – it was a source of pleasure, to be enjoyed as a diversion rather than as serious drama with a message anyone would take seriously (Ang 1985) – and how viewers in Israel retold the plot of certain episodes to fit their own moral views, filtering out potentially offensive material (Katz and Liebes 1990). Audiences, such studies found, do not sit back to absorb any material thrown at them but instead actively select and critically watch the shows on offer. They recognize fiction as fiction and at the same time try to apply stories to their own lives (Barker 1997: 124). Though such findings surprised scholars, neither viewers nor broadcasters would consider them earthshaking. Both know all too well that certain shows, however heavily promoted, simply fail to capture any attention. In the end, the audience is in charge.

But is it? In fact, programs do not simply flow to audiences in response to their demand. In the international television market, network executives serve as the key gatekeepers who must sort through an enormous supply of content to compose their schedules (Havens 2006). Due to advances in TV technology and policy changes in the 1980s and 1990s, those schedules expanded: more channels had more time to fill, and broadcasters felt the pangs of a "hunger for programmes" (Sinclair et al. 1996: 3). Only the US could provide enough shows to its many channels; everyone else became that much more dependent on everyone else. The TV trade boomed. In deciding what to import, programmers use various strategies (Havens 2006). Most of them construe their audience in national terms and therefore have ideas about what shows will fit "the" national culture as they see it. As a rule of thumb, cultural proximity works better: more Mexican *telenovelas* go south rather than north. Executives also rely on long-standing relationships, especially with prestigious American "majors" who have a track record of success. For that reason, America's historic advantage as a content producer breeds greater advantage, reflected in the 75 percent of total export revenues claimed by the US (29) and the great imbalance in program trade between the US and other regions (see figure 4.1).

Some American products, such as prime Hollywood movies, universally appeal to audiences and therefore always attract programmers' interest. They also watch each other, for example to learn which shows or formats or genres might be turning into a global fad. Jumping on bandwagons helps them to reduce the uncertainty they always feel about the prospects of any new material. Some of this happens at the three major annual TV tradeshows, two in France, one in Los Angeles or Las

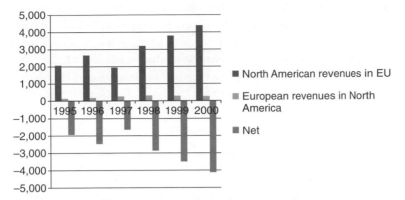

Figure 4.1 Estimates of trade in TV programs, European Union – North America, 1995–2000, in millions of US dollars
Source: European Audiovisual Observatory; UNESCO 2005a: 48

Vegas, that bring producers and buyers together in a kind of ritual deal-making dance. Producers try to brand their products or create a buzz while buyers try to take advantage of their relationships to beat their local competition for the most attractive material. Of course, what they end up buying depends as much on the very specific holes in their schedule that they need to fill, and above all on their resources. Hungarian programmers, for example, cannot pay top dollar for daytime shows.

Overall, then, TV executives from around the world work in very similar ways in an increasingly integrated marketplace still dominated by Western producers. Yet the market is also quite diverse and growing more diverse. Some products flow from small powers to large ones, such as Dutch reality show formats that make it in the US. Some things now travel from the former periphery to the center, as illustrated by *telenovelas* that succeeded in southern Europe. Some programs cross cultural boundaries, such as Japanese animation that flourishes on children's channels in the US. As the jargon has it, the flows are "multidirectional" (Sinclair et al. 1996: 5). Each region also has its own dynamics (ibid.). As a subcontinent, India is in fact a region in itself. So is Latin America. Parts of Europe also function as distinct regions. What gets produced and consumed varies from one such region to another. Multiple flows across various regions create "global, regional, national, and even local circuits of program exchange [that] overlap and interact in a multifaceted way" (ibid.). The "multifaceted" exchanges within and across regions produce even more diverse results in local programming due to the many specific factors that shape programmers' decisions, ranging from their own images of their target audience to the amount of money they have to spend to the number of competing channels in the domestic market. For all the material they import, they typically still reserve primetime slots for distinctive homegrown drama or event coverage, adding local flavor to even the most globally dependent schedules.

Commerce itself is nothing new in television. The US favored commercial broadcasting from the outset, much of Latin American television has operated commercially for decades, and even India's DD used to earn some of its income from advertising. Yet at the end of the twentieth century the rules of the media game changed in many places. When cable and satellite technology promised access to many more channels, it made less sense for states that had monopolized broadcasting to hold on to the old ways. Many did not want to do so either: as in India, a policy revolution swept across many countries to limit the role of government in the economy and open more sectors to competitive private enterprise. Of course, media corporations helped usher in the revolution, for example by lobbying for change, since they stood to benefit most. Various regulators also contributed, not least the European Union, which adopted more market-oriented media policies starting in the 1980s. As a result of this "neoliberal" paradigm shift (see Chapter 5), governments "opted for policies of breaking monopolies in media and communications and privatizing as much as possible" (Van Cuilenburg and McQuail 2003: 181). Policy had to follow "the logic of the marketplace and the technology and the wishes of consumers" (200). Thanks to new technology and new rules, the organization of global media changed enormously in recent decades: deregulated media would operate as a market, in which mostly privately owned providers compete both globally and locally to satisfy the demands of consumers and attract sufficient advertising revenue. The key players – states, corporations, media producers of various sorts – thus settled on common norms to govern their business. As students of international relations put it, they formed a "transnational media regime" (Bennett 2004: 128).

Not everyone was eager to join the new dispensation. Many authoritarian states tried to keep tight control of their media (Bennett 2004: 129). More liberal places also displayed some ambivalence. As noted, India restricted ownership of media companies even as it opened up the sector. In the Netherlands, commercial cable channels took advantage of European media rules to enter the Dutch market against the wishes of the political establishment at the time, and once they had breached the dikes of government protection flooded the country with many new offerings to compete with the publicly subsidized channels, which lost substantial market share (Lechner 2008: ch. 7). The relative decline of public service broadcasting, and the political handwringing over what to do about it, were not unique to the Netherlands. Officials in most countries tried to preserve some form of high-minded, publicly funded television, in an effort to make viewers eat their media vegetables, or at least put them on the menu. Others imposed some content restrictions, for example by requiring channels to broadcast a certain amount of domestically produced material. Another common restriction applied to ownership, adopted even in the otherwise market-friendly US and justified as a way to guard the national culture against overly intrusive foreign influences. In liberalizing Europe, countries still insisted on a special exemption for cultural goods in free-trade agreements that had intended to limit state favoritism for local products (Beale 2002).

Exactly how they "engaged" the transnational regime varied from country to country (Bennett 2004: 134). While the regime has become more neoliberal in the sense that media have turned into a market, states remain the key players. To be sure, for most state officials it has become more difficult to keep private networks or foreign content or dissenting voices out of their media. Fewer countries now have single channels charged with expressing the "view of the government," as DD once did in India. More messages flow across borders, and states cannot stop them altogether. But for the most part, officials still can channel the flows to suit their national needs. Thanks to the interaction of many players in many places, the transnational regime takes locally diverse forms. *Internet - all media*

In fact, local markets are becoming more alike in becoming more diverse. Following the transnational trend, most have opened up to new channels, brought in new competition, imported more programming, and increased the sheer supply of TV content. More viewers have more to watch during most of the day and night. In some cases, supply may outstrip demand. In the Netherlands, for example, the mix of public, private, and specialty channels by the early 2000s offered nearly maximum diversity while viewing time barely budged – the Dutch had more to watch but did not necessarily watch more. The premature demise of a new commercial channel founded by *Big Brother* producer John de Mol signaled limits to the market's carrying capacity in a country of 16 million that already enjoyed access to six major channels. How many channels a market can accommodate, or how many kinds of programming, depends, once again, on many local factors. But while bigger and wealthier countries with more liberal policies may see more competition and a higher overall supply, the trend across markets moves in the same direction; only the extent of their pluralism varies.

Interpreting Global Television

Section on this.

In the new global media culture, billions of viewers become more alike in being forced to choose. The couch has turned into a site of consumption. Of course, just as media buyers have ways to simplify their choices, so do consumers. They may stay with familiar channels or genres, even if they could zap to something new and potentially exciting. The habits of many consumers faced with many options typically segment the market, dividing audiences by age, gender, class, and other markers of taste. That makes it difficult to generalize about the media culture of any one country, let alone the world. Rather than serving as a mass medium that inculcates a standard culture, television increasingly means different things to different people. Some common threads cut across the segments. Certain spectacles, such as the World Cup or the Olympics, still draw a mass audience. Successful marketing of formats may create global fads that many people want to sample. Some Hollywood products still have fairly universal appeal. The segments are also linked across space. For example, young boys everywhere know the characters in Pokémon and some soaps create a virtual solidarity among older women in different places. Sports fans exposed to the televised exploits of their heroes form a global community of sorts. Such global subcultures add diversity to the overall global media culture. All of them involve at least some minimal global awareness, the sharing of common views in more than one sense. That is not to say viewers have turned into cosmopolitan sophisticates. More plausibly, media globalization has added new dimensions to their experience, new common things to watch and new common ways to watch them. For lack of research, we can still only speculate about how much actual global awareness that involves.

Globalizing television thus shows a complex picture. More content diffuses across borders but audiences actively sift and sort, demanding at least some indigenization. Trade flourishes, creating at least some dependence on US producers in many markets, but the flows take many forms and directions, partly through regional channels. The media system as a whole crystallizes into a regime but this form of organization allows for many kinds of state engagement. A global television culture spreads but in particular markets, and for most viewers, the common culture comes across as greater variety. To media scholars, this suggests that globalization does not equal homogenization: critical audiences, regional dynamics, state initiatives, and consumer choice press for more diversity. They therefore favor a way of thinking about globalization that stresses such diversity, exemplified by the Indian-American anthropologist Arjun Appadurai's (1996) model of the "global cultural economy," a model no doubt influenced by his own bicultural experience.

His perspective suggests that we think of the things people exchange as flows of goods and symbols, of institutions as channels that direct these flows, and sectors in society as "scapes." In the global "financescape," for example, investors exchange money and information. The ethnoscape refers to the movement of people, the ideascape to the exchange of ideas, for example in science and literature. Of course, not all those flows and scapes work the same way – people globalize differently than money. They also intersect differently in different places – Japan may be open to money and ideas but it has been less hospitable toward potential migrants. Due to such "disjunctures" in the global cultural economy, individuals and countries experience globalization differently. Certainly they are exposed to common flows, and the local scapes feature some similar institutional channels – think of canned TV shows and commercial cable providers. But the nature of the channels, the context of other scapes, and the conflict among flows, all variable across countries and regions, make for a peculiar dynamic, an ongoing tension between homogenization and "heterogenization." For Appadurai, the tension is inherent in globalization generally, not just in media.

Simply talking about TV as creating "more sameness" or "more diversity" is therefore a bit beside the point. The point is to understand both, together, in tension, as they play out differently for different people (Rantanen 2005: 116), to capture the many "alternative, overlapping, intersecting processes" that make up cultural globalization (Curtin 2007: 23). This way of thinking about media and globalization implicitly challenges another model of globalization. Appadurai himself offers the complex picture of a "cultural economy" as a counterpoint to the idea that world society has a single center that sets the tone for all peripheries. Much of the research I have summarized has an even stronger polemical subtext: it tries to refute "cultural imperialism." Its scholarly ammunition has been aimed at what risked becoming a strawman position. To mix metaphors, recent media research has put several nails in this strawman's coffin. Inside, however, the creature is still stirring. The next section suggests that reviving it entirely may now be a hopeless quest, but that after some plastic surgery it may yet contribute to the ideascape of media research.

Cultural Imperialism and Beyond

The changes in India's TV scene dismayed some observers. To them, one villain in the piece was Rupert Murdoch, News Corp's quintessential global media mogul bent on expanding his corporate empire. With Star TV, he extended his reach into a new market, subjecting Indians to a form of commercial television that turned shows into commodities and channels into advertising platforms. Under their indigenous veneer, the programs on Star Plus followed a single script. *Millionaire*, for example, was a prototypical global format designed to draw commercially interesting audiences by appealing to contestants' consumerist urges. The competition among providers only helped to institute the new market approach to television broadcasting. Both content and form of the new media carried an ideological message: they promoted the rise of consumerism and the spread of neoliberal values (Harindranath 2003: 166). In this way, they helped to make the market from which they hoped to profit. The Indian government's feeble attempt to balance corporate power in the media sector could not really alter the landscape. From the critics' standpoint, the apparent freedom and diversity in India's media market really marked a power shift. Losing control over its own media and succumbing to foreign content, India's national culture was also at risk. At the same time, however, television offers new opportunities for national self-presentation – provided that bits of national culture are properly packaged as commodities for consumption and that all local programming "presents the marketplace as the central arena of choice" (Murdock 2006: 26). But if the West is still engaged in "hegemonic appropriation" of a developing country like India, it is not simply forcing Indians to go along – for one thing, a colluding local elite, the domestic "bourgeoisie," is eager to do its bidding (Harindranath 2003; Murdock 2006). In spite of that collaboration, the relationship is still unequal and exploitative, sufficiently so to inspire some of the critics to call for reviving the "cultural imperialism" argument to explain recent changes (Harindranath 2003: 155).

To its chief advocate, the Marxist Herbert Schiller, the argument had been very much alive all along. From his point of view, India's change hardly counted as progress: it represented one more arena in which "corporate media-cultural

Plate 4.1 News Corp Chairman and CEO Rupert Murdoch, in his office at News International in Wapping, London, 2007
Source: © Tom Stoddart/Getty Images

industries" have expanded (Schiller 2003 [1991]: 320). Once part of a strong Non-Aligned Movement, insisting on national sovereignty, it now had no choice but to accommodate the demands of capital (324). Like people everywhere, Indians became "exposed to the drumbeat of corporate consumerism," infected by the "consumerist virus" (324). Surrounded by a "totalizing" cultural space, confronting a juggernaut of similar images, audiences were hardly in a position to sift and sort critically (330). The indigenization of programs produced little more than "spiced up" copies of Western models, and the advance of Western forms of broadcasting, for example in the thorough commercialization of all sports, really constituted a "concerted assault of corporate marketing values on global consciousness" (329). Beneath the "shifts in surface appearance" of new cultural forms, such as the many new offerings in most media markets, the rules of the capitalist game had not changed at all (332). India may have become nominally independent, but like many places it now suffered from the continuation of imperialism by other means: this was "not yet the post-imperialist era" (318).

If anything, the imperial grip of corporate power on global media seemed to be strengthening through the 1990s (Herman and McChesney 1997: ch. 2). Not just in India but around the world, big media firms increasingly operated across borders – Bertelsmann controlled channels in the Netherlands, French-based Vivendi made a major move into the US, News Corp expanded its stake in the UK and the US – thus increasing their influence over indigenous media. In an effort to benefit from economies of scale, they integrated their holdings across different sorts of media – Disney branched out from movies and theme parks to television, Time Warner tried to add TV channels and an Internet provider to its movie, music, and publishing businesses. In some media markets, those conglomerates dominated all competition; for example, in music and movies, more than in television, most revenues flowed to a few key firms. Deregulation spurred concentration by enabling all the major players to add to their stakes in many new markets, creating the beginning of a global media oligopoly where power was concentrated in a small number of hands. For all their efforts to differentiate themselves, they in fact spread a particular kind of popular culture and implanted a commercial model of communication everywhere. Through their competition, they also shaped a common global media system that followed rules that fit their interests. Free markets, open competition, and consumer choice, hallmarks of global media change since the 1990s, were in fact ideological illusions. In a powerful capitalist media system, key corporate players made the market, fettered competition, and determined what consumers could choose in the first place. That system had become "an indispensable component of the globalizing market economy as a whole" (Herman and McChesney 1997: 189). To its critics, at any rate, the "cultural imperialism" label still fit.

The core of their argument had always been quite straightforward: in a world marked by inequality in wealth and power, some countries and classes exploit others, corporations seek new sources of profit, and the dominant values reflect the interests of the dominant groups. The argument reflects the old Marxist notion that forces of production shape the economic process and that economic power shapes both political and cultural institutions. In a capitalist system media must operate on capitalist terms; if capitalism becomes dominant worldwide, that will require all media to fit a capitalist model. Cultural imperialism, as Schiller put it, is therefore simply a "subset of the *general* system of imperialism," a way to use media to entrench a system of domination, maximize corporate profits, and support the ideology of the global ruling class (Schiller 2003 [1991]: 319). Cultural imperialism, in his definition, "describes the sum of processes by which a society is brought into the modern world system and how its dominating stratum is attracted, pressured, forced, and sometimes bribed into shaping social institutions to correspond to, or even promote, the values and structures of the dominant center of the system" (Schiller 1976: 9). From this standpoint, free markets, open competition, and consumer choice, hallmarks of global media change since the 1990s, were in fact ideological illusions. In a powerful capitalist media system, key corporate players made the market, fettered competition, and determined what consumers could choose in the first place. If any Indians felt liberated, they were suffering from false consciousness.

Because the cultural imperialism argument really follows from a distinct, Marxist-inspired worldview, more is at stake here than simply figuring out how global media work. Proponents of the argument are often skeptical of "globalization" itself, at least if the term is used to convey a widening web of connections in which people participate equally and voluntarily. The real thrust in global change, they would insist, is still the imperial imposition of an unequal and exploitative capitalist system. Media research tells us, however, that the imperial lens obscures too much (cf. Curtin 2007: Introduction). Its users appear to identify politically with the interests of "the people," but present any audiences not actively engaged in "resistance" as hapless consumers, easily conned into harmful consumption. Based on some of the research cited, we have good reason to think that viewers have a little more sense. Still beholden to an old center-periphery model, the imperialism argument also does not do justice to the "con-traflow" from different regions (Bicket 2005), and even as an account of the world market, it is therefore outdated. Influenced by the notion that states necessarily promote capitalist class interests, its proponents underestimate political and cultural barriers to corporate intrusions (Flew 2007); many states do not toe the corporate line. Viewed through the imperial lens, media culture appears boringly homogeneous, a view at odds with the enormously increased variety of programming now available in many places. The "neo-Marxist analysis of capitalist culture projected onto an international scale" paradoxically also "reinforce[s] Western influence by taking it as a given" (Sinclair et al. 1996: 7), surprising on the part of critical scholars looking for signs of its waning. In treating them as bribed or coerced collaborators, they show a particular disdain for non-Western elites, such as Indian or Chinese media entrepreneurs. The "agency" of such "others" deserves better.

Portraying corporations as distinct actors with their own goals and interests, imperialist arguments view them as imposing their will. That, after all, is what gives "imperialism" its sting. If any executive were to read their work, she might wish to have the power critical scholars attribute to her. In fact, she faces many constraints. She knows, of course, that many of her products do not make money: audiences are fickle, liable to reject a fair portion of her conglomerate's output. Even in sectors where her company is performing well, it does not have a monopoly and must fight constantly for market share; the size of its revenues or market value offers little protection (Flew 2007: 83). As she and her colleagues contemplate entering foreign markets, they are all too aware of the many regulatory hurdles the state will put in their way. Going global is tough in any case, and apart from Rupert Murdoch few competitors have really done it, instead reaping most revenues from their home market (82). Remembering Vivendi's miserable retreat from the American media market, she realizes that strategies that once seemed promising, such as integration, may not pay off, leaving the firms involved in dire straits. Like anyone in the business, she would know all about the turnover in personnel and the churning of companies, proof that media are risky business and corporations not as powerful as they are cracked up to be. Though perhaps not expert in Marxist logic, she might sense that as the forces of media production change, for example via the Internet, the relations of production, including old forms of corporate control, are likely to follow, as illustrated by online music exchanges that go against the express interests of record companies. In a rapidly changing global environment, the executive suite is no imperial throne.

Though the evidence casts doubt on hard-line cultural imperialism, my point is not to dismiss another body of work. Underneath the apparent discord among scholars lurk some reasons for agreement. On the side of media researchers, no one questions that corporations are major players, or that the West still dominates the flow of programming, or that liberalization has created a new regime in most markets, or that audiences watch more similar shows. Some current advocates of a form of cultural imperialism, though still critical of media trends, have softened the old hard line: one calls for its revival but in "novel theoretical garb" (Harindranath 2003: 155), others stress the complexity of global-national entwinement as opposed to one-way flows (Murdock 2006), and still other sympathizers move away from a picture of top-down imposition in an oppressive structure toward a more "dialecti-cal" model in which many players have a part (Kellner and Pierce 2007). This con-vergence in media studies is instructive. Looking at world media, we can see many changes that fit a capitalism-takes-over scenario, yet in studying those changes we also begin to see that globalization is more than the continuation of imperialism by new means. Part of the story of globalization is that Western domination spurs new forms of difference. How to make sense of both in tandem is essential to understanding the process, further illustrated by the case of India's movie industry.

From Bollywood to Bollyworld

Opening the Indian TV market proved profitable for its movie industry. More channels needed more content, preferably appealing to large groups of people, and showing more Indian movies was the logical solution. Even before the advent of television, India had a flourishing movie industry. At first limited to copying Hollywood silent films, Indian movie makers became more creative with sound, developing a distinctive format of musical movies that included a set number of songs and dances. Like Indian meals in which all sorts of dishes mingle, Indian popular movies did not just adopt one of Hollywood's standard genres but had to have "everything in it," according to the director Shyam Benegal – comedy, drama, and melodrama, romance and action, talk and music in one "all-encompassing genre" (cited in Bose 2006: 168). By crafting a distinct film formula, Indians could demonstrate what it meant to be Indian, at first in opposition to British rule, later as a claim to global recognition – from the beginning, as one writer put it, "the formula was with nationalism" (35). That was evident in the very language of the most popular movies, as Hindi served to unify a linguistically diverse audience, making movies a vehicle for nation-building. Produced mostly in Bombay, now Mumbai, the genre became India's answer to Hollywood: "Bollywood." While it once may have sounded demeaning to Indians, the industry itself has used the

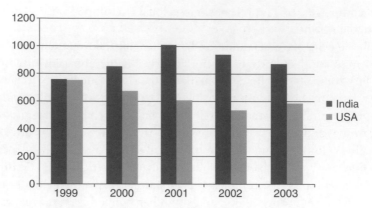

Figure 4.2 Number of films produced in India and the US, 1999–2003
Source: Motion Picture Association of America; UNESCO 2005a: 44

nickname to its advantage and made it a point of pride, both in India itself and in the global media market.

Bollywood's vitality, reflected in production numbers greater than those of Hollywood (see figure 4.2), reinforces what students of global television have found. It shows, most obviously, that Hollywood does not reign supreme everywhere; national distinction and national traditions, often quite deliberately cultivated as resistance to outside pressure (Tyrrell 1999: 265), still matter greatly. To some extent, content fits context; going a step further, some even count Bollywood song-and-dance sequences as strikes against cultural imperialism (262). Contrary to a model of media in which movies all flow one way, India, in particular, has the size and scale to make an alternative popular cinema flourish. That, of course, reflects the simple fact that audience preferences still vary enormously, filtering the reception of any foreign offerings. At the risk of being overly complimentary, some credit Indian audiences for being willing to deal with longer, more complex and "challenging" movies than their Western counterparts (273). Even in India, that judgment might be challenged by critics of Bollywood, who take issue with a restrictive formula that is tied to a certain kind of nationalism and exploited for mostly commercial purposes. Bollywood does not stand for all Indian movie-making.

Thinking of Bollywood as just an indigenous version of a global medium is also misleading because it has begun to make its way into the world at large, going beyond the Indian diaspora that had long taken an interest in popular fare from "home" – it is "no less an international industry than Hollywood" (Tyrrell 1999: 266). For many years, Bollywood has had success in countries ranging from Nigeria to China. In 1999, Amitabh Bachchan was voted star of the millennium in a BBC poll, the following year Bollywood export earnings topped $100 million, and in 2002 Andrew Lloyd Webber premiered a Bollywood-based musical, *Bombay Dreams*, and the movie *Lagaan* was nominated for an Academy Award in the non-English-language category (Govil 2007: 85). Conceived by the well-known

Bollywood star Aamir Khan, *Lagaan* was deliberately devised to succeed abroad, mixing Indian and British actors, Bollywood style and modernized music, an Indian theme and universal plot elements (Bose 2006). The story of Indian villagers beating a British regiment at its own game of cricket in order to earn forgiveness of land taxes took some liberties with historical accuracy but proved broadly appealing. Bollywood was not just an "Indian thing" anymore: more of its stars were known abroad, more of its movies attracted foreign viewers, a little more of its income came from exports, leading Shah Rukh Khan to predict that "one day Indian cinema will rule the world" (cited in Tyrell 1999: 261). Some Bollywood financiers have begun to back the prediction by pursuing projects in Hollywood itself, in an effort to make more money by changing its ways and creating a new "crossover" genre (Timmons 2008).

While Shah Rukh Khan's boast has yet to come true, slowly but surely Bollywood has turned into "Bollyworld," "at once located in the nation, but also out of the nation in its provenance, orientation and outreach" (Kaur and Sinha 2005: 16). The "contraflow" of Indian movies challenges the perceived dominance of Hollywood, up to a point, both in their home market and more globally, although even 10 *Lagaans* can hardly compete with one *Titanic*. The contraflow also feeds a backflow, as Bollywood's relations to the wider world in turn alter the genre, with changes that range from the very mundane, such as scene locations or characters' dress, to the more subtle, such as controversial treatment of sexual or political issues. Because Bollywood's audiences, style, relations to the world, and of course movie content continually change, no simple model of Bollywood-as-purely-Indian or Bollywood-as-inferior-Hollywood would make sense of it. As in the case of television, Appadurai's model, which may owe something to his own Indian experience, makes more sense. Like Indian television, Bollyworld reflects more diffusion filtered by critical audiences within a global film "regime" that fosters global awareness of movie styles and formats. Bollywood's record thus invites the same sort of analysis as Indian television, a way of thinking about globalization that balances the power of movie producers against the critical choices made by viewers, the homogenizing effect of diffusion against the diversity that results from fresh cultural encounters.

This thrust in studying media globalization has not yet convinced everyone. Neither Bollywood's domestic distinction nor its global aspirations are likely to convert adherents of the cultural imperialism argument. In movies, after all, America appears even more dominant than in TV, capturing about half of the French movie market but more than 90 percent in Britain and Australia, and supplying more than 80 percent of TV movies worldwide (Miller et al. 2005: 11, 22). Control over the production of major movies, and the profits that flow from them, is even more concentrated in the hands of the major studios, reflected in Hollywood's dominance of the annual and all-time lists of top-grossing movies (ibid.) (see table 4.1). In some ways, India is the exception proving the rule that Hollywood still rules the world, but even its paltry foreign cultural earnings pale compared to Hollywood's profits.

Table 4.1   Top all-time worldwide box office grosses, in unadjusted US dollars

Titanic (1997)	1,835,300,000
The Lord of the Rings: The Return of the King (2003)	1,129,219,252
Pirates of the Caribbean: Dead Man's Chest (2006)	1,060,332,628
Harry Potter and the Sorcerer's Stone (2001)	968,657,891
Pirates of the Caribbean: At World's End (2007)	958,404,152
Harry Potter and the Order of the Phoenix (2007)	937,000,866
Star Wars Episode I: The Phantom Menace (1999)	922,379,000
The Lord of the Rings: The Two Towers (2002)	921,600,000
Jurassic Park (1993)	919,700,000
Harry Potter and the Goblet of Fire (2005)	892,194,397

Source: imdb.com, July 2008

In the spirit of Herbert Schiller, his fellow Marxists interpret such facts as indicators of a "new international division of cultural labor," a variation on the world-system theme described in Chapter 2, in which the American core lords it over a largely poor and powerless cultural periphery (Miller et al. 2005: ch. 2). Taking Hollywood to task for maintaining this system by imposing its intellectual property rules on the rest of the world, they pitch a suggestion the Motion Picture Association might be shocked to hear, namely that Hollywood "should acknowledge piracy as a viable form of film distribution" (215). Challenging the notion that moviegoers are agents of choice, they portray them instead as objects of studio calculation and subjects of marketing surveillance (ch. 5). For movie makers, Marxian economics has a more mixed message: by its standards, movies themselves are merely commodities, but at the same time their value is determined not by the judgment of the audience but by the labor that went into producing them. Not just America's cinematic dominance offends hard-line Marxists, they also fault Americans for being "American," objecting to the way "Yanquis," their favorite appellation, have unfairly appropriated a name that should apply to a whole hemisphere (49). By their content and tone, such views cut against convergence of the sort noted above. Media scholars are not all of one mind.

Summary and Conclusion

Television has gone global through the diffusion of shows and formats, the interdependence of markets, the organization of a new "regime," and the more common awareness of audiences. Indian television, in particular, has joined the global "mediascape," absorbing foreign content and commercial formats while mixing them in the distinctively Indian context, thus adding "glocal" variety to that mediascape. Indian popular movies have long occupied their own rather large niche and now are moving out from it, adding variety to the global market as well. At the very least, they count against simple scenarios that equate globalization with homogenization. In the view of more subtle scholars, they also tell us something about the interplay between active audiences, local culture, and transnational flows, between domestic state management and transnational regimes. That interplay, creating different outcomes from different intersecting flows in different "scapes," marks one influential perspective on globalization.

By contrast, a substantial group of scholars reads the Indian record more critically, as at best a partial exception to the global rule of Western dominance that in fact continues old forms of imperialism by new means such as the special clout of major media corporations. Notwithstanding all the criticisms of Marx that have accumulated over the past century, in media studies a fairly orthodox Marxism remains prominent, centered on the overriding influence of capitalists and capitalist institutions, and this reinforces a lingering attachment to Marx-inspired critiques of globalization among academics and activists, which Chapter 13 takes up again. That both India's recent changes and overall media trends have provoked strong reactions from scholars on the left is not surprising: they rightly see global media as part and parcel of a larger system. India has joined a world economy that arouses their opposition. The next chapter describes some trends in that world economy as one of the key institutions of world society.

Questions

1 Going beyond the argument about variety in this chapter, the economist Tyler Cowen suggests in his book *Creative Destruction* that there is little need to worry about Hollywood's dominance in the global movie industry since it is limited to certain kinds of movies and allows many other kinds to flourish elsewhere. What evidence would count against or in favor of his argument?

2 The chapter focuses on two fairly traditional types of media, both of which have been challenged by the Internet. What impact is the Internet likely to have on the production and distribution of visual material? How will the business of television and movies change as a result? If the Internet becomes the dominant new medium, will that require proponents of the two kinds of perspectives summarized in the chapter to change their minds?

3 More than most media corporations, News Corp has followed a comprehensive global strategy. What sets it apart from competitors? How "global" are those rival companies? How could we measure the relative control of conglomerates over particular media sectors?

4 Measured by the extent to which people consume "content" produced in the countries where they live, different media sectors, from news to movies, vary in the extent to which they have globalized. Could intrinsic features of different kinds of content account for the variation, or are other factors (also) at work?

Further Reading

Arjun Appadurai, *Modernity at Large: Cultural Dimensions of Globalization* (University of Minnesota Press, 1996)

Michael Curtin, *Playing to the World's Biggest Audience: The Globalization of Chinese Film and TV* (University of California Press, 2007)

Timothy Havens, *Global Television Marketplace* (British Film Institute, 2006)

Edward S. Herman and Robert W. McChesney, *The Global Media: The New Missionaries of Global Capitalism* (Cassell, 1997)

Shanti Kumar, *Gandhi Meets Primetime: Globalization and Nationalism in Indian Television* (University of Illinois Press, 2006)

Lisa Parks and Shanti Kumar (eds.), *Planet TV: A Global Television Reader* (New York University Press, 2003)

— PART II —

GLOBAL INSTITUTIONS

5

THE GLOBAL ECONOMY AND THE POWER OF THE MARKET

- China in Globalization
- The World Economy After World War II
- Changes in the 1970s and Their Impact
- Integrating the World Economy
- Interpreting Economic Integration
- Neoliberalism and its Discontents
- Summary and Conclusion

China in Globalization

In the early years of the twenty-first century, an American consumer placing a web order for a new laptop computer was likely to trigger a chain reaction on the other side of the globe in China's Guangdong province, where women newly arrived from the countryside would assemble a machine to the customer's specifications, perhaps in a Foxconn or Inventec plant, before shipping it across the Pacific. Whatever brand she preferred, Guangdong could deliver: some factories in the area worked for several companies at the same time (Fallows 2007). Design and marketing were still mostly done in the US, but engineering and manufacture had already shifted to Chinese hands. When designs changed, factories could quickly retool. They had to, if they did not want to lose business to rivals nearby. And they were able to, not least because they enjoyed an ample supply of components from providers in the area. Being densely packed in the same region made for cutthroat competition but also gave Chinese producers an edge in the global market. In less than a generation, Guangdong turned from a poor backwater into an industrial workshop to the world (ibid.). Not just southern China took off: most of the country's east coast had become a giant industrial zone (Naughton 2007: 387). Not just computers led to greater riches: Western parents would have been hard put to avoid Chinese toys and baby clothes. As mundane as toys or laptops may seem to jaded consumers, they were part of the dramatic revival of the Chinese economy since the late 1970s. The rise of China is a global story, perhaps the most important of all, and how China changed tells us much about how the world economy changed in the third wave of globalization, the main theme of this chapter. After summarizing that story, the chapter puts it in context by assessing the extent and direction of economic globalization.

Though now often taken for granted, China's transformation is surprising. After all, until 1978 China was one of the most closed societies in the world. When relations with the Soviet Union soured in the late 1950s, China's former leader, Mao Zedong, had forced his country to try and build a distinctive socialist society in isolation. The strategy produced some benefits but also resulted in major disasters. Greatest of these was the Great Leap Forward in 1958–61, when the communist government madly pursued industrialization in the countryside while confiscating diminishing harvests, which caused widespread starvation that cost tens of millions of lives. The memory of such disasters motivated reformers, led by Deng Xiaoping, drastically to change course after Mao's death (Naughton 2007: 88ff.). The first step was local rather than global, namely to give peasant households responsibility for tending their own plots of land and allowing them to sell any surplus beyond official procurement targets in the open market. Tempted by the new incentives, farmers quickly increased production, enough to feed all Chinese, and they saved time and money to set up their own village enterprises, thus boosting the private sector. At the same time, the government also tried to "grow out of the plan," both by requiring state-owned enterprises to operate more rationally and by allowing new businesses to enter some industrial sectors. By setting up Special Economic Zones in coastal areas, separate from the rest of the economy and run by independent government bodies, it also hoped to lure foreign investors with the promise of low taxes, cheap labor, and easy regulations – a lure that proved strong for domestic companies as well. With those coastal zones, which ultimately blossomed into massive industrial regions like Guangdong, China adopted an explicitly global strategy, seeking export-led integration as the way to fuel its development (Guthrie 2006: 114).

After a downturn in 1989–90, followed by signs of an overheating economy, the Chinese leadership pursued reform with new vigor. Deng set the stage with a famous "southern tour" shortly before his death, during which he pressed for reforms to turn China into a "socialist market economy." The socialist characteristics faded more and more. For example, while state-owned enterprises had still been shielded in the 1980s, in the 1990s there would be "reform with losers." The market became that much more important. The Company Law of 1993 and a new constitutional provision later in the decade gave a stronger foundation to companies as market players, a process of "corporatization" (Naughton 2007: 313–5) that nevertheless stopped short of endorsing Western-style privatization. The government also reformed the way it did its own job, focusing macroeconomic policy on squelching inflation and restoring stability, and introducing new tax laws to secure its income. Banking reform slowly began to deal with bad loans in the public sector that might still pull down the house of cards, though this did not yet create an independent, competitive financial sector. Through the decade, Chinese entrepreneurs, often with foreign partners, started thousands of new companies, attracting

Table 5.1 Growth of China's per capita GDP, average annual percentage rates

	GDP	*Population*	*GDP per capita*
1952–78	6.0	1.9	4.1
1978–2005	9.6	1.1	8.5

Note: some scholars think official data overestimate China's growth rates (see Milanovic 2005: 188–194)

Source: Naughton 2007: 140

tens of millions of workers from rural to urban areas, including the women on the assembly lines in Guangdong. To affirm its commitment to market reform, China also sought membership in the World Trade Organization, in the process abolishing import quotas and lowering its average tariffs from over 40 percent to 11 percent between 1992 and 2003 (Wu 2005: 295, 313). After protracted negotiations with partners still skeptical of its intentions, it acceded in 2001. By that time, an apparently tentative, gradual strategy of "groping for stones to cross the river," in the words of a Chinese slogan, had created a wholly different kind of economy, fully engaged, according to another slogan, in "linking up with the international community." Mao would have shuddered at what amounted to the "marketization" of Chinese society. Still communist in name, the People's Republic had become a prime player in the capitalist world economy.

Not just the scope of its reforms makes China's record surprising; so does its sheer success. From 1952 to 1978, China's gross domestic product (GDP) grew at an estimated 6 percent annually, but from 1978 to 2005 that rate increased to 9.6 percent; because population growth declined from 1.9 to 1.1 percent, due in part to China's controversial one-child-per-family policy, GDP per capita grew more than twice as fast after Mao, at 8.5 percent per year (see table 5.1).

The impact on the poor has been especially dramatic: by China's own official calculations, "[p]ossibly never before in history have such a large number of people [approximately 250 million] been lifted out of absolute poverty" (Wu 2005: 212). After 1992, the "stream" of foreign investment turned into a "flood," rising to more than $60 billion by 2004 and 2005, for a total of more than half a trillion dollars (401–2, 405), making China one of the world's chief foreign direct investment (FDI) destinations. In 2004, it was the third-largest trading economy, after the US and Japan, with trade valued at $1.16 trillion (Guthrie 2006: 114). The ports of Hong Kong and Shenzhen alone shipped some 40 million 20-foot containers overseas in 2006 – about one per second (Fallows 2007: 50). Some individual Chinese have done extremely well, notably Yan Cheung, chairwoman of Nine Dragons Paper company, who earned billions from turning American waste into paper and packaging in which to transport goods. The scale of China's Special Economic Zones has come to dwarf similar export-processing zones in other Asian countries – several are at least a hundred times the size of Malaysia's model zone in Penang (Naughton 2007: 408). Emerging from fields and old housing projects in less than

Plate 5.1   Port of Shenzhen, China
Source: © John Van Hasselt/Corbis Sygma

a decade, the Pudong zone (East Shanghai) turned into "a high-tech urban land-scape" with a new skyline composed by very tall buildings (Guthrie 2006: 1), and farther to the south Shenzhen had grown a hundredfold to become an industrial powerhouse (Fallows 2007), both vividly illustrating the enormous momentum China had gained by the end of the twentieth century. Everything China did, it did larger and faster than others.

Yet outsized and extraordinary though it was, China also worked as a normal economy. The secret to its success was good old investment: the Chinese saved – both households and enterprises – and plowed much of the money back into business (Riedel et al. 2007: 150). In simple economic models, growth depends directly on investment, or the capital stock a country accumulates; since China consistently invested about 40 percent of its income, and never less than 25 percent, in the reform period, it is not surprising that its growth rate was also consistently high (Naughton 2007: 145–8). If this had been just a matter of adding equipment and facilities, the rate might have tapered off; in fact, however, China kept improving the quality of its capital, partly by transferring technology from abroad, and thus boosted its productivity. Like any developing country, it also made the most of its most abundant resource, namely labor, and labor-intensive industry became the leading edge of its economic advance. The reforms of the 1990s made China that much more "normal," as the government adopted firm policies to stem inflation and shore up the financial sector, thus making the business environment even more hospitable. Technically speaking, it still did not recognize private property and property rights remained "fuzzy" (121), a globally anomalous stance that in theory should have hampered business by reducing private incentives and causing uncertainty, yet in practice its legal reforms gave managers reasonably secure control over their companies and investors reasonably secure claims on profits – clearly enough to keep its economic engine oiled (Guthrie 2006).

Quite apart from its own economically rational decisions, the key to China's growth was a factor not derived from any economic theory: its access to the American market. Just as China shed its aversion to its old capitalist nemesis, American businesses and especially consumers, obviously with the backing of the US government, easily set aside any second thoughts they may have had about dealing with "communists." Business was business, and Americans did not want to pass up a good deal. American multinationals found their way into China, with companies like General Motors setting up shop there. Wal-Mart's customers got used to cheap goods, and the company built a retail empire by squeezing its suppliers to get the "China price." By some accounts, the effect may have been large enough to reduce inflation in the US. China greatly benefited from America's foreign investment and the knowledge it gained in the process. More subtly, the Chinese also benefited from contact with foreign enterprise, not just American, as it encouraged managers to run their affairs more transparently while treating workers better (Guthrie 2006). Most important to the Chinese, of course, was simply the chance to make money selling to Americans. In fact, China became so dependent on trade with the US, accounting for some 40 percent of its overall trade in the early 2000s, that a senior Chinese economist worried about "overconcentration" (Wu 2005: 318). The money it makes has further entwined China with the US. Since Chinese companies are required to exchange their dollar earnings for Renminbi (RMB) at a set rate through government-approved banks, those earnings ultimately add to the country's foreign reserves. To avoid overheating the economy and causing inflation by increasing the money supply, and to keep the RMB from gaining value against the dollar in a way that would hurt exports, the Chinese government "parks" much of its money, many hundreds of billions of dollars, in US Treasury securities that are safer than any Chinese investments, thus funding America's debt and underwriting American spending habits (Fallows 2008). Though it may seem to Americans that they can have their cake and eat it, buying things from the Chinese with dollars that are then recycled to their advantage, it is not a matter of charity, since China also benefits from the arrangement. That deep, mutual dependence supplies some of the glue for the world economy.

With the rise of China, the story of globalization also comes full circle. China, after all, helped to trigger the first wave. To exaggerate slightly, globalization as we understand it today is really the unintended consequence of the European pursuit of things Chinese – silk, porcelain, tea. Christopher Columbus's lucky detour incorporated the New World into a very loosely connected world society, and New World silver proved crucial for Europeans eager to gain access to the Chinese market. But while Europeans moved outward, China turned inward. Even so, some historians think China matched Western Europe's wealth and technology as late as the mid-eighteenth century, and only fell behind for lack of New World resources of its own and some of Britain's luck in pushing innovation (Pomeranz 2000). More recent research doubts that China was poised to lead in the second wave of globalization: even in advanced regions its standard of living was below that of Britain, it lacked not just technology but also institutions for early industrialization, and even if it had grown faster, its population would have grown as well, negating Britain's crucial advance in growth per capita (Voigtländer and Voth 2006; Clark 2007). Whatever might have been, the historical record is clear enough: the Rise of the West also meant the relative decline of the Middle Kingdom. Western exploitative inroads during the nineteenth century exacerbated China's disadvantage, setting the stage for later turmoil and the communist attempt to liberate China from all foreign exploitation. More than anything, China's return to the world market separates the third wave of globalization from the first two. Without the Chinese, "world society" would be a misnomer.

Its extraordinary history, size, and impact distinguish China from any other global player, yet it also has much in common with others. China's changes reflect and are part of global changes, as the next section elaborates. It joined a world economy that had been rebuilt after World War II at a time when broader reforms were sweeping the system. Communist China helped capitalism reboot globally, to the consternation of critics inspired by Karl Marx and Karl Polanyi, whose arguments about the weaknesses of capitalism still inform many current diagnoses; I briefly assess one such diagnosis in the concluding section. But this chapter obviously does not say the last word about China's role in globalization. Chapter 11 shows that China's growth may be tempering global inequality, Chapter 12 raises the question whether China's global strategy is ecologically viable, and Chapter 13 revisits critiques of the world economy.

The World Economy After World War II

When China began its reforms in the late 1970s, the world economy itself was poised for change. The Chinese caught the third wave just before it crested, and in distinctly Chinese acrobatic fashion pushed it along while riding it. But the wave did not start then. Since 1945, the world economy had already become much more integrated. China rejoined a world market very different than the one it had tried to leave after the Revolution of 1949.

This global transformation had happened partly by design. Even during World War II, the allies had begun to discuss ways to avoid the economic errors that had brought an ugly end to the second wave of globalization. Since in their eyes trade barriers, monetary instability, and limited investment were to blame, the Americans had three clear goals for the post-war order: to make trade flow more freely, to stabilize the world's financial system, and to encourage international investment (Frieden 2006: 254). Britain's key representative, the economist John Maynard Keynes, shared their goals and helped turn them into a feasible design. After some wrangling, the allies agreed at a famous conference in Bretton Woods, New Hampshire, to adopt new rules of the international economic game. Instead of returning to the gold standard, the new system would peg currencies to the dollar and link only the dollar to gold. With funds supplied by its members, a new International Monetary Fund (IMF) would monitor states' economic performance and step in with loan assistance if a serious imbalance would threaten a currency or cause a panic. The key point was to give all players enough confidence in the system that they would trade and invest freely, without undue concern for the future value of money – to create a virtuous spiral to replace the vicious one of the interwar period. Because many countries had been devastated by the war, the first order of business was to boost their reconstruction effort, a task handed to the new World Bank that would have authority to lend in support of development. Since protectionist sentiments still lurked, trade turned out to be a more sensitive issue. A proposed International Trade Organization never got off the ground, partly due to resistance in the US Congress, but major countries agreed to move forward via negotiations under the auspices of the General Agreement on Tariffs and Trade (GATT). The agreement prohibited signatories from giving some countries easier access than others, required countries to match tariff reductions by their partners, and gave them recourse against unfair practices like below-cost dumping. In the spirit of the agreement, but without a formal organization to promote free trade, countries realized that lowering tariffs would be wise, and in the following decades at least all of the industrialized countries steadily lowered their tariffs, to below 9 percent on non-agricultural goods by 1967 (288) and to about half that rate by 2000 (Findlay and O'Rourke 2007: 494–5).

In keeping currencies fairly stable and avoiding financial panics, the design worked largely as planned, though the IMF's role was weaker and the dollar's role more central than anticipated. The new world order had a stronger financial backbone. Reconstruction took a different course than planned because direct US aid in the 1940s turned out to be more important than the efforts of the World Bank, which before long shifted its attention to boosting development in what came to be called the "Third World." International trade exceeded everyone's expectations, not least because America had opened its market to European and newly ambitious Japanese producers, and already in the 1950s imported at a rate two or three times higher than before the war (Frieden 2006: 283). European exports went from $150 to $960 billion (in 2000 dollars) between 1950 and 1973, and trade had become nearly three times as important to every developed economy (289). Investment also skyrocketed; for example, US investment in Europe and Japan grew from $2 to $41 billion in the same period (283), and by 1973, multinational corporations had invested some $200 billion around the world, about half coming from the US (293). Even the Soviet Union joined in, increasing trade threefold in 25 years and attracting some foreign investment (328). As in the second wave, new technologies spurred integration – container ships reduced transport costs, jumbo jets that came into service in 1970 reduced travel times. For the West, all this international activity paid off spectacularly. The output of industrial countries grew threefold, poorer European countries nearly caught up with their neighbors, and Japan joined the club, growing so fast that it caught up with Western Europe (280–1). For many people, this was an economic golden age.

Though apart from a stray academic no one yet used the term globalization, it was in fact a global age – global, but not too global. Again, this was partly by design. The Bretton Woods architects worried that speculation might undermine currencies and make it difficult for governments to pursue their own goals, and they therefore granted states the power to impose capital controls (Helleiner 1994: 4–5). Instead of a fully liberal system, allowing completely free movement of goods and money, they laid the groundwork for a partly closed, state-managed "embedded liberalism" (Ruggie 1982), giving states sufficient clout to maintain their autonomy and devise social policies without fear of financial attack from without. Though economic ties tightened rapidly, by late-century standards the actual flows of money and goods were still modest. They mostly crossed the North Atlantic and one corridor in the Pacific, linking three regions rather than the world as a whole. In fact, "in many parts of the world the war set in motion forces that would isolate countries from international markets, rather than integrate them" (Findlay and O'Rourke 2007: 476). Again, deliberate policy played a role. Having been harmed by the pre-war crisis, and concerned about US dominance, Latin American countries disconnected from the larger economy via Import Substitution Industrialization – a strategy that for some time reaped great success in places like Brazil and Mexico. Partly to follow that example, newly independent countries in Africa as well as India embarked on a similar path, with results that initially seemed encouraging. In spite of modest overtures, most of the communist Second World remained behind the Iron Curtain. In the context of the time, Mao's retreat to autarky was just an extreme version of a widely practiced development strategy. It marked the limits of globalization, mid-century style.

Though American leaders would have preferred to pry open those relatively closed economies, it was in many ways a world made in or by America. At Bretton Woods, America set the tone and pushed its plans. It put Britain in its new, diminished place: British influence waned, the British Empire crumbled. After Bretton Woods, America provided the key impulse behind Europe's reconstruction, in part to stem a feared Soviet advance to the West. Of course, this was more than an economic exercise, and the US used the North Atlantic Treaty Organization (NATO) as a vehicle for leading a military anti-Soviet alliance. Both the lure of financial gain and pressing political concerns helped to solidify America's commitment to integration. By opening its markets to the world and having its companies venture farther than before, the US fueled global growth. Even though other countries grew faster, starting from a much lower base, America was the uncontested economic leader of the "embedded liberal" global order. Precisely because its role was so central,

changes affecting America reverberated throughout the world economy and ultimately would help to alter its very structure.

Changes in the 1970s and their Impact

The old order's Achilles heel was its reliance on the dollar. More than the Bretton
Woods negotiators anticipated, the dollar became the linchpin of the world's financial order. But for various reasons, banks and investors by the early 1970s had come
to think that it was overvalued and started to flee into the German mark or convert
dollar reserves into gold (Eichengreen 1996: 133). The US government faced a stark
choice: to maintain the dollar's value in gold ("convertibility"), it would have to
expend reserves and commit to austerity at home. In the end, in August 1971, the
Nixon administration chose to avoid domestic pain and break America's previous
international commitment by closing the "gold window," and subsequent negotiations with other countries led to a major devaluation. When America had to devalue
again in 1973, key European countries responded by letting their currencies float
as well, as the dollar already did. With its linchpin gone, the old financial order
imploded. A few years later, the US had also eliminated its capital controls, allowing
all market players to exchange dollars freely. Other advanced states had little choice
but to follow suit. By the early 1980s, a new world market for money emerged: key
currencies could be traded more easily than any commodity, their relative values
were set by traders judging countries' economic performance, and the dollar
regained status as a "reserve" currency without any backing in gold. Exposed to
that market, more and more countries had to "unpeg" their currencies, and only a
minority remained pegged by the early 1990s (Eichengreen 1996: 189). The market
was huge: in 1970, $17.5 trillion in currencies changed hands, but total turnover in
1995 had reached $297.5 trillion (Held et al. 1999: 209). *Daily* trading has since
exceeded $3 trillion. Finance took on a life of its own, as it were, with money flows
growing much more rapidly than world exports. Floating exchange rates and greater
capital mobility marked a new era of financial globalization.

Just as global finance was shifting course, OPEC, the cartel of oil-producing
countries, drastically raised the price of oil in 1973. Because the world ran on oil,
the increase shocked the system. In Western countries, prices of many goods rose
at a time when growth was already declining. Developing countries barely beyond
destitution could hardly afford to pay. Flush with new income, the exporters had
to decide how to deploy their funds. They recycled much of their money through
big banks that lent to countries that needed the money partly to pay for oil. For
lack of sufficient export income, import substituters incurred debt to fuel growth
and support government spending. When the US dealt with its own difficulties at
the end of the 1970s by raising interest rates to stem inflation, this added insult to
economic injury by increasing the cost of debt for everyone everywhere (Frieden
2006: 374–5). Latin American countries, in particular, faced heavy obligations they

could not meet, resulting in several crises, such as Mexico's near-default in 1982. As such countries got in trouble and tried to attract fresh capital, domestic investors often bailed out by moving their money abroad, further undermining currencies and making the healing job that much more difficult. The oil shocks – a second price increase in 1979 had aggravated the situation – brought to the fore a new form of global interdependence. Everyone was caught in a single web at risk of fraying.

Faced with new problems, the key players in the old Bretton Woods institutions asked the IMF and the World Bank to take on new tasks in managing financial instability, thus expanding their role. In exchange for loans, the IMF expected debtors to practice "structural adjustment" – live within their means, stop subsidizing unproductive sectors, and adjust policies to generate new income. Because states first got in trouble by spending more than they took in, partly due to their debt of course, the first order of business was typically to cut their budget. Since states often used the budget both to steer the private sector and to buy support through social benefits, this also required a "structural" change in how they spent their money. To get countries out of debt once and for all, they needed to generate more income, and the IMF's recipe for growth came down to another structural change: liberalization. Privatized state companies, business unencumbered by politics, more competition in the financial sector, and lower barriers to trade would have a salutary effect on the patient. The common ingredient in the prescriptions was the idea that the market would work best. Because some crises involved huge sums, the World Bank was drawn into the drama as well, providing supportive emergency loans. Until the late 1990s, it shared what was branded the "Washington consensus," a model for changing state policies to draw countries into a new global order (Williamson 1990; Rodrik 2006: 978). Since many countries had their own incentives to change course, and some did not reform as thoroughly in practice as they had agreed to do on paper, the actual impact of the IMF is still a matter of debate. In later years, it had to adjust structural adjustment when its recipes left a sour taste in many places (see box 5.1). Nonetheless, as interdependence rose, so did the clout of organizations trying to set new rules for the global game.

The oil shocks pushed many countries to the brink of economic disaster but even without this unwelcome assistance they typically faced significant challenges (Frieden 2006: chs. 13–14). The post-war strategies of different regions had run into trouble. Import substituters had industrialized successfully but after exhausting the "easy" opportunities they needed capital to buy new technology and grow further (Eichengreen 1996: 182). The Second World of communist countries had also managed to industrialize but ran into the limits of centralized planning as their economic system became more complex, failed to innovate, and could not deliver adequate consumer products. More isolated than most, China experienced an extreme version of common dilemmas. The oil shocks, of course, made the search for alternatives that much more urgent, a search joined by European countries as a result of their own troubles in providing generous welfare and full employment at a time of lower growth and threats of higher inflation. For different political

Box 5.1 Common prescriptions for economic policy, 1980s to 2000s: original and "augmented" Washington consensus – partial list

Original Washington consensus	*Augmented Washington consensus – original plus:*
Fiscal discipline	Anti-corruption measures
Financial liberalization	Good corporate governance
Trade liberalization	Independent central banks
Openness to FDI	WTO agreements
Deregulation	Social safety nets
Privatization	Targeted poverty reduction

Source: Rodrik 2006: Table 1

reasons and at very different levels of development, states in each region had tried to shield their domestic economies while carefully managing relationships with the outside world. Gradually, often reluctantly, at times under duress, their leaders decided that they could only solve their problems by "opening up" to seek new capital, new technology, and new opportunities. Import substitution fell by the wayside, liberalization took its place. More and more countries, including China of course, staked their fortunes on success in world markets. They bet that integration would make them better off. Globalization as it unfolded in the last decade of the twentieth century resulted from the choices they made.

As this short story shows, the third wave of globalization gathered strength due to a particular confluence of circumstances. The immediate post-war version of globalization had its weaknesses: trying to manage currencies by applying capital controls even as capital mobility increased, trying to have countries grow by themselves even as they came to rely on foreign funds and technologies, and trying to check the reverberations of price shocks in a system that relied on a single commodity, proved to be too difficult. Something had to give. Key players also did not want to keep the old system, and in this regard, once again, the US played a critical role: it made the Bretton Woods monetary system unravel, it pushed for further opening of markets, it precipitated the debt crisis and then led in pushing liberalization as a way to deal with it. Force of circumstance and American decisions set the stage for a new round of what came to be called globalization, or what some call "reglobalization" (Findlay and O'Rourke 2007: 496ff.) – a process of lowering barriers to spur trade and investment as a way to bring about closer integration. For its own reasons, China joined the game, enjoying the significant advantage of being debt-free. By the early 1980s, globalization was already going strong, with financial markets expanding, trade growing, and new rules of the game evolving. In one generation, the world economy did become far more integrated by any measure. Let us count the ways.

Integrating the World Economy

When McDonald's arrived in Tokyo and Hong Kong in the 1970s (Chapter 2), it was in the vanguard of a consumer revolution that would soon reach Beijing, where a 700-seat restaurant opened in 1992 (Yan 1997). From Taipei to Moscow, from Delhi to Paris, McDonald's opened more restaurants in more places serving more hamburgers, fries, and Cokes, as well as slightly more local fare, according to its standard production model, turning the company logo into a global icon by the end of the twentieth century. "Billions served" was more than just a snappy slogan. In a short time, the icon became a cliché, itself a marker of how rapidly certain products and experiences diffused globally. That diffusion took many forms, sometimes driven by specific companies, as in the case of McDonald's, sometimes more loosely responding to shifting demand, as in the case of sushi. In any of its many forms, such diffusion bolstered a very basic integration: as global markets expanded, more and more people liked, bought, and consumed the same sorts of things.

While McDonald's was building its global brand, a still-obscure sneaker company was plotting ways to market its shoes. Taking advantage of the American fitness craze in the late 1970s, and then promoting it heavily by associating itself with star athletes, Nike turned a simple commodity into an object of desire. Like McDonald's golden arches, Nike's swoosh became a global emblem in a short period, thanks to innovative advertising. Nike did not in fact make its shoes. At the outset, it had shoes produced by a Japanese partner, which shifted operations to Korea and Taiwan to avoid high Japanese labor costs; those countries made about 90 percent of Nike's supply by 1980, but contractors there increasingly moved into even lower-wage countries such as Indonesia, Thailand, and Vietnam, and in 1980 Nike had already begun to contract with Chinese factories as well, a good fit for the Chinese government at the time (Korzeniewicz 1994). American runners might wear shoes designed in Oregon but made by Indonesian women supervised by Korean managers. Just as it globalized production, it also globalized consumption by globalizing its marketing strategy, trying to reach new customers by sponsoring soccer events like the World Cup and great soccer teams like that of Brazil.

In Nike's case, the diffusion of a particular product and consumer taste rested on a global "commodity chain," or "value chain," in which different activities took place in different places to turn an idea into a commodity and then into a saleable item. Nike developed one way to "slice up the value chain," typical of buyer-driven networks in which apparel companies deal with contractors that directly steer work to subcontractors; in electronics, by contrast, producer-driven chains are more common, with supplies from many sources gathered at one site to be assembled into a final product at the direction of a single manufacturer (Gereffi 2005). If the components of a shoe – rubber, glue, stitching – already link several places, the supply chain "symphony" that results in notebook computers is even more intricate, as an American journalist discovered when he had Dell trace the components of the machine he ordered (Friedman 2007: 580–3). It so happened that his computer was assembled in Penang, Malaysia, one of six Dell production sites – it could have come from Ireland or China or Brazil, or even Nashville, Tennessee – using a design jointly produced by engineers in Texas and Taiwan. Within hours of the order, the Dell factory requested parts from its nearby supplier logistics center, which were quickly delivered for assembly. The parts themselves were a bit harder to trace, since Dell used multiple suppliers for 30 key components – the memory could have come from a Korean, Taiwanese, German, or Japanese factory, the Intel microprocessor from a factory in Malaysia, the Philippines, Costa Rica, or China, and so on. Just as Nike does not make shoes, as a "network enterprise" (Held et al. 1999: 264) Dell did not really make the computer – it developed the design, guided the assembly, processed the sale, and perhaps followed up with service (if that had not been outsourced to personnel in India at the time).

Nike and Dell were at the forefront of a global trend that greatly increased economic interdependence. In the last decades of the twentieth century, foreign direct investment by such companies, more than 50,000 altogether (Held et al. 1999: 245), outstripped the growth in trade or income: while world GDP increased at a 2.5 percent and exports at a 5.6 percent pace between 1985 and 1999, FDI inflows grew 17.7 percent annually (Barba Navaretti and Venables 2004: 3). Most of it still came from and went to advanced countries, whose inflows and outflows peaked at over $1 trillion in 2000 and after dipping briefly rose again to similar levels in 2006 (OECD 2007a: 18). Yet developing countries gradually attracted a higher share, growing to some $200 billion or 2.5 percent of GDP by 2004 (World Bank 2007GEP: 32; Barba Navaretti and Venables 2004: 9). Once upon a time, much FDI was a means to get around trade barriers – General Motors produced Opel cars in Germany in order to sell its products more easily there – but Nike and Dell illustrate how organizing production globally (or "vertically") can bring other gains besides market access. Not surprisingly, freer trade makes it easier for them to do more of it: multinationals certainly help to globalize the world, but there are many multinationals partly because the world is so globalized (278–9). Such multinationals typically perform better than rival firms in their home or host countries, expand their home activities thanks to gains abroad, and boost world income overall, leading two experts to conclude pithily that "[o]rganizing activities across the border works" (279). Whether the benefits of FDI inflows "spill over" to local firms and the local economy is less clear: places where firms adapt and consumers enjoy lower prices see net benefits, but multinationals that operate as islands of technological sophistication in less developed countries may not contribute as much (280).

As large and important as FDI has become, reaching $1.3 trillion in 2006, its scope still pales compared to the value of international trade, worth more than $14 trillion in the same year. One conventional way to measure trade's significance is to compare it to overall GDP. The trend is unmistakable that for individual countries and for the world as a whole, trade represents an ever-larger portion of GDP: except in 1985 and 2001, according to IMF data, trade grew faster than overall GDP in all the 25 years up to 2008 (cf. Held et al. 1999: 180–1). Because modern economies shift to services, many of which are less easily traded, the number if anything understates the true significance of trade. It is the lifeblood of many small countries, and the total value of imports and exports may actually exceed their GDP – in the Netherlands, for example, it stood at 139 percent in 2006 – but even for the big ones, trade is now absolutely essential, and in the US, the biggest economy of all, its contribution to GDP increased to 28 percent by 2006. Developed countries still dominate but developing countries sell more and more to each other, as in the case of Intel processors going from China to Malaysia. As the Dell case also illustrates, much of that trade does not take place in the open market but really occurs within industries or firms that manage the flow. Not only do more things move to more places, trade comprises more than "things" since services are taking on a greater role, a niche exploited by India with its back-office processing and computer service call centers. Thanks to higher levels of trade than ever before, a new "global trading system" has developed, featuring "an intensive network of trading relations embracing virtually all economies and . . . evolving global markets for many goods and some services" (Held et al. 1999: 176). Even without any policy changes that might lead to further opening, the World Bank expects trade to reach new heights: by 2030, it should rise from a fourth to about a third of world GDP, or about $27 trillion.

Tempting though it may be to think of this global trading system as led by an invisible hand, as the natural result of self-interested parties freely pursuing their own gain, some visible hands played a part as well. Of course, expanding trade had been the allies' prime goal at the end of World War II, and the GATT had promoted it to some extent. But the problems that mounted in the 1970s, along with changes in technology, caused widespread dissatisfaction with the old system and a sense of urgency to find a way out. A GATT ministerial meeting in 1982 set off a new round of negotiations – the so-called Uruguay round – that resulted in a new agreement among the parties in 1993 to form a World Trade Organization that would open for business in 1995. A late successor to the stillborn International Trade Organization, the WTO was intended to implement new rules for lowering barriers, serve as a forum for further negotiations, and settle disputes about infractions on free trade. It was vastly more ambitious: whereas the GATT texts comprised all of 80 pages, the Uruguay agreements required 26,000 pages or 200 kilos of text; the WTO would also have more than 60 councils and committees (Gallagher 2005: 7). It would have more power as well, especially in imposing sanctions on countries that were found unfairly to favor their own producers or to keep out foreign products. And it addressed new issues, for example by formulating rules for members' domestic laws

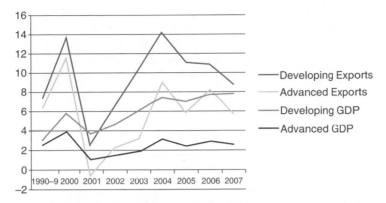

Figure 5.1 Development of real GDP (adjusted for inflation) and trade (exports only) in developing and advanced economies, 1990/99–2007, in percentage rates (decade average for 1990–99)
Note: 1. Developing-country growth rates in mid-2000s exceeded average growth rates for 1990s. 2. Developing-country exports grew faster on average than advanced country exports, one way developing countries "globalized" faster. 3. Developing-country GDP grew faster on average than advanced GDP, hence developing countries overall "caught up." 4. Trade grew faster on average than real GDP, hence trade became relatively more important in global economic activity.
Source: IMF 2008, Tables A1 and A9

dealing with intellectual property. It was also more comprehensive: it included 112 members at the outset in 1995, and when China joined six years later it became the 143rd member. In its first decade, the WTO struggled with controversial issues, such as how to treat agriculture, and became a lightning rod for globalization critics, as Chapter 13 explains, but for all its difficulties it clearly acquired authority, granted by states, to organize the trading system. By the early 2000s, that system had a deliberately arranged framework of rules, another mark of integration.

Along with global trade and production, global finance took off as well. In its most frenzied precincts, many of them a virtual reality of traders deploying fancy computer systems, trillions in currencies changed "hands" every day. Only slightly less dramatic were ordinary capital flows that reached $1.5 trillion in 1995, representing 6 percent of world GDP, but a decade later had swelled to $6 trillion or 12 percent of total GDP, according to an IMF Survey of Global Capital Flows. FDI, of course, was part of those flows; so were portfolio investments in securities abroad. Strikingly, the value of all those foreign assets nearly came to match annual world GDP (Obstfeld and Taylor 2004: 53). Reversing previous trends, developing countries became capital magnets, drawing in close to $1 trillion or 12 percent of their GDP in 2004 (World Bank 2007GEP: 32). With confidence in their sunny prospects, institutional investors put more of their money to work in "emerging markets," which represented some 16 percent of their assets in 2006, nearly double the rate of a decade before (IFC 2006). That confidence paid off in the early 2000s

Table 5.2 Organizing the world economy: three key institutions

	IMF	*World Bank*	*WTO*
Origin	Bretton Woods, 1944	Bretton Woods, 1944	GATT rounds since 1948
Founded	1945	1945	1995
President (2008)	D. Strauss-Kahn (France)	R. Zoellick (US)	P. Lamy (France)
Members	185 countries	185 countries	152 countries
Headquarters	Washington, DC	Washington, DC	Geneva
Main goals	stable exchange rates, monetary cooperation, balanced growth	poverty reduction and sustained growth	promote free trade, fair competition, dispute resolution
Main method	lending from members' capital subscriptions to countries with balance of payment problems	lending from own funds and financial market borrowing for development projects and policy reform	dispute settlement via consultations or judgments by expert panels
Some other activities	surveillance/ oversight of monetary system; technical assistance for reform; research	grants for debt relief; research	provide forum for negotiations (e.g., about trade in agricultural goods); administer agreements
Some numbers	$16.1 billion in loans outstanding in 2008	$24.7 billion lent for 301 projects, 2007	332 cases brought, of which 132 submitted to panels, 1995–2005

Sources: institutional information

as such markets saw spectacular gains far exceeding those in more mature counterparts, boosting their market capitalization from $2 to $5 trillion between 1995 and 2006 (ibid.), before concerns about a bubble surfaced and emerging market stock values retreated in 2008 as part of a broader economic retrenchment.

Among the winners prior to that point were Western retirees who enjoyed higher returns on their pension investments and American students who enjoyed the financial aid that trickled down from growing university endowments. Global finance hit home just as tangibly for people seeking a mortgage when American financial institutions started offering them better terms on risky loans, expecting to turn such loans into securities that could be packaged into groups or "pools" and sold to global investors – a strategy that went sour in 2007–8 when those securities turned out quite insecure as more people holding sub-prime mortgages defaulted. Though that episode raised questions about money managers' judgment, with more funds at risk in more assets, more currencies, and more places, they had in fact been looking for ways to hedge their bets. Each step toward financial globalization carried risk: emerging bubbles might burst, newfangled securities go bust, or currencies plummet. To deal with these and other risks, financial innovators devised new ways to cushion potential blows with new financial instruments. Taking advantage of better tools to assess risk, so-called hedge funds became major, multibillion dollar global players, quickly moving their money across borders and asset categories. They were just one group of global operators among many others. By the early twenty-first century, often without quite realizing it, more people in more places had become dependent on each other through the intricate workings of much larger and more complex global financial markets, as the downturn of 2008 made all too clear.

Interpreting Economic Integration

In spite of its apparent "deterritorialization," even money was still tied to space, for example because investors in most countries kept focusing on domestic stocks and bonds. If they were truly global players, they would have had to diversify their assets much more than they had in fact. By the same token, most countries still derived most of their investment from domestic sources. For all their foreign ties, economies retained a distinctly national cast. That was even more evident in trade. Take the case of the US and Canada: the countries are similar in many ways, they share a long border, they are mostly on friendly terms, so if borders did not matter, Ontario would trade more with New York State than with British Columbia. Yet the border turns out to be very wide: it dampens trade and adds price variability as much as a distance of at least 2,500 miles within either country (Engel and Rogers 1996). Where culture, law, and language differ more than in North America, borders are bound to be wider still. Apart from such political barriers, sheer distance continued to play a role. The "gravity model" of trade says that the farther apart countries are, the less they will trade with each other, and in fact for each additional 1 percent in distance, trade turns out to fall between 0.7 and 1.0 percent (Frankel 2000: 53). Clearly, space still entails costs. Ocean transport may actually have become more expensive since World War II, an effect partly offset by increased air shipments; faster transport for light goods also reduced storage costs while goods were in transit, but these still imposed the equivalent of a hefty 9 percent tariff in 1998 (Findlay and O'Rourke 2007: 504–5). Just as distance carries costs, proximity has its benefits, as managers in Guangdong or Penang well knew. Even, or perhaps especially, in an era of vertical production with components coming from many places, having an ample supply nearby is critical to efficient assembly. Similarly, many industries and services, from New York finance to Bollywood movies to

Silicon Valley high-tech, need a critical mass of partners and competitors within reach of face-to-face contact to enjoy the fruits of agglomeration. In an age of deterritorialization, many businesses still have to be in just the right place.

Granted the spatial limits to economic globalization, why did the world economy "go global" at all? Economic history suggests some answers, economic theory suggests others, but no one has quite solved the puzzle. Part of the reason was that for most countries not going global was worse, since previous strategies seemed to have run their course. But apart from the push of old problems, magnified in the turmoil of the 1970s, countries also felt the pull of potential gains: opening up to the world market might just work better. To most economists, there was good reason to believe it would. They had long thought that in free exchange all parties win, and that therefore trade is inherently beneficial. Their old doctrine of comparative advantage argues more specifically that if two countries freely trade and compete, they will both be better off – that is, their overall joint output will be greater at a given effort – if each specializes in the line(s) of business in which it is most efficient relative to others it might pursue. Applied globally, this implies big gains for trading compared to secluded or import-substituting countries, which are bound to be stuck in inefficiency. According to a more modern version of the argument, by contrast with counterproductive government interventions "[a] high rate of interaction with the rest of the world speeds the absorption of frontier technologies and global management best practices, spurs innovation and cost-cutting, and competes away monopoly" (Frankel 2000: 60), producing not just growth but a higher rate of growth. More competition and access to larger markets account for some of the effect. Probably even more important is the learning across borders inherent in technology transfer, and according to one economic model "world GDP would be only 6% of its current level . . . if countries did not share ideas" (Klenow and Rodríguez-Clare 2005: 856). Of course, basic economic theory also suggests that lowering the cost of transactions will stimulate more of them, and when states around the world lowered barriers, lo and behold, trade and investment indeed took off. Technical advances, such as the beginnings of jet travel and the incipient computer revolution, had similar effects, especially in coordinating production across borders, enabling massive capital flows, and creating wholly new financial products. Open markets put a premium on continued improvement in such transaction technologies, which further improves efficiency and stimulates growth. These markets are non-zero-sum games: everybody who plays can win. To enhance its appeal, as the next section explains, some economists marketed the idea of the market with special zeal, giving global integration a strong intellectual push.

What exactly has integration achieved? At the risk of committing a tautology, integration is an achievement in itself. Globalization, once started, triggered more globalization. As a result, the web of the world economy is now thicker and stronger. World society has a distinct economy. The second achievement is a vast increase in output, thanks to old players improving their game but also to new players entering. Leaving aside the issue of how best to measure world income (see Chapter 11), the annual value of all goods and services reached over $50 trillion by the early 2000s – a

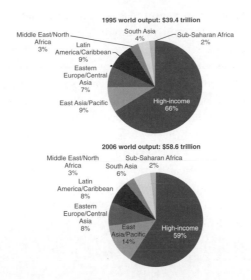

Figure 5.2   Increase in developing economies' share in world output, 1995–2006
Source: World Bank 2008a: 193

staggering sum. Of course, it would be rash to credit all of it to globalization, yet the era of globalization has seen a great expansion. After 2000, that expansion got a further boost as many developing-country economies boomed for several years. At least potentially, the strengthening web can also keep its parts from swinging wildly and thereby reduce volatility, for example because high-performing places can make up for trouble in another spot and because the system itself has devised ways to manage risk to the web's strands. Even very large recent crises, such as the Asian debt crisis of 1997–8, left few permanent scars on the world economy, however traumatic the event was for people in several Asian countries at the time. But it may be too early to cheer: precisely what tests the web can withstand, and under what conditions its strong ties might actually amplify risks, is less clear – a concern highlighted during the credit crisis that cascaded across countries in 2008.

Broad measures of integration's impact are well and good, but did openness pay off for participants? Not across the board: some Latin American countries, for example, struggled to regain their footing even as they practiced reform. As their experience shows, openness is not sufficient for growth, an issue Chapter 11 revisits. But it is increasingly clear that openness is necessary. For example, in the 1990s nearly all the countries that caught up with the developed core were open to trade and investment, and two that fell short in liberalizing, India and China, had become much more open than before (Findlay and O'Rourke 2007: 523). From 1995 to 2005, "countries that opened up to trade also performed better on growth," and those that did not saw their GDP shrink on average (World Bank 2007WDI: 2). Relatively high growth, already clear in figure 5.1, meant that some countries, especially in Asia, claimed a larger share of world output and income – a bigger slice of a growing pie. That, in turn, had implications for inequality, as Chapter 11 shows.

But the sunny picture of integration, expansion, and the fruits of openness may be a bit too bright. Globalization may have helped to lift some countries out of previous problems, but until the turn of the century its growth benefits did not measure up to the immediate post-war boom in several regions. For all the dynamism of globalization, Europe and North America settled for a growth rate of about 2 percent. Sub-Saharan Africa, Latin America, and Eastern Europe did better in the 1960s than in the 1990s (Findlay and O'Rourke 2007: 519). Even there, however, the beginning of the new century brought new economic vigor (World Bank 2007GEP: 53). Yet the very fact that growth fluctuates across time and space shows that the global path is by no means smooth. Critics go a step further, to argue that it leads in entirely the wrong direction.

Neoliberalism and its Discontents

Deng Xiaoping might have shuddered at the cover of a critical history of the globalization era in which he played such a major role: it pictures Deng between Ronald Reagan and Augusto Pinochet, flanked on the far right by Margaret Thatcher (Harvey 2005). After all, Pinochet was the Chilean dictator who had forcefully removed the government of Marxist president Salvador Allende in 1973 before turning Chile into a leader in market reform. Thatcher had become prime minister of Britain in 1979 determined to reduce the role of government and to break the power of unions that in her view had held the economy hostage. Taking office as president of the US at a time of crisis in 1981, Reagan supported the strong medicine of high interest rates administered by the Federal Reserve Bank at the expense of the unemployed, pushed for the lowering of top tax rates, and laid down the law to workers by firing members of PATCO, the air traffic controllers' union that engaged in an illegal strike. They form unusual company for a Chinese communist, to say the least. Or do they? Deng himself, David Harvey avers, might have been a "capitalist roader" all along, as Mao had suspected (120). The reforms he ushered in followed the "neoliberal" path that his cover mates were blazing at the same time. In a way, they were doing the same sort of thing under very different circumstances. The global transformation since China's turn is a "history of neoliberalism."

The plot of the story resembles that of the previous section, but Harvey gives it his own twist. When "capital accumulation," hampered by the social democratic welfare state, sputtered in the 1970s, countries could have taken the socialist path of greater state control, Harvey suggests somewhat nostalgically, but instead they stumbled toward a neoliberal path that required reducing the role of the state and giving free rein to the market (12–13). Guided by utopian ideologues inspired by economists like Friedrich von Hayek, who loathed the state as inherently oppressive, leaders like Reagan and Thatcher proceeded to reform capitalism at home and abroad. Though none may have uttered the phrase, Harvey suggests that they promoted the slogan "what is good for Wall Street is all that matters" (33). At the urging of big banks and corporations, the US government revived its "imperial tradition" to pry open foreign markets (27). This was a political project: the point of neoliberal globalization was to restore "class power," the power of the owners of capital. In this reading of history, Deng Xiaoping was an unwitting participant in that capitalist project.

Prime villain in this tale of woe is the IMF. As one country after another exposed to the harsh pressures of reviving capitalism suffered financial crises – Mexico in 1982 and 1995, Thailand in 1997, Brazil in 1999, Argentina in 2001, and so on – the IMF invariably stepped in to demand further liberalization as the universal tonic, at the expense of local control over domestic affairs and the welfare of citizens (see also table 5.2). Harvey shares the diagnosis of Joseph Stiglitz (2002), former World Bank economist and Nobel Memorial Prize winner, who has chided the IMF for harming its patients with poisonous medicine. In the case of the Asian crisis of the late 1990s, according to Stiglitz (99ff.), the patients got sick in part due to IMF policies that urged greater openness to capital flows, which then led to imprudent lending as Asian banks borrowed dollars, lent to local companies in local currency, and then could not repay when business slowed, the currency declined, and the dollar loans became bigger burdens. But in response the IMF prescribed more of the same: less control of capital flows. It also unwisely insisted on lowering deficits at a time economies needed stimulation (105–6). The money the IMF provided in effect bailed out foreign lenders while leaving Asian workers to deal with the fallout of higher unemployment (95–7). Equally telling was the IMF's treatment of Ethiopia in 1997. As a condition for a new loan, the IMF told the country to lower its budget, declining to count foreign aid as income, even though according to Stiglitz such aid is more reliable than ordinary taxes (28–9). It also asked Ethiopia to break up its largest bank, hoping that competition would make loans available more easily, but according to Stiglitz this risked foreign takeovers that would squelch competition (30–2). Instead of applying a one-size-fits-all version of "market fundamentalism," Stiglitz wanted the IMF to be more sensitive to Ethiopia's special challenges and well-intentioned government.

Such market fundamentalism, Harvey argues, is nothing new. In fact, the current phase of globalization looks remarkably like that of the nineteenth century, as interpreted by Karl Polanyi (1957), whose diagnosis he finds "particularly appropriate to our contemporary condition" (Harvey 2005: 37). Then, as now, ideologues sang the praises of a self-regulating market. Then, as now, land, capital, and especially labor were turned into mere commodities in ever-wider markets. Then, as now, collective support for the poor declined as economic relations were "disembedded" from their social context. Prior to Britain's free-market conversion, the Poor Law had prescribed welfare payments to be paid from communal funds, but in Polanyi's view (1957: 82–3), the Reform Act of 1834 stripped poor workers of social protection by abolishing the "right to live" and leaving many of the most needy "to their fate." Under the gold standard, a global free market briefly prevailed that allowed capital to flow freely but prevented states from interfering in economic affairs for social purposes. It was a rough system that provoked resistance, calls for the protection of society against the depredations of the market. Although in practice it at first took destructive forms, the resulting "double movement" would replace an unsustainable economic utopia with a more just and cohesive society. Not surprisingly, this analysis inspires left-leaning critics of globalization, more of whom we will encounter in Chapter 13. Just as neoliberals follow in the footsteps of their nineteenth-century liberal predecessors to advocate a more open world economy, its critics follow in Karl Polanyi's footsteps in viewing the contemporary phase of globalization as the Second Great Transformation. And just as they view globalization as a political project, their analysis has a political thrust as well. Like Polanyi, they want to indict a system they abhor. Just as Polanyi attacked the false freedom to "exploit one's fellows" or "make inordinate gains," Harvey laments with more passion than good grammar that "[o]bligated to live as appendages of the market and of capital accumulation rather than as expressive beings, the realm of freedom shrinks before the awful logic and the hollow intensity of market involvements" (185). Though he does not go as far as Harvey, Stiglitz joins the critique by blaming the IMF for imposing that "awful logic" on innocent countries.

The logic may be awful but critics of the critique might counter that the alternatives could be worse. In the case of Ethiopia, for example, the IMF had good reason to doubt that a government that relied on aid would carry out meaningful reform and raise its future income. IMF officials familiar with the record of other African countries that had failed along these lines might have savored the irony of being lectured by Stiglitz, not known for his African expertise, on the need to understand local conditions. The subsequent resumption of a wasteful war against Eritrea no doubt reinforced that feeling. Similarly, breaking up politically exploited banks may harm officeholders with good connections, but maintaining their monopoly harms local entrepreneurs who might prefer the awful logic of the market to continued poverty. In the Asian case, the IMF undoubtedly made missteps, but the real source of the trouble lay in the decisions of many market players. Again, some IMF officials may have savored the irony of being dubbed market fundamentalists even as their actions cushioned the full effect of market processes that had led countries to seek assistance in the first place. By neoliberal standards, a third irony that might amuse its officials, the IMF itself is an anti-neoliberal institution, since it is used by governments to shield states and businesses from the effect of bad decisions, a form of moral hazard that in fact encourages imprudent risk-taking and thus distorts the operation of the world market. Asia's substantial recovery was a complex process, and IMF actions may well have retarded it, but it makes a moot point of the sweeping claim that they caused a permanent setback. In China the IMF never had much influence in the first place, which puts its role in perspective.

The critics' indictment of the IMF and its sister institutions is only one part of their attack on "market fundamentalism." In China, Deng and his colleagues had to overcome similar skepticism from establishment opponents steeped in Marxist thinking. In China, too, Deng knew the alternative to market reform could be worse – more than Harvey, he knew the destruction wrought by really existing communism, which had attempted to "disembed" people from their communities more drastically than capitalism ever attempted. Deng could have argued that for the Chinese it was better to be an "appendage" of the market than to suffer destitution in the countryside. And he might have restated his own pragmatic, rather than "fundamentalist," case for market reform by saying that the color of the cat does not matter as long as it catches mice. When it comes to the power of the market in improving the well-being of workers, including many of the low-skilled, a latter-day Deng could plausibly claim that China's record speaks for itself. That is not to argue, of course, that the workers' choices were entirely "free," or that "the market" gets credit for all of China's progress. That progress is itself due to many forces, not fully captured in the simple picture of globalization-as-neoliberal-project.

Summary and Conclusion

When China's leaders decided to change course in 1978, their country rejoined a world economy already undergoing major shifts. China's remarkable record since then coincides with, and greatly contributed to, a new thrust toward integration in the world economy – a thrust that economists typically refer to when they use the term "globalization." Products and techniques diffused, countries became even more interdependent through trade, some institutions took on an organizing role, and all actors were more aware of playing one global game according to a common set of rules. The reasons for the global turn are complex but it represented a world-wide effort to cope with the problems the world ran into at the end of the immediate post-war phase of economic integration. Many economists think globalization pays off for participating countries, above all in the form of higher growth, but critics of "neoliberalism," the marketization of economic affairs at the expense of the state, take a more jaundiced view.

Had he seen the company assigned to him by Harvey's book cover, Deng undoubtedly would have denied being a "neoliberal." The market was not a matter of faith to him or the Chinese leadership, nor did he try to turn China into a "market society." Its government has kept tight control over currency transactions, restricted the movement of workers to cities, left private property in legal limbo, imposed considerable burdens on foreign investors, and stood ready to intervene in the economy at any time. Far from being market fundamentalists, China's leaders have used the market to advance development and thereby secure their own power. In global perspective, both the development and the power are unusual but the role of the state is not. In many ways, large and small, states still steer and channel economic activity. When France legislates a 35-hour work-week, or the Dutch government hesitates to permit firing workers without judicial approval, or British "neoliberal" reformers leave the UK's healthcare sector in government hands, or the US imposes strict accounting standards on corporations, or Argentina tries to increase export taxes on farm produce – examples that could be multiplied a thousandfold – this implies that many markets are deeply embedded in a web of rules. Events in

2008 reinforced the point even more dramatically: already a key force in the housing and mortgage markets though subsidies and regulation, the US federal government greatly expanded its role by intervening in financial markets in response to widespread defaults – an episode interpreted by some as the beginning of the end of neoliberal globalization. However, describing economic globalization since the 1970s as neoliberal in fact mistakes an ideological model for a more complex reality. In the real world economy, as the next chapter shows, the effects of Polanyi's protective "double movement" have hardly disappeared and states retain a major role.

Questions

1   This chapter, like the book as a whole, treats the whole post-World War II period as part of the "third wave" of globalization. Yet events in the 1970s spurred changes that altered the course of the world economy. Would it make sense to speak of the post-1980 period as a fourth wave, and if so, what would be its main distinctive features?

2   China's development since 1978 is usually treated as a success story. But what are its downsides? Is it sustainable? What reforms would China have to carry out to make it more sustainable?

3   By definition, globalization involves greater interdependence. With economic interdependence come new risks and uncertainty. In what ways might the economic integration of the past generation expose workers, consumers, or countries to new risks? What tools or institutions does the world economy have to manage major risks, and how might we judge their effectiveness?

4   Is Harvey's critical diagnosis of neoliberal tendencies compatible with the world-system view of capitalist development summarized in Chapter 2? If so, how does neoliberalism work in and for that system?

Further Reading

Jeffry A. Frieden, *Global Capitalism: Its Fall and Rise in the Twentieth Century* (W. W. Norton, 2006)

David Harvey, *A Brief History of Neoliberalism* (Oxford University Press, 2005)

Barry Naughton, *The Chinese Economy: Transitions and Growth* (MIT Press, 2007)

Maurice Obstfeld and Alan M. Taylor, *Global Capital Markets: Integration, Crisis, and Growth* (Cambridge University Press, 2004)

Joseph E. Stiglitz, *Globalization and Its Discontents* (W. W. Norton, 2002)

Martin Wolf, *Why Globalization Works* (Yale University Press, 2004)

6

GLOBAL STATES AND THE SPECTER OF RETREAT

- The Rise of Welfare States
- Interpreting the Rise of Welfare States
- Globalization and "Retrenchment"
- What Happened to Welfare States?
- Did Globalization Matter?
- Resilient States in Globalization
- The Education State
- Summary and Conclusion

The Rise of Welfare States

An unlikely figure deserves credit for setting Western countries on the path toward the welfare state: Otto von Bismarck, chancellor of Germany in the late nineteenth century. A cool and calculating politician, always focused on the interests of the state he had helped to unify, he was not known for undue sentiment toward the underprivileged. Yet in the 1870s he turned his attention toward social legislation, introducing an accident insurance bill in 1881, soon followed by a health insurance bill. After much wrangling and debate, the German Parliament passed these initiatives, the health bill in 1883, the accident bill a year later (Zöllner 1982; Pflanze 1990). With these pioneering laws, Bismarck meant to show the state's concern for the welfare of industrial workers. While the moral impulse of what he called "practical Christianity" may have prodded him, his main reason for making this commitment was more mundane (Rimlinger 1971: 112–13). Germany's strength depended on its fast-growing industries, which in turn depended on legions of workers. In the new industries, they were exposed to injuries and other risks that traditional poor relief organized by villages could not match. Worker discontent gave social democrats an opportunity to agitate for radical change, a danger to Germany's stability. Rather than simply using repressive laws prohibiting worker mobilization, Bismarck thought he also needed tools to gain the loyalty of workers and counter socialist temptations (113–14).

Plate 6.1   Prince Otto von Bismarck (1815–1898), chancellor of Germany, 1871–1890
Source: © The Art Archive/Culver Pictures

Plate 6.2   William Beveridge (1879–1963), British economist, author of the Beveridge Report on social insurance (1942)
Source: © Topical Press Agency/Getty Images

Social legislation was that tool. It required employers to pay premiums to funds administered by employer associations, supervised by a state agency, that would disburse money to sick or injured workers to make up for some lost wages. At least initially, Bismarck's gamble did not pay off, since in the 1884 national elections social democrats made great gains. Yet together with old age and disability laws passed later in the decade, Bismarck's "path-breaking" and "unmatched" steps (Pflanze 1990: 171) laid the foundation of a welfare state edifice that served as a model for others in years to come. This chapter shows how many states followed the model in their own way, contributing to rather than opposing globalization by political means. Turning welfare into a state project was only one part of a still-larger process of state-building that proceeded vigorously well into the third wave. In world society, as this chapter elaborates, normal states have become subject to global norms on how to be "welfare states," "education states," and the like. Globalization, in other words, operates partly in and through the work of states.

Germany was first but it was not alone. Inspired by the German example, British prime minister Lloyd George and his Liberal and Labour allies pushed through a National Insurance Act in 1911, a "triumph" of social legislation that culminated a series of smaller initiatives (Ogus 1982). The Act introduced compulsory health insurance for manual workers and unemployment benefits for certain groups of workers. For Britain, it marked a decisive departure from the liberal practices of the nineteenth century that had limited state involvement in worker welfare. On a more modest scale, other European countries also adopted protective laws in the same period. On the eve of World War I, social protection, still weak by contemporary standards, had grown definite roots in many places. The trend was part of a larger movement: at the end of the second wave of globalization, Western states had grown stronger, their bureaucracies larger, their agenda more expansive. Even though they did not grow as rapidly as the booming private sector (Mann 1993: 395), as they participated in globalization states also accumulated tasks and resources.

That trend would continue more strongly in the post-war years, when, as this chapter shows, states bolstered globalization and globalization relied on states. In the United States, the federal government had already become involved in social legislation by providing support to veterans and their families (Skocpol 1992). In the watershed decade of the 1930s, the Roosevelt administration went several steps further, introducing unemployment insurance, Aid to Families with Dependent Children, and a national pension scheme called Social Security. During World War II, leading figures in Britain began to think about an even more ambitious welfare state. Their famous Beveridge Report laid out a vision of comprehensive state services to protect citizens against all sorts of risks, a vision partly realized by new institutions such as Britain's National Health Service. After the war, other countries also accelerated their welfare initiatives. The Netherlands, for example, first caught up with others by introducing a national pension scheme in 1956, then outpaced them in building its welfare state. Spurred by the energy of Gerard Veldkamp, a Christian Democratic minister, it added laws providing child support to families and ample benefits to people whose disability, regardless of cause, prevented them from working. Though less generous in state expenditures than its European counterparts, the United States also expanded its welfare offerings, notably with the introduction in 1965 of Medicaid and Medicare, health insurance programs for the poor and the elderly. From country to country, in the different "worlds of welfare capitalism" (Esping-Andersen 1990), the details and benefits of such programs varied. Their focus also varied – countries in the Bismarck mold especially supported male breadwinners, the Beveridge model fostered a kind of social citizenship for all, and the United States gave most attention to the needs of the elderly. Yet by the late 1960s, the idea of state responsibility for the welfare of citizens was firmly ensconced across the industrialized countries, and all of them devoted a growing portion of their growing budgets to social programs.

Interpreting the Rise of Welfare States

It is tempting to think of the expanding welfare state as part of what Karl Polanyi (1957) has called the "double movement," the self-protective response of societies faced with the depredations of free-market capitalism. In the nineteenth century, to reiterate the argument summarized in the previous chapter, Western countries lib-eralized by turning to markets to satisfy human needs. Even labor became a market commodity. As economic relations "disembedded" from real communities, society lost its ability to support those who could not fend for themselves. But free markets imposed high costs, reducing many to poverty and others to great insecurity. To mend the fabric of society and cushion the insecurity, different groups proposed ways of reining in the market. The welfare state stands out as the most enduring of these, the most successful effort to "decommodify" the lives of workers and citizens. Because nineteenth-century liberalization was in effect a global process, intertwining major countries across large distances, the story also has a global element: the welfare state served not only a domestic purpose, it compensated for the troubles caused by world markets as well. As part of the double movement, budding welfare states chal-lenged the idea that society, at home and worldwide, could be a market society. But, at least at first, they did not derail globalization. Instead, the double movement altered its course, reembedding economic forces in political structures. At the crest of the second wave of globalization, states also advanced.

As a historical account of welfare states, this leaves a bit to be desired. Bismarck, for one, hardly fits the double movement scenario. His main motives were political, not economic. Germany had only recently begun to liberalize and never matched British enthusiasm for free markets. At least in Prussia, a strong state had long been taken for granted. By adopting "justified" socialist demands in social legislation (Zöllner 1982: 13), Bismarck also meant to prevent any disruption to capitalist expansion. The Roosevelt revolution in the US fits better. Faced with a major depression, policymakers and people at large had become skeptical about capital-ism. They had faith in the ability of the state to free people from fear. But this phase of welfare state growth does not fit the notion that welfare states cushion the shocks of world markets. The Great Depression, after all, was marked by countries drawing inward and putting up new barriers. "Deglobalization" may have contributed to the economic malaise, and to welfare expansion, but this is a different story than that of globalization triggering expansion. In spite of such historical caveats, the Polanyi argument has a point: welfare states, both in embryonic form and in their full 1960s glory, grew alongside globalization and did not undermine it. By the same token, globalization may have helped to foster welfare states but it did not fatally weaken them.

But is that still true? The gnawing question of the third wave of globalization is whether welfare states are still viable. Though the term globalization was not yet widely used at the time, the question started to gnaw in the 1970s. Generously drafted social programs attracted many takers, unexpectedly raising the costs of welfare. Shocked by a rise in oil prices, many Western countries suffered recessions that further increased demand for social support while cramping state resources. The tools of economic policy, such as the Keynesian effort to prop up demand by government spending, did not seem to make much difference. What began as a financial drama turned into a more ideological struggle in the 1980s (Rosanvallon 2000). With the support of voters, leaders like Margaret Thatcher and Ronald

Reagan, who already figured in the previous chapter, began to question the very premises of the welfare state and advocate a reversal in the inexorable growth of government. Changes in the world at large added to the drama. Whereas the welfare state first got in trouble by "doing things badly or bringing about unwelcome consequences," said one of its prime defenders (Esping-Andersen 1999: 3), the "crisis" of the 1990s was "essentially a manifestation of exogenous shocks that put into question the longer-term viability of the welfare state." Globalization threw new problems on the path of welfare states while depriving them of tools to clear it. They threatened to become an endangered political species.

But are they really? Answering the question helps to shed light on a still bigger one: does globalization spell the "retreat of the state" (Strange 1996)? There is ample reason to think it might. In a much more complex world society, individual states cannot control their own fate. More people use more kinds of power across state boundaries – power diffuses. New organizations go underneath, above, and beyond the grasp of states, whether mafias or accounting firms, multinationals or nongovernmental organizations (NGOs). Both "blind" market forces and new rules of all sorts hem states in. Subsequent chapters explore some of these ways in which globalization limits states. They show that developed states may indeed lose some of their old hold on the social lives of citizens. But reports of their demise, or even retreat, are premature. As their welfare record shows, states are also resilient. To show how and why, focusing on an area in which states might be most vulnerable, I first recapitulate the key arguments about the "retrenchment" of welfare states, then describe actual changes in them, and finish by asking how we can best make sense of the changes. With a few caveats, I offer a both-and rather than an either-or argument: globalization and welfare states can develop in tandem. The larger message in the welfare state experience is that in the global age states still have much to do. In fact, as I illustrate further in the case of the "education state," we can think of globalization as a process that also builds up states as key actors with a lot of responsibility. In several ways, beyond welfare, globalization helps states advance rather than retreat.

Globalization and "Retrenchment"

Welfare states got in trouble in a period of intense economic globalization. Not surprisingly, many people turned correlation into causation. Globalization thus contributed to the crisis atmosphere that surrounded welfare states toward the turn of the twentieth century. But is globalization to blame for their troubles? Why exactly should globalization diminish states' welfare effort? One reason may be that welfare is expensive. To fund it, states impose premiums on employers or taxes on citizens. Directly or indirectly, that raises the cost of production. The "social wage" is higher than a straight market wage would be. But this gives an advantage to competitors from places where wages are low. More competition from more such places puts pressure on the cushy wages in welfare states. Either they lower their (welfare) costs or they lose jobs. In some countries, this hits home with special force: the more a country produces for export, the greater its risks. Countries that are very open and depend on trade, such as smaller European welfare states, are especially vulnerable. They must adjust. Openness also hurts because it makes it harder for states to intervene in their domestic economies. For example, if a state tries to buy growth through more government spending, it may simply boost demand for imports rather than domestic production, creating trade deficits and other troubles. Open capital markets add further problems. If state taxes on capital are higher than elsewhere, companies or investors can leave more easily. If regulations are too tough, business is in a stronger position to demand softening. In effect, states may be competing with each other to see who can best cater to business. This may turn into a race to the bottom of a deregulated, stripped-down welfare state.

Even if they manage to stay away from that race, states cannot afford to make mistakes. For example, if they spend too much on stimulating the economy or funding welfare, they must borrow more; but this will tend to increase interest rates, which hampers investment, and it will likely raise demand for the currency, making it more expensive and thus hurting businesses that depend on export. In deciding where to build or invest, the people who make up "the market" in effect punish bad government. And just when capital is in a stronger position, labor loses clout. It typically cannot or does not leave; because it cannot exit, it also has less voice. It therefore cannot push its demand for welfare quite as much. The shifting balance of economic power leaves the welfare state more fragile. In a way that fragility feeds on itself. If "the market" is perceived as "the solution" to a wide range of problems, it becomes more difficult to reassert the claims of the state. Weakened welfare states are at risk of getting weaker.

Globalization can thus affect welfare states in many ways: through trade and competition, through greater capital mobility, through a new balance of power, or through new rules of the economic game (Hicks 1999: 204–5; Huber and Stephens 2001: 224–5; Glatzer and Rueschemeyer 2005: 3; Stephens 2005: 52–4). The optimistic, "neoliberal" take on this is that globalization pushes efficiency: when welfare states lose, the well-being of more people improves. The social democratic alternative, by contrast, views welfare losses as just that – a net loss (Stephens 2005: 53). But is it reasonable to expect globalization to have such a big impact in the first place? After all, much depends on factors not directly related to globalization. For example, welfare may pad wages, which may put certain companies at a competitive disadvantage, but if their workers increase their productivity enough to moderate the wage cost per product, they will greatly alleviate the problem. The greater productivity growth, the less welfare spending should be a burden. The level of spending itself depends on other factors as well. The big driver may be unemployment (Stephens 2005): the more people are out of work, the more will claim benefits. Some of the unemployed may have lost their jobs to foreign competition, but most typically fall victim to technical change or the business cycle – there are better ways to do their job or demand dries up – neither of which reflects the impact of globalization directly. The idea that welfare states will readily surrender to economic forces, global or otherwise, is implausible to begin with. They are a political enterprise with a political constituency. Many people have a vested interest in their programs and policies. Those people will therefore resist retrenchment, and politicians ignore that at their peril (Pierson 1994). Even if globalization dampens welfare spending, such domestic conditions, economic or political, filter its impact. If they are significant enough – and arguments about globalization cannot tell us when they are – they could conceivably cancel any such impact. Skeptics could well argue that globalization may have no effect at all.

But the issue of unemployment also suggests a very different reaction to the retreat-of-the-welfare-state scenario. What if the reverse is true? Might globalization actually strengthen welfare states? Suppose globalization does increase risks to many businesses and economic sectors. Suppose it actually does throw some people out of work and makes others really fear for their jobs. A logical reaction would be for the affected groups to clamor for help – welfare as compensation. The more a country opens up, the higher the potential risk to more groups, the greater their concern about their future, the stronger their demand for state protection. In democratic welfare states, that demand will attract a political supply of parties promising to ride to the rescue. Globalization thus creates a political opportunity for left-leaning groups to strengthen rather than weaken the welfare state (Garrett 1998). In countries that give a strong voice to workers, for example by involving unions in economic decision-making, the demand is likely to be that much more effective, bolstering the fortunes of the welfare state (Swank 2001).

But the welfare state does not just work for workers; it is good for business too. By guaranteeing some minimal stability in people's lives and thus preventing unrest among workers, it makes it easier for labor to cooperate with management (Manow 2001). Workers who know that they have a welfare cushion to fall back on will be more likely to adjust to change, take risks, or pursue new opportunities. In fact, welfare states may be a "beneficial constraint" on the economy (Streeck 1997). An even more ambitious version of the argument goes a step further: welfare states are not just "beneficial" to markets, they are essential to globalization itself (Rieger and Leibfried 2003). It is no accident, according to its proponents, that "not until the expansion of the welfare state in the first three decades following the Second World War were the governments of the most advanced industrial societies in a position to lower, lessen or eliminate import barriers" (50). What started as a rejection of free-market capitalism became a "pivotal precondition" for its international expansion (8). Globalization may thus be the "coincidental by-product of the welfare-democratic revolution" in the developed countries (6). Far from globalization dampening welfare, it needs all the welfare effort it can get. If anything, according to this line of argument, globalization, not the welfare state, is in danger.

The three types of arguments I have summarized thus far – implying that the welfare state might retrench, not change much, or even strengthen in globalization – assume that globalization has a static link to the welfare state. But should it? Perhaps the link itself varies. For example, some proponents of the strength argument recognize that welfare states do not just take the shape they do thanks to the way they assist the economy; they also rely on distinct cultural values that prevail in different countries – where social support is associated with families rather than the state, as in much of East Asia, welfare states will tend to remain more skimpy (Rieger and Leibfried 2003: ch. 5). It may also vary across regions simply because states have different abilities to deal with globalization – for example, we might expect Latin America to have more trouble keeping up welfare spending than Europe (Huber 2005). Or the link might vary over time. For example, welfare effort could support globalization up to a certain level but then turn into a stifling constraint when the state's financial resources become too strained. Case in point is the Dutch labor disability program (WAO): when nearly 1 million people in a population of about 16 million claimed benefits in the early 1990s, the program itself threatened to become disabling. After years of expansion, the Dutch "WAO crisis" provoked a dramatic response that gradually curtailed benefit levels and claims (Lechner 2008: ch. 6). The Dutch case may also illustrate another dynamic in welfare state growth: once it has "grown to limits," by claiming some large portion of people's income and spending some large percentage of GDP, it faces limits to growth (Flora 1986). If welfare states reach those limits in a globalizing period, globalization may appear to be the cause, even when the link is actually spurious.

As often happens in serious scholarship on globalization, many of these arguments are quite plausible on their face. Which is correct? What actually happened to welfare states, and why? Answering those questions turns out to be tricky. It requires evidence on the globalization experience of countries, on their welfare record, and ideally on the actual link between the two. In spite of much scholarly detective work, which I describe next to illustrate the way research tries to come to terms with the real complexities of globalization, the plot of the whodunit is not yet entirely clear. Let me try to clarify that lack of clarity.

What Happened to Welfare States?

An obvious place to start in unraveling the plot is to look at what governments spend: if spending goes down, that might be a sign of retrenchment. Did government spending decline in Western countries over recent decades? When students of welfare states first looked at the issue, they did not find what they might have expected. From 1960 to 1995, one scholar showed, total government outlays as a percentage of GDP actually increased by 75 percent (Castles 1998: 100). The US government share went up from 27.2 to 33.3 percent, the Netherlands rose from 33.7 to 50.9 percent, and champion Denmark increased from 24.8 to a whopping 62.4 percent (101). Clearly, government was still big business well into the age of globalization. Was welfare – broadly defined as social security, public health, and education – still part of that business? Yes, definitely: on average, members of the Organization for Economic Cooperation and Development (OECD) – the club of industrialized countries – spent 63.7 percent of their budgets on welfare in the early 1990s, versus 54.3 percent in 1960 (103).

If spending kept rising, was there even a "crime" to solve? Perhaps investigators arrived on the scene too early and the real deed was done later. Taking in more data from the 1990s shows a different picture: by some measures, overall welfare expenditures in the broad sense and social security transfers for specific benefit programs, both taken as a percentage of GDP, did start to taper off slightly in the early 1990s (Brady et al. 2005: 934). Investigators also discovered new evidence. For example, just as important as spending levels is the extent to which people can rely on the state to replace their income in time of trouble, and this replacement rate or "decommodification" score did in fact drop substantially across OECD countries since the late 1980s (ibid.), a sign that fewer people were eligible for lower benefits. This matches another piece of the puzzle detected by another investigator, namely that while overall spending was still rising into the early 1990s, spending per person in need (e.g., an unemployed worker or retiree) had begun to decline (Hicks 1999: 182–3).

Though such leads indicate that welfare states changed in the way they worked, they do not show that any serious harm was done. Through the 1980s and 1990s, two leading investigators concluded, "cutbacks in benefits were widespread but in large part modest, or at least not system transforming" (Huber and Stephens 2001: 300). In the US those cutbacks took the form of overhauling social assistance programs like Aid to Families with Dependent Children – with Republican support, the Clinton administration ended "welfare as we know it" – and raising the age at which people may draw full Social Security benefits. In the Netherlands, the labor disability program was reformed in phases to tighten medical eligibility and lower benefits. Several countries organized their welfare schemes differently, for example by introducing some privatization. In the UK and New Zealand, changes were more drastic, hitting pensions, sick pay, and unemployment insurance (ibid.). Overall, however, "there were very few programs in any country where benefits in the mid-1990s were more than marginally lower than they had been in 1970" (302).

Other investigators second the judgment, finding "high levels of stability" in conservative welfare states on the European continent, little movement toward the "neoliberal model" in Nordic welfare states in spite of some "nontrivial" cuts, and "moderate to substantial" retrenchment in the US and especially the UK (Swank 2002: 167, 156, 227, 229–32). In some cases, even the modest cutbacks were offset by increases. In the US, for example, the Earned Income Tax Credit for low-income workers and drug benefits for the elderly added to Medicare raised the country's net social expenditures. Swinging the political pendulum slightly to the left, a German coalition government in 2007–8 partly reversed modest reforms in unemployment benefits and public pensions that its predecessor had passed. Even where it occurred, then, retrenchment was by no means a relentless downhill slide. In fact, it often "did no more than reduce the increase in welfare state expenditures" (Stephens 2005: 64) – leveling off rather than actually sliding (Hicks 1999: 197).

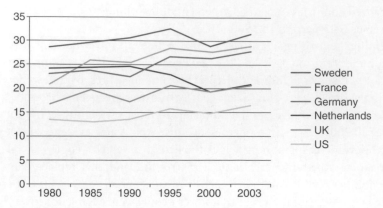

Figure 6.1 Development of public social spending (cash and in-kind benefits), 1980–2003, in selected countries, as a percentage of current GDP
Note: 1. Sweden had the highest level of public social spending throughout the period, the US the lowest. 2. Spending declined slightly in several countries in some periods but increased in the early 2000s. 3. Except in the Netherlands, spending was higher in 2003 than in 1980.
Source: OECD Social Expenditure Database 2007

Welfare states may have been injured in some cases, but none suffered a fatal assault.

Judging by long-term trends, any injuries were relatively minor. From 1980 to 2003, the most thorough compilation of the relevant data shows, public social spending actually increased in most industrialized countries from about 16 to 21 percent of GDP (see figure 6.1). To be sure, such spending dipped in many countries at one time or another, and in the Netherlands that decline persisted. But around 2000, the ratio of public spending to GDP generally started rising again, to about one-fifth of GDP on average, with Sweden on top at 31.3 percent and Korea bringing up the rear at 5.7 percent (ibid.). That states still actively cushioned social risks was also evident in other ways. For example, in spite of the drop in "decommodification," people who were unemployed for a long period could still count on replacing about 40 percent of their income on average (OECD 2007c: 63).

Many governments were doing even more than the figures on public social spending revealed. Especially low-spending countries like the United States give citizens many "tax breaks for social purposes," both mandatory and voluntary, in the form of tax deductions for children, health insurance, or retirement savings. In practice, this simply means that taxpayers keep more of the money they earn, but since government could have chosen to collect the money instead, and in some countries governments in fact spend money directly for similar purposes, it is nevertheless fair to include this in a country's overall social expenditures. At the same time, traditionally high-spending countries like Denmark and Sweden were not quite as generous as they seemed because they took back in taxes some of the money they granted in benefits (OECD 2007b: 31). Taking into account both the tax-

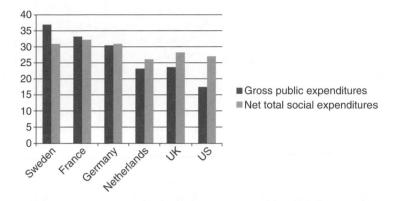

Figure 6.2   Levels of gross public social expenditures and net total social expenditures (gross public expenditures, minus taxes on benefits, plus tax breaks for social purposes and private social expenditures) in selected countries, as percentage of current GDP, 2003
Source: OECD 2007b: Table 5.5

subsidized private social spending in places like the US and the relatively high taxes in places like Sweden closes the gap between top and bottom – at 27.0 percent of GDP, US "net" social expenditure in 2003 was only slightly lower than the 30.9 percent spent by Sweden (figure 6.2). Handing out cash was not the only way states supported the welfare of their citizens.

Did Globalization Matter?

With retrenchment itself in doubt, the search for the culprit might be moot. Not that he made much effort to hide. As the previous chapter already showed, global-ization ran strong in the OECD countries since the 1970s. A comparison of the period 1960–73 with 1990–4 shows a dramatic increase across the board: all OECD countries eased their capital controls, lowered tariffs, engaged in outward direct foreign investment, and borrowed more on international capital markets (Huber and Stephens 2001: 228–9). The average trade openness score, for example, went from 48.8 to 63.3, the borrowing score from 0.52 to 4.25. In the eighties, both trade and investment already "skyrocketed" (Hicks 1999: 208). The trend continued strongly in subsequent years, when both investment and trade flows rose. If we measure investment as the sum of direct and portfolio investments, both inward and outward, and if we think of trade openness simply as the sum of imports and exports, and we then add up both kinds of openness, we get a measure of "total globalization" (Brady et al. 2005). In 1975, total globalization stood at 58.3 percent of GDP in the OECD, by 2000 it was up to 141.1 percent, declining to 123.8 in the recession year 2001 (933). Not every country joined the trend every single year, but they all became much more intertwined in the world economy than before.

But do we have the right suspect? Investigators have their doubts. One way to start the interrogation is to look for a direct link between measures of globalization and welfare spending. Plotting countries' rate of exports against their rate of social spending gives us a rough correlation of .26 – meaning that spending *increases* along with exports (Rieger and Leibfried 2003: 85). That scores a point for the strength scenario but it does not tell us much about what causes what. A fuller model can help to judge the possible role of all the relevant suspects together. Doing so still shows that trade has mostly positive effects, without reaching a threshold beyond which it dampens welfare effort, but at the same time suggests that investment openness may bolster welfare states up to a point – but not beyond (Hicks 1999: 212–13). However, focusing not on overall spending but on the actual points at which spending tapers off, the same investigator finds that trade first promotes, then resists retrenchment, while investment openness actually counters it (217). That again gives some support to the compensation thesis, but only tentatively: the analysis really shows a "complex, contradictory pattern of globalization effects" (218).

An updated version of this approach, focusing on episodes of welfare reversal rather than spending levels, confirms the key results: more openness and financial liberalization lead to a lower incidence of retrenchments, although the outflow of capital may promote retrenchment (Hicks and Zorn 2005: 648, 657). A similar analysis focusing on capital mobility reveals that international borrowing and liberalizing capital controls relate positively to welfare spending, even taking many other factors into account (Swank 2002: 86). This also supports the compensation thesis more than the efficiency argument, but again there are caveats: the effects are not large, since a big jump in liberalization may only increase spending by 1 percent of GDP, and there are hints that capital markets do not take kindly to budget deficits that get out of control, indirectly spurring some retrenchment (89, 94). Yet, overall, such evidence exonerates globalization.

Further investigation slightly complicates the picture. One of the most thorough studies of the crime scene looks at many aspects of globalization, distinguishes three kinds of welfare effort, and uses data on 17 affluent countries from 1975 to 2001 (Brady et al. 2005). It starts with a "baseline model" that includes variables that typically influence welfare state growth. Not surprisingly, the authors find that countries with more left-leaning cabinets or a more elderly population do more with regard to decommodification, welfare expenditures, and transfer programs. They then clarify what happened to the presumed victim. By their reckoning, welfare expenditures and cash transfer programs peaked in the early 1990s and had hardly declined by 2000 whereas decommodification declined a bit from an earlier peak but still ended up higher than it was in the 1970s. Whether this counts as a crime or not, they still ask if globalization had anything to do with it. The way they answer the question is to add features of globalization, such as trade and foreign investment, as variables to their baseline model with regard to all three kinds of welfare effort. Does globalization make a big difference? The results fail to support a clear verdict. A bit despairingly, the authors conclude that their evidence "defies a simple interpretation" (935). Globalization turns out to have positive and negative effects, but these do not closely fit any of the usual views of globalization. For example, countries that export more than they import tend to do better on decommodification but not as well on keeping up their welfare expenditures. Liberalizing a country's capital accounts helps to expand social security transfers. Greater openness to foreign direct investment may first hamper social security transfers but subsequently bolster them – one instance of a "curvilinear effect." As this mix of results suggests, no theory of globalization's link to welfare state retrenchment is clearly supported. Even the statistically significant effects are "substantively small" (939) – i.e., they have little actual causal impact. This hardly gives us enough evidence to prosecute the case with confidence.

Contamination of the crime scene hinders investigators on the trail of globalization. Like Brady and his colleagues, they consistently find other things present that may have caused welfare state injuries. Unemployment is one obvious factor: if more people are unemployed, demand for benefits greatly increases, which at some point becomes too much and leads to efforts to rein in spending. This is one instance of "self-limiting immoderation" by welfare states that indulge in raising welfare spending until they simply must cut back to keep from becoming insolvent or impose ruinous taxes. Some states that retrench are repeat offenders, since there is evidence that retrenchment at one point dampens later spending (Hicks and Zorn 2005). By the same token, some states may suffer fewer injuries thanks to corporatist institutions that involve labor in economic policy and setting wages, or universalistic programs that give everyone a stake in maintaining them, or a strong central government that can steer society as a whole. The less universalistic a country's programs, and the more it disperses power, the more likely it is to experience some retrenchment (Swank 2001). The presumed victims may thus contribute to their own injuries.

Resilient States in Globalization

The fact that many things affect the many things welfare states do brings to mind the sociological truism, all too evident in good quantitative research, that everything matters a little. In thinking about welfare states, it is nothing new: even before the wave of globalization studies, when scholars simply focused on trying to explain welfare effort, no single theory or set of variables did the explanatory job by itself (Hicks 1999: 180). Even on issues that states and scholars track intensely, and that have generated mountains of data, it turns out to be hard to say what happened. Making sense of the welfare state record is a very complex task. But this also tells us something useful about globalization: for indictments of the process there is no proof beyond a reasonable doubt. If anything, the data tell us to watch out for the globalization fallacy, since globalization is often not to blame. The less-than-clear picture in the data also contains a clear and convincing lesson about states: they stay in business. They have much to do and many resources to do it with. For all the controversy about the viability of welfare states, most have been quite resilient. The story of welfare states in globalization is not either-or but both-and: they can flourish jointly.

That story is unfinished. The research thus far does not offer a firm conclusion. Scholars favor the both-and plotline but it, too, faces reasonable suspicions. The evidence we typically use to judge globalization's effect on welfare states covers a limited period at the end of the twentieth century. Extrapolating to the twenty-first is hazardous. The evidence usually comes from Western democracies. Whether globalization will help to strengthen or weaken potential welfare states elsewhere, trying to emulate their predecessors but with more modest means, is an open question. The continued strength of welfare states where they have fully evolved may depend on domestic institutions that are themselves likely to change; for example, corporatist decision-making that grants a major voice to unions may not work as well when fewer workers care to belong to unions. Finally, even the hard-nosed literature on welfare states contains a bit of wishful thinking, in that scholars typically support the arrangements they describe. As a result, they are inclined to think, as two of them put it, that the welfare state has an "unassailable competitive advantage" over markets in granting individuals social rights that allow them to claim a specific resource or opportunity – something secure and guaranteed (Rieger and Leibfried 2003: 334). In several sectors, that advantage may not prove "unassailable." As populations age, many governments will scale back seemingly secure public pension benefits, while alternative, market-based, though often tax-subsidized, private pension schemes give beneficiaries more legally secure claims to their retirement resources. As old welfare states and newly affluent countries experiment with ways to support the good life of their residents, traditional welfare state arrangements are likely to face competition.

Whatever the outcome of such competition, welfare states have already shown their resilience. Most of the explanations after the fact focus on their political function, such as the way they satisfy demands or reflect institutional pressures. But states' welfare projects do not just persist because they happen to be useful in some way. Such domestic uses could not fully account for the fact that states with very different political backgrounds nevertheless all took on broadly similar welfare responsibilities. Even the Polanyi argument to the effect that they represent a "natural" protective reaction to disruptive challenges that all states faced only goes so far in explaining the convergence. According to the way of thinking about globalization derived from the neoinstitutionalist "world polity theory" (Meyer, Boli, et al. 1997) already briefly stated in Chapter 3, that resilience is no fluke for another reason. The decentralized world polity, divided into many sovereign units without a commanding power, that crystallized in the latest rounds of globalization assigns new tasks to states. Not only do states have more to do, they have to do more. From this point of view, the scholarly defense of the welfare state against the supposed onslaught of globalization sounds, well, too defensive: globalization also strengthens states, and deterritorialization also involves new territorial authority. Out of initially ad hoc efforts to contain social problems grew new models for how to be a proper state.

The Bismarcks and Beveridges thus helped to write a script that their successors enacted. More than a political expedient, "doing welfare" by following a globally applicable script became a way for states and their officials to show that they were legitimate, that they belonged to the club of "good guys" (Meyer 2004). From this neoinstitutionalist point of view, globalization means that world society gets organized in part by putting more and more normative pressure on states to behave a certain way. Even if many states are deviant in fact, the pressure is real nonetheless. Case in point is the global educational revolution.

The Education State

Visiting a classroom outside of Lilongwe in the African country of Malawi some years ago, the American scholar Bruce Fuller found the seventh-grade civics teacher asking "How does the government get money?" and the students responding in unison, "Income tax, customs duties . . ." (Fuller 1991: 111). For lack of a textbook, they read off a list written on the blackboard, for example to identify the six types of police in Malawi. To keep the interest of his 47 pupils, the teacher occasionally deviated from the call-and-response pattern to question individual students. In a southern Malawi primary school, Fuller saw how a science teacher joined the regular teacher to instruct a class of 100 students in the properties of different types of soil, managing to give pairs of students bits of soil while eliciting choral responses in English. In another school, he observed a math teacher stating a problem on the board, in English, then engaging in call-and-response before having the 72 students do individual exercises in silence, which the teacher then checked one by one while the students remained seated on the concrete floor. Civics, science, math, English – in spite of the concrete floors and rooms open to the elements, even without proper textbooks, these classes had all the trappings of a modern education. In coping with large groups of students, the teachers had to enforce strict discipline – evident in the mechanical collective exercises, and even in requiring students to kneel before asking permission to go outside to urinate. The sheer scale of the classrooms made it difficult to teach students individually, and the kids' individual interests did not rank high in the teachers' priorities, yet Fuller found that the teachers' authority was unmistakable. With limited resources, they ran a modern system, following the state's guidelines to the extent possible. In the years after those observations, Malawi's resources if anything shrank further, as droughts aggravated poverty and HIV/AIDS depleted the ranks of teachers. In view of those dire circumstances in one of the world's poorest countries, described further in Chapter 11, the striking thing about education as observed by Fuller is not simply how it was done but that it was done at all. However modestly and incompletely, even Malawi tried to become an education state.

So did Botswana. Enjoying a higher standard of living thanks to diamond, copper, and nickel exports, Botswana has been able to invest more in its education system. From the late 1960s to the early 1990s, student enrollment increased fivefold, from about 80,000 to 400,000, in a country of 1 million, a mass of students served by hundreds of new schools (Meyer et al. 1993: 456). When the country decided to expand junior secondary education in the 1980s, no one objected. Local communities eagerly fell in line, even when the central government took over local schools and while the overall program remained somewhat hazy (461). With the help of outside organizations and consultants, Botswana steadily modernized and centralized its system. As in Malawi, the results were sometimes at odds with the plans – at least by the early 1990s, teacher quality and student achievement remained low, and many classrooms were still run in a very traditional fashion. Yet Botswana's commitment to modern education was beyond question. Mass schooling, organized by the state, was the way to turn the country into a proper nation-state and its people into suitable citizens. Botswana would be, and has in fact become, an education state.

Malawi and Botswana have joined a global revolution (Meyer et al. 1977). Around the world, after World War II, countries built thousands of schools, attended by hundreds of millions of children. In 1950, nearly every child of primary-school age in rich countries already went to school but only 44 percent in poorer countries did; the latter were catching up by 1975, raising enrollment to 80 percent (Ramirez and Boli 1987a: 152). In rich countries, secondary education enrollment rose from 26.7 percent in 1950 to 66.9 percent in 1975; poor countries, many of them newly independent, quintupled enrollment in the same period, from 5.3 to 24.7 percent (ibid.). Both at the primary and secondary levels, enrollment continued to increase in the following years: on average, nine of ten young children in developing countries overall and about seven of ten in Sub-Saharan Africa were in school in 2005 (figure 6.3). Naturally, their "education expectancy," or years of schooling they would be expected to complete, kept rising as well (figure 6.4). Starting from more modest levels – only some 500,000 students were enrolled in higher-education institutions in the whole world in 1900 – tertiary education increased at an even faster rate in the immediate post-war period, from 3.7 to 18.9 percent in rich countries and from 0.6 to 4.5 percent in poor ones, with subsequent spurts later in the century (ibid.; Schofer and Meyer 2005).

Some of the data may overstate the case – not every child counted as enrolled in Malawi would attend continuously, and attendance itself means something different in classes of 100 or 20 students. Nonetheless, for some decades now such data have told a clear and consistent story: most children in most places spent much of their early lives in school as a matter of course. The fact that the data exist, collected and analyzed by the international organization UNESCO, attests to the revolution: it is now globally important to keep track of who does what in education, as important as keeping track of welfare effort.

Any proper state now needs a high-quality education system (Baker and LeTendre 2005: 1). Everywhere, states fund education. Everywhere, states set rules

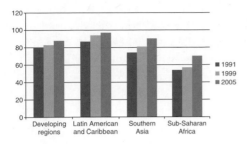

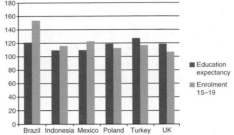

Figure 6.3 Trends in total net enrollment in primary education (as percentage of population in relevant age group), for developing countries and selected regions, 1991–2005
Source: UN 2007MDG: 10

Figure 6.4 Change in education expectancy (expected years of education, all students) and enrollment rate (15- to 19-year-olds as percentage of age-group population) in selected countries, measured as index for 2002/3 over base year 1995/6 = 100
Note: 1. Index over 100 indicates growth compared to base year. 2. Expected years of education and enrolment past primary education age keep increasing in most countries.
Source: UNESCO 2005b: Tables 1.4 and 1.6

for schools. Everywhere, kids must attend. Viewed from a global vantage point, different states do much the same thing: instituting formal mass schooling, erecting a state bureaucracy to manage it, imposing professional requirements on teachers, inculcating a certain body of modern knowledge, thereby molding children into citizens. In effect they follow a "singular model" (6). As neoinstitutionalist scholars would put it, they enact yet another script, written elsewhere though legitimate everywhere. Partly due to this global endorsement, education typically carries a lot of symbolic weight. For most states and their officials, education is the essential national enterprise, essential to holding the country together by giving kids a common culture and essential to making the economy grow by giving them skills to become productive. According to the "ideological order" that motivates the global revolution, the rational structure that fosters their individual development also serves that nation as a whole: as the texts of constitutions attest, which often link individuals' right to education to the state's duty to provide it, "individualism and statism develop hand in hand" (Ramirez and Boli 1987a: 159). You cannot be a nation-state without also being an education state.

Of course, just like the welfare effort of different states, the actual quality of education still varies. Research on student performance shows wide disparities across countries, even in areas like mathematics where the content is not tied to local cultures (Baker and LeTendre 2005). Not surprisingly, rich countries spend more per student than poor countries, which translates into nicer classrooms, smaller classes, and more highly trained teachers. But even more strikingly than in the case of welfare, the singular model has taken hold regardless of such differences. When it comes to education, measured by yardsticks such as enrollment, it hardly matters how wealthy a country is or how "advanced" in other ways. Bureaucratized, formal, national, mass schooling becomes entrenched regardless.

Precisely because it is so taken for granted, even more than social welfare an obviously good thing for states to do, hardly anyone thinks of globalization causing any retreat of the education state. Particular countries may contemplate new opportunities for private education, or they may trim their budgets a bit in tough times, but no state officials anywhere argue that their citizens should get less education, that their states should provide less education, or that education has somehow become a less important state task. There is no debate about the "retrenchment of the education state." It is not a live issue in political practice or in scholarly research. In fact, experts are decidedly "bullish" on the education state's prospects (Baker and LeTendre 2005: 174). To coin a global adage, once an education state, always an education state.

Like the welfare state, we may owe the education state to the Prussians. Even before it became the core of a united Germany, Prussia was one of the first European states to mandate public education in 1763, and in the era of European nation-building others soon followed (Ramirez and Boli 1987b). In the late eighteenth and nineteenth centuries, European polities turned into nation-states, at the time a new way of organizing society. Becoming a national state meant turning people into citizens, under the canopy of a common national culture, and that is what education was meant to do. Liberal nations also intended to develop the capacities of individuals – again a task for the budding education systems. In the competitive European arena, the emerging nation-states competed politically, militarily, and culturally, and education at least seemed to bolster the status of each one, even if it did not in fact strengthen a state. European states therefore "became engaged in authorizing, funding, and managing mass schooling as part of an endeavor to construct a unified national polity" (3). The new institution fit the new reality. Because the European definition of societal reality spread worldwide in the twentieth century, and the world as a whole turned into a collection of nation-states, education spread along with it. Just as the second wave of globalization was an era of nation-building, so was the third. Naturally, education played its part.

Thus path dependence is one reason for the resilience of the education state, in the sense that the "core" of the world was already organized along nation-state lines, with education a key institution, before the latest wave of globalization. The system already in place expanded to channel that wave. The global educational revolution of the third wave of globalization has its roots in the institutional innovations of the second wave. But the third wave has added something. What was common practice in Europe has become a global norm, an expectation imposed by the world polity on any aspiring nation-state. It has become ever more difficult to deviate from the "singular model." The more countries adopt it, the more they reinforce it. National sentiment does not arise as a matter of course but takes institutional work to develop. Where mass schooling does its job, it fosters national sentiments, which then help to tie people and institutions to states and the territories they manage. The attachment people feel in turn helps state institutions stay on the well-worn path. Even in the global age, successful national education creates a demand for more of the same.

Summary and Conclusion

The education state is such a standard feature of the world scene that it calls into question the whole idea of a "retreat" of the state. With respect to both welfare and education, this chapter has shown, the state has steadily advanced during the third wave globalization. This advance suggests that the resilience of the state may be more than a historical accident that happened to persist. Students of the welfare state, as we have seen, believe that it provides a setting in which globalizing business can flourish and that it helps people venture forth into a globalizing world by compensating for risks they face; the mixed evidence on retrenchment gives them at least some support. The previous chapter noted that even "neoliberal" economic trends still require states to do much sensible work, not least to provide a secure and predictable framework in which to transact business. The strength of the welfare and education state, at least in the most developed countries, reinforces the point that a state managing a place and a people may actually support globalization. Globalization does not go "beyond" the state or force it to "retreat," but instead depends on it. To sum up in a formula: no deterritorialization without territorial organization.

Up to a point, the formula contains a useful lesson. For states it does not imply that anything goes. Some overly generous welfare states may be at risk in globalization, some inept educational states risk falling farther behind. In a more intensely globalizing world, simply having the trappings of a "progressive" welfare state or a "modern" educational state may no longer suffice to keep up a state's standing. The world polity that evolved from the European model may well evolve further to impose more restrictions on the "proper" way to manage people and places. That applies not just to the old core but even more to states in developing countries, where building up state capacities is a greater challenge than preventing a retreat from prior strength. For them, retreat may take the form of not keeping up with potentially more demanding norms, a relative decline in capacity that adds to their vulnerability. The neoinstitutionalist picture of globalization in which many players enact global scripts certainly allows for the possibility that globally mandated practices, like some classroom routines in Malawi, may be irrelevant to or "decoupled" from local circumstances but at the same time gives little guidance as to how an inexperienced state actor can fully follow the script on the global stage. Role failure is a real risk. "The" state does not have to retreat but individual states, North or South, very well may.

Retreat could also occur in another way. Even if the value of education remains uncontested, the form of mass schooling need not. In fact, it has had critics throughout its history. However strong the current global impulse to organize education along national lines in order to socialize children into citizens, it is entirely conceivable that new technological developments will create new educational models that do not fit the old molds. Perhaps one day children in Malawi will enjoy distance learning via the Internet that exceeds whatever the damp and drafty classrooms of old had to offer. Just as the welfare state has few "unassailable advantages," so too has state-organized mass schooling. For children in Malawi, clear alternatives may be a long way off. But elsewhere, beyond the primary level, the education state no longer has a monopoly. Korean high school students traveling to the US with their families to improve their chances in college admission are a case in point. In higher education, a global market already operates, in which private American institutions effectively compete with state-run rivals elsewhere. The mere evolution of such a market does not signal the retreat of the state. But globalization, among other forces, helps to foster innovations in global education that may loosen the grip of the old European model.

For now, this chapter implies, such caveats are a bit speculative. The state is alive and well, illustrated empirically by the rather modest cuts in the social spending of developed countries up to 2000 and the slight rise in subsequent years. Its proven resilience also serves globalization. The resilience itself follows global norms: states are not at liberty to operate any way they like, but are subject to global expectations. States advance within a global setting not of their own making. The both-and plot I have sketched allows for state growth in an increasingly complex and demanding global environment. In that environment, new rules and new players constantly emerge. The following chapters explore whether those create a new form of global governance that shifts power away from states.

Questions

1   Many arguments about globalization and retrenchment focus on the cost of social spending. Program design is a different issue. If a, perhaps the, prime function of welfare states is to cushion the risk of participating in the global economy, might some kinds of social spending do the job better than others? What kinds of programs would help workers, or potential workers, more than others? Would a welfare state focused on competing effectively put its resources into programs for the elderly?

2   In developing countries, states face the challenge of building up some kind of social security rather than preventing its retrenchment. Apart from a current lack of state income, what would they have to do to follow the example of OECD countries? States at different levels of development have

in fact adopted some similar institutions – formal education is a case in point. Are they also likely to become more similar in types and levels of social spending?

3   The chapter focuses on two kinds of state activity, one clearly exposed to global flows, the other less so. What about other state responsibilities, for example in the areas of law enforcement and national security. What would count as "retreat" in those spheres, what forces might lead to retreat, and what kind of evidence would we need to assess relevant arguments?

Further Reading

David P. Baker and Gerald K. LeTendre, *National Differences, Global Similarities: World Culture and the Future of Schooling* (Stanford University Press, 2005)

Gøsta Esping-Andersen, *The Three Worlds of Welfare Capitalism* (Princeton University Press, 1990)

Miguel Glatzer and Dietrich Rueschemeyer (eds.), *Globalization and the Future of the Welfare State* (University of Pittsburgh Press, 2005)

Alexander Hicks, *Social Democracy and Welfare Capitalism: A Century of Income Security Politics* (Cornell University Press, 1999)

Evelyne Huber and John D. Stephens, *Development and Crisis of the Welfare State: Parties and Policies in Global Markets* (University of Chicago Press, 2001)

Susan Strange, *The Retreat of the State: The Diffusion of Power in the World Economy* (Cambridge University Press, 1996)

7

GLOBAL GOVERNANCE AND THE PROSPECTS OF WORLD LAW

- Global Governance from Bosnia to The Hague
- Interpreting Trends in Global Governance
- The United Nations in Global Governance
- The United Nations and World Law
- Governance Beyond States
- The United States in Global Governance
- Summary and Conclusion

Global Governance from Bosnia to The Hague

On July 11, 1995, Dutch troops stood by as Bosnian Serb forces occupied the town of Srebrenica and proceeded to round up the local Muslim population, sending away the women and children in a hasty evacuation while forcing the men to march off as prisoners. The Serbian assault culminated a brief offensive ostensibly aimed at removing the threat of attack from Bosnian government forces in the area. Representing the United Nations Protection Force (UNPROFOR) – the UN effort to keep the peace between Bosnia's ethnic groups – the Dutch contingent had tried in vain to block the Serbian advance. As an officially neutral party, the Dutch could not fire unless fired upon and so offered little resistance. Overrunning Dutch positions, the Serbs had taken some peacekeepers prisoner, in effect using them as hostages. The Dutch commander in the area had tried to call in air support to stop the Serbs, but some of his requests failed to make it up the chain of command, and the key UN official refused to grant permission for such military action. Not inclined to risk their lives, the Dutch retreated into the relative safety of their compound while the Serbs took control outside. In the days to follow, escalating Serbian reprisals against Muslim fighters led to a wholesale massacre of more than 5,000 men and boys. When word of the most massive slaughter in post-war Europe trickled out, the horror helped to galvanize the international community into more forceful action to stem Serb aggression, including a US-led bombing campaign that finally triggered serious negotiations. The humiliating peacekeeping debacle long reverberated in the Netherlands, where an official report recounting the dreary details and criticizing government ineptitude led to the belated fall of a cabinet in 2003 (Blom and Romijn 2002). Within the UN, too, Srebrenica had led to some soul-searching, resulting in a withering report in 1999 (UN 1999), though no official ever saw fit to take personal responsibility. For the world as a whole and the Dutch in particular, Srebrenica became a byword for collective failure in preventing the most serious crimes.

Even as they volunteered for their ill-conceived mission, the Dutch were already involved in Bosnian affairs in a way that illustrates an important thrust in globalization examined further in this chapter, namely the effort, often labeled "global governance," to build institutions that organize some aspect of world affairs without direct state control. In The Hague, their seat of government, they hosted the International Criminal Tribunal for the former Yugoslavia (ICTY), an institution established in 1993 by the UN Security Council with the lofty goal of contributing to peace and security by holding anyone in the relevant area accountable for breaches of the Geneva Conventions, crimes against humanity, and genocide. The ICTY soon commanded an ample budget, comprising some 10 percent of overall UN expenditures and growing to over $200 million in the early 2000s, when the tribunal had more than 1,000 employees (ICTY 2008). Distinguished figures lent their prestige – the leading Italian jurist Antonio Cassese served as the tribunal's president, Richard Goldstone from South Africa, a well-known prospective Constitutional Court justice in his country, agreed to be the first prosecutor. Reluctant to get directly involved in the Balkans until late 1995, the US took a major role in jump-starting the ICTY.

Yet for all its ambition to bring the rule of law to an apparently lawless situation, the tribunal had a slow start, lacking the means to conduct investigations on the ground or to arrest key suspects. When it began operating in earnest, it still moved glacially, taking four years to process its first case, that of a low-level Serbian police officer, Dusko Tadic, who had worked at brutal detention camps in Prijedor (Hagan 2003: 72, 83). In spite of the many hurdles it had to overcome, from recruiting suitable personnel to defining the exact rules it would apply, the tribunal compiled a series of convictions against war criminals from all sides in the Yugoslav conflagration. In the process, it created new precedents for dealing with war crimes and defined new types of crime, for example by treating deliberate sexual violence as a distinct offense. One of its signature accomplishments was the prosecution of Radislav Krstic, a Bosnian Serb general involved in the Srebrenica massacre who in 2001 was sentenced to 46 years in prison, a punishment reduced to 35 years on appeal (154–74). The tribunal was handed even bigger fish when in June 2001 the Serbian government, under pressure from the US, transferred its former president, Slobodan Milosevic, to ICTY custody. But what should have been a capstone achievement turned into a drawn-out tug-of-war when Milosevic craftily challenged the court's authority and prosecutors struggled to establish his responsibility for Serbian crimes. Even after hundreds of witnesses had appeared, the case was far from over when Milosevic died in 2006. At that point, two key figures in the Srebrenica massacre, General Ratko Mladic and Bosnian Serb leader Radovan Karadzic, were still at large. Only in 2008 was the latter finally arrested and put on trial. As the tribunal prepared to deal with his case, it was still unclear whether it would be able to hold both Karadzic and Mladic accountable for their actions.

Together, UNPROFOR and the ICTY illustrate the pitfalls and promise of two ways in which many countries have joined in recent years to devise new methods to deal with shared problems in the global age. "Global governance" is one name for the norms and institutions that result from such joint action to shape world society in a way that does not rely directly or exclusively on states. The very term equivocates, because it refers to rules not managed by an actual government yet endowed with some authority. It hints at the question of how exactly rules can rule without a ruler to enforce them. A similar question has long bedeviled international law, often derided as an oxymoron by those "positivists" who equate law with the commands of a sovereign power and see no semblance of it in the anarchic international arena. Yet as the examples also show, law in some form is at the center of global governance, for without rules backed by sanctions there can be no new governance. With due attention to skeptical objections, inspired by the sobering events in the Balkans and the uneven history of the ICTY, this chapter argues nevertheless that international law is steadily expanding into "world law" (Berman 1995, 2005), a configuration of rules that govern more than state relations and anchor diverse and significant forms of governance. Reviewing the record of the United Nations and some examples of less state-centered governance, I show that attempts to channel globalization and organize world society are themselves still quite haphazard – or as scholars might put it, "multilayered" and "disaggregated" (Slaughter 2004: ch. 4; Rosenau 2000: 183). The jumble of transnational institutions that "unbundle" the territorial control of nation-states (Ruggie 1993) resembles the polity of the European Middle Ages, when coexisting, overlapping, and often competing centers of power claimed authority over different matters within the same space. This picture of global governance also serves as a counterpoint to arguments, addressed in the conclusion, that it really does have a single structure, operating at the behest of the American hegemonic power.

It was no accident that The Hague would host the ICTY. The city had long been a key site in the evolution of global governance and especially of international law (Van Krieken and McKay 2005). Just as the Dutch took their UN peacekeeping role as a point of pride, so they had come to think of hospitality to legal institutions as the contribution a small country could make to a more peaceful world. That tradition goes back to at least the end of the nineteenth century, when leaders of major powers concerned about an intensifying arms race sought a place to negotiate disarmament and find ways to settle disputes. Gathered at the Hague Peace Conference for three months in 1899, diplomats formulated a new convention on the laws of land war and even more strikingly agreed on a Convention for the Pacific Settlement of International Disputes, complete with a Permanent Court of Arbitration (PCA) whose "judges" would be potential arbitrators used voluntarily by state parties to resolve conflicts (Eyffinger 2005: 36–7; Shifman 2005: 128–37). Of course, the PCA would operate from The Hague, where Andrew Carnegie helped to fund construction of a proper home, now called the Peace Palace. The 1899 conference made less headway on disarmament, as states like the US preferred to preserve their military prerogatives. The spirit of The Hague, embodied in the PCA and strengthened by a second major conference in 1907, obviously also could not prevent the outbreak of the Great War in 1914. When in its aftermath the major powers tried again to find a framework for peaceful coexistence in the form of the League of Nations, the legal branch of the new organization, the Permanent Court of International Justice (PCIJ), naturally found its home in The Hague, as a neighbor of the PCA in the Peace Palace. A full-fledged court where individual states could seek recourse, though still dependent on consent of state parties for its jurisdiction in any dispute, the PCIJ would decide a number of important cases before the troubles of the 1930s paralyzed its work (Rosenne 2005).

After World War II, the founders of the United Nations decided to give international law a fresh start, instituting the International Court of Justice (ICJ) to replace the PCIJ – to be seated, of course, in The Hague. Formally a part of the UN as its "principal judicial organ," its statute is annexed to the UN Charter, all UN members are parties to it, and its 15 judges are approved by the General Assembly. Yet the ICJ also operates quite independently, focusing on typical state issues like border disputes and access to fisheries while gradually expanding its reach, for example by issuing advisory opinions at the request of UN organs. The ICJ got involved in the Balkan mess in 1999 when in a series of cases Serbia and Montenegro tried to challenge the legality of the use of force by Western countries, though the court declined to take provisional measures to stop them. Since the mid-1980s, as the Serbian actions indicate, it has had a "heavy docket," one sign of its increasing importance (Rosenne 2005: 201). States from Eastern Europe, Africa, and Central America brought new and different sorts of cases, dealing with military activities, environmental effects of dams and mining operations, and the like (Crawford and Grant 2007: 203). As the court thus solidified its role in international law, it also had to face the limits of its traditional approach: in many disputes, the coalitions of states or the international organizations that played a major role could not appear as parties, and the real issues at stake did not just concern the behavior of states. The Balkan troubles brought home the point.

In the 1990s, those troubles, and similar ones elsewhere, created widespread frustration. Focused on bilateral disputes between states, the ICJ was useless as a tool to hold individual war criminals accountable. Trying to arbitrate the conflict through the PCA was a non-starter. As an ad hoc institution, the ICTY did its job up to a point, but its temporary status seemed at odds with its claim to further the rule of law. UN-organized actions in the Balkans gave some relief to the weakest parties but focused on political rather than legal goals. It seemed obvious that grave crimes were committed in the Balkans and in other hotspots, and a body of international humanitarian law had developed over a century to identify such breaches of common principles, yet the world had no regular institution to address the problem by pursuing justice. Guided by a sense that "there ought to be a court," proposals for a standing international criminal tribunal floated in the early 1990s developed under UN auspices into a full-fledged draft treaty discussed at a major conference in Rome in 1998, where after long arguments a majority of countries agreed to found the International Criminal Court (ICC) (Lechner and Boli 2005: ch. 10). Unlike the ICJ, it would have jurisdiction over individuals suspected of war crimes, crimes against humanity, and genocide, in cases where domestic courts were unwilling or unable to act. More than his counterpart at the ICTY, its prosecutor would have clear independent authority. By contrast with both the ICTY and the Nuremberg trials of the 1940s, the ICC would be free of the taint of imposing victors' justice. After 60 countries ratified the Treaty of Rome, the ICC was officially born in early 2002, just days after the start of the Milosevic trial (Hagan 2003: 204). It opened for business several months later – in The Hague, naturally.

Interpreting Trends in Global Governance

Calling The Hague the "legal capital of the world" (Van Krieken and McKay 2005) flatters the Dutch perhaps a bit too much. For one thing, however important the legal affairs conducted there may be, their scale still pales compared to that in domestic courts. Each of its legal institutions also suffers from distinct limitations, especially due to states that jealously guard their sovereignty. Those institutions still depend on states, especially powerful states, to gain compliance, as illustrated by America's pressure on Serbia in the Milosevic case. Yet international law has come a long way, with more institutions applying more rules to more issues in more authoritative ways. The fact that, compared to a century ago, the image of The Hague as legal capital does not induce people to smile at Dutch self-congratulation – that there may be some kernels of truth in the idea that "the world" now has common institutions with real authority that operate from a single place but have near-universal reach – shows how far global governance has come. Due to institutional globalization, international law is not what it used to be.

What it used to be, at least in the skeptical or "realist" view that has roots in the nineteenth century, was a tool of great powers pursuing their interests without any binding external constraint except the countervailing power of others or specific obligations assumed via treaties. From an older perspective, that view of an anarchical "international system" was always misguided. Even in the supposed heyday of great power politics, after all, many states and private parties tried to promote an international community bound by a common "standard of civiliza-tion" (Gong 1984). The spirit of internationalism took form in several new inter-national organizations and wafted through the 1899 conference as well. In the alternative view, "international society" refers to a society of states bound by common rules and institutions, established by dialogue and consent, whose members are committed to maintaining it (Kingsbury and Roberts 1990; Buzan 2004: 7–9). "International society" in this sense, as the very term obviously sug-gests, refers to a real community, at least among states, their representatives, and others acting in some official capacity – all those who help to manage "interna-tional relations." One way to describe trends in governance, then, is to say that, after the disasters of the long wars of the twentieth century, a nucleus of interna-tional society that existed in the late 1800s expanded into a more vigorous and diverse set of institutions.

The term international society, and the thinking about international affairs that informs it, is now often associated with one of the founders of international law as a distinct field of study and practice, the Dutch scholar and lawyer Hugo de Groot (1583–1645) (Bull 2000). "Grotius," the Latinized name common in his day and still in use for easier pronunciation, was active in The Hague early in his career, where he became a prominent figure in the United Provinces that broke away from Spanish imperial rule and witnessed the rise of what might have been the first modern nation. Being on the losing side in a Dutch political struggle, he was put in prison and then famously escaped into exile in France, where he wrote his masterpiece, *The Rights of War and Peace* (Grotius 2005). He later served as Sweden's ambassador to France during the Thirty Year War in Germany, the cauldron in which Europe's religious divisions and modern political order took definite shape. In this time of turmoil, when the medieval order was breaking up in the first wave of globalization, Grotius drew on Scripture and the annals of antiquity to argue in his classic work that sovereign powers were bound by rules derived from natural law, grounded in divine commands and common to all people regardless of religion. Only under limited circumstances could one state make war on another; even more rarely were subjects justified in resisting their superiors (Jeffery 2006: 41). Strikingly, Grotius did allow for a state to attack another when it undermines the common good by violating the basic norms of international society or inflicting unwarranted treatment on its subjects (Kingsbury and Roberts 1990: 16, 38–40), an "interventionary" argument (Tuck in Grotius 2005: xxvii) that might have heartened Western leaders as they con-templated military action in the Balkans or later in Iraq. Such collective law enforcement is one mark of solidarity in an international society that Grotius regarded as universal, based on natural law, and not limited to states (Bull 1990: 78–91). In recognition of his work and his way of thinking, attendees at the 1899 conference gathered at the Nieuwe Kerk in Grotius's birthplace of Delft to lay a wreath at his tomb (Vreeland 1917: 239–40).

They realized, of course, that Grotius did not foresee the exact shape of global affairs in their day. Nor did he predict their current shape. In fact, he did not even use the term "international law," invented only in the late eighteenth century by the British scholar Jeremy Bentham to distinguish inter-state law from both natural and private law, at the dawn of the second wave. In short, invoking Grotius does not mean that he anticipated all the challenges we face today. Yet Grotian insights still capture the thrust of global governance as a move toward institutionalizing shared norms in different ways beyond the control of single states in an international society that exhibits some basic solidarity. What we may call, with a bit of interpretive license, the "Grotian model" tells us that global governance has evolved to entangle states in a web of norms and that among those norms is the requirement that the actions of global actors must center on upholding rights. As was the case in Grotius's work, those actors include not just states but also individuals (Bull 2000: 108) – at least in principle, in international society everyone has rights and duties. Through trial and error, the evolution of global governance has now also produced something Grotius might have hoped for but that was still largely absent in the international society of his day, namely common institutions (Bull 1990: 89–91). Among those institutions are the ones in The Hague, and even more important are those of the United Nations proper, as the next section describes.

Whether Grotius can be so easily identified with a single vision of what we now call global governance is open to question, since his thinking was complex and his extensive writings lend themselves to different readings: Grotian doctrine has a protean quality. Among those writings were many theological tracts in which Grotius aspired to reunite Christianity torn asunder by the Reformation. The natural law of nations, properly understood and applied, would serve a more tolerant and harmonious Christian society based on universal core truths. In this regard, Grotius's project resonates with the efforts of modern scholars eager to promote world law as a critical institution in a united world society aware of the underlying commonalities in different faith traditions (Berman 1995, 2005). In other words, Grotius may serve as a source not just for a vision of solidary-but-anarchic international society but also for more ambitious, "Kantian" visions of a "world society," used in this case as a term of art to capture visions of law constituting the fabric of a peaceful human commonwealth rooted in shared values among the peoples of the world (Buzan 2004: 9). The upshot of this chapter is that those visions have not yet been realized – we do not live in a "Kantian" world society. At least, not yet: those more ambitious visions are very much at work in the recent evolution of global governance, which is propelled in part by the views of its interpreters even if it falls short of their high ideals.

The United Nations in Global Governance

UNPROFOR was only one of more than 40 peacekeeping operations the UN undertook since the late 1980s (Doyle and Sambanis 2007: 328–32). Blue helmets got involved in rough places ranging from Cambodia to East Timor to Congo. Their funding far exceeded the standard UN budget, and for a time peacekeeping became big business within the UN. For some of its smaller members, sending troops served to demonstrate their cosmopolitan credentials or to earn some hard currency. Each operation faced its own difficulties, though even among the tough spots, the multiple faultlines of Bosnia made it one of the worst (Durch and Schear 1996). But the actions had one thing in common: they would have surprised the UN's founders. The Charter, after all, does not mention peacekeeping (Fleischhauer 1995: 237). It grants the Security Council expansive powers but intervention in domestic or civil conflicts is not among them. Strictly speaking, the Charter even appears to prohibit such intervention in Article 2–7: "Nothing contained in the present Charter shall authorize the United Nations to intervene in matters which are essentially within the domestic jurisdiction of any state" (cf. Kennedy 2006: 78). Originally, peacekeeping that kept state combatants apart fit the Charter's prime purpose of maintaining international peace and security by taking "effective collective measures for the prevention and removal of threats to the peace," as in the classic case of blue helmets separating Israel and Egypt after the Suez conflict of 1956. But after the end of the Cold War, when many countries imploded and the Soviet Union no longer blocked UN action, the UN's missions expanded in scope and scale. In authorizing new-style peacekeeping operations, sometimes without consent from all local parties involved, the Security Council stretched the terms of its mandate. Accordingly, much of what the UN did in the third wave of globalization did not follow from the Charter.

On the other hand, the UN rarely did what its founders thought it was supposed to do. As the Preamble to the Charter says, they meant to "save succeeding generations from the scourge of war, which twice in our lifetime has brought untold sorrow to mankind." To prevent and suppress acts of aggression between countries, they enabled the Security Council, in Chapter VII of the Charter, to determine whether the peace had been breached and to take measures to restore the peace, including the use of force. They contemplated a new apparatus to guarantee collective security, comprising a Military Staff Committee and "national air-force contingents" held ready by members for "combined international enforcement action." The founders had high hopes; US president Harry Truman even thought that after 1945 the UN would eradicate war altogether. But the UN air force never took flight. The organization itself never carried out any enforcement action. In spite of their obligations under the Charter, many of its members have in fact engaged in wars of aggression. Though the Charter also provides for expulsion of any state that violates its obligations, no state ever lost its membership for warlike behavior. On the key issue, therefore, the UN proved nearly powerless. On only two occasions did it put muscle behind its message. While the Soviet Union was unwisely boycotting meetings in 1950 and thus could not exercise its veto, the Security Council decided to respond to the communist attack on South Korea by authorizing forceful protection. The following "police action" flew the UN flag but operated under US command. After Iraq invaded Kuwait in 1990, the Security Council resolved to expel the aggressor by force if necessary. Another US-led coalition did the job in 1991. But the exceptions prove the rule that the UN has done little to live up to its prime purpose.

Much as they might have hoped for a different result, that should not have surprised the founders. Since both the US and the Soviet Union were loath to join an organization that might infringe on their sovereignty, they insisted at the outset on having veto power in the crucial Security Council. This became a recipe for political stalemate. Though the United Nations Organization was meant to extend the wartime alliance of United Nations, even in 1945 some cracks were already evident. As the US and the Soviet Union formed their respective blocs to begin the Cold War, the UN turned from a tool of cooperation into a forum for confrontation. The security apparatus envisioned in 1945 was stillborn, due to a distinct lack of enthusiasm by UN members. The UN would never have "its" forces ready for deployment and instead had to seek ad hoc support from members for any new venture. All peacekeeping efforts of the late twentieth century were such ad hoc ventures, cobbled together by an inexperienced organization from limited resources supplied by willing countries. Many began under inauspicious circumstances, where there was no peace to keep but also no clear way to separate warring parties. UN rules further aggravated the problems: eager to stay neutral even in the face of overwhelming wrongdoing by one side, the UN undermined its moral authority and, according to a self-criticism of its Bosnian record, at times broached appeasement of war criminals. Chastened by failure to restore order in some tough places, notably in Somalia in the early 1990s, the Security Council, the Secretary General, and key member states inexcusably hesitated to get involved in Rwanda in 1994, where a small UN contingent proved utterly unable to stop the genocide by Hutus against Tutsis. To its sins of commission and omission we can add that of irrelevance. In some instances where the UN might have played a key role, other parties in fact did the heavy lifting. For example, in 1999 NATO pushed back a Serbian attack on Muslims in the province of Kosovo, seeking UN approval and requesting UN supervision of the province after the fact (Traub 2006: 116–7).

Aided and abetted by the UN, Kosovo, a province of a sovereign country, claimed the right to self-determination and eventually declared independence in 2008, followed by quick recognition from several major countries. Not all missions were as controversial and intrusive as those in the former Yugoslavia; at times, the UN could leverage its prestige or bring enough pressure to bear to enforce actual peace, as in the cases of Haiti, Mozambique, and El Salvador. However much this wide range of missions varied in degree of difficulty or success, they had something in common besides the surprising departure from the intent of the founders: each greatly intruded on a state's space. Even as it remains beholden to the interests of sovereign great powers, the UN also has insinuated itself into the affairs of some of its members. Through its peacekeeping ventures, however inconsistently, the UN has claimed in effect that everyone has a stake in what members do to their own citizens (cf. Franda 2006: 227). In a way that might have surprised the founders, the shell of sovereignty has been pierced.

Just as UNPROFOR was an unorthodox mission, the Security Council made an equally unorthodox move in establishing the ICTY. The Council justified it as a necessary step toward peace and security in the region, but while Chapter VII of the Charter gives it broad authority to decide on "measures not involving the use of armed force" to carry out its decisions, few of the founders would have envisioned such a step. By empowering the tribunal, the Council itself indirectly became a law-making body. It thus added to the "panoply of unorthodox means of promulgating norms" that had evolved within the UN (Kirgis 1995: 110), adding the special twist of targeting individuals rather than addressing only states. It was just one measure that helped to erode "the foundations of absolute conceptions of state sovereignty . . . , fundamentally altering the way in which many see the relationship between state and citizen" (Malone 2007: 117). In traditional international law, by contrast, orthodoxy stood for the body of rules derived from treaties agreed on or customs followed by states. The founders meant to keep it that way, defining neither the UN as a whole nor any of its agencies as a legislative body (Schachter 1995: 2). In fact, proposals to authorize the General Assembly to enact binding rules of international law were soundly defeated in 1945, and instead the Charter only vaguely allows it to initiate studies and make recommendations to encourage the development of international law (Franda 2006: 6). The Charter "was not intended to be an instrument for governing the world," and it deliberately did not copy the three-branch structure of many ordinary governments (Alvarez 2007: 58). The ICJ would serve as the legal organ of the UN, with jurisdiction over disputes between states if parties gave consent. When in legal doubt, UN agencies could seek an "advisory opinion" from the court. While the ICJ played its part more or less as intended, the UN took a different course, expanding its role in global governance in a way that significantly affected the sovereignty of states.

The United Nations and World Law

The UN's very existence had legal effects. The Charter itself became a super-treaty, taking precedence over anything else states wished to do among themselves, increasingly regarded as a kind of global constitution that casts a long shadow over all aspects of international law (Alvarez 2007: 59). To become fully involved in international society, a proper subject of international law, any state had to seek UN membership, which required adherence to the Charter (McNeely 1995). Instead of simply being a tool of states, the UN thus took an unexpected role in creating and legitimating states, most obviously during the period of decolonization. Subjecting themselves to the Charter, states also assumed open-ended obligations to the organization, for example because Chapter VII required them to help enforce any Security Council decisions, a provision used to good effect in the ICTY founding. Once established, organs that were not supposed to act as legislatures felt a strong temptation to do so, often pushed by demand from member states, and they produced many "texts of legal import" (Schachter 1995: 2). Among these texts were many declarations that fell short of being formal conventions, adopted and ratified by members, but nonetheless gained law-like weight as expressions of state custom that could be cited as a rule or standard of international law, as illustrated by the General Assembly's 1970 Declaration on Friendly Relations that restricted the use of force and urged the peaceful settlement of disputes. States had to respect the UN as having legal personality in its own right, after the ICJ explicitly granted that status in a 1949 case brought by the UN to claim reparations from Israel after UN representatives had been assassinated there. That precedent carried over to other international organizations within the UN system, which now complements the system of states. Though still a creation of its members, the UN took on a life of its own. Of the "ostensible limits on the UN's legal powers," few "remain operative" (Alvarez 2007: 59).

The rights revolution illustrates the dramatic shift. The Charter's Preamble already expressed the founders' wish to "reaffirm faith in fundamental human rights, in the dignity and worth of the human person," but precisely how to promote them remained nebulous. For the great powers, human rights were not a priority; at the time of the founding, they formed merely "a glimmering thread in the web of power and interest" (Glendon 2001: 19). Further discussion beyond the terms of the Charter was relegated to a commission that would draw up an international bill of rights. Sensitive to the difficulty of getting a binding bill or convention adopted by key UN members, the commission chair, Eleanor Roosevelt, widow of America's wartime president, steered its work toward a less demanding declaration of principles. After revising numerous drafts and negotiating individual articles, the commission presented its Universal Declaration of Human Rights for approval by the General Assembly, which adopted it unanimously with only countries like the Soviet Union, Saudi Arabia, and South Africa abstaining (169–70). Neither a treaty nor a law, the high-minded Universal Declaration craftily combined continental ideas about the right to equality and social protection with Anglo-American notions of liberty and political rights (xvii, 177). It quickly gained stature, and over time many provisions ripened into international customary law (Hannum 1995: 326–7). It also served as the basis for further negotiations on actual conventions that would codify its principles, negotiations that broke the Universal Declaration's synthesis by ultimately producing one covenant on Civil and Political Rights, and one on Economic, Social, and Cultural Rights, both adopted in 1966. By that time, the General Assembly had become an engine of international law by gathering members for multilateral treaty negotiations (Alvarez 2007: 61). Among the fruits of its law-making activity were several more conventions defining basic rights – one

Plate 7.1   Eleanor Roosevelt (1884–1962) holding United Nations Universal Declaration of Human Rights, 1949
Source: © Topham/United Nations

on the elimination of racial discrimination, another requiring equal treatment of women.

Through dozens of such "instruments," international law changed its character. This was partly a matter of scope: international law simply became much more complex, covering many more issues with many different sorts of norms, rules, and standards – the variety of terms itself offers a measure of the change. In the UN era, it ranged from the "black letter" of ratified treaties to the "gray" implications of UN custom, from the "hard" or "shall" demands of Chapter VII in the Charter to the "soft" or "should" demands of, say, the UN's Global Compact initiative intended to spur companies toward taking on more corporate social responsibility. It was also a matter of process: bilateral treaty negotiations did not disappear, of course, but increasingly the expectation grew that the big common issues needed to be addressed in the one universal forum where all could participate and where those issues could be resolved in the form of a multilateral treaty. In many cases, such treaties also created new commissions, panels, or tribunals with authority to resolve disputes and interpret rules, enormously expanding the apparatus of international law. The change in international law was also a matter of substance: once focused only on the mutual obligations of states, international law increasingly dealt with the rights of individuals in relation to those states. And it was a matter of impact: whereas the consent of states had historically limited the reach of international law, it now became plausible to argue that key rules also applied to those that had not given their explicit approval (Schachter 1995: 3–4).

In the case of the most prominent and politically sensitive human rights agreements, that broad authority remained controversial; some countries finessed the problem by ratifying treaties with numerous reservations, as Islamic countries did in signing on to the Convention on the Elimination of All Forms of Discrimination against Women (CEDAW). But in the actual practice of less glamorous international organizations in the UN family, limits on consent are increasingly taken for granted (Kirgis 1995). In the International Labour Organization's "super-treaty system," conventions are not signed but adopted by majority vote in plenary session; they become a kind of common law, influencing even states that do not ratify in spite of considerable peer pressure (115–6). Universal Postal Union conventions enter into force provisionally even before members have ratified them (118). Many organizations assume tacit consent to new agreements and make it hard for any state to "opt out," as does the International Civil Aviation Organization, leaving little room for deviance in air safety. Some law-like standards – such as the daunting 200-plus standards and 40 codes for food safety in the 25-volume Codex Alimentarius, established by the Food and Agriculture Organization (FAO) and the World Health Organization (WHO) – sidestep the need for full consent and instead allow different degrees of acceptance, but even for lukewarm adopters they serve as an authoritative guide if they wish to participate in international trade (Braithwaite and Drahos 2000: 401). Thus the UN and its agencies "channel members' conduct in discrete areas," often "without the express consent of each member to each norm they promulgate," an ability that is "reasonably effective even as to passive participants in the system" and thus moves global governance toward "a flexible concept of international legal obligation" (Kirgis 1995: 161).

The UN has come a long way. But what might have caused consternation among the founders heartens Kantian believers in universal world law. They see evidence that governance is moving in the right direction: states are ensnared in legal nets not entirely of their own making, subject to the authority of organizations that represent the global community, beholden to common principles such as human rights. They applaud breaking the state monopoly on rule-making. They view the UN's surprising growth as a virtuous spiral: new-found authority leads to new common rules that spur further expansion of authority into new arenas. More people with more authority work on behalf of world society rather than any particular nation-states. In this way, the UN brightens the prospects of world law.

At the same time, the actual UN record gives much critical ammunition to old-fashioned realists for whom states remain the key actors. The organization failed miserably to keep the peace in places like Bosnia, they would say, and even more obviously fell short of guaranteeing "collective security." With respect to its prime goal, it must defer to powerful members. Busy as the UN has been to make new rules and facilitate new agreements, in the end those rules and agreements must serve the needs of members. In certain technical areas, where clear rules are convenient for all, they might be willing to give much leeway to international organizations that have appropriate expertise, but when deeper political interests are at stake they will revert to old habits. Even the supposedly legal actions of the Security Council, such as instituting the ICTY or denying authority for the war in Iraq, are simply the continuation of ordinary politics by other means. The presumed power of the UN is a legal fiction in any case: with rare exceptions, it cannot enforce its demands, and violators of major rules remain members in good standing. Notoriously unable to reform itself into an efficient and transparent body, the UN cannot police itself either, as illustrated by the Oil-for-Food corruption scandal that siphoned money to the regime of Saddam Hussein as well as some UN officials, and by repeated instances of peacekeepers sexually abusing those they were sent to protect.

Great lawyer though he was, Grotius would not be able to settle this dispute, if only for the simple reason that global governance in fact often moves in opposing directions and seesaws between contending models. In some ways it is still an institutional house of cards, built by states for their convenience but always at risk of being blown apart by its builders. In other ways, the structure of the house is getting more intricate and the glue that holds it together is getting stronger. Though Grotius obviously did not anticipate the founding of the UN, the organization still inhabits a world he would recognize, a world in which states also form a world society, in which sovereign power is also bound by common rules, and in which conflict itself is governed by norms. This world has devised more ways to develop common customs, for example via UN deliberations, and some of its principles have acquired the status of quasi-natural law, most notably the whole theory of human rights. In a slightly more concrete way than in Grotius's time, though still imperfectly at best, international law can now rely on his second rule of nature, namely that "What the common consent of mankind has shown to be the will of all, that is law" (Jeffery 2006: 38). But this world is not a single community; it contains multiple cultures, multiple centers of authority – even the UN system is internally diverse. From a Grotian point of view, that complexity is not a problem. At the dawn of the modern nation-state system, Grotius's analysis of international law still included several players that were not states, which only adds to the complexity of governance, then and now. Grotius even allowed for the occasional legitimacy of private wars, for example to retrieve property or settle debts. Though few would go this far with him today, the role of private parties in global governance is also very much back on the agenda, as the next section explains.

Box 7.1   Features of global governance

Legal framework

Charter of the United Nations (1945)

Universal Declaration of Human Rights (1948)

Geneva Conventions (1949)

International Covenant on Civil and Political Rights (1966, entered into force 1976)

International Covenant on Economic, Social, and Cultural Rights (1966, entered into force 1976)

Convention on the Elimination of All Forms of Discrimination Against Women (1979, entered into force 1981)

UN Convention on the Law of the Sea (1982, entered into force 1994)

WTO Agreement, including 1948 General Agreement on Tariffs and Trade (1994, took effect 1995)

Rome Statute of the International Criminal Court (1998, entered into force 2002)

Key institutions

UN General Assembly

UN Security Council

International Court of Justice

International Criminal Court

International Criminal Tribunal for the former Yugoslavia

International Monetary Fund

Permanent Court of Arbitration

World Bank

World Trade Organization

Governance Beyond States

Grotius made his legal reputation with a work he wrote in his twenties on the freedom of the sea. It was in effect part of a sophisticated brief written on behalf of a client that was the most powerful business organization in the Netherlands, the United East India Company (or VOC, in its Dutch acronym). The VOC wanted to trade in Asia but was forcefully rebuffed by the Portuguese, who were eager to protect their monopoly there. Grotius helped defend the VOC's claim to booty seized by a Dutch captain from a Portuguese cargo ship in Asian waters, arguing that freedom to trade is part of natural law, as is freedom to travel across the ocean, a part of the earth no one can own. The law of nations encompassed both freedoms, and the VOC was therefore in the right. The law of nations pertaining to "foreign" activities thus spanned more than "international" law in the modern sense. For Grotius, it covered all rules that applied to all interactions among peoples at large distances beyond the reach of their respective sovereigns. Like many contemporaries in those pre-national days, Grotius did not assume that law consisted only of what a ruler in a particular place happened to command. *Ius gentium*, the law of nations – or, better, peoples – was inherently global. In different ways, global governance is recapturing features of that era.

Grotius's success as an author attests to the existence of a network of professionals and officials who shared his concerns and recognized his contribution. Writing in Latin, he could reasonably assume that fellow lawyers and scholars would be able to read his work. He was part of what we might now call an "epistemic community," a grouping of experts who looked at the world in similar ways, drawing on similar knowledge and skills. That epistemic community never quite disappeared. Even in the "nationalist" nineteenth century, activist scholars took the initiative to set up the International Law Association. One of them, the Dutch lawyer Tobias Asser, arranged the 1893 Conference on Private International Law – in The Hague, of course, thus setting a precedent for its future role in international law – to reflect on ways to unify disparate national approaches; for his efforts he earned the Nobel Peace Prize in 1911. Yet it is fair to say that after the national turn of the second wave of globalization the transnational epistemic community began to flourish again in the third wave. Across national borders, more and more judges are engaged in a "self-conscious conversation" forming a "community of courts" (Slaughter 2004: 68, 74), learning from each other about similar constitutional conundrums, how to apply human rights law, and how to resolve transnational disputes. In response to demand from multinational corporations, law firms on both sides of the Atlantic, but especially in the UK, have begun to work much more transnationally, in the process also creating more transnational legal business, for example in mergers and acquisitions (Morgan 2006). Around institutions like the ICTY, a transnational community of legal experts has formed, dealing with international criminal and human rights law as distinct areas of expertise. Certainly, most lawyers work within the confines of their respective countries, but ever more legal work crosses borders. In many such epistemic communities, global governance is attracting its own personnel.

One reason that professionals understood each other in Grotius' day is that an important part of the law had evolved through the activities of merchants. To do business abroad, they had to be sure that their partners understood contracts the same way. Instead of paying cash, merchants long preferred to use paper money or bills of exchange or letters of credit, which again required that everyone in a transaction treated those financial tools the same way. If there were disputes, it helped if everyone knew in advance how they were to be resolved, preferably short of direct violence or breaking off the relationship. To manage the special risks involved, long-distance trade thus fostered legal innovation. A transnational community of traders independently developed a near-universal, customary commercial law (Berman 1988: 2). This was not entirely private law, since public authorities were often involved in enforcing claims, but the *lex mercatoria* was nonetheless mostly the product of professionals minding their own business. In the second wave of globalization, much of this was nationalized via statutes enacted in different countries. This nationalization of commercial law created a demand for clearer common rules. On the initiative of the International Law Association, conferences in The Hague in 1910 and 1912 led to a new convention on bills of exchange, never ratified due to the outbreak of war. From the 1920s, the International Chamber of Commerce (ICC) agitated for unification, for example by developing its code on Uniform Customs and Practice for Documentary Credits, which was applied in 173 countries by 1966; more indirectly the ICC effort paid off in the 1964 Uniform Law on the International Sale of Goods and a related law on forming contracts, adopted at a state conference in The Hague, the first subsequently revised in the UN Convention on Contracts for the International Sale of Goods of 1980 (Braithwaite and Drahos 2000: 51–3). Several special international organizations, such as the UN Commission on International Trade Law and the more independent International Institute for the Unification of Private Law (UNIDROIT), devote their attention to working out the rules of international commerce. Following second-wave precedent, the Hague Conference on Private International Law became a permanent intergovernmental organization in the 1950s, focusing on both commercial and family law. On a parallel track, a "new" law merchant in the third wave still relies on the customs of traders, ship owners, bankers, and insurers to organize transactions (Berman 1988: 7). In this arena, global governance has become much more complex, involving different sorts of groups and many more rules, but to some extent it still is a form of self-governance as well.

Grotius's early client, the VOC, was an enterprising outfit in more ways than one. As a joint-stock company, it pioneered a modern form of business organization. Learning from Italian predecessors, it applied essentially modern forms of bookkeeping. It benefited from the emerging stock market in Amsterdam, where its shares could be sold. Over time, each became a global institution in its own right (Braithwaite and Drahos 2000). Stock markets served as engines of the second wave of globalization, when London and New York overtook Amsterdam, and then again of the more geographically diverse third wave. Nearly everywhere, corporations now dominate economic life, pooling capital in common, legally recognized fashion. To list shares on major capital markets, corporations typically must meet internationally accepted accounting standards, redefined in the 1990s by the International Organization of Securities Commissions and the International Accounting Standards Committee. But rules of the global economic game are not just new versions of old ones. For example, although he was a very successful author, whose theological works were translated into several languages, Grotius depended financially on the favor of political patrons. In the absence of internationally recognized copyright, the immediate rewards of literary success were probably quite meager. In the second wave, by contrast, countries began to take intellectual property more seriously, first through bilateral treaties, then through the Paris Convention of 1883 and the Berne Convention of 1886, which protected artistic works and industrial property, respectively, complete with an International Bureau that turned into the World Intellectual Property Organization (WIPO) in 1967 (Braithwaite and Drahos 2000: 59–60). Partly thanks to WIPO, defining and protecting intellectual property has become a critical area of governance in the third wave of globalization, as affirmed by the Agreement on Trade Related Aspects of Intellectual Property Rights (TRIPS), adopted in 1994 as a cornerstone of the newly formed World Trade Organization. From movies to pharmaceuticals to software to books by Grotius's successors, key goods of the modern world economy now earn higher rewards for their creators. It represents just one important way in which global governance has extended more tentacles more widely than would have been possible in the first wave of globalization.

Dependent on the sea for food and trade, Grotius and his fellow Hollanders took a special interest in the law of the sea. In his time, it was quite minimal; in the third wave, it has expanded enormously. By comparison with the days of the VOC, marine insurance contracts have become much more standardized under the influence of Lloyd's of London. In another instance of "private" governance, Lloyd's Register competes with dozens of private classification societies, which specialize in inspecting and monitoring ship quality, in a way few states care to match (Braithwaite and Drahos 2000: 422). The Strait of Malacca, already a flashpoint in Grotius's day, is one area covered by rules of the International Marine Organization (IMO), which no one is free to disobey, intended to keep ships safely apart in their own lanes – just one elementary provision in the 40 conventions and protocols the IMO has produced (426). In the first wave, piracy was still an accepted tool of state policy, but thanks mainly to the British Navy the oceans had become more peaceful in the twentieth century. Most stunning to a visitor from the 1600s would be the "regime" that governs the oceans themselves. Under the terms of the Law of the Sea Convention, the result of many years of negotiation, states can claim control over a certain part of their coastal waters but exploration of ocean resources elsewhere is subject to treaty rules, adjudicated by a special tribunal. Most of the oceans still cannot be owned in a conventional sense, but the Law of the Sea allows for exploitation of what it treats as the "common heritage of mankind" – a concept that Grotius would have appreciated.

Of course, some current experiments in global governance are entirely beyond Grotius's imagining. Yet what makes them striking to us might not be as surprising to his lingering ghost. For Grotius, global rules for use of the sea, global business regulation, and global legal epistemic communities might be recognizable extensions of practices in his day. Today, however, we measure global change against the intervening record of nation-states. In the second wave of globalization and again early in the third wave, states took on many responsibilities. Now, many of these responsibilities are thoroughly intertwined with global institutions, whether in combating illegal drugs, protecting food safety, or regulating securities. In 13 types of business regulation alone, the principle of national sovereignty has gradually lost ground (Braithwaite and Drahos 2000: 508–11). In the second wave, modern states became unitary actors, or at least acted as if they were. Now, states have become "disaggregated" as different agencies get involved in different global ventures for different reasons (Slaughter 2004). Some of those ventures have roots in the second wave, and in the third many more arose, at a time when developed states still maintained at least a façade of tidy coherence. By comparison, global governance looks chaotic – like a "striped" order of narrow compartments, each focused on its own special task (Ahrne and Brunsson 2006: 94) or a series of circles fanning out from a small core of UN institutions (Koenig-Archibugi 2002: 64). Municipal law within states was never all of a kind, but constitutions, codes, and cases make reasonably clear what the law is and what it expects of citizens. In international law, the very fabric of global governance, the status of "the" law is far less clear – the global legal system is "messier" (Slaughter 2004: 67), the realm of global regulation is "highly ambiguous" (Jacobsson and Sahlin-Andersson 2006: 254).

There are reasons for the messiness. One is simply that different problems call for distinct solutions – different sorts of rules make sense for sea transport or intellectual property or corporate accounting. Many actors are involved in formulating rules across a wide range of issues – food companies play a special role in the commission dealing with the food safety codex, the Basel club of central bankers figures prominently in financial regulation, and international organizations have the strongest voice on issues like civil aviation. In each domain, the actors also have to balance different principles as they try to decide whether to deregulate a practice or move toward stricter rule compliance, whether to harmonize rules across countries or require them to treat locals and foreigners the same according to national rules (Braithwaite and Drahos 2000: 508–9). Methods for creating new forms of governance also vary, ranging from long sticks to sweet carrots, from direct coercion by powerful states to persuasive modeling by entrepreneurial leaders to creating incentives for future adoption. The actual shape of any particular governance institution typically depends on the outcome of tricky negotiations, in which the relative strength of the many parties, bold action by energetic individuals, or simply accidental circumstances can make a great difference. No wonder, then, that global governance looks chaotic, that the organization of world society seems just slightly disorganized. Global governance may take the form of expanding "webs of dialogue" (Braithwaite and Drahos 2000: 553) but the conversation is often not easy to follow.

This picture of a world society with modest but growing powers of organization, a system of states embedded in new sorts of webs, fits neither the old realist model in which rationally acting states command all authority nor the rosy Kantian view that discerns seeds of world government. The "Grotian" label better fits the messier, quasi-medieval twenty-first-century state of world organization.

But is it all that messy in the end? A different sort of challenge holds that there is a method to it.

The United States in Global Governance

Though the Dutch play a disproportionate role in the story of global governance, they are not the central characters. The ICTY would not have been founded without US support. UNPROFOR floundered until the US decided to send in the bombers. Of course, these were only two late episodes in a history that goes back decades. The UN itself owes its birth and design to the US. The American president Franklin Roosevelt was "consumed" with the idea of founding the organization at the end of World War II (Traub 2006: 5), America hosted the preparatory meetings, the terms of the Charter built on American ideas, and the organization found its home in New York City. The US played an equally dominant role in the Bretton Woods institutions, the IMF and the World Bank, both in defining their purpose and in guaranteeing America's voting power – and they would also have their headquarters in the US. By the same token, American opposition could be crucial, too, as was evident in the failure of the planned International Trade Organization. Overall, a United Nations that still strongly protected state sovereignty and a financial architecture that would promote capitalist expansion certainly served American interests. As the clear, relatively unscathed victor in World War II, America had the clout to push its vision. After the end of the Cold War in the early 1990s, it enjoyed another short period of unrivalled strength or political "hegemony." More than any other country, America has left its mark on global governance. To the extent that it has, and still does, global governance may not be as disorganized as it seems. Global governance, in other words, might just be a way for the US to leverage its power to promote its values and interests, an instance of a more general process that favors strong states in the world system (Arrighi and Silver 1999).

No doubt this motivated American leaders to support the UN. But in this respect, as in so many others, the UN would frustrate the intent of some founders. Roosevelt had grossly misjudged the future, and the wartime alliance the UN was supposed to institutionalize soon fell apart (Traub 2006: 5–7). In the UN's early years, the Soviet Union often wielded its veto power to stymie UN efforts supported by the US. Easily swayed by the US in the 1950s, the General Assembly became a much more unruly arena in the 1960s as newly independent countries banded together to assert their views. Particular controversies, such as member animosity toward Israel that culminated in a resolution equating Zionism with racism, further soured American political sentiment toward the UN. Though still influential, the US lost control of the UN agenda, reflected in major world summits on issues such as the environment or population that put the US on the defensive. In some of the specialized agencies, America's discontent grew even more, for example when UNESCO promoted a "New International Information Order" that appeared to favor state control over a free press and became a factor in America's withdrawal from the organization in 1984. Both in UNESCO and in the UN at large, shoddy management became an issue as well, especially for the US Congress, which repeatedly threatened to withhold funds in an effort to make the UN more efficient and transparent. In 2003, tensions rose again when France, almost accidentally included as a veto-wielding member of the Security Council in 1945, played a prime role in resisting US efforts strictly to enforce UN resolutions that had threatened Saddam Hussein with "serious consequences" if he did not comply with UN demands. The UN thus gave a strong voice to America's adversaries, spawned policies America disagreed with, built an unaccountable bureaucracy, opposed American initiatives, and as a result came to upset American political conservatives most concerned about America's relative strength in the world – all while expecting American funding for about a quarter of its budget (cf. Muravchik 2005). In retrospect, the UN turned out to be an odd way to bolster American hegemony. A more cynical and calculating hegemon could have done without.

From the outset, the IMF had built in more safeguards for the US: by virtue of its greater financial contribution, it would in effect have a veto. By convention, the World Bank had an American president, guaranteeing US influence in a tangible way. Though their actions suited American goals in the immediate post-war period, they played an even more prominent role in the "neoliberal" phase of global expansion after 1980, promoting a set of policies linked to the appropriately named "Washington consensus" (see Chapter 5) that clearly tracked American thinking about the world economy. At crucial junctures, for example to deal with defaults in major countries, American policymakers mobilized the institutions for their benefit. The institutions thus served a political as much as an economic purpose. More clearly than the UN, they reflected and served American power. Even in these institutions, American influence has varied over time – the US had more leverage in the 1990s, when IMF/World Bank clients also had unusually great needs, but the institutions' lending power diminished after 2000 and the Washington consensus itself frayed. When the GATT finally made way for the WTO, it fit American wishes but also limited the US, since decision-making required consensus by all parties and the US had to agree to abide by the decisions of WTO panels, some of which in fact did turn against it. Across the spectrum of business regulation, American influence also varies – it is very great in areas like competition law, where the US can exert direct pressure, but moderate in banking regulation, where more consensual procedures prevail. The US remains uniquely able to advance its point of view through direct pressure or more subtle blandishments but even in the area where it enjoys the greatest advantage it has become dependent on many partners in many settings.

When that dependence rankles, the US often tries to pursue its goals outside of governance institutions where many partners might stand in the way, a strategy called "forum shifting." Even while large-scale trade negotiations move slowly, the US can seek deals with specific partner countries, as happened in a series of free-trade agreements in the early 2000s. Concerned that the ICC might affect Americans in spite of American opposition, the US negotiated exemptions to ICC provisions for its personnel with many countries in which it was involved militarily. As the Cold War heated up and the UN proved useless in dealing with security, the US moved to establish NATO with a group of close allies, in effect creating an entirely different "forum" for military cooperation. In the latter case, the US and its partners did not have much choice, since from their point of view the existing governance institution simply could not do the job. At other times, the US has good reason to find another forum because it can better exploit its size advantage in one-on-one rather than large-scale negotiations. More than most countries, the US can extricate itself from the webs of obligation that global governance has spun. It jealously guards its sovereignty, and has for a long time, as Senate rejection of membership in the League of Nations attested. Yet the fact that it has to try and shift fora in the first place also means that even the US now must take into account new constraints on its behavior. More than in the days of the League, global governance grows in ways and places the US would prefer to ignore. Increasingly, even the hegemon must take heed.

That was evident on one particular occasion in The Hague in 1986. Nicaragua had brought suit against the US in the International Court of Justice, arguing that the mining of Managua's harbor by the CIA and American support for the rebel Contras breached its sovereignty and therefore violated international law. Initially, the US responded that it took action to help its partner El Salvador stem Nicaraguan supplies to the rebel FMLN (Farabundo Martí National Liberation Front), thus assisting its defense against foreign intrusion. But as the court moved to decide the case, the US hurried to temporarily suspend its agreement of 1946 to accept "compulsory jurisdiction." The suspension was later followed by permanent withdrawal of consent. The ICJ nonetheless decided to decide, based on America's original consent and a treaty between the US and Nicaragua. It held that America had engaged in "unlawful use of force" and had illegally intervened in the affairs of another country, and it called for reparations (ICJ 1986). At the time, the decision marked a strong assertion of judicial authority, precisely because it dealt with a superpower. However, the court could only do so much: the US refused to comply, even using a veto in the Security Council to block resolutions calling for compliance, at great cost to its ostensible interest in the international rule of law. At least implicitly, it did not recognize the legitimacy of Nicaragua's Sandinista government, which had taken power by force, or of the 1984 elections that gave it a majority. While the court struck a blow for international law, in the actual political dispute the US had the last laugh: the Sandinista government decisively lost the elections of 1990, prelude to a period of democratic reform in the country.

Neither the ICJ nor, for that matter, the ICC is intended to restrain the US. Their officials would rightly reject the thought. At the same time, to the extent that global governance evolves new forms of power, new sorts of standards, and new potential sanctions, this may also serve to tame the hegemon. For some of its advocates, at least, that seems a worthwhile fringe benefit. Yet America, though deeply involved in global governance, resists taming.

Summary and Conclusion

Starting with the sobering UN travails in the former Yugoslavia, this chapter has argued that both within and outside the UN system new forms of governance are emerging, some with the force of law. Centered in The Hague, among other places, a diverse range of relatively new institutions are carrying out the business of world society. For all its faults and limitations, the UN in particular has taken on a larger law-making role than its founders had envisioned. More "private" regulation of transnational activities, for example in business, also challenges state authority in some ways. The clout of global governance institutions still varies enormously, and they rarely reflect a consensus among relevant states or experts or stakeholders in an issue. Yet the direction of change is toward more organization of more different fields above and beyond states.

In this process of change the US still exercises great influence, and much of global governance develops at America's urging or direction, but America also stands aside in cases where it fears limits to its sovereignty. In spite of its own skepticism about, and occasional rejection of, new steps toward global governance, its overall shape matches America's view of the world, to the extent that a big country with variable foreign policies can have a single view. Even the messiness works for America, as it avoids a form of centralized power that fits uneasily in the American political tradition and instead divides global power in a way that resembles a series of checks and balances. Of course, that lack of centralization also preserves America's preeminence. America matters for governance in yet another way. Governance in the Grotian sense may flourish in a still mostly anarchic world, yet it also depends on a minimal global order immunized against destructive great-power conflict by a hegemonic country providing some security for all. When one country carries the big stick, others are free to act more kindly and gently.

Among them are actors in civil society, key figures in the next chapter, who have tried to become a voice and force for global change. The growth of global civil society, to which world law owes some of its impetus, complements that of global governance.

Questions

1   The International Criminal Court is intended to be a more permanent body with broader jurisdiction than the International Criminal Tribunal for the former Yugoslavia. What are the advantages of institutionalizing global criminal law in that way? Is there still, or should there be, room for ad hoc, improvised governance institutions as well?

2   This chapter reflects a thrust in recent scholarship by picturing global governance as "disaggregated" and "multilayered." Does this contradict the arguments of world polity theory to the effect that in a decentralized system of states

there are likely to be strong pressures toward convergence or "isomorphism" in the practices of many organizations?

3 Both UN-related bodies and other governance institutions appear to have pierced states' shell of sovereignty. Does this mark a "retreat of the state" after all? Is sovereignty itself now conditional upon states fulfilling certain domestic or international obligations?

4 The chapter hedges its bets by endorsing a Grotian rather than a Kantian picture of governance. But actual global governance and world law are in flux. What would count as major steps toward a more "Kantian" world? What reforms in the structure or behavior of the UN would move governance in that direction?

Further Reading

John Braithwaite and Peter Drahos, *Global Business Regulation* (Cambridge University Press, 2000)

Antonio Cassese, Paola Gaeta, and John R. W. D. Jones, *The Rome Statute of the International Criminal Court: A Commentary* (3 vols.) (Oxford University Press, 2002)

Mary Ann Glendon, *A World Made New: Eleanor Roosevelt and the Universal Declaration of Human Rights* (Random House, 2001)

John Hagan, *Justice in the Balkans: Prosecuting War Crimes in the Hague Tribunal* (University of Chicago Press, 2003)

Anne-Marie Slaughter, *A New World Order* (Princeton University Press, 2004)

Thomas G. Weiss and Sam Daws, *Oxford Handbook on the United Nations* (Oxford University Press, 2007)

8

GLOBAL CIVIL SOCIETY AND THE VOICES OF CHANGE

- Violence Against Women as a Global Problem
- Women Mobilizing for Change
- The Global Association Revolution
- Interpreting Global Civil Society
- Power Shift?
- Summary and Conclusion

Violence Against Women as a Global Problem

In the summer of 2007, Egyptian leaders mounted a strong public campaign against their country's entrenched tradition of cutting girls' genitals before marriage (Slackman 2007). Religious figures, government officials, and women activists united to denounce the practice and support an outright ban. They faced opposition in many traditional communities where families were reluctant to risk dishonor by deviating from an old norm. A reporter visiting a clinic that had been shut down after a girl died there due to careless cutting of her clitoris found villagers unapologetic. "They will not stop us," shouted one local shop owner, "We support circumcision!" (ibid.). To many Egyptians like him, cutting was still the natural thing to do. So it was in local practice: by some estimates, 90 percent of Egyptian women had experienced the procedure. But the campaign gained ground, bolstered by arguments that Islam did not sanctify the practice. Egypt was poised to make a change, going beyond a ban imposed in 1996 that had left a large loophole for "emergency" circumcisions.

The earlier ban shows that the issue itself was not new. At the time, Egypt had acted under pressure (Boyle 2002: 2–3). Having ratified the 1979 Convention on the Elimination of All Forms of Discrimination against Women (CEDAW), it had been criticized for failing to protect girls. When it hosted a UN conference on population in 1994, many attendees took the Egyptian government to task for tolerating an abhorrent practice. The ban-with-loopholes enabled Egypt to claim adherence to global norms while still accommodating local preferences. But its effect proved limited, foreign dismay did not let up, and within the country itself critics became more numerous. Though fueled by domestic concern, the 2007 campaign against female genital cutting (FGC), also called mutilation, was not merely a spontaneous domestic affair. Cutting had been the focus of an international movement for decades, a movement that united critics, mobilized opposition, formulated new principles, and stigmatized the practice. The critique had been incorporated in the policies of intergovernmental organizations (IGOs), like the World Health Organization (WHO), and adopted by several governments as part of their foreign policy. Acting on their own moral fervor, Egyptian circumcision opponents joined a broader movement, reflecting a new way of thinking about women's place in world society.

That broader movement was itself part of an emerging global civil society, which complements the institutions of world society discussed in previous chapters. Conventionally, "civil society" refers to "the sphere of institutions, organizations and individuals located between the family, the state and the market in which people associate voluntarily to advance common interests" (Anheier 2004: 22). "Global civil society" stretches the term but preserves the idea of voluntary associations beyond states and markets or corporations, as a "third force" on the world stage (Florini 2000). This civil society grows through globalization and its participants in turn are active globalizers, within limits this chapter describes.

The women's movement's roots reach back to at least the mid-1970s. For a decade or more, feminists in many Western countries had already been agitating for greater gender equality. Realizing they had a common cause, various women's groups had also begun to bundle their efforts internationally. When the UN declared 1975–85 the Decade for Women, itself a reflection of how its collective consciousness had been raised, such bundling became that much easier. Major conferences on women in 1975, 1980, and 1985 not only drew diplomats representing the various UN member countries but also provided an unofficial platform for nongovernmental organizations (NGOs) to raise their voices, get connected, and organize joint efforts. Among those efforts was an attempt to eliminate FGC, a manifest result of old-fashioned patriarchy and a clear violation of women's equality in the eyes of most liberal feminists. As early as 1976, for example, many participants in the First International Tribune on Crimes against Women in Brussels spoke out against FGC (Keck and Sikkink 1998: 175). Through such actions, women's groups played a critical role in raising international interest in the issue (Boyle 2002: 45), and that interest in turn helped to fuel the women's movement itself.

On some occasions, such as a boycott of an FGC session at a major NGO meeting in 1980, African women took exception, accusing Western liberals of unfairly targeting a legitimate cultural tradition (Boyle 2002: 67). Partly to skirt such sensitivities, some feminist activists and their allies in international organizations shifted to scientific arguments, claiming that FGC should be banned for medical reasons. While this introduced individualistic values, focused on the well-being of women as individuals, into the debate, it also gave cover to FGC practitioners who simply adopted "forms of cutting with less severe health consequences" (OCHA/IRIN 2005: 58). Not satisfied with limited reform, many women's NGOs therefore stuck with a more confrontational approach, trying to use the media to shame or force states to reform (Boyle 2002: 71). Critical to their work was a new line of argument: women's rights were human rights, human rights encompassed each individual's right to be free from violence, and since human rights were also universal, states were responsible for protecting them (53). FGC became a prime instance of "violence against women," a focal point of international women's activism since the 1990s that challenged the many ways in which women suffered "broken bodies," from trafficking to domestic abuse to rape in wartime (OCHA/IRIN 2005). As the new norm took hold in the international arena, countries like Egypt could not ignore it altogether. Its national struggle to deal with it, first in the mid-1990s and then again by 2007, was in part the culmination of a transnational campaign.

Women Mobilizing for Change

The campaign took different forms. For example, in 1991 the Center for Women's Global Leadership, led by Charlotte Bunch, started a drive to advocate women's human rights at the upcoming 1993 UN human rights conference in Vienna. Activists gathered by the Center developed the idea of an annual campaign of 16 Days of Activism Against Gender Violence, the first of which spawned a petition to the world conference to focus on women's rights and gender violence, a demand supported by some 1,000 groups (Bunch and Reilly 1994: 4–5). Not confident that Vienna would take women seriously, Bunch and her colleagues in the emerging self-styled Global Campaign for Women's Human Rights prepared to stage a Global Tribunal on Violations of Women's Human Rights to coincide with the world conference (9). An International Coordinating Committee organized the tribunal as an extended consciousness-raising session that would feature disturbing testimony on violence against women in the family, war crimes against women, violations of women's bodily integrity, and political persecution of women. More important perhaps than the outcome of the tribunal – not surprisingly, the judges recruited for the tribunal condemned the violations – was its impact in shaping the human rights agenda. As a key event in a "catalyst campaign," it helped to strengthen the women's networks and heighten global awareness (Keck and Sikkink 1998: 181), soon expressed in another major UN declaration. A problem that had been absent from international policy agendas in 1975 became a significant issue by the mid-1980s and crystallized into new global norms a decade later – with "remarkable speed" it had become the shared concern of feminist activists and an integral part of the global policy agenda (192–5).

The global campaign exemplified by the Vienna tribunal grew out of the broader movement of international women's activism embodied in "transnational feminist networks" (Moghadam 2005) since the 1970s. The numbers are striking: in the period after World War II until 1974, some 59 women's international nongovernmental organizations (WINGOs) were founded, in just the following decade 80 more joined them (Berkovitch 1999: 160). The UN Decade for Women and its world conferences deserve much of the credit, since they directly spurred the founding of many organizations, such as the African Women's Task Force charged with guiding African NGO efforts to implement decisions taken at Nairobi in 1985 (161). By the end of the Decade for Women, the international women's movement had grown tremendously, not just in size but also in the range of issues, places, and peoples it represented – it "had become truly international" (166). By comparison with earlier periods, more women from the global South participated in and even led NGO activities (Tripp 2006: 59, 69). By comparison with the feminist agenda of the 1960s, NGO concerns also expanded under "Southern" influence: going beyond gender equality, the Decade for Women refashioned the movement agenda to focus on women's rights and roles in development. In the 1980s, the frame widened still further, as activists like Bunch, soon followed by officials, proposed treating women's rights as human rights, in an effort "to make women's claims more indisputable" by presenting them as universal, indivisible, and inalienable (Bunch 2001: 131). Not only did the irresistible aura of human rights inspire support, it also enabled the international movement to straddle North–South divisions between those who were most concerned about women's civil rights and those focused on their social or economic advancement. For all its diverse issues and causes, the transnational women's movement thus also shared a common set of principles and commitments.

As its leaders would readily acknowledge, they shared a history as well. Since the mid-nineteenth century, women had joined in common causes across boundaries. Over several decades, initially informal links gradually took more definite shape. In 1878, for example, a group of women held the first international congress devoted to women's rights, in connection with the World Fair in Paris; a second such meeting in Washington, DC, in 1888 gave birth to "the first lasting multipurpose transnational women's organization, the International Council of Women" (ICW) (Rupp 1997: 14–15). Strikingly, its international structure came first and the seeding of domestic chapters followed. Led by Lady Aberdeen for many years, the ICW was devoted to "internationalism" among women. Among the issues it addressed were problems such as trafficking in women that would reappear on the agenda after World War II. While suffragists had helped to form the organization, it shied away from taking a position on the hot topic of women's voting rights and actually included antisuffragists in its meetings. Partly for that reason some women activists founded an alternative organization in 1904, the International Alliance of Women (IAW), dedicated first and foremost to promoting women's suffrage. Judging the ICW too conservative, Alliance leaders did not care to form strong ties with their sister organization (25). With the outbreak of World War I, a long-standing pacifist strain among women's groups came to the fore, leading to the founding of the Women's International League for Peace and Freedom. By that time, women had already been involved in a number of transnational moral causes. For example, the American utopian socialist Frances Willard and British temperance leader Lady Isabella Somerset had jointly founded the World Woman's Christian Temperance

Union in 1883, and its missionaries quickly took the message of "drug-free living, sexual purity and women's rights" to places like Australia, New Zealand, and Japan (Grimshaw 2001: 35; Hayakawa 2001). With moral and spiritual goals in mind, fellow Christians had formed the World Young Women's Christian Association in 1894.

All of these women's groups and networks held their own conferences, published various materials, and advocated their positions to a wider public. Though some of their activism looks familiar to contemporary feminists, they differed in other ways. Most of these early groups consisted of well-to-do Europeans and Americans; few, if any, Southern women participated. Slower travel and communication made their networking more cumbersome. One strand of early feminism stressed women's rights as mothers rather than full citizens, arguing for "self-determination via protection" (Berkovitch 1999; Lake 2001: 254). In the context of their time, however, even women's groups using arguments that later fell out of favor constituted a progressive force that joined the larger sweep of internationalist and idealist organizing fervor marking the second wave of globalization. Some of these groups in fact incubated ideas that would flourish again later, moving toward a vision of "equality via non-discrimination" (Lake 2001). For example, IAW leader Margery I. Corbett Ashby argued in 1928 that "[t]he greatest freedom won by women is surely precisely this equal right with men to effective interest in the whole of life." Anticipating the rhetoric of human rights, the IAW declared on the eve of World War II that "[t]he woman's battle is that of all mankind" and that "[t]he sacredness of human personality has always been the keystone of the woman's movement" (Offen 2001: 244, 251).

Inheriting the nineteenth- and early twentieth-century legacy of their predecessors, contemporary women's groups comprise an important segment of global civil society, the welter of voluntary associations formed by people from several countries who work on global causes across and beyond state borders. This segment of civil society also has close ties to states and IGOs; for example, some WINGOs were actually founded by the UN (Berkovitch 1999: 161). Since few organizations have members who pay dues, many derive part of their funding from ordinary taxes, funneled through government or UN subsidies – UNIFEM, the UN Development Fund for Women, has given much direct assistance to NGOs, making the UN an "unlikely godmother" to the women's movement (Snyder 2006). Though many women's groups operated in an oppositional mode, understandably so in the case of groups like Women Living Under Muslim Laws, they were often in sync with what many governments and IGOs were doing anyway. Many countries had begun adopting laws guaranteeing equity for women or establishing ministries to focus on their concerns (Berkovitch 1999). IGOs like the World Bank took such concerns more seriously by focusing on women's education as a way to promote development. FGC was very much on their agenda: in 1997 the WHO adopted a plan to eliminate it, which helped to shape legislative change in several African countries, though enforcement there often remains poor (OCHA/IRIN 2005: 56). Soon after women's groups took up violence as a salient cause, the UN issued a Declaration on the Elimination of Violence against Women. The 1995 Beijing Declaration, adopted at the Fourth Conference on Women, affirmed countries' collective commitment to "the empowerment and advancement of women," to the principle that "women's rights are human rights," to the right of women "to control all aspects of their health" – and to the importance of the "contribution of all actors of civil society." Even if several governments of Islamic countries registered reservations in Beijing, partly out of concern that women's autonomy might trump Islamic norms, the declaration showed that treating women as full citizens was not just an idea pushed by oppositional activists but in fact represented a broader thrust in world culture (Lechner and Boli 2005: ch. 4), forcing countries like Egypt to engage.

In Beijing hundreds of state delegates attended the official conference while thousands of NGO representatives held their own separate meeting nearby. The scale of the proceedings indicated how far the women's movement had come. The declaration marked a victory of sorts for activists in global civil society. Yet the effervescence of the peak event stands in contrast to the routine of their everyday work. Examined more closely, transnational feminist networks pursue big issues on a modest scale with modest resources (Moghadam 2005). Founded in 1985, Women in Development in Europe (WIDE) uses a small staff in Brussels and volunteers around the continent to lobby governments with critiques of their trade and development policies. Since the early 1990s, the Women's Environment and Development Organization (WEDO), has used its small core of professionals in New York to educate women in workshops and lobby other organizations to promote its solutions to women's problems. Development Alternatives with Women for a New Era (DAWN), which originated in a meeting in India in 1984, lacks such professional personnel but claims a constituency of over 4,000 women around the world, all interested in promoting gender justice in development and reproductive rights of women in the Third World. Formed in 1984 by a group of Muslim women led by Algerian activist Marième Hélie-Lucas, Women Living under Muslim Laws (WLUML) has collected information about and supported women' struggles against discrimination in Islamic countries, operating with a small Paris staff and some similarly small offices in places like Nigeria. All these groups spend much time doing research, writing reports, educating fellow activists, and attending meetings. Given their intellectual bent, it is not surprising that scholars play a prominent role – Charlotte Bunch, for example, has long been based at Rutgers University, Hélie-Lucas was a scholar in Algiers before moving to France, and a sociologist started WLUML's Nigeria office. For lack of members, several groups also need to ask big donors for money – Henry Ford might have been surprised to learn that the foundation that carries his name funds the distinctly anticapitalist activity of some women's groups. That activity also shows that women's groups do not just deal with women anymore: like some of their predecessors in the second wave of globalization, many have branched out to join larger causes, notably the global justice movement that opposes neoliberalism (Moghadam 2005), discussed in Chapter 13.

In spite of this larger agenda, women's groups still stand out by virtue of their focus on gender and their feminist inspiration. Yet they also embody key features of global civil society. They include many loosely linked organizations with different but overlapping agendas and competing leaders, creating segmented networks that are common in other sectors of civil society as well. As their record of the last few decades shows, they have also framed their work in terms of broad, universal principles. They share roots in the nineteenth century with many different kinds of organizations. Globalization has helped them as it has fostered the growth of civil society more generally (Ferree 2006): connecting transnationally has just become that much easier for everyone. Their structure, culture, and history therefore exemplify what is happening in global civil society. Going beyond the women's case, the next section examines global civil society more generally, showing how a "global association revolution" (Anheier 2004) has helped to form a distinct new sector of world society. I conclude by considering whether the growth of global civil society represents a "power shift," a process in which citizens take matters away from state control and into their own hands. Because civil society has spread its tentacles far and wide, we will encounter it again in later chapters. For example, civil society groups are key players in global environmentalism (Chapter 12) and in the global justice movement (Chapter 13).

The Global Association Revolution

From FGC to the thickness of credit cards is a big leap. Yet travelers and business people need their cards to work abroad. Banks count on their customers having universal access to credit. Many daily transactions around the world depend on standards that apply across states. It so happens that the thickness of credit cards has something in common with the more dramatic, occasionally front-page, issues pursued by the women's movement: both fall under the purview of volunteers working for international organizations. For credit cards, it is the International Organization for Standardization, which confusingly derives its name, ISO, from the Greek word for "equal." Working together in its technical committees, engineers and other experts from many countries regularly gather to set standards for anything from the pitch of screw threads to the requirement for manufacturing processes. Since its founding in 1947, ISO has promulgated over 9,000 standards in more than 500,000 documents (Loya and Boli 1999: 169). Some, like credit or phone card standards, affect people's daily lives; others, typically more obscure, mainly affect business. In many sectors of world society, corporations and governments ignore the work of ISO, and of its sister organization, the International Electrotechnical Commission, at their peril – in those fields, anyone who wants to enter business, or trade internationally, or qualify as a reputable enterprise has to toe the ISO line. European corporations typically expect trading partners to comply with ISO 9000 certification standards. For many businesses, such compliance also becomes a point of pride, or at least an opportunity to publicize their global bona fides, as is evident in home repair trucks in the Atlanta area that display their adherence to ISO standards.

Since ISO has only a small staff of less than 200 at its Swiss headquarters, volunteers do much of its work. Usually, they are delegates supplied by corporations that have a stake in the outcome and belong to national standard-setting bodies. The volunteers are therefore not starry-eyed idealists acting on their own accord: their role is really part of doing business, and their employers are keenly interested in the results of their work. Yet in working for ISO, they are expected to act as impartial experts serving "universalistic purposes" (Loya and Boli 1999: 177), to find rational solutions that work across the world for the benefit of humanity. Politicking is frowned upon. ISO guards its autonomy by not catering to special interests, and that stance grants it a special authority. Its devotion to rational progress, reliance on scientific expertise, and involvement of impartial delegates not beholden to any party's interest confer legitimacy that translates into real influence. That influence is palpable. By comparison with the women's groups, which must work hard to gain a hearing, ISO and its sister organization in effect constitute a whole sector of world society. Within its spheres of operation, its rules rule.

ISO's work may set it apart from the women's groups but in other ways it is similar. As noted, volunteer-delegates make it run. It addresses global problems. It flourishes in a dense network of organizations, including hundreds of other INGOs and 40 IGOs (Loya and Boli 1999: 176). It derives some authority from its commitment to universal principles, as a carrier of world culture. It exercises real power. But if by global civil society we mean associations that develop between market and state, aiming neither to make money nor to achieve state power, ISO exists at its very edge. Though not interested in profit, it depends on business and has a direct impact on business. Though not itself a government, it has close ties to government agencies. Both market and state circumscribe its reach, since its impact depends implicitly on agreement among states and corporations that following ISO is more advantageous than negotiating formal treaties or solving problems via private contracts. Far from being an oppositional advocacy network, like many women's groups, it functions as part of the global "establishment," closely intertwined with other global economic and political institutions. In this respect, it represents a large swath of global civil society, the thousands of organizations focused on technical, scientific, and professional matters that help to make world society work. Together with associations that represent business sectors, such as the hospitality industry, and organizations like FIFA that manage certain leisure activities, they constitute by far the largest segment of global civil society. They are the kinds of organizations that rarely raise their voices, and typically do not have to. The very fact that their work is routine, even boring to outsiders, tells us something important about the state of world society.

Like the women's groups, ISO also traces its roots to the nineteenth century. As examples from the sports world, discussed in Chapter 3, already showed, at a time when Western powers built their nations and strengthened their states, international organizing also increased. Some of it undoubtedly seemed innocuous to state officials. But even in the early days civil society really showed its mettle by addressing problems at the heart of state affairs. That is the moral of the story of the International Committee of the Red Cross (ICRC), which became the very model of an international nongovernmental organization (Finnemore 1999), though the organization may regard itself as a particular kind of voluntary organization under Swiss law. After Swiss banker Henry Dunant happened to see the suffering of wounded soldiers after the 1859 battle of Solferino between French and Austrian forces, so goes the familiar story, he wrote a memoir describing the horrors he had seen and calling for the founding of relief societies that might take care of the wounded in future wars. Moved by Dunant's observations, influential figures joined him to set up a committee that would organize such relief societies internationally. Gathering state representatives at a series of meetings, the committee helped to fashion agreement on the 1864 Geneva Convention that protected neutral medical personnel in wartime and set standards for care of the wounded. At the outset, then, the Red Cross served as a catalyst for making new rules, thereby altering state relations. After founding relief societies around the world, it also became a service provider, responding to many emergencies short of war. Over the years, of course, the Red Cross and its Islamic counterpart, the Red Crescent, have become global icons.

To gain influence, Dunant and his colleagues did not appeal primarily to states' interests – casualties did not seem to matter greatly from a military perspective – but instead approached officials as Christian leaders representing civilized nations (Finnemore 1999: 164). For Dunant, already a member of the Young Men's Christian Association, this came naturally. Emphasizing the neutrality of the ICRC and its primary commitment to humanitarian purposes helped to establish it as a key organization among states battling for power. Its story served as an inspiring example of how voluntary efforts by concerned citizens, acting on a sense of high principle while disregarding national loyalties, could make states change course for the benefit of humanity. Though Dunant himself had lapsed into obscurity by 1901, living very simply in a hospice in a small village, it was no accident that he received the first Nobel Peace Prize that year, along with a renowned French peace activist. As it branched out across the globe, the ICRC in alliance with a federation of national societies in what it called the International Red Cross and Red Crescent Movement, the Red Cross gradually lost its Christian connotations, presenting itself instead as a generic humanitarian organization professing commitment to world-cultural principles of individualism and universalism, of voluntaristic authority in the service of progress and world citizenship (Boli and Thomas 1997). By the late-twentieth century, it explicitly claimed "humanity" (ensuring respect of all human beings), "impartiality" (eschewing discrimination), "independence" (autonomy from governments), "voluntary service" (relief not prompted by gain), and "universality" (a worldwide movement in which all societies have equal status) as its core tenets. Already a model for other organizations shortly after its founding, the ICRC thus remained an exemplary member of global civil society, rewarded with three more Nobels after Dunant's.

In 1997 another organization devoted to alleviating the effects of war, the International Campaign to Ban Landmines (ICBL), along with its coordinator, Jody Williams, received the Nobel Peace Prize for their work on a convention banning the use of antipersonnel landmines. There was a problem in awarding the prize: since the ICBL had no address and no bank account, the Nobel committee had no place to send its check (Mekata 2000: 143, 172). The problem illustrates the nature of the ICBL. Unlike ISO and the Red Cross, it lacked a definite organization and instead operated as a more nebulous, loosely connected network of different groups, roughly in the manner of the women's campaign against violence. Launched in 1992 by six groups, including Medico International and the Vietnam Veterans of America Foundation, the ICBL held its first NGO conference in London the following year (146–7). Its media campaign to raise public awareness, aided by celebrities and victims speaking up for the cause, quickly percolated through international organizations and several governments, putting the issue firmly on the agenda of international discussion. The ICBL ballooned rapidly as well, mobilizing 350 NGOs from 32 countries at the time of an international diplomatic conference on weapons issues in Vienna in 1995 (155). When some countries appeared to oppose adding a ban on landmines to the existing Convention on Prohibitions or Restrictions on the Use of Certain Conventional Weapons (CCW), proponents pursued the unconventional strategy of bringing together willing governments and NGOs in a new forum, beginning with a meeting hosted by Canada in Ottawa. With ICBL representatives involved in drafting treaty language, the "Ottawa process" yielded agreement on a new treaty in Oslo, subsequently signed by 122 countries in Ottawa in December 1997, and going into force in March 1999. While some major countries, such as the US, Russia, and China declined to sign, eight years of activism by a diverse coalition had led to a concrete result in the form of a new treaty. No wonder that Jody Williams declared the ICBL to be a "super power" in its own right (174).

In the campaign, hundreds of domestic groups joined forces to address a common concern – they were in a sense ready to be mobilized. One of the founding groups was Human Rights Watch, illustrating the importance of invoking human rights in addressing new global problems. Paralleling strategies of their counterparts in the women's movement, the ICBL used media images of horror and more sober analyses of the effect of landmines to stigmatize their production and use. Turning landmines into a moral taboo gave an impetus to the diplomatic and legal efforts to do something about them. To effect change, NGOs worked closely with states and IGOs, especially the UN. States like Canada, eager to take on moral leadership on a humanitarian issue, provided essential support for the cause. As an advocacy network, the ICBL put pressure on governments, urging them to do something they might have been reluctant to consider, but at the same time it was not simply

Plate 8.1 Nobel peace prize laureates Wangari Mathai (R) of Kenya, Shirin Ebadi (C) of Iran, and Jody Williams of the US at the Mine-Free World summit, December 2004, Nairobi, Kenya
Source: © Simon Maina/AFP/Getty Images

comprised of outsiders shouting from the sidelines. On this issue, as on many others, civil society advocates and state officials, voluntary associations and inter-governmental organizations, became wrapped up in shared work and a shared way of thinking – part of the same "world community," as Jody Williams put it (Mekata 2000: 174). Even as critics of "the system," civil society activists also became part of it.

From ISO engineers compiling technical manuals to Red Cross medics providing relief to ICBL activists criticizing international weapons policy, global civil society comprises a wide range of activities carried out by volunteers acting as world citizens. They follow trails blazed by nineteenth-century pioneers while also going off in new directions. As figure 8.1 and table 8.1 illustrate, many more people are now involved in the "global association revolution" (Anheier 2004). However staid their purpose may be, INGOs fuel that revolution, having grown more rapidly than IGOs and states (Boli and Thomas 1997). Add the more temporary, improvised ties like those among domestic groups united in the ICBL, and the scope of global civil society looks even more impressive. As a conduit for information, global civil society helps to diffuse all sorts of practices, such as best ways to treat the wounded in war zones. Civil society is in the business of connecting people across borders,

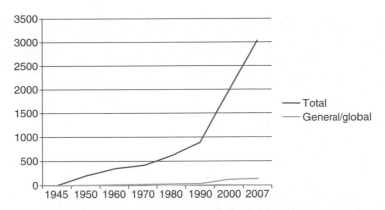

Figure 8.1 NGOs in consultative status with the UN Economic and Social Council, 1945–2007

Note: 1. Total number includes regional and specialist NGOs. 2. General/global NGOs reached 10 in 1960, 30 in 1980 and 120 in 2000.

Sources: Willetts 1996 and http://www.staff.city.ac.uk/p.willetts/NGOs/NGO-GRPH.HTM and UN Department of Economic and Social Affairs NGO database

Table 8.1 INGO growth by category, 1990–2000

Purpose	1990	2000	Growth (percent)
Culture and recreation	2,169	2,733	26.0
Education	1,485	1,839	23.8
Research	7,675	8,467	10.3
Health	1,357	2,036	50.0
Social services	2,361	4,215	78.5
Environment	979	1,170	19.5
Economic development	9,582	9,614	0.3
Law, policy, advocacy	2,712	3,864	42.5
Religion	1,407	1,869	32.8
Defense	244	234	−4.1
Politics	1,275	1,240	−2.7
Total	31,246	37,281	19.3

Source: Anheier et al. 2001, UN Human Development Report 2002: 103

making their interdependence more tangible. It also provides a model for organizing those connections, emphasizing the independence and neutrality of voluntary associations. The inhabitants of global civil society also think globally while trying to live up to a set of world-cultural principles typically focused on the rights of individuals and the needs of humanity. In all these ways, global civil society embodies globalization. Its main "effect" is simply to develop one core feature of world society.

Interpreting Global Civil Society

According to John Keane's formal definition, this global civil society consists of a "dynamic non-governmental system of interconnected socio-economic institutions that straddle the whole earth, and that have complex effects that are felt in its four corners" (Keane 2003: 8). Strictly speaking, then, for-profit corporations might qualify as members. From a historical point of view, that makes good sense, since the concept of civil society served at one time to capture all social activities outside the family that were not controlled by the state. Business counts as a form of voluntary, nongovernmental association. In practice, of course, the for-profit world differs enormously from the non-profit sector. The latter is complex enough in its own right. Even with business left out, Keane has reason to claim that because global civil society takes so many different forms, in so many different connections focused on so many different sorts of activities, it is "the most complex society in the history of the human species" (17). The movements of global civil society comprise "a clutter of intersecting forms: face-to-face encounters, spider-web-like networks, pyramid-shaped organizations, hub-and-spoke structures, bridges and organisational chains" (60). Though its pluralism prevents any sort of easy consensus across its many networks, its "cross-border patterns have the power to stimulate awareness among the world's inhabitants that mutual understanding of different ways of life is a practical necessity, that we are being drawn into the first genuinely bottom-up transnational order" (17). That ringing endorsement would seem to make the question mark in the title of his work – *Global Civil Society?* – moot. In fact, the endorsement comes with caveats. While the idea that civil society might persuade "the world's inhabitants" of the necessity of "mutual understanding of different ways of life" conveys a whiff of romantic faith, Keane himself also counsels against a view of civil society as the home of the globe's good guys and gals, of a "world proletariat in civvies" busy "righting the world's wrongs" (65–6).

Since global civil society embodies globalization, and in a way simply forms one kind of global connectivity, it is not surprising that other features of world society bolster it. As the examples have already shown, civil society does not operate apart from the state system. Far from being implacably opposed to states, many civil society groups receive state support and work closely with governments. NGOs that want to be taken seriously often strive to achieve "consultative" status within the UN system, one way in which intergovernmental bodies endow nongovernmental ones with legitimacy. Markets also serve the interests of non-profit organizations by helping to produce more resources, strengthening communication across large distances, and carving out a space for entrepreneurial activity. In fact, global civil society "could not survive for more than a few days without the market forces unleashed by turbocapitalism," which themselves depend on civil society institutions (Keane 2003: 78). To take one of the earlier examples, ISO is by no means the only organization to benefit from corporate interest in supporting independent organizations. A third global force, the educational revolution, may also pay off for civil society. A larger, more educated middle class will supply more potential experts to staff civil society organizations. With perhaps a bit of academic self-congratulation, Keane thinks that higher education, in particular, "helps to stabilise and strengthen global civil society" (138). The very tradition of civil society, going back to the second wave of globalization in the nineteenth century, reinforces its expansion, providing a path for new groups to follow as they address new problems. The concept of civil society itself has traveled as well, inspiring people to associate freely and creatively even in places that otherwise do not welcome such dangerous independence. As the first case in point, Keane cites the revolt of the colonized against British power in America (35). Thanks to this diffusion, more people in more places have come to think that they can link up to tackle their shared problems. Civil society has become a global model for how to organize globally.

In this way it resembles the scripts for state-building that neoinstitutionalists think account for great similarities across very differently situated countries (Chapter 6). In world society, they would argue, the public space between and beyond states allows groups of people to organize voluntarily, bootstrapping into an authoritative role, as it were. Their activities follow a script, already described above: they choose to mobilize as world citizens, claim to act for the common good, often rely on special expertise, and legitimate their actions in terms of some universal principles (Boli and Thomas 1997). While enacting scripts, they also improvise extensions or venture into full-blown scriptwriting. INGOs are constrained by the actually existing world culture but also push its limits. At the risk of mixing metaphors, they are part of the "software" of world society (Lechner and Boli 2005: ch. 5) but also develop new code. In the neoinstitutionalist picture of world society, this helps to account for change. Instead of state, and non-state, actors always operating on the basis of already-written scripts, which would stifle world society, new ideas also come to the fore through the self-motivated creativity of civil society. And instead of all actors agreeing on how scripts should be interpreted, civil society creates room for disagreement and tension. In short, civil society provides breaths of fresh air in an otherwise potentially stale structure.

Civil society, if one more metaphor will serve, is an engine of world society. From a neoinstitutionalist standpoint, it complements states, which have their own distinct tasks and shape. The size and scope of global civil society has tempted more enthusiastic observers to speak of a "power shift" in world society away from states. The next section asks whether that enthusiasm is justified.

Power Shift?

The hundreds of NGOs present in Vienna in 1993 and the hundreds of thousands of women gathered near Beijing in 1995 left an impression. Their mass meetings made the growth of civil society tangible. Civil society also seemed to produce results, evident in the Beijing Declaration or the landmine ban. By the mid-1990s, then, civil society was riding high. As one influential observer put it, "in numbers and in impact, nonstate actors have never before approached their current strength" (Mathews 1997). But what has civil society achieved? What difference does it really make?

The questions are difficult to answer because the power of civil society takes many forms. Doctors Without Borders goes into areas where states fear to tread. Amnesty International pressures governments to release political prisoners. Transparency International measures state corruption in a way that individual states would be reluctant to do. Such INGOs, key elements in civil society, thus do things that states cannot do, or can do but prefer not to, or just want to leave to others altogether. Simply by virtue of their scope and number, civil society organizations indeed have assumed broad responsibility for global tasks of all sorts. Each activity involves a little bit of power, at least in the minimal sense of shaping the behavior of others. But very rarely do INGOs directly "shift power" by assuming a power states used to have but were forced to relinquish. They also typically lack the traditional trappings of power: they possess no tanks or aircraft carriers, and they cannot collect taxes. Their very presence on the global scene makes them a force to be reckoned with but the actual extent of their power is more difficult to gauge.

In the case of organizations like ISO, however, that power is quite obvious. It makes rules that stick, and it commands support from states and business. In principle, of course, states or companies could negotiate similar rules through official treaties or private contracts, and therefore ISO power depends implicitly on their assent, but the ISO forum has advantages for all parties involved and ISO power would be hard for any single party to dislodge. ISO stands for many organizations that have considerable autonomy and in effect constitute the field they organize (Boli 1999: 268, 289). Most international sports federations, discussed in Chapter 3, have such autonomy: they make their own rules, run their own competitions, decide on who may or may not participate, and so on. Some of the rules, or at least their enforcement, depend on state authority. Banning athletes from international competition due to illegal drug use is one thing, bringing criminal charges based on state law quite another. But beyond such borderlands between sports and the "real" world, federations have a lot of sway, if only because states do not really care how long a game in volleyball should be or how the offside rule in soccer should be interpreted. If all such organizations gain power and states let them, the balance tilts toward civil society. But not much actual control changes hands: in this sector of global civil society, we see some power, not much shift.

More than the autonomous organizations, the ICRC must work with states. Its signature service in wartime requires official consent. It achieved its first historic accomplishment, the Geneva Convention, by persuading, even cajoling, states to go along. Calling the Geneva Convention a Red Cross accomplishment may already overstate the case, since it was a treaty that resulted from diplomatic negotiations among willing states. True, without the ICRC they might not have reached agreement, or they might have postponed the whole process, and in that sense the ICRC's persuasive power had a clear catalytic effect. Yet its power was "collateral," inextricably dependent on the joint efforts of state parties (Boli 1999: 269–70). The ICBL similarly needed states to go along and IGOs to support its work. Certainly, the ICBL made it more difficult for individual parties to stall the international effort to ban landmines, and it helped propel the process by formulating possible terms of state agreement. The excitement of quick success made its leaders feel like a "superpower." But if the ICBL was a necessary element in the global effort to ban landmines, it was by no means sufficient. The ICRC and especially the ICBL stand for many civil society organizations and networks whose indirect power is contingent on many factors, complicating any effort to assign precise credit. In this broad sector of civil society, we see some shifts, but not as much direct power.

What might boost the power of organizations that have "only" collateral authority? The answer depends first on what they try to accomplish. Both the ICRC and the ICBL purposely achieved a concrete result, in the form of an international agreement. For other organizations, such as some of the women's groups, the immediate effect they strive for is less tangible – it may be to "raise awareness" or "put issues on the agenda." In practice, of course, organizations may have mixed motives, but different factors are likely to shape their ability to affect state action or to have a more symbolic impact. Though there is no strategic golden rule, more "symbolic" organizations may adopt a more confrontational approach, stressing moral outrage at a certain practice, while organizations aiming for more concrete outcomes typically get involved in more routine negotiations. Making a big symbolic splash requires getting public attention; working on concrete agreements requires getting official respect. The tactic must fit the goal, and any tactical choice carries disadvantages.

In one way or another, civil society organizations legitimate their work in terms of principles at the core of world culture, a point illustrated especially in the case of the ICRC. Promoting "progress," relying on "science," working with volunteers for some "universal" aim earns INGOs goodwill and support. In specific campaigns, they may apply "frames" that make a problem stand out as uncommonly serious and in need of immediate action. For several decades, "human rights" has served as the quintessential frame of transnational networks. The campaign against violence against women, a creative application of an old idea, fits the pattern. By invoking human rights, it moved beyond an issue that could have been treated as "merely" of interest to women. It put the burden of proof on opponents, for, after all, who could be opposed to human rights? Acting under the banner of human rights also attracted natural allies interested in the same broad issue, which helped to build new networks. As in the case of civil society tactics, however, there is no framing formula that always boosts power. In fact, because any number of initiatives can now invoke the mantra of human rights, that particular concept risks losing impact due to inflation. If everything is a matter of human rights, nothing is.

Especially INGOs and networks that focus on controversial issues must deal with many players. The ICBL contained different groups, each rooted in a national setting; it interacted with numerous governments and pursued its agenda in IGOs as well. In the case of violence against women, women's groups initially argued among themselves, the WHO approach differed from that of feminist leaders, and several key governments were quite recalcitrant. Success in such complicated settings depends on leaders who can exploit opportunities available in the particular structure of power relations, a factor that experts on social movements often emphasize. At a minimum, the structure needs to be reasonably democratic: global civil society flourishes only on a foundation of domestic openness, as we will see again in Chapter 12 on the environment. Without such openness, there is little opportunity to begin with. On the transnational level, unfortunately, the opportunity in the structure often only becomes clear after the fact, once someone has taken advantage of it. With the benefit of hindsight, Charlotte Bunch and Jody Williams made the right moves, but to some extent such activists create the opportunities that help their cause. Their relative success also depends on the contingent state of play with regard to an issue, and more specifically on the relative strength of the players. The ICBL benefited from the support of states like Canada; actual implementation of a landmine ban ran into opposition from the real superpowers. FGC became globally taboo, and various African countries ostensibly fell in line with laws banning it, but implementation left much to be desired due to domestic opposition. Only rarely can global civil society organizations force the issue.

While they sometimes lack local clout, such organizations can also exploit their very globality. Egyptian women activists can go "around" local opposition or official hesitations by appealing directly to outsiders, mobilizing their support, and thereby bring critical pressure to bear at home. Were a ban on FGC submitted to a popular referendum in Egypt, the outcome might dismay feminist activists. If Egypt's ban were to become truly effective, this could have more to do with US congressional threats of withholding funds than with pressure from an INGO like WLUML. Yet the lack of "real" implementation, and cases where implementation is due to due to forces outside of civil society, do not refute the idea of a "power shift" altogether. The fact that Egypt has moved on the issue at all is ultimately due to a change in the climate of global opinion, which was undoubtedly shaped by women's activism. In the same vein, figures like Shirin Ebadi, an Iranian feminist who won a Nobel Prize for her work, may not command a huge domestic following but can occasionally parlay their global credit into local influence. These are instances of the "boomerang effect," when locals go global for greater local effect (Keck and Sikkink 1998). This does not always work, of course. At times, the barriers are high, for example when it comes to women's rights in Arab-Muslim countries. Across the region, survey data indicate, Muslims harbor reservations about giving women fully equal rights (Inglehart and Norris 2003). But the ground is shifting. Benefiting from some air currents in the region itself, the boomerang is on its return path.

Almost by necessity, activist INGOs that pursue a particular cause are "unrepresentative," and this has been a focus of criticism. They claim to speak for humanity but in fact only represent themselves. They may work "for the people" but usually are not "of the people" and do not operate "by the people." Critics who might sympathize with particular INGO causes nevertheless are skeptical of what they consider a structural flaw in global civil society. The term itself implies an analogy: that cross-border crusading or do-gooding organizations are just like their coun- terparts in the civil societies of democratic countries. But strictly speaking, this analogy does not work, for the single-issue fervor of country NGOs is typically tested and filtered by the democratic political process, a process that world society lacks thus far (Anderson and Rieff 2005). Because world society is undemocratic, the pretensions of global civil society groups are hollow: their unstated claim to "represent" the public good simply "elevates the status and reach and importance of what are otherwise merely international NGO's advocating and acting for what they see as the right and the good" (30). But "ballot-free" legitimacy ultimately rests on quicksand; the "universal" claims of advocacy INGOs are mostly an effort to globalize the preconceptions of a particular, especially European, elite (33–4). This does not imply that they are therefore wrong, for INGOs may do good even if their own opinion of the good they do is a bit too high; FGC opponents, moreover, are well aware that their principles are not strictly "universal" yet can make a strong case for their position nonetheless. The "unrepresentative" charge is easy to test in democratic settings, where the ballot box provides an answer to even such well- organized, transnational, and popular movements as the European anti-nuclear movement of the 1980s, which could not dislodge several pro-nuclear parties, and the even more intense anti-war movement of the early 2000s, which could not prevent the re-election of the American president who started the vilified war in Iraq, but the charge is more difficult to apply to groups that address problems in states that are themselves undemocratic, for there the boomerang may in fact strengthen the voiceless.

Summary and Conclusion

Global civil society encompasses a wide spectrum of groups, from activists opposing violence against women to engineers setting standards for manufacturing to net- works forming to ban landmines. They are globalizers who also energize globaliza- tion. Their impartiality and independence, among other virtues, has given them new authority, but as we have seen the extent of the "power shift" in their direction varies from case to case.

As described in this chapter global civil society was mostly the work of secular figures pursuing secular purposes. From the critique summarized in the previous section follows a slightly different way of looking at it, at least at the part that advo- cates great moral and political causes rather than the no-less important specialized and "autonomous" organizations that focus on technical, professional, business, or athletic issues. In some ways they continue old religious movements by other means: they are "nineteenth-century missionaries in modern dress" (Anderson and

Rieff 2005: 32). But thinking of human rights organizations as the Jesuits of the third wave, or development organizations as the Maryknoll Order, reminds us that in the past many voluntary associations devoted to public causes and inspired by universal principles were religiously motivated. Anti-Slavery International, perhaps the first modern transnational movement organization, owed much to its evangelical leadership. The very name of the original Red Cross is telling. Several of the second-wave women's movements, described earlier, were also seriously Christian. More religiously focused groups were among the pioneers in global civil society. Real Christian missionaries traveled as much as later quasi-missionaries: along with Sufi orders and Buddhist monks they long-ago carried their message and example "across vast spaces before those places became nation-states or even states," and "[s]uch religious peripatetics *were* versions of civil society" (Rudolph 1997: 1; emphasis in original).

That it is now common to equate civil society with secular activism, and the analogy to missionaries might in fact cause offense, itself reflects the outcome of a cultural struggle that took place in many Western societies, which diminished the social role of religion. But, of course, religion has by no means disappeared from the global scene. In fact, as global civil society in the sense of this chapter grew, so did religious associations. As table 8.1 indicated, religious INGOs are going strong, reaching nearly 2,000 in 2000. A more fine-grained count in data for 1994 actually found more than 3,000 religious international nongovernmental organizations (RINGOs), from the International Christian Cycling Club to the World Council of Churches, with Christian RINGOs making up about four-fifths of the total (Boli and Brewington 2007). RINGOs still differ from other INGOs in that many are obviously dedicated to spreading a particular faith and recruit fellow adherents only, but even more than the religious orders of old many are also devoted to doing good in this world, adapting their religious commitments to the dominant institutions of secular world society (223).

The rise of RINGOs is only part of the story of the changing role of religion in world society. The next chapter picks up that story to consider how religious traditions can flourish in globalization and find their place in world society.

Questions

1   The prime actors in global civil society are international nongovernmental organizations (INGOs) yet some transborder campaigns, like the International Campaign to Ban Landmines, take the form of linking mainly state-based NGOs. What might be the advantages of one or the other form of organization? Are both equally "global" in word and deed?

2   Relying on authors like John Keane and John Boli, the chapter discusses some conditions that make civil society actors more or less effective. Could a civil society entrepreneur derive some advice from that discussion? What organization and strategy would work well to advance a specific new cause?

3   Critics charge that the unrepresentativeness of some global civil society organizations is a special problem because they typically do not have to face the critical sifting that occurs in domestic political arenas. Does the claim that INGOs are "carriers" of great world-cultural principles, that they independently serve a universal cause with special expertise, offset that criticism? Could some critical sifting of INGO proposals occur transnationally?

Further Reading

John Boli and George M. Thomas (eds.), *Constructing World Culture: International Nongovernmental Organizations Since 1875* (Stanford University Press, 1999)

Elizabeth Heger Boyle, *Female Genital Cutting: Cultural Conflict in the Global Community* (Johns Hopkins University Press, 2002)

Ann M. Florini (ed.), *The Third Force: The Rise of Transnational Civil Society* (Japan Center for International Exchange, 2000)

John Keane, *Global Civil Society?* (Cambridge University Press, 2003)

Margaret E. Keck and Kathryn Sikkink, *Activists beyond Borders: Advocacy Networks in International Politics* (Cornell University Press, 1998)

Valentine M. Moghadam, *Globalizing Women: Transnational Feminist Networks* (Johns Hopkins University Press, 2005)

9

GLOBAL RELIGION AND THE IMPACT OF FAITH

- The Catholic Church Globalizes
- How the Church Went Global
- A Global Movement of the Spirit
- Islam versus Islamism as a Global Struggle
- A New Role for Religion in World Society?
- Summary and Conclusion

The Catholic Church Globalizes

In June 1979, Pope John Paul II made a historic pilgrimage to Poland. On this first visit to his homeland after being elected pope the previous year, he drew enormous crowds, organized by church volunteers rather than the communist authorities (Maguire 2003: 48). Throughout his stay, he challenged the Polish regime. When its leader praised the alliance with the Soviet Union at a meeting with John Paul, he replied that peace required respect for human rights, including a nation's right to freedom (Weigel 1992: 131). On other occasions, he objected to an ideology that viewed man as a means of production, imposed a deadening conformity, and denied the right to real self-determination (132–3). In his inaugural mass, he had already inspired his countrymen with the ringing phrase, "Be not afraid." At a Warsaw event, he electrified them by calling on God to let his spirit descend "to renew the face of the earth – this earth" (Maguire 2003). All Poles knew what he meant. The pope's actions spoke as loudly as his words: praying at shrines like that of the Black Madonna of Czestochowa, John Paul displayed the strong bond between nation and faith, reinforcing the role of the Catholic Church as embodiment of the country's traditions. The visit had a great impact, both on Poland and on the world at large. It gave Polish workers the courage to confront the regime the following year, when the Solidarity union led by Lech Wałęsa, a pious electrician from Gdansk, began "a workers' revolution against a 'Workers' State'" (Garton Ash, cited in Weigel 1992: 140). A nine-day act of defiance, the pilgrimage also exposed the ideological hollowness of the Polish regime and its Soviet patron. By helping to undermine Marxism-Leninism as doctrine and ethic (Weigel 1992: 35), it marked the

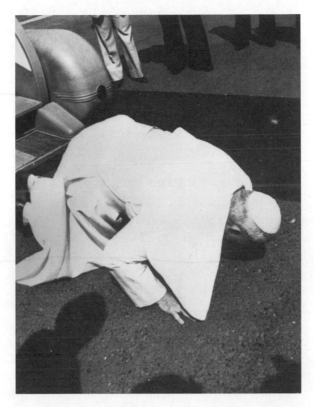

Plate 9.1 Pope John Paul II (1920–2005) kissing the ground after arriving in Warsaw, 1979
Source: © Keystone/Getty images

beginning of the end for Soviet-style communism and therefore of the Cold War. If only for his contribution to that process, which broke down old divisions and set the stage for a new round of global integration, John Paul II gets credit as a key actor in recent globalization.

That was not the only part he played. When he took office, the Catholic Church was in some turmoil. In many Western countries, priestly vocations and attendance at mass had dropped. Liberal Catholics were disappointed about the waning influence of the Second Vatican Council. In Latin America, progressive theologians channeled the spirit of Karl Marx. As befits a pope, supreme leader of a hierarchical organization, John Paul II's first concern was therefore the Church itself. He and his team could not solve all its problems, notably in secularizing Western Europe, but during his tenure from 1978 to 2005 he gave it fresh energy and coherence. However, the challenges were not just internal. In Latin America, for example, where the Church has long been the dominant religious institution, it faced competition from evangelical Protestants who offered a more vibrant and emotionally satisfying faith that they vigorously promoted through networks of independent congregations. In Africa and the Philippines, too, the Church had to deal with mostly Pentecostal upstarts that supplied a version of Christianity well suited to various local needs. Clearly, if only from an organizational standpoint, the Church had to do something, and during John Paul II's tenure it embarked on a "Southern strategy."

In a globalizing world, the Church's relations with other religions rose to the fore again as well. Islam, in particular, posed a problem to the Church: it spread to the Christian heartland in Europe, the overall number of Muslims grew steadily to exceed that of Catholics, and Muslims affected world affairs in dramatically new ways. Church leaders had to think hard about how to position their universal institution in an obviously pluralistic world, and in doing so gave up on old aspirations to worldly dominance and instead took a new place in global civil society. By examining these various challenges, this chapter shows how John Paul II further globalized the Church, "one of the oldest and largest transnational actors of all" (Ryall 2001: 41), and gave it a stronger global voice. Using recent Catholic experience as a particular vantage point from which selectively to discuss changes in world religion, it first describes how he invigorated the institution to take on its competitors in a complex religious landscape, then focuses on Pentecostalism and Islam to describe other parts of that landscape.

In retrospect, the Church turned out to be lucky in its choice of leader – some Catholics might claim that Providence was involved. Karol Wojtyła, the former archbishop of Krakow, was the first non-Italian pope since Adrian VI in the 1520s, well suited to guiding the Church in reaching out beyond the borders of Western Europe. Displaying the talents of the amateur actor he once was, he brought enormous personal charisma to the job of leading the Church, using many hundreds of speeches and television coverage of public events to communicate not just with the faithful but also with a wider audience. With great energy, he devoted himself to "reaching across borders" (Pullella 2002): circling the globe altogether at least 28 times on more than 100 trips to some 129 countries, he covered longer distances than all his 263 predecessors combined. Removing himself from the Vatican – during his tenure he spent about a year and a half elsewhere – he showed by example that the Church was not an institution bound to a physical center but instead a universal community of faith. That became even more tangibly clear in his new appointments to the College of Cardinals, the leading "princes of the Church" responsible for electing a new pope, nearly half of whom hailed from developing countries. Though Poland had his special attention, both the pope's travels and his appointments reflected the shift in the Church's center of gravity: like Christianity as a whole, the Church moved South (Jenkins 2002). Using all modern media, he also preached a new kind of message, engaging the world in a different way than most of his predecessors. Via speeches and encyclicals, he committed the Church to the pursuit of human rights, the defense of religious liberty, and the cultivation of global solidarity – addressing what he viewed as the needs of humanity rather than only of Catholics. In this way, a more global institution led by a global celebrity advanced a distinctly global message.

How the Church Went Global

Though John Paul II changed the Church, he built on the work of his predecessors. Just as major figures rebuilt the world economy after World War II, Church leaders began to think about how to adapt its old ways to a new world. In 1962, Pope John XXIII convened the Second Vatican Council (Vatican II), a gathering of bishops that would reconsider Church doctrine on a wide range of issues. His encyclical *Pacem in Terris* (1963), which adopted much of the Universal Declaration of Human Rights as properly Catholic, helped to set a liberal tone. At Vatican II, Europeans were already in the minority: the American delegation was the largest, with over 200 bishops, and Asia and Africa sent 228 (Casanova 1997: 135). After much debate in four three-month sessions over four years, it issued 16 major documents that took decidedly progressive steps in calling for translations of the Latin liturgy into the modern languages, affirming the collegiality of bishops and pope, encouraging dialogue with other Christians, and addressing the secular world in a realistic manner, without triumphalism or condemnation (Bokenkotter 1977: 387–9). Upon taking office after the untimely death of John XXIII, Pope Paul VI appeared to side with the progressives when he opened the second session of the Council by emphasizing the need to renew the Church, unite all Christians, and engage in dialogue with the world (383). Between the third and final sessions, he traveled to a Eucharistic Congress in Bombay, where he enjoyed an enthusiastic reception from large Indian crowds, and as the Council discussed peace and the community of nations in its final session in 1965, he traveled to New York to address the UN, setting a precedent for his successor. In the spirit of Vatican II and long before John Paul II, he reached out to the world. So did the Council itself. Perhaps most strikingly, its 1965 Declaration on Religious Freedom, *Dignitatis Humanae*, affirmed the importance of human rights in Catholic social doctrine, which thus absorbed and expanded a key global value.

Thanks to the Council, the Church of the mid-1960s seemed fully prepared to participate in the third wave of globalization by internationalizing its own affairs, especially by granting more authority to bishops, and by accommodating national differences, particularly through the language of the mass. As envisioned, the accommodation would be no mere concession to the world; rather, Church leaders aimed for what came to be called "inculturation," a process strikingly analogous to secular instances of "glocalization," in which the Christian message would transform a culture but in turn be transformed by it (Burns 2001: 84–6). The Council, then, was "the occasion of a fundamental shift in the Church's understanding of its social and institutional place in a pluralistic world": as a "transnational" Church, it was no longer committed to the ideal "of a single ideal religious order in which Catholicism would hold a privileged place," nor to the ideal of a "single normative model of political and economic order" (Hollenbach 1998: 88–90).

Yet the Church did not sail smoothly from Vatican II to John Paul II. Though committed to the spirit of Vatican II, Pope Paul VI appeared to distance the Church from its secular surroundings and in the process reasserted papal authority against the majority leanings among the bishops when he issued the encyclical *Humanae Vitae* in 1968, which took a conservative stance on sexual matters and birth control. At least to critics, it seemed that through these and other actions "Romanization" soon balanced the promised internationalization or transnationalization of the Church (Casanova 1997: 134–5). Karol Wojtyła, an active figure at the Council sessions, thus inherited a complex legacy, as he tried to apply many of its teachings in the spirit of John XXIII while also continuing to tighten the reins as Paul VI had begun to do. Following Paul, he tended the central roots of the institution while enabling it to branch out. Like any Catholic leader, he believed deeply in the core of the faith – the unique saving power of Jesus Christ and the unique role of the Church in bringing humanity closer to God. In matters of Church policy, such as the celibacy of priests, or matters of moral teaching, such as the condemnation of abortion, he steered a traditionalist course. He further dashed liberal hopes by limiting the autonomy of bishops and appointing people in his own conservative mold. At the same time, following John, he also used his unique pulpit to preach the dignity and rights of every person as a universal principle for all humanity, becoming, so to speak, "the high priest of a new universal civil religion of humanity" (125–6). Following both his predecessors, he continued the dialogue with other religions, albeit from a specifically Christian standpoint, emphasizing how they showed "the unity of humankind with regard to the eternal and ultimate destiny of man" (cited in Sherwin and Kasimow 1999: 27). Out of the elements of Church tradition, he fashioned a new global role.

An older legacy shaped his tenure as well. In the nineteenth century, during the second wave of globalization, the Church experienced a revival in Europe when conservatives flocked to it as a bulwark against the godless modernization attempted by the liberals who ran many states (Bokenkotter 1977: ch. 25). Priests at risk of becoming civil servants looked to the pope for protection, strengthening his hand within the Church. After much military wrangling, the pope had to give up his traditional territorial claims when Italy unified as a nation, and as liberal states tightened their grip on people and land, the Church and the papacy had no choice but to "deterritorialize." But as they were losing temporal authority, the popes worked hard to heighten their spiritual power. The key figure was Pius IX, in office from 1846 to 1878. Through audiences that enabled ordinary believers to get close to him, he cultivated personal devotion to the pope as a key element of Catholic practice. He revived devotion to Mary as integral to the faith and in 1854 proclaimed the dogma of the Immaculate Conception. A die-hard conservative, he famously denounced the ways of the modern world, including rationalism and socialism, in his *Syllabus of Errors* (1864). To solidify his exclusive authority over Church affairs, he convened the First Vatican Council in 1869, which the following year adopted the dogma holding that the pope was infallible when speaking as supreme pastor on key matters of doctrine. Pius's successor, Leo XIII, was hardly a liberal, but especially through his signature encyclical *Rerum Novarum* (1891) began to lift the Church's "state of siege," formulating a "social Catholic" approach to the most pressing political issues of the day that steered between liberalism and socialism. At the same time, the Church also benefited from the missionary energies stirred up by Gregory XVI (1831–46) and religious orders founded over several decades, which rededicated the Church to the conversion of heathens, especially in Asia – and by the end of Leo's pontificate in 1903, for example, there were 20 bishops in India (Bokenkotter 1977: 337). As the second wave of globalization crashed, the Church was already a formidable apparatus led by one supreme leader but also deeply involved in social questions and mobilized to spread the faith. During that crash, at the time of World War I, Benedict XV spoke forcefully about peace, claiming a new spiritual authority that earned the Church a wide hearing. In becoming a global figure, John Paul II wove together elements of that older, second-wave legacy – Gregory's missionizing fervor, Pius's devotion and strict authority, Leo's social engagement with the world, and Benedict's way of addressing all humanity.

In an institution as long-lived as the Catholic Church, nothing is ever entirely new. The nineteenth-century reforms themselves had precedents in the sixteenth century, when the Church faced its greatest crisis with the rise of Protestantism at the very time that Europe's secular powers began to make their mark on the rest of the world. As in the later eras, Church leaders met in Council, at Trent (1545–64), a drawn-out affair that ultimately succeeded in formulating tenets of the faith and the content of the mass in a way that would serve for several centuries, right up to Vatican II. In Rome, several popes set Church affairs in order by reforming the Curia, the Roman bureaucracy. With other fervent Catholics, Ignatius of Loyola (1540) founded the Society of Jesus, which would take on an important role in spreading the faith and become a model for transnational orders operating within and alongside the main Church – a prototypical RINGO, in the language of Chapter 8. Other relatively new orders, such as the Franciscan and Dominican friars, also became active in missions: "[l]egions of them went forth and did all that seemed necessary for the spreading of the faith" (Griffin 1997: 66). They had help, since "the Catholic religion was carried wherever the Spaniards, Portuguese and French had possessions" (67). To manage the global missionary enterprise, the Church eventually instituted in 1622 the Sacred Congregation de Propaganda Fide (for the Propagation of the Faith), until 1908 the second-highest authority over the US Church, long considered to be in mission territory (57).

By the end of the first wave of globalization, the Church had sunk deep roots in South America and the Philippines. However, in spite of the best efforts of talented Jesuits, it had gained few converts, let alone a major presence, in China. Africa and

Islamic lands were still mostly untouched. Though only selectively successful in its first global ventures, in riding its own wave of globalization the Church made its old universal self-image a little more real. By the time John Paul II was elected, his "reaching out across borders," though new for a pope, was already an old Church habit. In fact, the habit is as old as the Church itself, one reason religion can be called the "original globalizer" (Lehmann 2002: 299). Adding to ancient precedent with new global means, John Paul II made mission his mission, illustrated by his renaming of Propaganda Fide as the Congregation for the Evangelization of Peoples in 1988.

When John Paul died in 2005, he left a Church very different than the one he found: an organization at once more centralized and more colorful had a new élan and a stronger global voice. As he well knew, it was one voice among many. As the following sections explain, the Church enhanced its global impact while competing with other religious forces. Especially in Latin America and Africa, evangelical Protestants made inroads with a livelier, more spirited kind of Christianity. Charismatic Catholics brought some of the same fervor into the Church but could not immunize it entirely. While the Catholic Church still could claim the bigger numbers, with about 1.1 billion adherents and more than 1 million employees, generous estimates reached over 80 million for Pentecostal denominations and over 300 million for the fuzzier group of baptized "neocharismatics" outside self-described Pentecostal bodies (though for convenience I will use the term Pentecostal to cover both). As noted, Islam posed a challenge as well. Thanks mainly to population growth, the world counted more Muslims, about 1.4 billion people or one fifth of humanity, than Catholics by 2008. They had also spread widely, not just southward into Africa but also northward into Europe. Across the West, Muslims built mosques as church buildings were torn down or put to new uses. Even without the Muslim influx, Europe's Christian roots had weakened, but the Muslim presence made clear that a globalizing Church had much work to do in its old heartland.

The number and distribution of adherents tells us that in contemporary world society more different believers live in more different places, and in that sense religion, too, is deterritorializing. But religion also matters for world society in a different way. Religious traditions carry certain images of the world and religious communities help their members make sense of the world in specific ways. None of the communities is wholly monolithic, and their interaction with others further tugs at their core, but they all have their own voices. Through their different visions of world society they mark its culture as inherently diverse if not deeply divided. That among these voices the Catholic one gained strength is only partly due to John Paul's personal qualities. By contrast with other faiths, Catholicism had the advantage of having one leader who could mobilize a formidable apparatus and speak for millions – no Pentecostal preacher or Islamic scholar comes close. In the aftermath of Vatican II, by virtue of tradition and creative adaptation, the Church also found a way to negotiate a common dilemma in world society, namely how to particularize its universal message while uniting the particularities

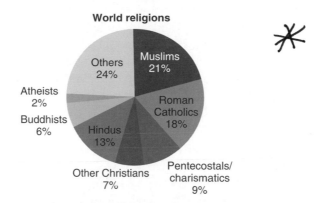

Figure 9.1   Distribution of world religions in 2005 as percentage of global population (6.5 billion)
Note: 1. Numbers and percentages (rounded) are estimates, based on limited data for some regions, subject to measurement error. 2. In absolute numbers: All Christians: 2,172,766,009; Muslims: 1,358,263,004. 3. Others include Sikhs at 0.35% and Jews at 0.23%.
Sources: World Christian Database, worldchristiandatabase.org; David Barrett, George Thomas Kurian, Todd M. Johnson, *World Christian Encyclopedia*, Oxford 2001; also http://www.bible.ca/global-religion-statistics-world-christian-encyclopedia.htm for percentage of Catholic and Pentecostals/charismatics

of its parts within a universal fold. John Paul showed Catholics a new way to relate to the world. But the competition did not sit still, as the next sections describe.

Apart from dealing with the religious competition, the Church faced more secular challenges that I take up in the concluding section. This was obvious in Poland and other parts of Eastern Europe behind the old Iron Curtain, though in retrospect the Polish communists were easy prey. Marx-inspired Catholics, like liberation theologians, presented thornier problems, for they seemed to challenge the Church from the inside. John Paul cleaned house by rooting out the more radical theological strains, on the grounds they had adopted false secular tools and therefore strayed from the true path. At the same time, he adapted the tradition of Catholic social thought, derived from Leo XIII's *Rerum Novarum*, to formulate his own critique of economic globalization and define a distinct Church position on key issues in world society. The "preferential option for the poor," dogma of the Catholic left, found a place in official teaching as well. While he stifled a certain kind of critical spirit within the Church, John Paul also gave the Church itself a somewhat critical posture in relation to secular world society. But, for several reasons, its precise impact is difficult to gauge. In spite of its public visibility at the top, the Church struggled to sustain sufficient personnel in many Western countries – in many places it was weak "on the ground." Church-related groups participated in several civil society ventures, such as movements for peace and justice, but joining secular partners often diluted any specifically religious influence. The sheer variety of Catholic groups, many loosely linked to the institutional Church, meant that even Catholicism did not speak with one voice. Overall, the Church has assumed a spiritual role less focused on influencing worldly institutions, deliberately distancing itself from the nation-state, and defining itself instead as the premier institution of civil society (Casanova 1997: 137). Even if its practical effect is hard to gauge, it has thus set an example that is hard to ignore. Its voluntary disestablishment, a legacy of Vatican II, may well become a model for how to "do" religion in world society, by claiming a distinct "niche" while leaving much leeway for secular institutions.

A Global Movement of the Spirit

His travel schedule reflected John Paul II's special interest in Latin America: he visited Mexico five, Brazil four, and Guatemala three times. The first two countries seem obvious destinations, since they are among the largest Church provinces. But the pope had good reason to attend to tiny Guatemala as well, for in a way it was a spiritual battleground where the future of the Church was at stake. Whereas the country counted barely more than a few percent Protestants in the early 1960s, they comprised about a third of the population around the time of his visits, and evangelical groups were multiplying at a "staggering" rate (Brouwer et al. 1996: 47, 58). Most were Pentecostal, a substantial minority belonging to the Assemblies of God or the Church of God (61). They sprouted in rural and urban areas. They attracted the poor but also the middle class, including prominent politicians. Through the religious enthusiasm that swept across the country, Guatemala was at the cutting edge of a "global movement" (Martin 1990: vii), the "phenomenal growth" of transnational Pentecostalism (Corten and Marshall-Fratani 2001: 1). Rapidly spreading to many places, loosely organized in networks, and instilling a new global awareness in its adherents, Pentecostalism represents religious globalization in action. Obviously, the Catholic Church had to be concerned.

Even within Guatemala, the movement has many parts, and across the globe it is still more diverse (Lechner and Boli 2005: 173–6). The largest single congregation in the world, the independent Yoido Full Gospel Church in Seoul, Korea, led by pastor David Yonggi Cho, belongs to it, with its more than half a million members, a huge campus and auditorium, simultaneous translation at services, and a force of missionaries (Cox 1995). Another part is the International Central Gospel Church in Accra, Ghana, led by pastor Mensa Otabil, who preaches God's plans for humanity in English to a mostly middle-class audience of thousands (Gifford 1994). A third is the Toronto Airport Christian Fellowship, which evolved out of the so-called Toronto Blessing, a series of mass ecstasies at a Toronto church in the 1990s that turned into a long-term revival attracting thousands of Pentecostal pilgrims to the conveniently located site (Richter 1997). While these are internationally

Table 9.1 Pentecostal and charismatic populations in selected countries, as percentage of total population, 2006

	Pentecostals	*Charismatics*	*Total*
United States	5	18	23
Brazil	15	34	49
Guatemala	20	40	60
Kenya	33	23	56
Nigeria	18	8	26
South Africa	10	24	34
Philippines	4	40	44
South Korea	2	9	11

Note: "Pentecostals" belong to Pentecostal denominations, "charismatics" do not belong to such denominations but describe themselves as charismatic or Pentecostal Christians or regularly speak in tongues.

Source: PEW 2006: 2

prominent congregations, and Cho has even been called "arguably the most influential minister in [his] denomination globally" (Anderson 2004: 116), more typical of the movement is the Assembly of God in Campo Alegre, Brazil, where perhaps 200 worshipers of modest means in an equally modest building make up for their lack of worldly goods with gifts of the spirit – the *charismata* that give the overall movement one of its names – singing intensely, giving praise, attesting to miraculous healings, and speaking in tongues at prayer services (Ireland 1991). Campo Alegre illustrates one difference in a movement that counts many megachurches. Pentecostals also vary in style: Campo Alegre might look most familiar to revivalists from the early twentieth century, while in some "neo-Pentecostal" and independent churches ministers no longer lay on hands to heal the sick and they frown at those who feel called to speak in tongues. Their prime symbols also differ: missing in Brazil are Cho's invocations of Korean shamanism or Otabil's reliance on African spirituality. Across the continents, the Spirit has moved millions in hundreds of different ways.

What, then, makes them a "movement"? Some of the parts are in fact connected, not just in denominations like the Assemblies but also in newly created networks, which enable many Pentecostals to get to know each other and work together (Lehmann 2002: 307). Missionaries, whether sent from Seoul or San Antonio, also build bridges. Powerful speakers, like the German-born preacher Reinhard Bonnke who leads massive crusades in Africa, ride a circuit of evangelical events, linking believers in yet another way (Gifford 1987). Mixing modern technology with old-time religion, many key figures also use the Internet to spread the Word. Still, most congregations go their own way, and even more than other Protestants, Pentecostals are proud not to bow to any pope. The movement has no center or leader, no plan or program. Yet for all their diversity, not to mention the distances that separate them, the parts share a common cause. Though lacking the core teaching of the Catholic catechism, Pentecostals have a universal message, namely that Jesus Christ is Lord and Savior, that the Bible is the literal word of God, and that in a new Pentecost the Holy Spirit is bringing worldly blessings and future salvation. Though lacking a strict Catholic liturgy, they also share a common worship style, in which the Spirit descends to move people, physically and emotionally, through song and praise and dance, through incantations that may take the form of foreign tongues. Though lacking Catholic organizational prowess, Pentecostal communities take a similar form as independent congregations led by strong, authoritative ministers that also demand active involvement from members. At the base of it all is the shared faith that true conversion, being "born again" in the Spirit, transforms the individual and puts her on the path to salvation.

More than any other type of Christian practice, Pentecostalism is both "biblical" and "experiential," embracing "the whole person and the whole world" (Poewe 1994: xii). Yet in the end it is the "fire from heaven" (Cox 1995) that matters most: the sacred text is true, but the experience is the thing. Guatemalan Pentecostals visiting Campo Alegre or Toronto or Accra or even Seoul might be surprised at the differences in scale, or perhaps at the relative restraint of the Koreans, but in the many family resemblances they would recognize kindred souls. The similarities are reflected in Pentecostal attitudes: by comparison with fellow believers, they are more likely to think that the Bible is the literal word of God, to assume that Jesus will return to take the faithful to heaven before the end of the world, to have witnessed healings and exorcisms, and to oppose homosexuality and drinking alcohol (Pew 2006). As Christianity moves South, such attitudes gain great global weight (Jenkins 2002).

From the believers' point of view, the power of the Spirit explains their success. Even in more secular terms, the intrinsic Pentecostal appeal seems obvious: it offers not a merely formal ritual but a deep religious experience that totally involves the individual, connecting her with a transcendent reality and an enveloping community. Its structure, or lack thereof, also helps, since any entrepreneur, or any group of converts, can start on their own; no cardinal or bishop will stop them. Of course, Pentecostals are confident in the Spirit's ability to help people transcend language barriers, and their message is as universal as the pope's. More than Catholic doctrine, the message also adapts easily to different contexts – Pentecostals are expert at "indigenization," giving the Spirit a Korean or Ghanaian or Brazilian form even as they vocally oppose being tainted by local tradition. Flexible in form and content, Pentecostalism "works" in different ways for different groups. Some groups, to be sure, prove more receptive than others. Pentecostalism counts many poor people among its converts, and this has tempted some to see it as solace for the dispossessed, as a haven in a heartless world – a simple, satisfying spirituality that serves as the opium of the people. At the very least, that cannot be the whole story, since, as in Guatemala, its appeal has spread to middle-class audiences as well and many apparently poor members are in fact moving up from destitution – it must be "more than opium" (Boudewijnse et al. 1998). It is not so simple either, since being born again usually requires people to change their conduct and separate from society, a price converts are willing to pay to receive blessings in health and wealth as well as the mutual aid that comes from the new community they join. For women, the majority of new members, Pentecostalism "works" in yet another way, for an ostensibly patriarchal religion that reserves authority for men at the same time supports women in holding men tempted by drink or dissipation accountable for their actions as fathers and husbands – making men more moral is the key (Brusco 1993).

Beyond the motives of converts, some larger forces play a role as well. As a deeply individualistic faith, centered first and foremost on the individual's choice to convert and desire to connect with the sacred, Pentecostalism is unlikely to flourish where people are still firmly attached to traditional communities and their customs; only where that fabric breaks down do individuals gain the spiritual breathing space needed to turn Pentecostal. In that way, social change spurs religious change. Even if religion is more than a spiritual drug, Pentecostalism may have had special appeal in Guatemala due to the sheer hardship and violence associated with its long-standing political divisions. The new faith offered a cocoon of sorts. Its adoption depended on many local factors, as illustrated by the different religious tracks followed by communities within small regions in Guatemala (Martin 1990: 215–20). As in Guatemala, so in the world at large: global Pentecostalism follows no single formula. Of course, Guatemala also had a Christian tradition, making the new faith less alien to potential converts. Across the globe in fact, with some exceptions, Pentecostal success is greatest in countries that have been evangelized before.

The Holy Spirit had human help. To some extent, Pentecostal diffusion is a result of deliberate effort. Certainly in Guatemala outsiders have made conversion their mission. For example, American evangelists have long supported Pentecostal institutions and broadcast the Word directly to the country. Perhaps the most ambitious effort was "Proyecto Luz" (Project Light), an evangelical campaign in 1990 organized by the Christian Broadcasting Network belonging to American TV preacher and entrepreneur Pat Robertson. This involved a media blitz on most television stations that culminated in a *telenovela*-style show of conversion stories recounting, as the title indicated, how people had been "rescued from hell" (Vázquez and Marquardt 2003: ch. 8). More than 4 million Guatemalans, some 60 percent of the potential audience, watched, but to the disappointment of the organizers the high ratings of their carefully "glocalized" programming did not translate into a wave of people committing themselves to Christ. The initially lackluster results of that major American push into Guatemala offer just one bit of evidence that it is an overstatement to view Pentecostalism as "exporting the American gospel," a gospel peddled by Americans that also happens to glorify America itself (Brouwer et al. 1996). In most places, Pentecostalism grows by local effort, as in the case of Brazil's large home-grown denominations, and by most accounts, "America" barely figures in actual Pentecostal practice. As in global media, "multilateral flows" and "local expressions of global culture" better capture Pentecostal growth (Freston 1997: 185).

Though in the third wave of globalization Pentecostalism does not depend on American money or American ideas, it nevertheless has American roots in the second wave. Pentecostals typically trace their origins to a 1906 revival in a building on Azusa Street in Los Angeles, led by the black preacher William Seymour, where the spirit seized growing crowds that went forth to spread word of the new Pentecost. Global Pentecostalism thus grew from inauspicious circumstances, among poor and uneducated folk. In a way, 1906 is an arbitrary date, for Azusa Street was just one of many similar events: throughout the nineteenth century, the US witnessed religious revivals that captivated believers, instilling a particular kind of religious enthusiasm linked to personal moral discipline. That enthusiasm in turn has roots in British Methodism, the deeply felt faith of eighteenth-century believers who left the Church of England. Methodism already had many of the trappings of modern Pentecostalism – the seeking of the Holy Spirit, the independent congregations, the itinerant preaching and revivals, the soulful music. Methodists set up churches outside the Church of England, effecting a definite disestablishment – yet another precedent for Pentecostals in Latin America. From a grand historical perspective, the third wave helps to globalize the first-wave Methodist model as developed by Americans in the second wave, in a creative replay on a larger scale (Martin 1990). Pentecostalism germinated at a time when all kinds of Protestants, from both sides of the Atlantic, were already deeply involved in spreading their faith, both to save the heathens and to beat Catholics to the punch. The Protestant–Catholic competition of recent decades thus also replays another second-wave precedent. The enormous Protestant missionary effort took many forms in many places, too complex to recount here, but it firmly planted churches in several places, including Korea and across West Africa. Pentecostals got into the game quickly too, with Swedish missionaries, according to the standard story, taking the faith to Brazil in 1911. But the large-scale conversion Protestant leaders had long envisioned did not occur; China, for example, once again proved to be "stony ground" (Varg 1958: 5). Second-wave religious globalization, though dramatic in many ways, did not match economic globalization. By comparison, the third wave makes possible what second-wave missionaries had hoped. With Pentecostals variously estimated in the tens of millions, trailed by perhaps 12 million Catholics, even Chinese territory is no longer quite so religiously "stony" (Allen 2007).

The pope's travels, then, partly served to counter the "invasion of the sects," as he put it, and the appeal of a competing brand of Christianity, by reaffirming the tenets of the faith, energizing his troops, and inspiring his followers. But his global advantage in marshaling the resources of a large institution could not fully overcome some local disadvantages. In Guatemala, as in other parts of Latin America, the Church had long been associated with repressive regimes, and at times of political conflict had suffered from the perception of being on the wrong side. Its cadre of priests had traditionally been small, serving a nominally Catholic population without fully inculcating the faith. For many people, their Catholic religious identity was mainly a "comfortable reference point," "a matter of baptism and custom in the form of personal devotions" rather than regular attendance or strict adherence (Brouwer et al. 1996: 53). Since the 1950s, a growing number of priests and laymen united in the so-called Catholic Action had used community projects and other kinds of outreach to turn nominal Catholics into full members, and in some ways they rejuvenated the Church, but their efforts came late in the game, at a time when Protestants were already making inroads. Particular parishes went charismatic, infusing the Spirit into Catholic molds, and this helped to preserve a Catholic presence. Progressive laymen and some priests started "base communities" dedicated to reaching ordinary people and serving their social needs. Thanks to such initiatives, the Catholic Church held on in many places and among a majority of people in Latin America. But as in the case of America's lumbering Big Three car companies in the 1970s, the lazy monopoly of the seemingly imposing but actually weak old Church helped the upstart competitors.

With the benefit of hindsight, Pentecostalism seems to "fit" a globalizing world (Droogers 2001: 54): the bodily experience of the Spirit is both personally intimate and easily shared, Pentecostals are cultural "polyglots" eager to cross borders, and they have a vision of humanity united by faith as an intimation of the universal Kingdom of God. Above and beyond the local competition with Catholics, Pentecostalism presents a different challenge as well, by offering a different way for people to relate to the world at large, a different vision of world society. But Pentecostals do not just fit into a world already made; they also change it. To be sure, they tend to be peaceful, and in their daily lives they are typically hard working and law abiding – and some critics charge that they go along too easily. While the exact effects of the charismatic explosion on politics and economics in places like Guatemala are still being debated, one effect is undeniably clear: there and elsewhere, Pentecostals "pluralize" religion (Prokopy and Smith 1999: 15). Pentecostalism breaks up establishments and the very idea of establishment: where the Spirit descends, religion becomes a matter of choice, exercised by individual believers in voluntary communities, accountable to no secular authority. Focusing on the spiritual needs of individuals and the world as a whole, it claims independence from Church and state alike. It creates a "free space" for the faithful, outside socially enforced traditions or politically imposed frameworks, and therefore further "differentiates" religion from society, both the local community and the wider political sphere (Martin 1990: 43, 279). "Cultural," as opposed to socially influential, religion belongs in civil society only. From the traditional Catholic Church, especially in Latin America, this required painful concessions. But for all their ostensible competition and the still-major theological differences between them, Catholics and Pentecostals have actually grown closer in the way they deal with globalization: both peacefully proclaim their faith in the context of an inherently pluralistic world society, endorsing religious freedom and social differentiation as religiously valuable. The religious "fit" with global trends thus also channels those trends in a particular direction. Precisely with regard to the place of religion in world society, an issue on which large groups of Christians may be reaching some agreement, Muslims have had far greater misgivings.

Islam versus Islamism as a Global Struggle

On a visit to Syria in 2001, John Paul II prayed in a mosque, the first pope ever to do so. He had met with Muslims on many other occasions, when he gave a speech to young Moroccans in 1985, for example, or when he talked to Muslim clerics on a visit to Egypt in 2000. For him, these were chances to reach out in "interreligious dialogue" to people who both shared his belief in one God yet strongly resisted his specific faith in Christ. Vatican II had explicitly encouraged such dialogue, illustrating its recognition of the world's religious diversity. Exactly how much actual dialogue occurred on these occasions is less clear, since for the pope dialogue remained a means of evangelizing. For all the apparent openness, he still viewed Islam as a religion that "reduces divine revelation," has "no room for the Cross," and therefore "is not a religion of redemption" (cited in Kasimow 1999: 14). At the fifth centenary of the birth of Pius V, who mobilized Christian forces to defeat the Ottomans at Lepanto in 1571, the Church's chief historian added more pointed criticism of Islam's historic tendency to impose conversion through the use of force, its "all-embracing conception of religion and political authority" reflected in "an entire way of life, sanctioned even at the political level," and the consequent refusal of Islamic countries to accept the full panoply of human rights (Brandmüller 2005). John Paul's successor, Benedict XVI, who as Cardinal Joseph Ratzinger had been instrumental in charting Church doctrine for many years, challenged Islam even more directly in a speech at Regensburg, Germany, in 2006, when he quoted the Byzantine emperor at the time of the siege of Constantinople as saying that Muhammad's new teachings only contained "evil and inhuman" things, "such as his command to spread by the sword the faith he preached," presumably indicating Islam's deficient regard for human reason itself (Benedict XVI 2006). The speech provoked Muslim protest and led the new pope to issue apologies. Church statements on Islam nevertheless display a long memory of rivalry and a certain aversion to Islamic tradition itself. Both the sense of rivalry and the aversion reflect a widely shared perception of Islam's place in the world among non-Muslims. In that perception, Islam is an alien element in an integrating world, distinctly prone to violence, unwilling to accept universal values, and incapable of putting religion in its proper, circumscribed place. That perception has some basis in fact but also greatly underestimates the changing involvement of Muslims in globalization.

Two events helped to foster the perception. On September 11, 2001, a group of Muslims hijacked airplanes in the US and flew them into the World Trade Center in New York and the Pentagon in Washington, DC. Of course, it soon became apparent that they were members of al-Qaeda, a group centered in Afghanistan and led by the Saudi Osama bin Laden. It had been given shelter by the Taliban, the regime that had imposed a particularly strict version of Islamic law in that country. The attack was not the first it had carried out but it was the most dramatic and therefore focused world attention on a new kind of global jihad by a new global network of Muslim militants. Follow-up attacks by related groups in places like Madrid and London intensified the perception, especially in the West, that a new sort of battle was afoot, a replay of the rivalry that concerned Catholic leaders except on a larger scale. The other event took place much earlier. On February 1, 1979, Ayatollah Ruhollah Khomeini returned from exile in Paris to claim victory in the Islamic revolution that had toppled the Shah of Iran. Quite unexpectedly, in less than a year, protests by rather diverse groups with different motives had crystallized into a full-fledged rebellion, led by a cleric with radical ideas about establishing an Islamic state (Arjomand 1988; Kurzman 2004). He was serious: soon after his return, the new Islamic Republic instituted rule by clerics, with a pious jurist at the top, and made sharia the law of the land. Its founders had high hopes of spreading the revolution as a way to thwart America, the Great Satan. As prelude, Iranian students took US embassy personnel hostage, getting the attention of the American public. Long before bin Laden, Khomeini had demonstrated the impact of a certain version of Islamic faith.

The events obviously differ greatly. Iran is mostly Shiite, al-Qaeda a Sunni enterprise. Khomeini was an established, though not a highly ranked, cleric, bin Laden a freelance radical. The Islamic Republic instituted sharia in one nation, al-Qaeda tried to take jihad global. In spite of differences in doctrine and strategy, a similar vision of Islam connects them, once commonly called fundamentalist, more recently labeled Islamist. Bin Laden and his second-in-command, the Egyptian Ayman al-Zawahiri, drew on a particular legacy of Sunni thought, to which Khomeini contributed from his Shiite standpoint. That legacy had been created in the decades prior to the two events by Muslim thinkers – Sayyid Abul Ala Maududi (1903–1979) in South Asia and Sayyid Qutb in Egypt (1906–1966) prominent among them – who had formulated a diagnosis of Muslim troubles, a call for renewal, and a plan of action. In their diagnosis, recent history is a history of defeat for Islam: after being attacked "with sword as well as with pen" Muslims found "the foundations of the Islamic civilizations shaken," exposed not just to political but to "intellectual subjugation" (Maudoodi 1991: ch. 1, 14). Khomeini agreed, lamenting how for centuries "the foul claws of imperialism have clutched at the heart of the lands of the people of the Quran" (Khomeini and Algar 1985: 195). In the common diagnosis, the crusaders' culture corrodes the essence of Islam: it universalizes Europe's original "division between religion and the world," thereby undermining Islam's commitment to "unite earth and heaven in a single system, present both in the heart of the individual and the actuality of society," a system that "reckons all the activities of life as comprehending worship in themselves" (Qutb 2000: 23, 26–8). Again, Khomeini agreed, charging that the "imperialists" deliberately advanced the idea of division (Khomeini and Algar 1985: 38). Much as they scandalize Islamists, alcohol consumption and women in revealing dress are therefore merely symptoms of the larger syndrome.

To combat the disease, Islamists echo the stern call to the Muslims of Arabia made by Muhammad Abd al-Wahhab (1703–1791), to renew their faith by returning to its pure origins, to go back "directly" to the Quran and the Sunna, the sayings of the Prophet (Algar 2001: 10, 31). More than reforming individual conduct, the renewal must change society as a whole: the proper task for believers is to establish an Islamic state applying Islamic law, a state that "cannot evidently restrict the scope of its activities" and where instead "no one can regard any field of his affairs as personal and private" (Maududi, cited in Arjomand 1993: 113). It will be a state based on some "eternal" principles, specifically "the worship of God alone, the foundation of human relationships on the belief in the Oneness of God . . . and in all affairs of this [human] viceregency the rule of God's law and the way of life prescribed by Him," prescriptions that include "the principles of belief, principles of administration and justice, principles of morality and human relationships, and principles of knowledge" (Qutb 1981: 104, 107). Again, Khomeini agreed, calling the sharia a blueprint for a "complete social system" (Khomeini and Algar 1985: 43). To bring about the renewal, Muslims must "wrest the locomotive's control from the atheists" (Maudoodi 1991: 16) and put themselves at the head of the caravan "where we may grasp the leading rein" (Qutb 2000: 318). More concretely, this will involve jihad, or a public struggle "striving to make [Islam's] system of life dominant in the world," in which a vanguard of the committed may have to use "physical power" against the poisonous secular system, in order to "establish God's authority in the earth; to arrange human affairs according to the true guidance provided by God" (Qutb 1981: 12, 55, 70, 75–6). And once again Khomeini agreed at least in principle, for example by urging that "we must strive to export our revolution" (Khomeini and Algar 1985: 286).

Of course, so-called fundamentalists often disagreed among themselves. Dozens of major figures arguing over several decades did not all think alike. In jihadist practice, the main Sunni branch, presuming to represent the 90 percent Sunni majority of Muslims, generally regarded Shiites as enemies. It is nevertheless fair to recognize a shared thrust in Islam*ism*, a term that captures a variety of militant traditionalists, since the variety also crystallized into a commonly understood and widely shared critique. In the latter part of the twentieth century that critique resonated among many Muslims, from Algeria and Egypt to Pakistan and Indonesia. One reason was that the Islamists benefited from historical precedent, since they seemed to follow the example of earlier reform efforts, going back all the way to the Hanbalist movement of the mid-ninth century, the "prototype of Islamic fundamentalism" (Arjomand 2003: 31). At least parts of their message also had a certain simple intrinsic appeal – for many Muslims, the Oneness of God, the importance of law, and the need for jihad all sound eminently plausible. The message fell on fertile ground in societies undergoing rapid change, where especially young people living in cities who were now able to read religious texts and exposed to religious media proved receptive to a strict version of scriptural Islam (32–3). In many places, modernization brought instability, a change in customs, a loosening of the link between faith and community that Muslims had long taken for granted

– Islamists, so to speak, put their finger on a sore spot. Because they called for radical change, they presented a threat to governments, which often responded with repression – Qutb was hanged, Algeria's government waged a civil war – but at times that repression intensified the commitment of a minority. Islamism also had its uses: it gave Khomeini and his colleagues the ideal ideological umbrella for an otherwise disparate revolutionary coalition, and it gave bin Laden a means to claim leadership among radical groups. Such reasons for Islamism's rise to global prominence help to show that the incidents that most shaped Western perception of "Islam" were no accident.

As promising as Islamism's program may have seemed to eager militants seeking certainty, in practice it ran into several difficulties, quite apart from the instances of effective state repression. The Islamic Republic, the one seemingly successful Islamist experiment, claimed to institute a pure version of Islam but in fact innovated from the outset – the Quran does not specify the idea of a republic or a constitution, and both suspiciously resembled models from the reviled West (Arjomand 1993). In trying to hold on to power, Khomeini deviated from Shiite tradition by claiming that the Republic needed the ultimate guidance of an unelected supreme jurist, with effective veto power over key decisions of the Republic's democratic bodies – and his own ascent to that position came as no surprise. The Republic instituted sharia after a fashion, including close control of gender relations, but this provoked resentment among Iranians who disagreed with the authorities' heavy-handed edicts (Haeri 1993). Iran tried to foment resistance among Shiite groups elsewhere but across Islamic countries demand for its revolutionary export proved minimal.

On the Sunni side, al-Qaeda was a much more modest force to begin with, a minority within a minority of mostly peaceful Islamists, a larger group that al-Qaeda failed to rally to its cause. It also had to innovate, building a loose global network by defining violent jihad as a Muslim's personal duty and focusing the struggle on the "far enemy," the US (Gerges 2005), which after the 9/11 terrorist attacks in New York and Washington proceeded to rout al-Qaeda from its former base in Afghanistan. For several years, it managed to recruit new adherents to the cause but it never was able to organize its global network into a coherent strike force or incite the larger masses to rise up alongside it, and 9/11 in particular failed to trigger the desired response among Muslims at large. Apart from improvised attacks in Europe and bombings of mostly Muslim sites, al-Qaeda obviously had no strategic plan to follow up on its US action, ceding the initiative to its opponents (Roy 2004: 55). When partner groups like those led by Abu al-Zarqawi attempted to broaden the struggle by getting involved in the war in Iraq, using terror against Shiites and even arranging the infamous bombing of a wedding in Amman, this strengthened a backlash, both locally in Iraq among former Sunni supporters and more widely among former sympathizers elsewhere who challenged the al-Qaeda version of jihad. A "rebellion within" began to fracture the movement (Wright 2008); with the departure of former comrades it was at risk of "unraveling" (Bergen and Cruickshank 2008).

The radical Islamists were bound to fail. According to critics, politicizing Islam is bad for politics but worse for religion, for it makes obedience to a particular state or policy a mark of being a good Muslim and stretches religious precepts beyond their traditional bounds to justify specific decisions by specific leaders (Tibi 2002). The whole model of restoring Islam in the form of an Islamic state is inherently unworkable, and Islamists have been largely unable to build an Islamic state at all. Where they have done most, in Iran, politicization entailed "desacralization," stripping Islam of its aura by turning it into a mere tool of politics (Roy 2004: 61, 89). Though imagining a return to authentic Islam, the more violent Islamists in fact owe less to the Quran than to the Western revolutionary tradition, which since the "Jacobin" phase of the French Revolution fostered faith in the total transformation of society (Eisenstadt 1999). Pure defenders of the faith are thus always already infected by the foreign virus. Especially in its Sunni version, Islamism is a symptom of the way globalization has already changed the bond of religion and society, and the far-flung network of al-Qaeda and its affiliates demonstrates how Islam is no longer the culture of a coherent community but instead the "deterritorialized" religion of uprooted people (Roy 2004). It may appeal to Muslims living among non-Muslim majorities, as in parts of Europe, but turning Islam into a religion to be adopted by the individual, and then deliberately applied to the problems of society, already assumes one of the premises of Western-style secularization (Roy 2004). Once the unity of faith, place, and community shatters, as it has in modernizing Islamic countries and especially among migrants, there is no putting it together: in its most radical forms, Islamism peddles an illusion.

Most Muslims do not share the illusion. The vast majority does not think faith is central to politics, rejects Islamist parties, and shares democratic values (Bonney 2004: xiii; Inglehart and Norris 2003). Islamism is everywhere a minority taste. Many predominantly Muslim countries have already devised ways of affirming their identity without imposing one faith, as in the case of Indonesia's evolution toward a "civil Islam" that allows for democratic competition, a fairly independent civil society, and a minimal tolerance toward nonbelievers (Hefner 2000). Neither Saudi Arabia nor Iran serves as a model for all to follow. Many Muslim intellectuals have long been supplying ideas for rethinking the current meaning of old traditions. For example, they have argued for limiting the meaning of jihad to the defense of Islam within definite strictures (Bonney 2004; Kelsay 2007), advocated reviving the form of Islamic legal reasoning that allows new solutions to be derived from fixed old rules (Rahman 1982), made a case for a positive Islamic understanding of human rights (Mayer 2007), and even turned the tables on the Islamists entirely by arguing that true Islam can only flourish in a secular state (An-Na'im 2008).

To be sure, such "liberal" arguments face resistance, but the ensuing debate about the meaning of Islam makes clear that there is no single voice or authority that can claim to speak for the whole Islamic community or *ummah*. Partly under the influence of a more liberal discourse, many peaceful Islamists have themselves moved in a different direction as well. The Wasat Party in Egypt, for example, has tried to distance itself from its origins in the old-style Islamist Muslim Brotherhood to enter the rough-and-tumble of political competition, though whether it has truly converted to the civil-democratic gospel is still in question (Rosefsky Wickham 2005). In other countries, too, Islamist groups have entered normal politics, claiming legitimacy as part of "civil society" and seeking public support while being held accountable for results, perhaps the most effective moderating factor of all (Roy 2004). Political Islam takes many different forms, too many to recount here, but demonstrates by the mere fact of its diversity that no single Islamist bloc is taking root (Rubin 2007). Altogether, the force of public opinion, the experience of particular countries, the push of liberalizing intellectuals, and the changing direction of peaceful Islamists add up to an ongoing "moderation" of or even "reformation" within Islam. One implication is clear: the perception of Islamism as representing Islam is a misperception.

Yet the very idea of a "reformation" – with or without capital "R," to invoke parallels with prior Christian experience – is contested. It is contested empirically, in the eyes of outsiders, by cases like that of Saudi Arabia, which may have ceased indirect funding for militants abroad and clamped down on militants at home but still holds to a rather unreformed Wahhabi version of Islamic law. It is contested in practice, among Muslims, by those who disparage the very need for reform in an unchangingly perfect religion – and quite apart from trying to provoke "civilizational" conflict, terrorist violence in the name of Islam serves as an "argument" in an intra-Islamic civil war on this very point. It is contested intellectually, not just by Catholic leaders but even by a renowned liberal Catholic far more sympathetic to Islam than any popes, the German theologian Hans Küng, who still thinks that Islamic tradition makes it difficult for Muslims to accept the key change required of modern societies, namely to differentiate various parts of society as independent institutions and give up the idea that religion could be an unchanging institution "set over the social system to guarantee its unity" (Küng 2007: 648). He thinks Islam needs a "paradigm shift" to really come to terms with the modern world, but more than the popes he is an optimist in this regard and considers a reformation of sorts possible: just as Catholics were able to shed the "integralism" of the nineteenth century, he predicts "[i]n Islamic countries, too, politics, law and the economy, science, education and art will slowly develop into autonomous, secular spheres that can no longer be controlled by religion but have been emancipated in a worldly way. This process has already, imperceptibly, begun" (649).

Whether the paradigm will shift is still in some doubt. Even if a kind of reformation does unfold, the outcome, of course, need not be a copy of Western-Christian precedents – Muslims will have to find their own versions of global models. But if globalization is as deeply invasive as this book implies, they will have to do at least that. Chances are, they will do it willingly. If Küng's judgment turns out to be more valid than that of the popes, Islam will contribute constructively as one faith among others to a world of secular institutions (Gould 2008).

A New Role for Religion in World Society?

Shortly after arriving at the airport of Managua, Nicaragua, in March 1983, Pope John Paul II encountered the priest and culture minister Ernesto Cardenal, who knelt before him. Alluding to previous Vatican criticism of priests serving in public office, especially in the leftist Sandinista government, the pope wagged his finger at Cardenal and told him in Spanish to "straighten out" his position in the Church (Pullella 2003: 94–5). It was only one incident during a trip marked by confrontation, with the Sandinistas trying to drown out the pope's message and the pope trying bolster the Catholic Church against the Popular Church instituted by the Sandinistas. The confrontation in Nicaragua, shaped by the country's domestic politics at the time, also brought to the fore a struggle within the Church. Since the 1960s, a group of Latin American bishops, priests, and theologians had been rethinking the meaning of the Gospel in the context of poor countries, increasingly relying on Marxist ideas, expressing a "preferential option for the poor," and allying themselves with left-leaning political groups – a thrust appropriately tagged with the label "liberation theology" (Gutiérrez 1973). Cardenal had simply taken the logical last step. But Rome had long been concerned. Of course, part of the problem had to do with authority: some progressives did not toe Rome's line. Part of it had to do with substance: Marx and Jesus mixed uneasily. But also at issue was the Church's relation to society: if the Church was to claim autonomy, it could not fully join any secular power. From that point of view, Cardenal in particular had gone too far, at a time when the post-Vatican II Church had begun to shed its "integralist" pretension to worldly involvement. It had to, and wanted to, keep a critical distance, as an independent institution of civil society.

Independent did not mean irrelevant. The distance was critical in more ways than one. To the dismay of the Sandinistas, Nicaraguan archbishop Obando y Bravo proved a consistent defender of democratic values. Of course, John Paul himself had already demonstrated the power of the critical distance of the Church as a civil actor in Poland. On a more global scale, too, the Catholic Church sought to find its voice while working within the constraints of a secular environment and a religiously pluralistic culture. How it did so serves as just one example of a track other faith communities, including Islam, may well follow.

One public issue on which Catholics gained a voice was poor-country debt, a persistent global problem since the early 1980s, as Chapter 5 mentioned. When President Bill Clinton signed a foreign aid bill in 2000 that funded debt relief for developing countries, the Office of Social Development and World Peace of the US Catholic bishops cheered that "We won on debt!" and attributed the "tremendous victory" to a grassroots campaign led by religious groups (Lechner 2005: 118). The campaign was a branch of a global effort called Jubilee 2000, started in Britain in the 1990s, that drew inspiration from the biblical injunction to "hallow the fiftieth year and proclaim liberty throughout all the land to all the inhabitants thereof: it shall be a jubilee to you; and you shall return every man to his possession, and you shall return every man to his family." Addressing Jubilee campaigners in 1999 with apparent approval, John Paul reminded them that the original Jubilee "was a time in which the entire community was called to make efforts to restore to human relations the original harmony which God had given to his creation . . . During the Jubilee, the burdens that oppressed and excluded the weakest members of society were to be removed" (120). The biblical Jubilee, prophetically invoked by religious leaders, served to rally support from the faithful and framed the issue in a way that resonated in the halls of power as well. Though secular debt activists and public officials played their own roles, the religious voice emanating from civil society had a distinct impact in this particular case, giving a marked impetus to debt relief as a way of fostering development. Clearly, religious actors were able to "engage the demands" of civil society and through their actions became implicated in it (Thomas 2001: 532).

To John Paul, Jubilee 2000 was no isolated cause. While obviously critical of liberation theology within Catholic ranks and of Marxism in theory and practice, he also kept a critical distance from globalization generally. On a 1998 visit to Cuba, of all places, he criticized systems that "presumed to relegate religion to the merely private sphere" and lamented the "resurgence of a certain capitalist neoliberalism which subordinates the human person to blind market forces," a neoliberalism that "often places unbearable burdens upon less favored countries" and therefore leaves "a small number of countries growing exceedingly rich at the cost of the increasing impoverishment of a great number of other countries" – adding, lest his host Fidel Castro took too much comfort from these words, that the Church provides an answer in its "social Gospel," which "sets before the world a new justice" (Lechner 2005: 122). The problem was perhaps not globalization as such – which he described on other occasions as in itself "neither good nor bad," "basically ambivalent," and with implications that could be "positive or negative" – but lay in "absolutizing" the economy, a tendency, in the words of the encyclical *Centesimus Annus*, to make "the production and consumption of goods . . . the entire of social life and society's only value . . . [while] ignoring the ethical and religious dimension" (123). Made autonomous, the encyclical said, "economic freedom loses its necessary relationship to the human person and ends up by alienating and oppressing him." Elaborating and acting on such tenets of Catholic social thought, many groups affiliated with the Church have become deeply involved in social justice issues. Just as important to the pope, it seems, was to be able to cast critical judgment on the economy as a secular enterprise. Not only is religion a "player" in civil society, it helps to carve out that free space itself.

The pope's judgment was part of a vision of globalization. John Paul thought the process offered "exceptional and promising opportunities, precisely with a view to enabling humanity to become a single family, built on the values of justice, equity and solidarity" (Lechner 2005: 126). Building on the Catechism's statement that the unity of the human family implies a universal common good, he argued that "[t]o give positive bearings to developing globalization, a deep commitment to building a 'globalization of solidarity' is needed by means of a new culture, new norms and new institutions at national and international levels" (127). Combined with the Church's post-Vatican II commitment to human rights and religious freedom, this amounts to a distinct "solidaristic" image of what world society ought to be. It affirms and legitimates certain secular elements of world culture but also envisions a direction for world society rooted in a belief in another world. If recent Catholic experience is any indication, religion may no longer be "set over the social system to guarantee its unity," but now at a certain distance from worldly affairs provides an inherently plural world society with a transcendent and holistic image of itself. Even in mostly secular world society, then, religion has by no means retreated to the "merely private sphere."

Summary and Conclusion

As this chapter has shown by example, world society is in some ways very religious: billions believe, churches and mosques arise in new places, and many faith communities have real vitality. Yet world society is also quite secular: its guiding principles cut across faith traditions, its main institutions do not defer to religious authority, and religions themselves are carving out distinct niches. Religions that once might have had a vision of one encompassing order guided by the one true faith must come to terms with a world society that is socially complex and culturally diverse. But world society does not sideline religion. Religious leaders, and the faithful themselves, are bound to create new global institutions that address the problems of the world from a special vantage point. That this role may be less socially significant than some faith traditions used to prescribe does not mean that it is insignificant. Coming from different directions, Catholicism and Pentecostalism have moved toward a similar track; whether Islam can join them is less certain.

How religion finds its place in world society does not only depend on religiously inspired activism, the creation of a religious free space, or grander pronouncements about the state of the world, as illustrated in the case of the Catholic leadership. By moving to distant places, actual believers help religion to globalize in yet another way. The next chapter takes up migration as a major facet of globalization.

Questions

1 Among the traditions not addressed in the chapter, Buddhism stands out as notably "portable." What organizational or doctrinal features might have helped strands of Buddhism to "deterritorialize," first within Asia and then more globally? How does global Buddhism differ from the traditions discussed in the chapter?

2　Many observers are struck by the vitality of religion outside Europe. Assuming they are right, does globalization get credit for this spiritual awakening, for example because it facilitates the diffusion of faith or because it creates new spiritual demand or because globally competing religions are bound to attract more believers?

3　Globalizing religious traditions also inevitably "glocalize." But in what different ways, in the structure and content of the faith, do they link the global and the local aspects of religious practice?

4　Liberal Christians in the global North and more conservative, and increasingly numerous, Christians from the global South differ in several ways. Within the Anglican Church, for example, Southerners have objected to leadership roles for gay men within the Church and equal rights for gays in society at large. How will such differences affect Christian unity? How might they affect Christian influence on moral issues around the world? Are the Catholic and Pentecostal churches, or even Islam, likely to encounter the same kind of divisive turmoil as the Anglicans?

Further Reading

Abdullahi A. An-Na'im, *Islam and the Secular State: Negotiating the Future of Shar'ia* (Harvard University Press, 2008)

Peter Beyer, *Religions in Global Society* (Routledge, 2006)

Philip Jenkins, *The Next Christendom: The Coming of Global Christianity* (Oxford University Press, 2002) revised paperback edn., 2007

Mark Juergensmeyer (ed.), *Religion in Global Civil Society* (Oxford University Press, 2005)

David Martin, *Tongues of Fire: The Explosion of Protestantism in Latin America* (Blackwell, 1990)

Olivier Roy, *Globalized Islam: The Search for a New Ummah* (Columbia University Press, 2004)

— PART III —

GLOBAL PROBLEMS

10

GLOBAL MIGRATION: HOW NEW PEOPLE CHANGE OLD PLACES

- America and Global Migration
- People on the Move
- To Move or Not to Move
- Integration and its Discontents
- Comparing Ways of Coping
- Living Transnationally
- Who are We?
- Summary and Conclusion

America and Global Migration

Along the roads in my neighborhood, church signs announce services in Korean. Bus-stop advertisements for more earthly pleasures tempt riders in Spanish. A Salvadoran restaurant and a barbershop run by a Vietnamese family adjoin the small local supermarket. That store itself has gone bilingual, labeling its beef as *bistec* or *picadillo*. At the gas station across the street from it, a group of Hispanic men often waits throughout the day to be picked up for jobs. Five minutes down the road, a formerly run-down shopping center has been revived as Plaza Fiesta, catering to immigrants. It is just one of many such centers and strip malls along a major artery serving customers from Asia and Latin America by offering a wide range of exotic ingredients, wholly familiar to their clientele of course, and an equally wide range of services in foreign languages, the native tongues of the many locals who speak them. They are only the most public evidence of the way my fellow immigrants and I have changed the Atlanta metropolitan area in less than a generation, one particular instance of the global phenomenon this chapter describes. As "new people" settle in "old places," they transform those places, and themselves as well, thus unsettling the identities of both.

At the neighborhood elementary school, the children of immigrants make up a third of the once black and white student body. To assist newcomers, the school offers a program for kids learning English as a second language. A hallway map proudly displays the many countries represented by the children and their parents. Like most of its peers, the school celebrates its diversity, especially on its annual International Night. With the support of parent translators and a principal who invested in her language skills, important announcements go out in English and Spanish. In recent years, kids whose parents came from Eastern Europe or Ghana have been among the top students. Yet the school has a thoroughly "American" feel: it is taken for granted that everyone should read, speak, and write proper English, students recite the Pledge of Allegiance every morning and at major events, and the curriculum aims to prepare students for success in American society. By all appearances, most immigrant parents would not have it any other way.

In the early 2000s, some 10 percent of the students in DeKalb County schools like ours were immigrants. As the county changed, so did the larger region and the state of Georgia. In the 1990s, census figures show, the state had become a magnet for immigrants, a "new settlement" state: only North Carolina exceeded Georgia's 233.4 percent growth in its foreign-born population (Bump et al. 2005: 22–3). Here, as elsewhere in the US, most were Mexican, but the Atlanta area also attracted large groups from Vietnam, Korea, India, and Nigeria. As the "flow" of immigrants increased, their "stock" obviously rose, too, reaching 7 percent of the total population by 2000. Settled in particular enclaves, such as the corridor near my neighborhood, early pioneers made it easier for others to join them. In different ways, stores, banks, restaurants, and churches – many run by immigrants themselves – adapted to their new clientele and helped ease the transition. Hospitals and courts hired translators. More than a dozen groups could take driving license exams in their own language. Locally, immigrants became mainstays of construction or landscaping crews and domestic cleaning services; around the state, they took on other heavy-duty work in the carpet industry and in chicken processing. In the workforce and in the wider community, they changed Georgia's complexion, long marked by a black–white racial divide.

My neighborhood, Atlanta, and Georgia thus experienced the advance of the "third wave" of immigration that had already washed across other regions of America. California and New York, Texas and Illinois had preceded us. In 1965, amendments to federal immigration law had relaxed previous national origin quotas limiting the number and sources of newcomers, replacing them with a uniform 20,000 cap per country as well as overall limits by hemisphere, thus enabling more immigrants from Asia and the Caribbean to enter the country. Thanks to provisions encouraging family unification, entries soon exceeded the caps, not least from Latin America. Even if the law did not "cause" the flow, it declared, in effect, that the US was "prepared to accept newcomers from all over the world" (Alba and Nee 2003: 176). When millions who entered illegally obtained amnesty thanks to a subsequent 1986 law, their families added a wavelet of their own. Initially, most settled in and around some major cities, such as Los Angeles and New York; later, as Georgia could attest, they spread out. In some ways, the post-1960s wave was very different from earlier streams of immigrants: more spoke Spanish, more came from Korea,

Plate 10.1 New American citizens pledging allegiance to the United States of America during a naturalization ceremony at Miami's Orange Bowl Stadium, 1985
Source: © Bettmann/CORBIS

the Philippines, and India. At the same time, a larger proportion came from a single country, Mexico, than in the past. Their collective impact on America was dramatic. After a mid-twentieth-century interlude of relatively closed borders, the country opened up again. By 2000, immigrants already made up 11 percent of the US population, only slightly lower than the proportion of 13.2 percent reached in 1920 at the end of the second wave. In the years following 2000, immigration steadily approached the latter figure.

The American experience in turn is part of a wider global process. For several decades now, migration has increased around the world – though not everywhere – affecting not just traditional countries of immigration like the US but many others as well. Migrants are the quintessential global actors, linking more people across larger distances in more different ways. But how many people are moving where? Who exactly is moving, and why? What happens to "old" places when "new" people arrive? What is new about the new people and their impact? And how are they bridging old and new in their own lives? This chapter takes up these questions. It also illustrates how globalization can become a "problem." The point is not that immigration is intrinsically harmful. But when new people arrive, old-timers must adapt somehow – often an uncomfortable experience, at times a source of serious conflict. How to change institutions, how to incorporate (or exclude) "others," how to define who "we" are when "we" begin to look and sound different, are contentious issues many countries now confront. This chapter is therefore also a case study in ways of coping with globalization.

Though the sheer scale of immigration was new to DeKalb County, it coped in familiar American fashion. Adult immigrants integrated mainly through the labor market. For them, becoming American meant first and foremost pursuing opportunity through hard work. Their families also integrated through the many churches in the area, invigorating especially the Catholic Church – just one of the ways in which "civil society," the web of voluntary associations, envelops newcomers. Government was involved, too. The local public school system provided some services, such as the language program in the schools. So did state government, as illustrated by driving tests issued in a dozen or so languages and the translators hired by the courts. The federal government played a role as well. Though it gave little direct financial aid, some of its programs, such as subsidized school lunches for children from poor families, also benefited immigrants. Federal law conferred other benefits: children born in the US were automatically citizens (an instance of *ius soli*, the "right of the soil" or birthright citizenship), and, according to a Supreme Court decision, children of illegal residents could not be excluded from public education. What government did not do also made a difference: neither state nor federal agencies zealously enforced immigration law, enabling those who had entered illegally to live with little risk of discovery and expulsion. No officials stood in their way – quite the opposite.

For some local institutions, integration also meant hard work. Characteristically, schools were once again a focal point. The staff of schools in areas with "transient" rental housing occasionally faced a sudden influx of hundreds of new students with limited language skills. The sheer scale of immigration in a short period presented one kind of problem. Within and between schools, test scores of native-born and many foreign-born kids varied greatly, challenging teachers to help students at both ends of the spectrum. Inequalities in the classroom reflected larger ones. The school district as a whole had to respond to new demands for immigrant services while also adding facilities in the rapidly growing predominantly African-American part of the county – an emerging source of ethnic tension. Of course, such issues are not limited to DeKalb County. How to become part of a new community and how to adapt old institutions to newcomers – how to "do" integration – is a common global challenge.

People on the Move

Just as immigrants flocked to the Atlanta area, they made their mark in many other places as well. In the 1960s, guest workers from Turkey started coming to Germany, and with their families and descendants they topped 2 million by the mid-1990s. In the years after independence, many people from India and Pakistan left for the colonial motherland, turning the UK into a multiracial society. After the oil boom

Table 10.1 Evolution of the number, growth, and percentage of international migrants in the world and major areas, 1970–2000

Major area	Number of migrants (millions)				Average annual growth rate			Migrants as % of population	
	1970	1980	1990	2000	1970–80	1980–90	1990–2000	1970	2000
World	81.5	99.8	154.0	174.9	2.0	4.3	1.3	2.2	2.9
Developed	38.3	47/7	89.7	110.3	2.2	6.3	2.1	3.6	8.7
Developing	43.2	52.1	64.3	64.6	1.8	2.1	0.0	1.6	1.3
North America	13.0	18.1	27.6	40.8	3.3	4.2	3.9	5.6	12.9
Europe	18.7	22.2	26.3	32.8	1.7	1.7	2.2	4.1	6.4

Source: IOM 2005: 396

of the early 1970s, newly rich states in the Middle East attracted workers from India and the Philippines, who even as laborers on temporary contracts soon made up a substantial portion of the population – up to three-quarters in the United Arab Emirates (UAE). Besides the US, other traditional countries of immigration, such as Australia and Canada, also witnessed a larger and more diverse flow of migrants, first from Europe, later from Asia. Particular places changed even more dramatically, as Jewish Iranians settled in Beverly Hills, or Berbers from Morocco in the suburbs of Amsterdam, or South-Asian Muslims in Birmingham or Bradford. Like Atlanta, urban areas in nearly every developed country now contain large "foreign" sections. America's third wave was part of a global wave.

In 2005, the International Organization for Migration and the UN estimate, about 190 million migrants lived outside their countries of birth. Comprising 3 percent of the world population, they would have formed the fifth-largest nation at the time. Up to 40 million more were "unauthorized," living in the shadow of host country laws; more than 8 million were refugees who escaped from trouble at home, down from some 18 million a decade before. Since the 1960s, growth in migration had outstripped population growth: while the world population doubled, the flow of migrants grew more than twofold. In the decades after 1960, the top receiving countries in percentage terms were the UAE and Qatar, with average net-migration rates of 3.42 percent and 3.15 percent, respectively. Israel also ranked high with more than a quarter of its population foreign-born. In absolute terms, the US remained the immigration champion from the 1960s to the 1990s, with a 20 million average, followed by Germany, Canada, Saudi Arabia, and France (Massey 2006: 43–4, table 2; Zlotnik 2004). Since an estimated one-third of immigrants lived in the US illegally, the country led in that category as well. Mexico topped the sending countries with 6.7 million emigrants on average for the period, followed by Afghanistan, Bangladesh, and the Philippines. In percentage terms, far smaller countries like Samoa, Suriname, and Guyana were out front.

The main global story behind these numbers is simple: more and more people moved from "South" to "North," from developing to developed countries (cf. Zlotnik 2004). If we count the former Soviet Union as a developed country, the proportion of migrants that moved to the developed rather than the developing world increased from 47 to 63 percent between 1970 and 2000. In North America their stock rose from 5.6 to 12.9 percent, in Europe from 4.1 to 6.4 percent (IOM 2005: ch. 23). But the simple story is not the whole story. For one thing, North-to-North migration is also important. When the issue became a public problem in Europe in the 1990s, more than one third of immigrants in European Union (EU) countries actually came from other EU countries. Specific events also affect the flow. When the former Soviet Union fell apart, the resettlement of millions of people that once would have been a merely domestic affair was counted as international migration in the 1990s. There, so to speak, borders moved across people (Massey and Taylor 2004a: 1). Political upheavals thus helped to swell the global numbers.

Measures of migration are mostly estimates – no one covers all borders to tally every single migrant, no one keeps track of every traveler who ends up staying abroad, and no census can accurately capture unauthorized residents. Allowing for some fuzziness, the numbers nevertheless show that, since the 1960s, more different people have gone from more different places to more different places – certainly an instance of globalization in action. More universal and more "salient," international migration "is part of a transnational revolution that is reshaping societies and politics round the world" (Castles and Miller 2003: 1, 7). But how global is contemporary migration really? If 3 percent of the world's people are on the move, the other 97 stay home. Obviously, then, most people are not being uprooted, their lives are not being "deterritorialized," at least not in this way. Judging simply by the scope of migration, we hardly live in a borderless world. Many of those who do move also stay close to home, Mexicans in the US being a prime case in point. Overall, three-quarters of those who venture abroad end up in just 28 countries. Far from being evenly global, migration thus varies by region, as Zlotnik (2006: 26, table 6) confirms. In Latin America, for example, migrants made up only 1.1 percent of the population in 2000 and their flow had slowed in the 1990s. In the last decades of the twentieth century, other figures suggest, the migrant stock of many countries actually declined; in developing countries overall, it dropped from 1.3 to 1.1 percent. The former Soviet Union and North America saw big gains, but immigrants comprised more than 10 percent of the total in only nine large countries with a population over 10 million (IOM 2005). Sizable in a few places, the global wave is therefore no more than a trickle elsewhere. Even assuming that official data understate the movement of people, and recognizing that tourists or people on temporary business abroad create their own cross-border ties, the total flow of migrants remains modest. DeKalb County may be the exception more than the rule.

For certain places in the American South the immigration experience may seem unfamiliar, but as a global phenomenon, some historians would insist, current migration is nothing new. By comparison with transatlantic migration in the nineteenth century, the latest wave is not as big and not as important. When European countries started sending people to the US, they lost a larger part of their population than many recent senders. The influx into the US was huge: the country admitted some 30 million people between the 1860s and 1920, and by 1910 some 15 percent of Americans were foreign-born. By their sheer numbers and concentration, immigrants affected Chicago and New York much more than they do Atlanta; Hispanic newcomers are unlikely to change this area as much as Irish Catholics once changed Boston. Only in the 1970s did the overall number of immigrants attain the level of just before World War I. Because the total population had grown as well, by 2005 their stock had not yet reached the level of a century earlier. The immigrants of old had a bigger impact: their labor fueled America's economic expansion, helping to usher in the "American century." Europe benefited as well: emigration lessened social tensions and brought in revenue. For a while, then, the Atlantic world was closely integrated. In the world of the second wave, more than in the third, borders were no barriers.

To Move or Not to Move

For theories of migration (Massey et al. 1998), the relatively modest scale of recent global flows actually constitutes a puzzle. Most of those theories focus on explaining why and where people move. One key idea is straightforward: people move to improve their lives. In some ways, life "over there" must be better than life back home – enough to justify the cost of moving. But if lots of poor people have a chance to move to richer countries, why don't more of them do it? Improvements in transportation and communication – the infrastructure of globalization – make moving that much easier. It is ever-less costly to get "over there" and to keep in touch with the home front. If incentives are healthy and costs decline, that should stimulate many more people to leave home. Why don't they?

In fairness to the theory that portrays migration as a result of rational choice, it does explain part of what happened in recent decades. After World War II, the developed countries increased their economic advantage over most developing countries. The growing gap meant that more people in the latter could improve their lives by moving to the former. Other things being equal, their rational calculations should have resulted in a larger South-to-North flow – and this indeed happened. But even in the global age, distance is costly, so one would expect greater flows where rich and poor are not far apart – an expectation roughly confirmed by the heavy migration from Mexico to the US, by the movement of people from North Africa and Turkey to Europe, and by the fact that most migrants in South Africa used to come from surrounding nations. Given the lure of getting rich and the constraints of distance, moving should make more sense to people with less to lose and more to gain than others in the same situation, which fits the unattached young men who are often a leading edge of migrant flows. Migration thus varies with age.

If costs go up, that should stem the flow a bit, and this is what several European countries found when they started raising income and language requirements for newcomers. In many ways, then, migrants are pretty rational actors, responding to changing incentives in their environment, which helps to explain the overall process.

But if we think of potential movers as rational actors, the key question for them is whether their likely benefits exceed their costs. Typically, those costs are still quite high, whether they take the form of an airfare from Manila, a long trek through the Mexican desert, or payments to a Chinese smuggling ring. Even when life does not treat them well, many people become attached to the place where they grow up, to the sights and sounds and smells; giving it up is hard to do, more so as one gets older. Starting over in a new language, without the support of family and friends, represents a sacrifice. Usually, migrants also have to overcome physical, legal, and social barriers to entry, another cost they must take into account. Those costs add up. From a strictly rational standpoint, then, it is not obvious that many more people should be on the move.

The decision to move is not just an individual choice. Often families deliberate about who should go. Young men who make their way from Monterrey to Atlanta or from Senegal to France carry with them the hopes of many others. Deciding to go means being sent; it represents a collective decision and investment. Some go so that others can stay behind. Money is a lure, of course, and the sheer scale of remittances, the money sent back, is proof – in the early 2000s, the total amount doubled to about $200 billion (see table 10.2). But the prospect of more money from higher wages by itself need not be the prime motive. The opportunity to work also serves as insurance against uncertainty back home or as a way to build up capital to invest there; for example, peasants may use their sojourn to make up for crop failure or eventually make their land more productive. A fair portion of migrants does not actually intend to migrate, since making it abroad often serves as a way to ease one's return, though of course plans can change. Just as ties at home shape the choice and pull many movers back, ties abroad smooth the path. Some migrants are pioneering adventurers, to be sure – West Africans sailing off in rickety boats trying to reach Spanish territory in the Canary Islands may not know where they will end up and risk their lives in the process. But many find their way in a new country with the help of distant family, friends of friends, or people from the old village. Migrants link nodes in a network. This also means that families and communities that successfully launch migrants may have more people move, while those that lack those network ties have a harder time sending their own. Once migrants get settled, whether intentionally or not, they may bring families from home or find new partners there, adding new people to the flow through their own network ties. Migration thus leads to more migration. All this is not to say that migrants do not make rational decisions or fail to weigh the costs and benefits of their actions. Network ties, for example, factor into those decisions by helping to lower the cost of moving. But their decisions are typically embedded in a complex social setting: seemingly

Table 10.2 Global flows of international remittances, in billions of US dollars, 2000–5

	2000	2005
Total	85	193
East Asia/Pacific	17	45
Europe/Central Asia	13	31
Latin America/Caribbean	20	48
Middle East/North Africa	13	24
South Asia	17	36
Sub-Saharan Africa	5	9

Source: World Bank 2007GDF: 54

personal choices are not just theirs to make. There are strings attached, in more ways than one.

As rational actors, potential migrants assess their options in view of the actual constraints they experience. Things beyond their control affect what they do. Perhaps the most important is some big structural change at home. Peasants may have their farms bought out or demand for their product dry up, forcing them off the land. New machinery or a deep recession may hurt workers, pushing more of them to leave. Similar big changes abroad add "pull" to the "push." For example, when native workers become reluctant to do heavy or dirty labor, say in harvesting strawberries in the US or asparagus in the Netherlands, they open new niches to willing foreign workers. In bursts of economic growth, labor markets usually expand, also creating opportunities for newcomers. Even in a more skill-based economy, business in certain sectors needs low-skill labor that is easy to hire and fire as demand fluctuates. This structural picture again does not deny that migrants act rationally – in fact, it assumes that they respond to changing constraints and incentives. But it does suggest that the real force behind their flow consists of more than just the hopes of individuals.

At times, the push and pull are a matter of policy. For some governments, export-ing workers makes economic sense, as a way to relieve tensions in the domestic labor market or increase revenue they might gain from "remittances," money sent home by migrants. Thus the Philippines has long assisted people in moving, setting up a registry for emigrants and a special agency to help them prepare. Faced with domestic shortages, governments can also make a point of attracting workers, as European countries once did via treaties that eased the entry of guest workers or as the US did by expanding quotas for skilled immigrants during its high-tech boom of the 1990s – Moroccans did not end up in Amsterdam or Indian engineers in Silicon Valley by mere personal choice. Though states do not have full control over who comes and goes, their requirements influence the size and direction of the flow. For example, when America began to favor family ties over work skills in granting visas it changed the make-up of its migrants by comparison with Canada, where a point system helped to select those likely to benefit the country. In all these ways, states can make entry easier or harder and turn their borders into barriers. The very fact that they do indicates that labor still does not move as freely as goods, money, and information. The freer movement of these other "factors of production" has fostered more migration as well, all part of an opening up of world society. But regulation of the global labor market also helps to stem the flow.

To sum up, then, migrants exercise choice, given the constraints they face, but that choice is shaped by their ties to others, by bigger changes that push or pull them abroad, and by specific state actions that favor or discourage movement. Current theories combine choice plus social context plus structural change plus policy to explain the "cumulative causation" (Massey et al. 1998: 100) that drives and perpetuates migration. In a way, these cumulative causes prove too much, if only because their joint effects still do not produce a very large flow. Implicitly, they point to limits on migration – limits inherent in the costs faced by migrants, their ties to others, or state barriers. Yet the cumulative causation model reflects some "basic truths" about migration (Massey and Taylor 2004b: 384ff.): it is not the poorest of the poor who move but people displaced due to economic development; people do not spread randomly but favor places to which they are somehow linked; migrants often aim to solve problems at home rather than settle, though with experience their motivations change; migrant networks help to generate "internal momentum" to keep the process going but flows from particular sending regions also come to an end when conditions there finally improve enough. That flows seem to have a limited "natural life" – whether this applies to Mexico as much as it does to the old European source countries remains to be seen – adds another constraint on global migration.

Both these truths and the key factors in current theories of migration fit one kind of migrant quite well, the relatively low-skilled young man from a relatively poor country making his way to a richer country. But the highly skilled are not all that different, though European scientists looking for work in the US or South African nurses preferring jobs in the UK obviously make slightly different calculations. Even refugees resemble other migrants in assessing their options, relying on social ties, and responding to state policies. In their case, of course, the nature of the choice can be quite different – sudden upheavals in their homeland, like the Taliban taking over in Afghanistan or civil war in Liberia, leave many families with the feeling that they really have no choice but to leave. State policies also differ in this case – refugees escaping political persecution can claim a right to entry yet states may also take action to make granting refugee status more onerous, as several European countries did in the 1990s. Still other migrants, like young Ukrainian women responding to advertisements for too-good-to-be-true jobs abroad, may start out as regular migrants seeking better opportunities, partly pushed by structural changes in their homeland though typically lacking ties to anyone abroad, but once in the clutches of criminal smugglers may be treated as near-slaves and forced into prostitution. The sheer scale of such forced migration, involving perhaps a million people world-wide, suggests that law enforcement has at best a tenuous grip on this transnational industry, itself just one sign of the limits of state policy in managing migration. As the examples of settlers, refugees, and coerced illegal immigrants show, the causes that drive migration thus "cumulate" differently for different sorts of people.

Even if global migration is limited in scale, regionally variable, hardly unprecedented, and less impressive than "cumulative causation" would lead us to expect, such points risk downplaying its significance. Some 200 million people are directly involved. Many more "back home" feel the impact through their ties with migrants. So do the communities where newcomers arrive. Precisely because migrants now go to select destinations, their influence in those places is that much greater. How countries cope is the topic of the next section.

Integration and its Discontents

On October 27, 2005, three teenagers running from police in the Paris suburb of Clichy-sous-Bois tried to hide in a transformer station, where two were electrocuted and the third badly injured. Blaming unfair police pursuit for the deaths, the community reacted with a silent march as well as more violent protests. Young people claiming that their peers "died for nothing" started burning cars and clashing with police at night. Officials responded that it was all due to a tragic misunderstanding rather than any police pursuit. The youngsters, from Mauritanian, Tunisian, and Turkish families, simply got scared when, after attending a soccer game, they heard sirens that in fact had nothing to do with them and, realizing they did not carry identity papers, tried to get away. Soon the fuzzy facts were overtaken by events. The protests turned into full-fledged riots, first near Paris, then across the country, making news around the world and forcing the authorities to crack down hard.

These riots were hardly the first of their kind. Since at least 1990, the *banlieues*, suburbs like Clichy-sous-Bois, had witnessed other disturbances, usually involving unemployed young people from immigrant families – *français issus d'immigration* or FII, as they were labeled – who burned cars and confronted police (Mucchielli and Le Goaziou 2006). By comparison with the Los Angeles riots of 1992 that had cost dozens of lives, some French officials insisted, the latest incidents were not so bad – one woman had been unable to escape from a bus set on fire, dozens of police officers and firemen had been injured. But the burning of some 10,000 cars, the nightly specter of police in battle with young people, and the sense that violence was spreading unsettled the French. Something was amiss in the French ghettos, the suburbs that housed many immigrants and their offspring, often in bleak apartment buildings. On the political right, the events confirmed a long-standing fear that aliens, and Muslims in particular, posed a threat to the French Republic, a fear National Front leader Jean-Marie Le Pen had previously exploited to garner one-fifth of the first-round votes and earn a place in the run-off in the presidential election of 2002. Others played down the cultural angle, stressing instead that the young rioters were in effect protesting their economic disadvantage, social exclusion, and lack of opportunity. All sides agreed, however, that the riots laid bare a serious faultline in French society, a sign that integration *à la française* was failing.

France has a history of immigration. As one of the early industrializing countries, it attracted immigrants from across the continent throughout the nineteenth century. Even more than America, France stirred them into a melting pot: it adopted a strong, secular-republican identity, identifying France with certain universal values, and expected all new citizens to assimilate, not least by exposing their children to the common public education run by the dominant central state. In principle, anyone could become a citizen, and anyone born in France automatically qualified. To the state, always in charge throughout French society, immigrants were simply individuals to be incorporated, regardless of their cultural background, to the point where even collecting evidence on ethnic groups was suspect.

Though as colonizers in Algeria the French had had an uneasy relationship with Islam, to say the least, they applied this "statist" integration model (Soysal 1994) to Muslim immigrants as well. About a million came as guest workers during the boom of the 1960s, mostly from the former colonies; as recruitment stopped in the early 1970s, they brought over families and had children, reaching more than 4 million prior to the riots. Most were citizens and adopted the values of the Republic, including the separation of church and state, but many were also stuck in segregated public housing projects and hit especially hard by economic stagnation, a predicament reflected in an unemployment rate three times as high as that of the native-born (Giry 2006). Much public debate had centered on the headscarves issue – whether girls should be allowed to wear the *hijab* in public schools – which was resolved in 2004 with a strict law against all religiously identifiable clothing, a law that affirmed French *laïcité*, the civil religion that relegates real religion to the private sphere only. Behind that issue lurked a fear of Muslim radicalism, a sense that discontent might turn into support for jihad. But French Muslims, said one leading expert (ibid.), had already become too diverse and too Gallic for such radicalization. Their immediate problems were more practical. Economic change had left many behind, past policies had kept many outside the mainstream, and for ideological reasons government had done little to address the situation. Not surprisingly, the riots prodded the French to question their model.

In slightly less dramatic fashion, Germany struggled with the same sorts of issues. Like France, it had drawn many immigrants even before World War II and during its post-war recovery it also attracted tens of thousands of guest workers, especially from Turkey, who decided to stay after the boom ended, but it even more strongly resisted viewing itself as a "country of immigration," instead holding on to an "ethnocultural" model of nationhood (Joppke 1999). For a long time, being German meant being born to German parents, hence children of immigrants born on German soil remained outsiders. Ethnic Germans who had lived in Russia for generations could naturally claim citizenship while "Turkish" kids born and raised in Germany itself could not. Apart from this engrained cultural preference, however, Germany did not have a clear, national model for incorporating strangers, a problem exacerbated by the federal structure that gave its different states independent authority to decide on residency rules (ibid.). But following a string of liberal court decisions that increasingly required treating "them" like "us," a 1990 law formally expanded the rights of foreign residents, specifically by making it even easier to bring in spouses and children. Around the same time, the large influx of ethnic Germans from the east, eager to leave the former Soviet Union, made the anomaly of the millions of resident strangers that much more palpable. A 1992 compromise on asylum took one step toward granting long-term residents the right to naturalize. After extensive debate, and against conservative opposition, a new law that went into effect in 2000 finally broke with the ethnocultural model, opening the door to citizenship even wider. Whether the potential new citizens would truly feel at home was another matter. Though not as concentrated in ghettos as in France, Germany's minorities still lagged in education and income. A string of violent attacks against minorities and the growth of new nationalist groups suggested that many had yet to accept the strangers as fellow Germans.

In Britain, post-war immigrants came mostly from the "New Commonwealth" countries in the unraveling empire, not as a result of deliberate guest worker recruitment. They happened to be brown and black, which stirred considerable public hostility. In response, Parliament via a series of laws increasingly restricted citizenship to those who had a substantial or ancestral connection to the UK – which initially excluded groups like Asians with British passports left stateless due to policy changes in Kenya – culminating in 1981 in the introduction of three forms of citizenship, only one of which carried the right of residence (Joppke 1999). Struggling with family unification after cutting off the primary thrust of immigration, the UK especially tried to limit the entry of South-Asian men, with limited success – by 2001 Asians in Britain numbered about 2.3 million. In the 1990s, the UK was similarly strict in dealing with "bogus" asylum claims. Throughout, Parliament and the government had ample discretion, neither hampered by courts, as in Germany, nor guided by a universalist philosophy, as in France. But while immigration policy remained quite "firm," as officials often stressed, Britain's approach to domestic minority issues turned more multicultural, recognizing different groups as ethnic minorities while at the same time extending the blessings of the welfare state to them. Over time, it supplemented early steps to overcome discrimination with "positive action" in favor of minorities as a way to manage British "race relations." Though obviously not a "racial" minority, Muslims gradually claimed and gained recognition as well, for example by mobilizing in favor of the 1989 Iranian fatwa against Salman Rushdie for writing *The Satanic Verses*. Offic
in-one-nation (Favell 2001) gave the UK no immunity: a sign
ity within the Muslim minority remained deeply disaffected
their ranks bombed the London Underground in 2005.

Like Britain, the Netherlands admitted many citizens from
of Indonesia (in the 1950s) and Suriname (in the 1970s), but
workers from southern Europe, Morocco, and Turkey also
of Dutch society. When Moroccan and Turkish workers bro

and started families, their numbers grew, to over 300,000 for each group in a population of slightly over 16 million. With the addition of 1990s refugees and asylum
seekers from other Muslim countries like Iraq and Somalia, Muslims reached 1
million or about 6 percent of the Dutch population. Like Germany, the Netherlands
hesitated to think of itself as a country of immigration but began to do so in the
1980s. Without much fanfare, it extended benefits to migrant families, such as
generous housing subsidies and worker disability insurance. It also promoted a
form of emancipation that allowed immigrants to preserve their identities, for
example by paying for classes in their languages and subsidizing minority organizations. When this Dutch multicultural approach failed to close gaps with the native-
born and fostered instead a certain ethnic segregation, the country shifted course
toward more stringent civic integration, imposing new language and financial
requirements on newcomers as a way to foster internal integration (Entzinger 2003,
2006). The continuing disparities and the failures of integration policy became the
subject of intense debate. Populist politicians – first Pim Fortuyn, assassinated by
an animal rights activist in 2002, then former liberal MP Geert Wilders in 2006 –
mobilized against the perceived "Islamization" of Dutch society. As in Britain, a
minority of radicalized Muslims departed further from mainstream culture, most
dramatically with the 2004 murder of filmmaker Theo van Gogh by Moroccan-
Dutch Mohammed Bouyeri in the streets of Amsterdam. But while official policy
focused more intently on integration in the early twenty-first century, the Dutch
did not entirely jettison their multiculturalism, as illustrated by state subsidies for
several dozen Islamic schools (Lechner 2008: ch. 5).

Comparing Ways of Coping

As these examples show, European countries, and many others as well, all have their
own "incorporation regimes" (Soysal 1994), their own "philosophies of integration" (Favell 2002), their own "models" (Castles and Miller 2003: 44). The "republican" French model contrasts with the formerly "ethnic" approach of Germany
and with the once imperial, later "multicultural" approach of the UK or, in part,
of the Netherlands. These reflect different ways of thinking about what the nation
stands for, who should belong, and how strangers can become insiders. France had
a particularly clear view in this regard. The regimes organize incorporation in distinctive ways, relying on their own political institutions. For instance, involving
minority organizations in political consultation or extending subsidies to religious
schools fits standard procedure in the Netherlands. The different integration
methods also involve their own trade-offs. France's centralizing universalism makes
it easy to treat strangers as equal citizens but more difficult to confront their economic and cultural difference head on. Treating immigrants as distinct groups for
the sake of giving them voice and resources may also have hampered their emancipation in the Netherlands. Positive action in British-style multiculturalism runs

counter to colorblind universalism that once characterized the welfare state. Each regime or model thus struggles with its own dilemmas.

Describing European and other ways of coping with migration in terms of "models" oversimplifies the situation. For one thing, as even the brief vignettes show, these regimes, philosophies, and models were rarely crafted carefully and consistently; they involved some "patchwork" improvisation that hardly fit a clear design (Freeman 2004). How they worked in practice also depended on where most migrants came from – English-speaking West Indians from a former colony had a different relationship to the UK than newly arrived Turks did to Germany. Nor are the models all that stable. In some ways, nations have trouble deviating from the path they happened to take at some point – national philosophies are sticky, political institutions change slowly (Brubaker 1992). But especially in dealing with dramatic new situations, like the arrival of millions of strangers – those strangers, at any rate, who by virtue of their culture, race, or otherwise present a "problem" – countries sometimes do deviate from their path. Germany is perhaps the best case in point, as it changed its collective perspective on the nation and citizenship quite drastically. The Netherlands, too, changed course, first trying to model immigrant incorporation after the example of native minorities, later stressing a form of civic integration that required more from potential citizens. The national variations therefore evolve. Sometimes elites learn from mistakes, as the French may do in examining their "ghetto problem" more forthrightly. Sometimes they simply improvise solutions to new problems, as in the case of the sudden surge in dubious asylum claims in the 1990s that severely stressed the already tight housing supply in several European countries.

These countries also have much in common. They play national variations on a global theme but they also sound alike. Everywhere, incorporation happened more smoothly when the economy did well, less so during times of recession that typically hit newcomers hardest. Even in the best of times, in every regime, many newcomers trailed the native-born in income, work, and education. The size of the gaps varied but not enough to declare any model superior. On indicators of social problems, minorities typically fare worse, as their overrepresentation among convicted criminals attests. Focusing on some immigrants as "problems" is itself something European countries have in common. In fact, many immigrants do not turn into "problems" at all, thanks to cultural similarity, economic success, or just white skin. In the EU, migrants who come from other EU countries were rarely an issue, until the "Polish plumber" raised the specter of cheap labor undercutting native workers in countries like France. In dealing with familiar problems, countries also watch and learn from each other. For example, when many Europeans felt around the turn of the century that integration was faltering and multiculturalism tearing at the fabric of the nation, many countries adopted similar assimilation policies, stressing that common membership also requires common values, in a manner critics labeled "repressive liberalism" (Joppke 2007). The influx of Muslims has heightened tensions across the continent, evident both in native hostility toward minorities and in public violence perpetrated by minorities.

At the same time that tensions have increased in some respects, native–immigrant relations have also improved in others. In part this is simply the result of integration "on the ground," as the second and third generation learn the local language better, gain more education, and so on. As a Dutch parliamentary commission once put it, integration proceeds even when policy fails (Lechner 2008: ch. 5). Even more striking is the fact that aliens have acquired substantial rights nearly everywhere. As welfare states, European countries typically grant "surprisingly open access" to a wide range of benefits even to people who are not full citizens (Freeman 2004: 955). When it comes to refugees, liberal states in Europe and elsewhere are bound by common treaty obligations they willingly assumed. Some scholars view this as the impact of world society, with global norms enforcing a new kind of proper state behavior (Soysal 1994). More concretely, in Europe such external pressure may stem from legal bodies like the European Court of Human Rights and the European Court of Justice, which, to cite one example, have faulted the UK for discriminatory provisions in its nationality and family unification rules. But the convergence on human rights also comes from within. Germany's own Basic Law already provides ample human rights protections, and the first provision in the Dutch constitution guarantees equal treatment to everyone. In the US, the Supreme Court derived a right to public education for illegal residents from its reading of the American constitution. Global norms result from, as much as they shape, such state practices.

State policy affects how many migrants move and what happens to them after they arrive. But many borders are porous. Determined migrants find a way. For various reasons, states themselves do not zealously try to stop the flow. Similarly, for all their minority policies and welfare expenditures, they can only do so much to "integrate" newcomers. Integration rarely happens by design. But integration, in the sense of fully joining a new nation, also becomes a less plausible outcome. Nation-states do not work as self-contained cages, if they ever did: they cannot keep others out, and many newcomers do not just live inside. Even when they integrate within, they often also integrate across state boundaries, creating new transnational lives, as the next section describes.

Living Transnationally

In the early 1990s, the 20-member Miraflores Development Committee met every Sunday in Jamaica Plain, Massachusetts, to discuss projects in their hometown, a village in the Dominican Republic (Levitt 2001: 180ff.). With tens of thousands of dollars raised from fellow Dominican migrants in the Boston area, they had built an aqueduct, renovated the village school, and, not least important from a Dominican perspective, planned a baseball stadium. Local leaders at a distance, they kept close tabs on the work in Miraflores, sometimes conferring with their counterparts there via conference call. The town gained more than buildings and money, for the knowledge migrants brought back helped townspeople cooperate more effectively, and presents like clothing conveyed US fashions in a way that influenced local styles – both forms of "social remittances." Of course, things did not always go smoothly, as when the sports committee in Miraflores hired replacement players to help the local team win in the new stadium, against the wishes of the Bostonians, who were less eager to win at all costs and wanted local men to benefit from playing there (194–5). As such episodes show, just as the Bostonians were deeply involved with the old village, the folks back home were very much aware of what their kin abroad were doing. On both ends, though obviously more so in Boston, they were becoming "transnational villagers."

The Development Committee was just one way that migrants stayed in touch. Many traveled back regularly. Parents who had left children behind with relatives naturally were keen to know how they fared. Most migrants at first intended to return, but even those who did often left again, becoming part of a circulation of migrants. Dominican political parties, such as the socialist Partido Revolucionario Dominico, tried to gain a foothold among migrants as a source of votes and money, thereby involving them in "domestic" politics. Already a global, well-connected institution, the Catholic Church enabled parishioners and priests to move quite seamlessly across borders, infusing Boston practice with some Latin spirit while making religious life back in the village a bit more formal and church-centered (Levitt 2001: 179).

In the manner of Miraflores, communities around the world join this transnational society through a home-grown tradition of moving. In Ecuador, both the southern province of Azuay and the northern area around Otavalo sent many people northward, motivated by "la YANY" (short for "I love New York"), while far fewer left the equally poor coastal areas (Kyle 2000). With the assistance of middlemen and accomplices abroad, people who no longer could make a living off the land in Azuayan villages found their way to New York to work for jewelers or in restaurants. As in Miraflores, their remittances had an impact back home, not least in new home construction. Since the migrants were mostly men, the villages became women's domain, empowering them by default while also challenging them to maintain a semblance of family life. The northerners, on the other hand, mostly left temporarily to engage in "ethnic" craft trading, not only in New York but also in other major American cities, creating a new kind of transnational enterprise. People from a village with only one telephone could travel to more than 20 countries in one year (202). In both regions, many movers do not "flow" one way but keep shuttling back and forth, many specialist middlemen help facilitate migration as a matter of course, and the livelihood of people "back home," whether as cottage artisans or remittance recipients, depends on keeping the process going. Like their Dominican counterparts, the Ecuadorans, too, have thus become "transnational peasants."

The Ticuani Solidarity Committee of New York, made up of people from the same hometown in southern Mexico (Ticuani is a pseudonym), undertook even more ambitious projects than the Dominicans in Boston, at one point raising some

$100,000 for a new potable water system back home, more than any government contributed (Smith 2006: 2–3). Perhaps 40 percent of migrants from the area are actively involved in such activities, affirming the primary Ticuani identity of the "absent ones who are always present," as a Ticuani expression puts it. They may travel home at least once every few years, contribute funds to worthy projects, even run for office, or give their kids a taste of the social life back home – and some teen migrants flee troubles in New York by taking up gang life in Ticuani, where few males are left to rebuke them (ibid.). As Ticuani turns into a "nursery and nursing home where the young and old await the return of their relatives in New York" for feasts and vacations (39), a place full of spiffy but empty new homes, the flow is bound to slow. Even as the many ties across the border seemed to consolidate by the early 2000s, they might not prove permanent and could attenuate (ibid.), as the second generation becomes more fully "American".

The Dominican, Ecuadoran, and Mexican experiences are not entirely new. As collections of letters attest, earlier European immigrants to the US kept in close touch with the old country; they had their own civic groups to promote "ethnic" well-being and stay politically involved; and perhaps as many as a third of them also returned eventually. But at least for legal migrants who can pass border controls, going home is easier now – a short flight from Boston, a bus ride from Atlanta. Conference calls or satellite TV programming bring home virtually closer. And even as nation-states have become more stringent in requiring proper authorization and pressing newcomers to integrate, at least some groups of migrants "move through" without "moving to." Some of the Ecuadorans engage in this kind of "incomplete migration." So do Polish workers temporarily going to the UK. But British pensioners retiring to the Spanish coast also fit. As not-quite-permanent "denizens," legal or not, they create a new category of people who have moved but not fully arrived. The "transnational society" (Castles and Miller 2003) created by migration partly consists of people living in this sort of limbo.

Not all immigrants are as deeply involved in two places at once as the Mexicans in New York. For example, Russian Jews who felt emancipated and more "Jewish" after moving to the Philadelphia area have little reason to stay in touch with the oppressive home they were glad to leave behind, and though Polish immigrants to the same city remain much more attached to their national identity and travel back quite frequently, they give only some financial support to relatives overseas without formally organizing their involvement like the Dominicans, who stand out for their strong involvement in their home country and think of themselves more as "sojourners" in the US (Morawska 2004). Some groups, then, have more regular and intense transnational contacts, due to "home" being closer and making more specific demands on migrants, but also due to their prospects in the host country, which welcomes some groups more than, say, the "black," working-class Dominicans. The organization of such contacts also varies greatly, depending on migrants' background. With the encouragement of the Colombian government, middle-class Colombian émigrés are deeply involved via formal clubs and Catholic philanthropies in charitable projects like supporting a home for the homeless run by nuns in

Bogotá; poorer, lower-class, and often "undocumented" Mexicans typically focus their efforts on hometown committees like those in Ticuani, partly matched by government assistance; and Dominicans participate in a range of activities, from the very political arranged by authorities in the home country to the local, civic ones sponsored in Miraflores – but regardless of such differences, across all these groups more established and better-educated migrants set the tone (Portes et al. 2007). Their impact is large and growing, evident in the amount of money sent home ($5 billion to Colombia, $16 billion to Mexico in 2004), in new causes that flourish, and in concrete projects built (ibid.).

Many immigrants, of course, only travel home occasionally. Gradually, they and their children become more focused on their destination rather than their origins. But as transnational ties expand, many others become "bifocal," actively concerned about and engaged in at least two places at once, living "here and there" at the same time (Vertovec 2004). "[I]ncorporation in a new state and enduring transnational attachments are not binary opposites," say two prominent scholars, and it therefore makes more sense to see the migrant experience as a kind of gauge that "pivots between a new land and a transnational incorporation" (Levitt and Glick Schiller 2004: 1011). Since those different places are situated in specific nations and bifocal migrants remain very much attached to their particular communities, the boundary-crossers do not live in some cosmopolitan nether land – calling their way of life "transnational" may be a misnomer (Waldinger and Fitzgerald 2004), "binational" a better label. Some of their fellow immigrants, in fact, are neither fully here nor there, such as Moroccan-Dutch "invisible parents" in Amsterdam who have lost touch with home but also are isolated from the host society, to the point where they do not know where their kids go to school (Kleijwegt 2005). All these ways of life are in flux as well – whether second- or third-generation immigrants keep up their (grand)parents' transnationalism remains to be seen.

Transnationalism itself is only one immigrant option. Among transnationals back-and-forth contact varies. Yet the presence of more people not fully part of the wider society, whose very identities are in some sense unbounded, adds to a predicament felt in many countries by the native majority. What will become of "us" is the question that lurks behind immigration debates. I take up the issue of national identity next.

Who are We?

According to Samuel Huntington, an influential American political scientist, the new immigration challenges America's national identity (Huntington 2004). More people, about two-thirds of immigrants, come from a single country, Mexico, which continues to pull them homeward thanks to its proximity. They are more likely to speak a single foreign language, Spanish, which undermines the use of English as the common national tongue. They concentrate in large numbers in major cities,

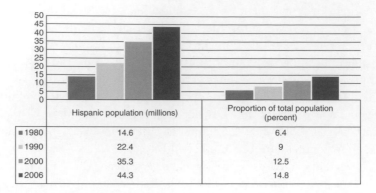

	Hispanic population (millions)	Proportion of total population (percent)
▪1980	14.6	6.4
▪1990	22.4	9
▪2000	35.3	12.5
▪2006	44.3	14.8

Figure 10.1 Growth of Hispanic population and proportion of Hispanics in US, 1980–2006
Source: US Census Bureau

asserting their clout in order to gain special recognition. They identify with their old nationality and their old hometowns rather than with the US, turning into a permanent, both subnational and transnational, minority. By virtue of their low skills and education, they differ enormously from the native population. Coming from a hierarchical, more traditional, Catholic-infused culture, they do not share the American creed rooted in an Anglo-Protestant culture. That creed expresses a commitment to America as a promised land in which liberty and equality flourish thanks to the disciplined hard work of its citizens. Once a culturally alien element reaches a critical mass, Huntington implies, the national identity built on that creed will crack. Immigration may thus lead to a "clash of civilizations" within one country. That is not all the immigrants' fault, according to Huntington: the national commitment of native-born elites is waning as well, making it easier for newcomers not to assimilate.

America's problem is a global problem, Huntington thinks. Everywhere countries – or at least their leading figures – face the question of who "we" are. While America grapples with "Hispanization," Europe deals with "Islamization." In each case, culturally distinct, economically disadvantaged, and socially segregated minorities do not fit in, over time causing the national identity to dissipate. That, at least, is the specter immigration critics fear. Are they right?

Language is one yardstick to judge whether the new immigrants fit in. The US has always been strongly monolingual, expecting all to use English in public, and to a large extent it still is. Not surprisingly, most immigrants follow a familiar path, learning at least some English soon and ensuring that their US-born children become fluent – who then often switch to speaking English exclusively at home. For Mexicans, the picture is a bit different: they switch to English-only at a lower rate than Asians, more US-born Mexican-Americans remain bilingual, and especially near the border just a small minority speaks only English at home (Alba and Nee 2003: 224–8). Spanish has also seeped into American public life more

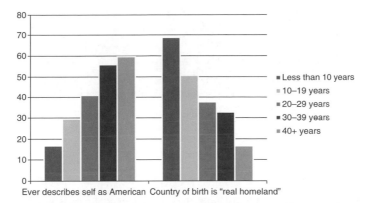

Less than 10 years
10–19 years
20–29 years
30–39 years
40+ years

Ever describes self as American   Country of birth is "real homeland"

Figure 10.2 Identity changes with time in country, measured in percent foreign-born Hispanics
Source: Waldinger 2007: 12

than any other foreign language. Even so, leading scholars do not share Huntington's fear, since they doubt that the power of monolingualism can be broken (ibid.).

When it comes to marriage, assimilation is also going strong in America, as it has historically: not only Asians and whites intermarry ever more frequently, so do Hispanics and whites, albeit at a lower rate. Due to the sheer scale of Hispanic immigration, some of their enclaves grow, but at the same time newcomers also settle in new places, including suburbs where they live closer to native whites. As in other groups, people in the second generation get more education and better jobs than their parents, though Mexican-Americans, in particular, are still far more likely not to complete high school and to remain in low-skilled jobs. Over time, then, Mexican-Americans gain more intimate contacts across group boundaries, though within limits; they do not settle exclusively in enclaves but spread out to some extent; many in the second and third generation advance socially but many others stagnate – they assimilate in some ways but remain more apart in others. Huntington thus seems partly right but mostly wrong. The ongoing arrival of low-skilled, unassimilated newcomers further complicates the picture. Even if a substantial portion of the Mexican community assimilates, snapshot impressions may continue to suggest deep gaps, feeding Huntingtonian fears even as America's immigration machine does its job. Evidence on Latino immigrants overall should dispel at least some of the fears: many keep in touch with family and friends back home, "trying to remain true to the people and places they have left behind," while "simultaneously shifting loyalties and allegiances to the US, where they see a bright future for themselves and their children and where they plan to stay for good" (Waldinger 2007: 22). Contrary to Huntington, those immigrants seem to find America "deeply appealing" and are capable of finding their way from "there" to "here" (22–3).

But nationalists like Huntington also fear that immigrants will break the national mold as they enter it. The idea of "one nation," he might argue, does not carry the same weight for "bifocal" people whose lifeworld spills over the edges of the mold. In his view, elites who celebrate "diversity" over unity exacerbate the problem. Huntington has a point, but the national mold proved strong enough to hold earlier diverse groups and the spillover need not crack the mold itself – there is breathing space, some room for variation within. Especially Hispanic immigrants, either Catholic or evangelical Protestant, would seem very comfortable with the idea of a nation "under God," one of the religious elements in the Anglo-Protestant creed. By contrast with European Muslims, they have much in common with the religious majority of the nation they join. The American creed views the country as always being under construction, a promise being fulfilled by hard work – and once again, judging by the sheer amount of work they do, immigrants appear to subscribe to it as much as the native-born. Catholic or Protestant, the modern version of the Protestant work ethic is entirely familiar to them. The creed revolves around some high principles of individualism and equality, but if Hispanic-Americans turn out to have slightly different views on the meaning of those principles, they are joining a centuries-long debate rather than breaking a fixed mold. If as new citizens they swear allegiance to the Constitution, that may evoke a different image for them than for Huntington, but the role of the Constitution, too, evolves constantly. The national mold expanded during the second wave of immigration and may do so again as a result of the third.

Summary and Conclusion

The third wave of globalization has witnessed a rise in migration: though a large majority of the world's population stays "home," more people move from more places, to some extent unsettling the communities where they arrive. The reasons behind migration are complex, leading scholars to speak of "cumulative causation." So are the reactions: "old" places, such as various European countries, adapt in different ways, each with its own trade-offs. As more immigrants live "transnationally," up to a point, the meaning of integration itself begins to shift as well. In globalization, nation-states lose some of their hold on "their" members. Not surprisingly, that often causes soul-searching among the native-born.

Some nationalists think the who-are-we question has a definite and fixed answer. That is part of how they see their national identity. They cherish the nation's roots. In historical practice, however, national cultures get replanted, reseeded, and cross-fertilized. National "imagined communities" re-imagine themselves repeatedly. In the process, some things get lost. Not surprisingly, many people object, either through academic writing, like Huntington, or in the more contentious political arena, where populist leaders like Jean-Marie Le Pen in France or Pim Fortuyn in the Netherlands stir up deep sentiments. But in the global age two options become less and less plausible: to preserve the national identity as it once was and to choke off the flow of strangers that threatens it. Another possible outcome, namely that nations will simply give up the ghost, is equally implausible, if only because they matter too much to too many people. Instead, their common challenge is to redefine their national identity.

The common challenge has no universal solution, because nations must find their own way in world society (Lechner 2008). Yet if migration research has it right, at minimum new versions of their national identities must leave ample room for ties to elsewhere. The idea of the nation, so to speak, must be "deterritorialized" a bit. For nations already defined by values and institutions, like the United States, that should prove less of a problem than for others that prize the particularity of a people in its place. But as with the supposed "retreat" of the state, rumors of the demise of the nation are premature in any case: globalization fosters not a straight loss but transformation.

Many migrants have more mundane concerns, of course: they want to improve their lives. Not surprisingly, much migration "flows" from South to North, along the gradient formed by global inequality. The next chapter examines how unequal world society is, and how globalization might affect that inequality.

Questions

1   The chapter explicitly summarizes several European "incorporation regimes" and describes the American version by example. How does the American approach to integration differ from its European counterparts? What do the differences tell us about the various countries' national self-conceptions?

2   Do the differences in integration strategies contradict the neoinstitutionalist argument that in the world polity common scripts will steer states toward similar policies on core issues? What kind of evidence in the treatment of migrants would indicate movement toward "isomorphism" in migration policy?

3   Many developed countries put up barriers, physical and/or legal, to poor foreigners who want to enter. But why exactly? How do the costs compare with the benefits? If countries otherwise committed to globalization put up such barriers, are they contradicting themselves in a way?

4   How might the evidence on global migration support skeptics who argue that space still constrains social life, that geography is destiny, and that therefore globalization is of limited significance for most people?

Further Reading

Richard Alba and Victor Nee, *Remaking the American Mainstream: Assimilation and Contemporary Immigration* (Harvard University Press, 2003)

Stephen Castles and Mark J. Miller, *The Age of Migration* (Guilford Press, 2003)

Christian Joppke, *Immigration and the Nation-State: The United States, Germany and Great Britain* (Oxford University Press, 1999)

Frank J. Lechner, *The Netherlands: Globalization and National Identity* (Routledge, 2008)

Peggy Levitt, *The Transnational Villagers* (University of California Press, 2001)

Douglas S. Massey, Joaquín Arango, Hugo Graeme, Ali Kouaouci, Adela Pellegrino, and J. Edward Taylor, *Worlds In Motion: Understanding International Migration at the End of the Millennium* (Clarendon Press, 1998)

11

GLOBAL INEQUALITY: WINNERS AND LOSERS IN GLOBALIZATION

An Unequal World: Malawi

When their country became independent in 1964, the people of Malawi were mostly poor and illiterate. Four decades later, they were still very poor and only a little less illiterate: the country had made "no appreciable progress" (Harrigan 2001: 1). In the small rural village of Dickisoni, for example, most families lived at the edge of subsistence in mud huts furnished only with a few pots and mats, and even the richest man, though the proud owner of a bicycle, could not afford soap at the beginning of harvest time and slept on a sometimes freezing floor (Wittenberg 2007). Few of the 300 villagers had ever visited Malawi's capital, Lilongwe, only 80 kilometers, or a 2.5 hour drive if they had had a car, down a bad road. Exhausted by constant worry and disease, the people of Dickisoni farmed small plots of exhausted land that produced barely enough food to eat, let alone to sell. In their dire circumstances, any adversity could turn into disaster.

The village was a microcosm of the country as a whole, which in turn attests to the stark inequality in the world as a whole, the subject of this chapter. In 2004, when the population had grown about threefold to over 10 million, Malawians' life expectancy at birth of 39.8 years was fourth lowest in the world, and in overall "human development" the country ranked 166th out of 177 countries (UN 2006: table 1). According to a major international study in 2005, Malawians on average only had $514 per person to consume, at a time when American per capita consumption reached nearly $32,000 – and of course, they were once again near the very bottom of the scale (World Bank 2008b). About three-quarters of Mala-wians lived on less than $2 a day and some two-fifths on less than $1 – including most people in Dickisoni – and per capita income had grown by a mere 0.2 percent per year for the previous 30 years (Conroy et al. 2006: 22). Not surprisingly, Malawi still depended on foreign aid, which at $377 million comprised more than 10 percent of its meager gross domestic product (GDP) (23). Only in education had there been a bit of "appreciable progress": about two-thirds of adults qualified as minimally literate (UN 2006).

If Malawi seemed stuck, it was not for lack of trying. After independence, the country tried to grow its way out of poverty by cultivating tea and tobacco for export. The government favored production on large estates that might bring in more foreign income while at the same time encouraging the majority of small farmers to grow enough food to supply the needs of the country. As farmers became more productive and some lost their land to government schemes, many men left to work abroad, for example in South Africa and Zimbabwe (Mhone 1992: xii), and sent home money. For a while, the early development effort made Malawi look good: well into the 1970s, it grew at an annual pace of over 5 percent, it invested in its future, and it avoided the overly ambitious industrialization projects that came to naught in other developing countries. Even in those days, all was not well. The picture painted by the official figures was too rosy since they overestimated how much Malawian peasants really produced (Harrigan 2001: 20–23). Though less corrupt than their colleagues elsewhere, Malawi's political elite eagerly enriched itself, with "Life President" Hastings Banda taking control of much of the economy through an overextended holding company whose tentacles reached most major businesses, and this predatory elite behavior helped to make Malawi one of the most unequal countries in the world. For all the progress the country had made by the late 1970s, it could not withstand the shocks of that era (Mhone 1992: 27–9). Just as the cost of fuel and fertilizer imports went up, the price of tea and tobacco declined, worsening "terms of trade" that hit especially hard because Malawi had come to rely on profitable exports by estates that required the now-expensive imports. The government tried to borrow money to cover sudden shortfalls but had to pay higher international interest rates, nearly quadrupling its debt payments in just a few years (Harrigan 2001: 40). A drought in 1979–80 forced the country to import food with money it did not have, making an already bad financial situation that much worse.

Like many other countries at the time, Malawi had little choice but to seek help from the IMF and the World Bank. In exchange for "structural adjustment" loans, the country agreed to carry out reforms to get the state's financial affairs in balance. Equally important, the outsiders helped to unravel the president's holding company, the impending collapse of which might have damaged the whole economy (Harri-gan 2001: 242). But the initial benefits of the adjustment program were short-lived: after an uptick in growth, the economy languished again, leaving the benefits of adjustment uncertain at best (241). After President Banda lost a referendum on the

Plate 11.1 Mphandula, a poor village without electricity or clean water, about 30 miles outside Lilongwe, Malawi
Source: © Per-Anders Pettersson/Getty Images

introduction of democracy in 1993, a newly elected democratic government took office the following year. It continued to abide by World Bank and IMF guidelines on liberalization but also focused with new energy on alleviating poverty, for example by lifting fees on public education and by trying to diversify the economy as a way to take the burden off the land. Small farmers no longer beholden to a single government buyer and free to export their products responded to new incentives by raising production dramatically (296–7). But diversification was hampered by the inefficiency of Malawi's modest industries (310). Even with the civil war in neighboring Mozambique being resolved, transportation costs remained very high for landlocked Malawi (Conroy et al. 2006: 107). HIV/AIDS swept through Malawi in the 1990s, infecting more than 10 percent of adults, killing some 50,000, and devastating many affected families (64–5). It proved difficult to tame the "fiscal deficit," the Malawi governments' habit of spending more than they took in, as politicians were tempted to use state funds to promote their political fortunes. When new droughts occurred in 2001–2, the country had few reserves with which to face the food crisis. The poor had to sell everything they had just to survive, and for women that often meant selling access to their bodies as well, which only aggravated the AIDS epidemic (11). Even deficit spending by the government, "out of control" in 2001–4, could do little to help, since the government still had barely more than $30 per person to spend on public services (25, 27). In the early 2000s, places like Dickisoni were thus especially vulnerable as they were trying to recover from yet another setback. Due to the combined "storm" of bad climate, deep poverty, and a new pandemic, Malawi was stuck in a "trap" (4).

From Malawi to Korea

The mixed metaphors convey the plight of people at the bottom of the global scale. They make unmistakably clear that even in an age of globalization, how well anyone lives depends first and foremost on where she is born: almost any American lives better than almost any Malawian. As Malawi's story starkly confirms, world society remains vastly unequal: as Americans got richer, many Malawians sank into deeper poverty. In fact, if we measure inequality by the share of income received by different segments of the world population, the world as a whole is more unequal than any individual country except Namibia (Sutcliffe 2004: 34). The inequality is so great that it calls into question whether there really is a "world society." America and Malawi might as well be on different planets. On one planet, people struggle to have enough to eat, on the other, the poor struggle with obesity. While on one planet, people were lucky to earn a few hundred dollars, on the other median household income was over $40,000, a quarter of households made more than $75,000, and GDP per capita was over $41,000 – more than 60 times that of Malawi. On one planet, a country stumbled from crisis to recovery to crisis; on the other, an already wealthy country enjoyed mostly low unemployment, modest inflation, and renewed productivity growth, rarely interrupted by a serious recession, for more than a generation. By contrast with the planet where people barely live better than their ancestors, on the other planet disposable income has grown by more than half and new technologies have transformed people's daily lives since the 1970s. Such simple comparisons still understate the gap for they do not quite capture the cushion of comfort and security that America's extraordinary wealth provides. And the gap is growing: the American economic engine revved up as Malawi's sputtered. The rich got richer, and the rich among the rich got richer faster. That made an unequal world society even more unequal.

At the time of Malawi's independence, South Korea was also among the world's poorest countries. Its GDP per capita was just $82 in 1960, its economy barely better than that of Congo (Pirie 2008: 1). Not yet recovered from a war against the North, the country got by on American aid. It had no natural resources and no great prospects. Forty years later, however, Korea had made more than appreciable progress: thanks to astonishingly rapid growth, it had become the global development champion. Its GDP per capita rose to $20,499 in 2004. Its population was almost universally literate. Its life expectancy of over 77 matched that of the developed countries. Its steel, ships, cars, and electronics had spread around the globe. Its top firms – Hyundai, Samsung, LG, and Daewoo – were larger than those of any other developing country (Amsden 2001: 198, 203). In fact, by the early 2000s Korea no longer thought of itself as a "developing country" at all. After decades of averaging over 26 percent annual export growth (162), highest in the world, it had caught up with the West. Not entirely, of course: Americans' standard of living was still about twice as high on average. But Korea had closed a once enormous gap and Koreans had fully joined world society.

How did they do it? Korea may have been in dire straits in 1960 but it had hidden strengths. More than the British in Malawi, the Japanese occupiers had trained a cadre of Korean officials to run the colonial bureaucracy. To support its own imperial designs, the Japanese had also begun to industrialize the country, again involving Korean managers. While the Korean elite had gained specialized skills (Amsden 2001: 101–5), Koreans overall were already far more literate than Malawians. The military government that seized power in 1961 thus did not have to start from scratch. To justify its rule, the regime had to make the country grow. Over the next decade, at first with little success, it began to build a classic "developmental state," a strong, independent bureaucracy devoted to development. Initially focused on domestic development (Lie 1998: 55–6) and infrastructure, it soon shifted to promoting exports, using the government's control of finance to provide special credits to favored firms. These were not yet the famous large *chaebol*, or business conglomerates, that emerged later but mostly smaller companies; wigs and plywood, rather than cars or television sets, were leading products, especially in the American market (66–7). As the Cold War was heating up, Korea also took advantage of the American "umbrella," for example by producing supplies for the Vietnam War. With money and licensed technology, both the US and Japan supported Korea's big push toward industrialization in the 1970s, financed by loans rather than direct foreign investment (82–3). Not only did the state protect infant industries, nurturing the *chaebol* conglomerates until they comprised nearly half of the economy, it also limited imports of consumer goods – no Japanese cars graced Korean streets in the 1970s (84–5). For some time, many Koreans did not share in the country's gains, since the authoritarian regime insisted on keeping wages low, but even so, Korea was never as unequal as Malawi, and in fact inequality declined during its period of rapid growth (Korzeniewicz and Moran 2007: 578). Like Malawi, Korea suffered an economic crisis around 1980, and again in the late 1990s, but unlike Malawi it adapted successfully, gradually shifting to a somewhat more "neoliberal" economic policy that effectively used the tools of state power to force business to meet market challenges (Pirie 2008). Painful as these episodes were for Koreans, they never suffered the hardships of Malawi. Once their country had taken off into self-sustained growth, it would not turn back.

Because by the early 2000s Koreans lived better than their grandparents a half century before and almost as well as people in the West, this stylized version of their experience complicates the picture of global poverty and inequality conveyed by the case of Malawi. The purpose of this chapter is to make that picture clearer. As the examples already suggest, my painterly exercise has an impressionistic quality, since the overall picture is composed of many country experiences, many dots of data. In a world of Malawis and Koreas, no single line or figure quite conveys what is happening to poverty and inequality. Yet in the global picture two patterns stand out: on one relatively bright side, more people now live better than before and fewer people suffer extreme poverty, but on the other, gloomier, side, the contrasts between rich and poor have faded only slightly or, in some cases, become more stark. "The era of globalization," concludes a World Bank economist, "has seen unprecedented poverty reduction and a modest decline in global inequality" (Dollar 2005: 117). The evidence for this big-picture argument, it turns out, is still somewhat uncertain – the brushes and paints we use to fill in the picture leave much to be desired, and there is much we do not know about poverty and inequality. As I show in a subsequent section, that also makes it difficult to credit or blame globalization for any trends in poverty and inequality. Some form of globalization is probably necessary for nations to advance, but as the initial examples already suggest, the role of globalization varies – it worked differently for Malawi, Korea, and the United States. If we want to reduce poverty and inequality, we in effect prefer a more "Korean" than "Malawian" world. But can Malawi be more like Korea, and, if it can, is globalization in some form more likely to be help or hindrance? The chapter concludes by reflecting on that issue.

Trends in Poverty and Inequality

At the end of the twentieth century, as Chapter 5 noted, many regions of the world were not flourishing. After the collapse of the Soviet Union, former communist countries at first got poorer. Latin America had been in the economic doldrums since the 1980s. For Africa as a whole, the 1990s were a tough decade on many fronts. Meanwhile, developed countries were moving forward. Malawi went one way, the US another. According to one popular phrase, the rich were getting richer and the poor poorer. Or were they? Around the turn of the century, more people began to see signs of progress. While the rich were getting richer, some of the poor also seemed to be getting richer. Some of the poor who stayed poor seemed less miserable than before. Some old gaps seemed to be closing. What exactly were those signs?

To burnish its credentials as an organization contributing to the common good, the UN set ambitious "Millennium Development Goals" (MDG) in 2000. The very first was also the most obvious: to halve the number of people living in "absolute poverty" between 1990 and 2015. The term referred to the notion that everyone needs minimal resources just to survive – anything less leads to starvation and death. Mere subsistence of this sort, the World Bank had calculated, required just over $1 a day per person (in 1993 dollars). Though the exact help the UN might give on this score remained a bit fuzzy, it soon appeared that the goal was well within reach. In 2004, agencies tracking poverty estimated that the number of absolutely poor people had fallen below 1 billion, down from 1.25 billion in 1990. Since the world population had increased in the meantime, the proportion of abso-

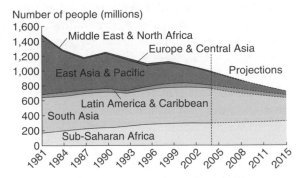

Figure 11.1 Trends in poverty, measured by number of people living on less than $1.08 (1993 dollars) a day, in millions, 1981–2004
Source: World Bank 2007GMR

Table 11.1 Trends in poverty, percentage of population living below $1 (PPP, 1993 dollars) a day, 1990–2004

	1990	*1999*	*2004*
Developing regions	31.6	23.4	19.2
Sub-Saharan Africa	46.8	45.9	41.1
Latin America and Caribbean	10.3	9.6	8.7
Eastern Asia	33.0	17.8	9.9
Southern Asia	41.1	33.4	29.5
South-Eastern Asia	20.8	8.9	6.8

Note: Numbers are not adjusted for PPP revisions based on International Comparison Program
Source: World Bank and UN 2007MDG

lutely poor people had declined even more, from nearly a third to less than a fifth (UN 2007: 4). Across all developing regions, the proportion of people in extreme poverty fell from 31.6 to 19.7 percent. Malawi's travails notwithstanding, even Africa showed signs of progress, with absolute poverty down slightly from 46.8 to 41.1 percent, though at that rate it would not meet the MDG target (7). The average income of people living on less than $1 a day also increased. At the beginning of the twenty-first century, such cold figures indicated, fewer people suffered absolute poverty, and those who did suffered slightly less. Of course, the fact that a very low bottom got raised a bit hardly implies that it approached the top: progress on poverty does not necessarily translate into less inequality.

How much people earn only tells us so much; to judge their well-being, we also want to know, at the very least, how well they live and how much they learn. The most striking fact here is that more people live longer. In Western countries, the "mortality revolution" started in the nineteenth century, eventually bringing life expectancy up to 77; in the twentieth century, developing countries followed suit – newborns there may now expect to live to 66 on average (PRB 2007). Because at a certain point life expectancy improves only very slowly – much as we would like to think otherwise, there is a ceiling effect – the greater longevity of people in poor countries has enabled them to catch up. In the early 1950s, for example, people at the tenth percentile in the world population could expect to live 34 years, those at the ninetieth percentile 69 years, but by 2000 the former were up to 54.3 years, for a gain of 20, while the latter had only gained 12 additional years (Wilson 2001: 162). More food and better care for children had much to do with it. Whereas 13 million children died before the age of five in 1990, thanks to a drop in the child mortality rate of about one quarter that number was down to a still-shocking 9.7 million by 2006 (UNICEF 2008). Even Malawi joined the trend, cutting child mortality by 29 percent between 2000 and 2004. In low-income countries, young children were still 15 times more likely to die before the age of five, one mark of persistent deep inequality, yet the trend pointed to smaller gaps here as well, if only because child mortality had not much room to fall further in high-income countries.

By official standards, more people were getting better educated as well. As noted in Chapter 6, mass schooling surged in the second half of the twentieth century, and enrollment in primary education continued to go up in most regions since the early 1990s, increasing from 54 to 70 percent by 2005 in Africa (UN 2007: 10). In many regions more than 90 percent of children regularly attend school, and by 2005 52 countries had achieved universal primary completion (World Bank 2007GMR). Of course, this did not mean that everyone learned equally well; on a sixth-grade reading test, for example, barely 30 percent of Malawian students displayed minimal literacy (7). Leaving aside such caveats, the global picture shows "sharp declines" in health and educational inequality (Firebaugh and Goesling 2007: 560). Apart from income, one bold scholar claimed, just about everything was converging by the early 2000s, ranging from the level of female literacy to how much beer people drank. He concluded that "quality of life has improved over the past 50 years worldwide, and . . . for 50 years, and sometimes longer, it has improved more rapidly in the developing world than in the developed world" (Kenny 2004: 10).

Did income gaps shrink as well? In one obvious way they did not: inequality between countries kept rising, reflecting widening overall gaps between Malawi and the US but also new gaps between Korea and Africa. However, there are at least four times as many Koreans as Malawians, and it makes sense in international comparisons to give more populous countries greater weight. If Korea advances rapidly while Malawi remains stuck, our overall measure of inequality ideally should reflect the relatively greater progress of the larger group. If more of the bigger countries do well while poor smaller countries do not, that means that for more people the income gap is shrinking. Around 2000, measures of the share of income going to countries at different income levels, adjusted for size, indeed seemed to

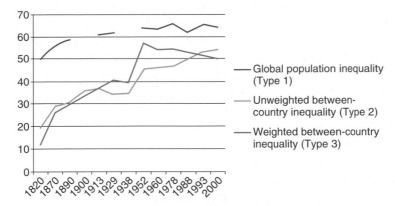

Figure 11.2 Trends in inequality: Gini indices, 1820–2000
Note: 1. Types of inequality and underlying data are explained in text, in the sections on inequality facts and measuring inequality. 2. Sample size and data quality differ by year; Type 1 data are missing for 1900 and 1938. 3. Overall trend shows sharply increasing inequality or "great divergence" since 1820, partial reversal in late-twentieth century.
Source: Milanovic 2005: 142, which relies on various sources

show a turnaround: having risen for decades, the global Gini coefficient or index, an income distribution yardstick explained below, finally declined a little, one sign of inequality tapering off (Sala-i-Martin 2002; Firebaugh 2003; Milanovic 2005). Different measures seemed to reinforce the message; for example, the ratio of the top 50 to the bottom 50 percent of the world income distribution, and of the top 10 to the bottom 10 percent, also declined, showing that the bottom was rising faster than the top (Sutcliffe 2004: 28). Since about 1990, perhaps a bit earlier, inequality between countries had been dropping (Korzeniewicz and Moran 2007: 566). If the nineteenth century witnessed a "great divergence" between the West and "the rest," some optimists viewed this latest trend as a "great reversal," in which the rest might indeed catch up with the West (Firebaugh 2003).

The main reason for the trend was no great secret, and Chapter 5 has reduced the suspense still further. Even more dramatically than Korea, on a slightly lower level but on a much larger scale, China has been growing rapidly since the late 1970s – much more rapidly than developed countries. As China industrialized, many peasants found work in factories. A new middle class of managers and entrepreneurs emerged. In just a few decades, hundreds of millions of Chinese rose from near-Malawian poverty. They still lived soberly by Western standards, but they were closing the gap. Because the biggest player gained the most, it changed the nature of the inequality contest. Inequality measures that adjust for population, taking China's sheer size into account, thus began to show a significant change. The "great reversal" was above all a "China effect." The gains of the second largest player, India, were at first less apparent in the data but also began to alter the contest, since India's growth might sustain the reversal brought about by China.

If many of the poor climb out of poverty more rapidly than the rich reach new heights of wealth, that should further reduce global inequality. Optimists found early signs that this might be happening in data from the late twentieth century, mostly in Asia, but trends in the 2000s added to their confidence. For several years, as Chapter 5 has already showed, most developing regions grew more rapidly than the developed countries – on average, 7.8 versus 3.0 percent in 2006 and 7.9 versus 2.7 percent in 2007 (IMF 2008). Median growth rates similarly hinted at the rise of "the rest" – 6.1 versus 3.4 percent in 2006 and 6.0 versus 3.5 percent in 2007. In a period when the value of the world's output increased enormously, from $39.4 trillion in 1995 to $58.6 trillion in 2006, especially the Asian rest claimed a larger share of it (see figure 5.2). In the booming world economy of the mid-2000s, "the rest" overall did especially well (see figure 5.1). Sustained over time, that promised to make not just the rich but also many of the non-rich richer.

The rosy scenario did not fully persuade skeptics. To them, the global inequality "reversal" was not all that "great" to begin with. For 200 years, after all, the West had been pulling away from the rest. In 1820, the richest country was about three times as well off as the poorest, by 1992 the advantage had widened to 72 to 1 (Milanovic 2005: 46). The comparison is an estimate, since we lack good information on the poor in the 1800s, but we can be sure that the poor did not keep up with the rich. Countries near the bottom and the top in the late twentieth century could not have grown at the same pace, for then those that were still barely above subsistence, like Ethiopia or Malawi, must have started well below – a logical impossibility (Pritchett 1997). Conclusion: today's world displays the result of "divergence, big time" (ibid.). Slightly less dramatic than that two-century process, but perhaps equally disturbing to the countries involved, is the more recent divergence between the countries that are now wealthy and the failed "contenders," countries well above the bottom that in 1960 were within striking distance of the West but by 2000 sank to Third World status at less than two-thirds of First World GDP per capita (e.g., Poland and Hungary) or even Fourth World status, defined as being at less than one-third of that First World level (e.g., Ghana, Nicaragua, and Jamaica) (Milanovic 2005: 63–8).

The Fourth World in fact swelled to include 71 countries, Malawi included of course, and only Botswana and Egypt managed to escape. Korea is the exception to the rule, the only country that was still Third World in 1978 but made it into the First World by 2000. The First and Fourth World were still "worlds apart," as the evocative title of a key study describes the global condition (Milanovic 2005). Because many countries had long been growing apart, any increase in the fortunes of those near the bottom at first simply helped countries make up for lost ground. But after the crisis of 1979–80, caused mainly by an oil shock combined with higher interest rates that affected both Malawi and Korea, rich countries recovered more quickly than poor ones, and this again hampered potential contenders. Latin America's "lost decade" in the 1980s, recession in the transition economies of Eastern Europe, and disastrous performance in much of Africa made inequality between countries worse (36–41). As a result, at the end of the twentieth century there was much inequality to reverse.

If we take population size into account, even skeptics would agree, overall income inequality has declined since the 1970s, dipping below the level of 1950 by 2000 (see figure 11.2). But it is China that makes the world look good. Strip away China, and the world looks very different: since 1980, inequality has been rising slightly once more; take out India as well, and the increase becomes more pronounced – ample reason for skeptics to be cautious about great global inequality reversals (Sutcliffe 2004; Milanovic 2005: 87). The China effect itself rests on murky data; if China did better before its recent growth spurt than official statistics suggest, then inequality declined less than optimists think (Milanovic 2005: 95). Even weighting for population does not really do justice to what is happening in China, since China's national figures veil deep domestic differences as people in cities improve their standard of living much more than those left behind in rural areas – the global China effect comes at the cost of greater internal inequality (Korzeniewicz and Moran 2007: 573–5). Precisely what is happening is difficult to gauge in any case, since most studies of China have relied on limited information about Chinese prices. When the World Bank obtained better information in an extensive study in 2005, it turned out that prices were higher than once thought, so that the Chinese could get less for their money, which meant that their effective incomes had been overstated (World Bank 2008b). According to the new figures, China's national income was 40 percent lower than previously thought, GDP per capita was less than one-tenth of that in the US, over 300 million Chinese still lived in extreme poverty, and Chinese consumers had $1,752 to spend compared to the $31,995 of Americans. Simply by judging China's economic prowess more precisely, the new figures enlarged the gap. For all its advances, China had a long way to go. Even if it did, optimists were willing to concede (Sala-i-Martin 2002), its equalizing effect might well dissipate, since a successful China would distance itself from the world's laggards. The Korea–Malawi gap, writ larger, would increase global inequality with a vengeance. To skeptics, then, China's rise offers little solace. If it continues strongly, they realize, it might upset the otherwise quite stable pattern of global inequality in a system that seemed to have reached "equilibrium," allowing individual countries to advance while not changing the rank order itself (Korzeniewicz and Moran 2007: 568, 584), but so far, viewed skeptically, the great reversal is at best a modest fluctuation.

For all the fuzziness of Chinese numbers, and for all the difficulties in determining who really is rock-bottom poor, even to skeptics the numbers of global poverty are pretty telling: the proportion of absolutely poor people, and probably their actual numbers as well, in the world is declining, as figure 11.1 and table 11.1 show (Wade 2004). We know also that more people live longer and fewer children die early – facts that brighten the positive side of the picture. Still, skeptics are inclined to redraw it. The mere fact that fewer people live at the edge of survival does not make the condition of the super-poor "bottom billion" (Collier 2007) any less horrifying. Global change makes their grim condition stand out more starkly, if only because more people become more aware of what they are missing. To globally conscious people, then, slightly less global poverty may accentuate stubborn global inequality, making inequality a bigger problem even as the well-being of many people improves. Skeptics might add that new developments can easily dim the bright big picture. After all, life expectancy in Malawi, and Africa as a whole, declined in much of the 1990s, reminding us that no gains are permanent. Things that look good in one period can regress in the next, regions that once flourished may retreat. In fact, many people in many places remain extremely vulnerable. Perversely, globalization in some forms may be dangerous to their health, as Malawi could attest in the crisis years around 1980 and again during the AIDS epidemic of the 1990s. Because globalization really means different things to different countries, skeptics insist, it would be a mistake to view it as a panacea for their troubles.

Before examining that claim more closely, I first take a short detour into the evidence behind the points I have just made. Unfortunately, while some big-picture trends are quite clear, the evidence does not yet allow us to fill in the picture with confidence.

Facts about Inequality Facts

To understand how well people live, we need to learn a lot about them. The previous section barely scratched the surface with data on life expectancy, education, and income. Those cover the basics: quality of life has little meaning if people do not live long, learning is a passport to a better life in modern society, and income gives us access to things we need and want. For most people in most places, however, they are not the whole story of a good life, for regardless of cultural differences most people also want access to clean water and medicine, a voice in a government that operates according to law, and civic peace that provides a sense of security. To capture differences along these lines, the UN has constructed a "Human Development Index" – the broad ranking in which Malawi fared so poorly. Even that index necessarily simplifies a complex reality. Taking one element out of the index, information pertaining just to differences in economic well-being, further truncates the complexity. But because money is a universal medium, income tells us much, though not everything, about the range of goods that might enhance a person's or a family's life. By the same token, differences in income indirectly tell us about differences in standard of living and in power. Assessing people's economic status as straightforwardly as possible is therefore obviously important. Yet measuring even such apparently clear concepts as poverty and economic inequality turns out to be hard enough.

What should count as "income," and how can we find out who earns what, on a global scale no less? Ideally, we would ask everyone on earth how much they receive from all sources and how much they spend on all goods and services. Assuming everyone answers truthfully and we can translate their answers into a common currency, we could then count exactly who gets what. If we plot the numbers very precisely along an income axis, from zero to several billion in common currency X, that would give us a nice picture of the global income distribution, the actual inequality among the people of the world. Let us call this Type 1 inequality. In addition to looking at the plot with untrained eyes, we could let statisticians loose to describe the shape of the distribution and tell us more exactly how unequal things are. If we repeat the process, say, every five years, we could also find out if the world is getting more or less unequal. Alas, our actual information falls short of the ideal (Milanovic 2005: ch. 2).

To start with, taking a poll of more than 6 billion people is difficult, and even if it were feasible, it would cost a lot. To reduce the cost of getting information, we can instead take shortcuts. The most common one is to rely on government figures about a country's economy and population. Since every country collects data on economic activity within its borders by compiling national accounts that give an overall sense of the value of the things its people produce, we can divide that number by the number of residents to calculate an average income in terms of a measure I have already used, "GDP per capita." This is handy for international comparisons since it sums up a country's status in one number that is calculated roughly the same way everywhere. If we want to know whether Malawi, Korea, and the US are moving farther apart or closer together, GDP per capita gives us an approximate answer. Of course, it expresses income simply as a national figure that depends on official records that may not be entirely accurate. It includes money spent by government or earned by business, not just the resources of actual house-holds, which especially affects the results for rich countries that spend more on public services like education and have more profitable companies. These national production data therefore overstate people's income, and because they make people in rich countries look even richer than they are, they also make global inequality look larger.

A more direct way to get at income is to ask a sample of real people selected from the larger population in a survey. Most countries have now in fact carried out at least one such survey; Africa joined only recently (Milanovic 2005: 104–6). Of course, even smaller-scale surveys are by no means easy – identifying people to interview, and then getting them to participate, poses a challenge. The rich, it turns out, are even more reluctant than the poor, potentially distorting survey results. But assuming we can reach the sample we need, what exactly should we ask people? If we simply ask how much they made, they might not tell us honestly, or they might not include things they receive in kind or as subsidies. An alternative way to get at economic well-being is to ask about what goods and services people actually acquire, since those household expenditures might give a less distorted view of their condition. But this is also tricky (Milanovic 2005: 16–7), for example because countries in which people rent rather than buy their homes would look much better off unless we adjust for the value of owner-occupied housing, and doing that is very complex. If a number of people in a sample buy large items like cars, their expenditure-based "income" might look unreasonably high unless we somehow spread out the value of that purchase over a number of years. To make things worse, many Western countries collect income data while Asia and Africa focus on expenditures, thus complicating any comparisons. Because these comparisons leave out the larger public expenditures in rich countries, they make households there look less well off than they are and therefore understate global inequality. Another part of such comparisons, by contrast, makes the gap look larger. If we get information from a single household member, and then simply divide the number she provides by the number of members in the household, without allowing for the possibility that larger families can provide for their members at lower cost on average, we might overstate income per capita in the rich countries where the cost of children, typically in smaller families, is higher (19). Measuring income is therefore much harder than it seems.

If getting good data is hard, comparing the results across the world is harder still. Behind the reasons I have already mentioned looms the even greater challenge of converting income data from many places with different currencies into a single common currency. Because the dollar has become the dominant currency in world affairs, it makes sense to try and turn any country's or person's income into a dollar equivalent. Not surprisingly, many studies have done this, and the previous section reports some of the results. But converting poses a dilemma: either we have to rely on common exchange rates, which vary greatly depending on market conditions, or we have to construct a more stable conversion rule, which presupposes that we know a lot about what money actually buys in different places. Choosing exchange rates is not unreasonable, because even in poor countries access to goods on the world market depends on their currencies' worth in the financial markets. To pay for oil imports, Malawi must first get dollars for its *kwachas* at current exchange rates, and if a middle-class Malawian wants to travel abroad, he will have to pay international prices. Yet many factors affect exchange rates so that they do not really capture a currency's buying power within a country. They also do not reflect the fact that the price of many goods is lower in poor countries, giving the poor more for their limited money and raising their well-being a bit beyond what exchange-rate comparisons would suggest.

To make sure we compare apples with apples, researchers have therefore devised a clever way of turning financial oranges and bananas into apples. Instead of asking how much the *kwacha* is worth in dollars if visitors try to exchange some Malawian bills at the airport in Lilongwe, we can ask how many *kwachas* it takes Malawians to buy a certain "basket" of goods that we know costs Americans a certain amount in dollars. Simply put, if purchasing a set of items that goes for $100 in the US takes 1,000 *kwachas* in Malawi, the "real" value of the *kwacha* is one-tenth of the US dollar. A Malawian income of 10,000 *kwachas* translates into a global dollar income of $1,000. If we put together a single basket, find its value both in the US and in local currencies around the globe, and then perform the same conversion for all currencies, we can calculate everyone's "purchasing power parity" or PPP dollar income, enabling us to do an apples-to-apples comparison. This is easier said than done. Deciding what goes into the single basket is hard because rich and poor typically purchase different sorts of things; including services that only the rich consume, typically at high prices, makes the poor seem richer if they just buy a very small amount, at the typically lower poor-country service prices (Pogge and Reddy 2005). Getting good data on local prices is hard because especially in large countries prices vary from place to place; national averages distort the cost of living, and therefore the "real" income, of many people. Finding a good basis for comparison is hard because relying on the US gives too much weight to local conditions there; the "average international price" calculated by the researchers of the World Bank's International Comparison Program still gives greater weight to rich-country choices, simply because the rich buy more of everything and therefore influence the average more.

Measuring Inequality

Even assuming we can get data and do comparisons, we still need to decide how to assess inequality itself, an issue addressed in detail by Milanovic (2005). One option, of course, is to focus exclusively on Type 1 inequality to rank the whole world population. Since much of that inequality is so closely tied to the performance of the countries where people live, another option is to measure the gaps between countries, what we might call Type 2 inequality. We can picture this as a parade in which each country is represented by an ambassador of a size that reflects its income. To describe the shape of the parade, we can subtract the size of Malawi's ambassador from Korea's, and Korea's from America's, and then add up the differences as a way to gauge "absolute" inequality between countries. That certainly captures some difference in well-being but fails fully to reflect Korea's progress. A slightly better gauge would measure the relative gaps between countries – relative to their own income or to average world income. At least the US–Korea comparison would show that Koreans now earn proportionally more than they once did, though the sum of these proportional changes might still show an increase if there are more Malawis than Koreas in the world. But this does not give us a good picture of global inequality either if the Koreas are much more populous than the Malawis. Korea should be able to send more representatives to the global parade than Malawi. If larger poor countries have been advancing more rapidly than the rich, in terms of GDP per capita, we would prefer a gauge that captures this population-weighted Type 3 inequality between countries. A logical way to do this is to multiply any differences between countries by their proportion of the world population. The standard measure for inequality between countries, the Gini coefficient named after an Italian economist, rests on this basic idea. But simply calculating between-country differences in this way still does not give us an accurate picture of global inequality because it leaves out what may be happening within countries. Again, much as inequality in Malawi remains disturbingly high, a good measure of inequality would give greater weight to big shifts in China. The "true" Gini measure of global inequality therefore must include the population-weighted sum of inequality levels within countries. In practice, it turns out that because inequality between countries is so much greater, inequality within countries does not add very much to the global total.

More intuitively, the Gini derives from data on what portion of total income individuals or countries receive. Returning to Type 2 inequality for illustration, let us assume we live in a world of 100 countries, take each country as a unit of equal size, and measure world income by adding all GDPs per capita and then dividing by 100. We can then display inequality across those countries in a figure composed of two axes: a horizontal axis indicating the cumulative percentage of countries and a vertical axis indicating the cumulative percentage of income they have received. If countries are completely equal, country 1 claims 1 percent of total income, country 2 another 1 percent, and so on. Since for each horizontal step (one additional country) we move up one vertical step (one additional percent of cumulative income), pure equality takes the form of a line that coincides with a straight line bisecting the plane at a 45-degree angle. At the other extreme, countries 1 through 99 would have no income and country 100 claims everything; in this case the curve runs along the horizontal axis (each additional country adds 0 percent of cumulative income) until it gets to country 100, where it shoots up. That curve produces the maximum space under the straight line at 45 degrees. The Gini coefficient is a number derived from the size of these spaces, 0 in the case of total equality, 1 in the case of total inequality (or, turning the coefficient into an index, between 0 and 100). Normally, the number is somewhere in between. Type 3, population-weighted world Gini stood at just about .50 (or alternatively, 50) in 2000. That fits a large area under the line of total equality – a technical reason for skeptics not to be too impressed with reversals in inequality.

One more twist complicates our task. As the discussion of the country examples showed, we are interested not just in how well countries do relative to others but also in whether they make progress compared to where they were before. If country A progresses faster than country B, for example in the sense that its GDP per capita is going up faster, then we could say, as I said about Korea, that it is "catching up." But here we risk comparing apples and oranges again by mixing country-to-country comparisons with domestic comparisons over time. For domestic comparisons, we want to know how income at time 2 compares to income at time 1, say a decade earlier. Even if actual production per person or actual buying power stays flat, the number at time 2 will be higher if the country experiences inflation. To gauge whether the higher number at time 2 really represents progress we have to "deflate" it to see, in effect, if the higher income reflects greater buying power. Because inflation has given the country a different currency at time 2, comparing it to the previous period requires creating a common currency, as it were, to express how much an amount of 100 at time 1 is worth if converted into time-2 currency. As in country-to-country comparisons, the best way to do this is to select a basket of goods and services, track their price from year to year, and then calculate a consumer price index (CPI) that enables us to convert the old into the new currency.

Suppose, for the sake of simplification, the standard basket that cost 100 units at time 1 now costs 110 units at time 2, for an inflation rate of 10 percent for the ten-year period; this means that each time-1 unit is equivalent to 11/10 of a time-2 unit and we should multiply time-1 incomes by 10 percent to get their time-2 equivalent. If it turns out that average nominal income at time 1 used to be 10,000 units per year, or 11,000 in real time-2 terms, and that average time-2 income has increased to 12,100, we should say that income has increased not 21 percent but 10 percent.

As in comparisons across countries, calculating inflation rates and deflating nominal incomes is actually hard, in this case because the basket changes. At time 1, it may have included prices of old-style boxy television sets, at time 2 everyone had shifted to flat panels – how, then, has the "price of televisions" changed? If the price of beef goes up and chicken stays flat, more consumers may choose chicken for dinner – how, then, does the changing price of beef affect the price of dinner? Because quality change and substitution through consumer choice affect what constitutes a representative basket, we have to make assumptions, for example, about how to value flat-screen TVs relative to older models, but this inevitably introduces some guesswork. In practice, in rich countries this often leads to over-stating price changes and understating real income growth, but expert opinions differ on how much this matters. Of course, estimating price changes assumes that we can get good data on prices across a country in the first place, which is no easy feat for many countries. If we simply stick to PPP comparisons to gauge inequality across countries, at time 1 and then again at time 2, each time using a distinct world basket, then inflation need not be a problem. If we try to use progress country A has made relative to its status at time 1 to gauge its advance over country B at time 1, then we are mixing the apple of a PPP-based country comparison with the orange of a CPI-based temporal comparison, which is confusing at best (Milanovic 2005: 14–5, citing Pogge and Reddy).

The hard work of comparing countries' GDP per capita, or of getting data from surveys around the world, still only gives a partial picture of economic inequality. In some ways, the situation is much worse than the standard data suggest. Snapshots of income across countries do not capture the experience typical of many people in rich countries that income fluctuates over time. Many young people, say graduate students in sociology, may start out poor but can reasonably expect to do much better in mid-life, unlike many low-income earners in less wealthy countries. Just as important as the actual income people receive or their expectations about the future is their access to credit, either to get them through a tight spot or to finance bigger purchases. Again, in richer countries more people can count on more sources of credit, which supplements the income they expect to earn. Typically, middle-class citizens in rich countries also gain considerable wealth over the lifecourse as they save for retirement or build equity in a home, another difference in economic status not captured in many measures of income inequality. An American who owns a home, can buy a car on credit, has saved a bit for retirement, and expects to receive a Social Security pension enjoys a quality of life that exceeds the one typical in

Malawi much more than mere income differences would suggest. At the same time, other good things in life tend to be more equally spread, for example because even poor Malawians without any material possessions to speak of may get some education or medication, and to that limited extent inequality in human misery may be less stark than income differences suggest.

All in all, this should give us pause in trying to generalize about trends in global income inequality. Grand claims about the topic all depend on a series of steps, each of which can be a misstep. In collecting data, measuring inequality, and comparing countries we have ample opportunity to stumble. That should inspire some humility in optimists and skeptics alike. This attitude may help as well in decoding the impact of globalization on inequality, discussed in the following section. The link between a big process and a complex set of inequality patterns, supported by somewhat shaky evidence, is likely to defy rash simplifications.

Globalization and Inequality

When Nike cast about for places to produce high-end sneakers after production in Japan had become too costly, Korea offered a good alternative (Korzeniewicz 1994). Reliable workers could produce fairly intricate shoes at low cost, at least until Korea's rising incomes priced its workers out of sneaker production. At that point, Koreans became managers of shoe factories in places like Vietnam, operating as subcontractors for Nike. In just a few decades, Korea's role in this particular global commodity chain shifted. That change is just one part of the larger story briefly summarized in the beginning of this chapter. Quite deliberately, Korea used exports to boost growth. After starting small, it placed big bets on heavy industry, entering key markets around the world. After borrowing technology from its allies, it began producing its own, keeping up with the cutting edge. After closing itself off to imports and direct investment, it gradually opened up to a greater foreign role in its economy. Though Korea related very differently to the world at large in 2000 than it had in 1970, its strategy of export-led growth had proved consistently successful. Globalization served Korea well.

To optimistic interpreters of globalization, as Chapter 5 already indicated, that is not surprising. To show that Korea is more rule than exception, they would cite China, of course, but also Vietnam or Uganda, as places where greater trade translated into higher incomes for many poor people (Dollar 2005: 120–21). At the end of the twenty-first century, countries that opened up more than others, measured by the rise in the proportion of GDP derived from trade, also enjoyed higher growth and this higher growth benefited the poor (106, 115). A bit more cautiously, they would make the same claim about freer movement of capital into a country: other things being equal, greater openness to direct and portfolio investment from abroad leads to higher growth, at least for countries that have already reached a certain level of development (Calomiris 2005: 61–2). Of course, they also think it is telling that there are no countries that stayed closed, either to trade or capital, and nevertheless caught up with the rich countries. Such evidence, then, suggests that globalization and poverty reduction, or globalization and the modest reversal in inequality, are not just correlated, but that globalization actually deserves credit for those effects because it fostered relatively higher growth in relatively poor countries.

The argument makes theoretical sense to economists who view globalization as the construction of an open world market, a position also encountered in Chapter 5. In an ideally open world, globalization should pay off, for reasons reviewed there. Trade helps workers compete abroad, enabling them to earn higher wages than they would have in domestic sectors. Foreign investment in principle should help to improve productivity and therefore wages by putting more capital at businesses' disposal. Similarly, diffusion of technology should help domestic businesses improve their performance, to the benefit of workers and the larger economy. In the long run, this should even out differences between countries and lead to economic convergence, just as there has been convergence in life expectancy and beer drinking.

As with celebrations of the performance of the open world economy and the blessings of neoliberal policies, skeptics challenge the notion that globalization has greatly contributed to poverty reduction and inequality reversals. For starters, the Korean case is more ambiguous than it seems. At first, Korea practiced one-way globalization: exports going out without consumer goods coming in. As noted, it had the good fortune to get financial and technical, not to mention military, support from its wealthy friends, the US and Japan, a form of favoritism not available to all participants in the world economy. Korea quite deliberately sought opportunity in the global market but until at least the late 1990s it did so under the guidance of a strong, "developmental" state whose success suggested that simply opening markets, in the manner preferred by economic theory, was not sufficient (Amsden 2001). Globalization took a peculiar form in Korea and only complemented other factors.

This skeptical response is fair as far as it goes. Yet precisely what it was about the developmental state that made it work, at least for a while, remains a question, since it did many things at once – protecting property, extending loans, restraining unions, and so on. The developmental state is an institution that worked in Korea under Korean conditions, and it placed bets on businesses that happened to pay off, but there is no formula that guarantees such success in other situations. In fact, Korea itself gradually dismantled it, first by becoming more democratic and therefore less top-heavy, then by moving in a more "neoliberal" direction, more closely following global policy norms (Pirie 2008). Korea's global engagement also occurred in a particular phase of globalization. Quite apart from the distinctive political support it enjoyed, Korea happened to have good timing in pursuing export-led growth in certain heavy industries, but making steel and building ships will not seem quite as attractive to others at a later stage. Under different market conditions, with different technologies, new contenders will have to make new choices. Korea's temporary self-protection raises the question whether all developing countries should be allowed some slack as they get ready to be contenders, but it does not refute the notion that globalization in some form is essential if a country wants to "catch up." The Korean case does show that countries are likely to engage globalization in their own way, with their own traditions, resources, and institutions. How they may benefit from globalization depends on the state of the world, that is, on the opportunities it presents and the forces of competition it unleashes at any particular time. Skeptics notwithstanding, there may indeed be some common ingredients in global success stories. Yet the moral I draw from the story is that globalization contributes to growth if, and only if, a country brings to bear ideas and policies and institutions that make it pay off. Globalization's benefit is contingent on a particular mix that can vary.

To quantitative evidence that globalizing countries or investment recipients grow most, skeptics respond that the data do not speak so clearly. For example, the point about the growth of globalizers counterintuitively suggests that countries that have long been very open but simply have not opened up further should enjoy slower growth than countries that came to the party late (Wade 2004). If the benefit lies in openness, then the rate of opening should not have a much greater effect than the level of openness. Even more complex is the picture of foreign investment. Its record turns out to be more mixed, perhaps because in comparisons across countries places that grew without much direct investment, like Korea, dampen the effect of places where such investment did work, but that in itself casts doubt on the universal benefit of foreign direct investment. Other quantitative evidence suggests that there is by no means a clear correlation between globalization and growth. The irregularity of the link is partly accounted for by the fact that globalization can also cause countries trouble. If a country stakes its fortune on coffee exports and new suppliers get into the business, lowering the world commodity price, or if a country that made a good living from textiles suddenly encounters new competition from across the globe, or if a country like Korea puts short-term foreign loans in hard currency to work in long-term domestic investments and then has trouble repaying debt when its currency plummets, the people in such places associate globalization with crisis. At least in certain periods or episodes, globalization can hurt. Again, to take issue with the skeptical line, this does not refute the notion that on balance globalization in some form is essential to growth and therefore to the closing of gaps. Yet on one point skeptics and globalization proponents have come to agree, namely the idea that globalization's effect is contingent on many other factors.

Should globalization lead to convergence? Without rehearsing the competing arguments discussed in Chapter 5, there is reason to think it will not. By putting great resources in the hands of the rich, globalization gives them greater clout in defining its rules and shaping its direction, which is just one reason that inequality can lead to greater inequality as the rich rig the game to their advantage (Pogge 2007). The forces of convergence do not fully account for the urge to accumulate capital that pervades the system and constantly spurs innovation to the advantage of some but not others: capitalism's creative destruction creates a constant drive toward new inequality, which at the very least counteracts the push toward convergence (Korzeniewicz and Moran 2007). But it is becoming more difficult to believe in a global "Matthew effect," that they who have shall receive, since Korea is by no means the only exception anymore. The drive toward inequality does capture some of the dynamism in the world economy but it does not refute the idea that convergence may also continue. In fact, assuming that both happen – at the same time, together and in opposition – is not a bad way to think about the challenge all countries face in the age of globalization.

So does globalization lead to less inequality? Not necessarily. Earlier waves of globalization in fact enlarged global gaps, as did the third wave until recently. Yet there are now signs that the old divergence may be done, that the system of inequality is no longer quite stable. This is neither a triumph of neoliberal globalization nor testimony to the brilliance of developmental states. Under certain conditions, both institutional and historical, globalization can pay off. As in more places more of those conditions prevail, inequality will decline further. "Globalization plus" is the only recipe we can sensibly prescribe. In one way, that is of course unsatisfying, since it leaves unclear just exactly what must be done. But it speaks to a larger point we have noted before: instead of thinking of globalization as a factor or cause that by itself can create a certain effect or change people's lives, it makes more sense to view deterritorialization, even in the mundane and specific form of trade and investment, as one aspect of a package of social and technical changes that are transforming the lives of billions. It offers the prospect of lower inequality. But it can only deliver if Malawians can join those billions. Will they?

Toward Lower Poverty and Inequality

Malawi is in a tough spot, literally and figuratively. Without easy access to oceans, its exports are always at a disadvantage. Short of natural resources, the country has no easy road to riches. Always at risk of drought, it suffers whenever the rains prove short. Since its neighbors are quite poor as well, it cannot piggyback on their strength. Its land cannot carry the load of feeding a larger population, growing exportable crops, and providing work and income to small farmers. Yet, since colonial days, the nation had looked to agriculture as the way to a better future, even as its products proved steadily less profitable in global markets. The colonial legacy of a strong central state also hampered progress, not least by tempting Malawi's elite to skim the meager gains the country made. Even as it improved its "human capital" by getting more kids into schools, it had to keep up with an outside world in which other kids were learning more as well. A globalizing world accentuated the disadvantages of backwardness. After Asia had taken off, it was that much harder for Malawi to make similar progress since it now had to compete with whole new groups of strong players. Certainly Korea faced some of the same challenges at one time, but in combination Malawi's are far more daunting.

Can Malawi at least do better than it has? Few prescriptions for development offer easy answers. One such prescription is that growth minimally requires protection of property rights, needed to attract investment that is key to growth. In the Malawian countryside that is easier said than done when any little surplus risks being poached by hungry neighbors. Another prescription focuses on education, since higher skills and human capital may translate into better jobs and wages. Holding on to educated people is another matter, as Malawi discovered when many doctors and nurses preferred to emigrate. A third prescription points to a government bound by law and accountable to the people as a way to avoid predatory elite behavior and create a more predictable economic environment. While Malawi has already taken strides in this direction, its experience with democracy has met with mixed development results. Malawi should lower tariffs and taxes to attract foreign investment rather than rely on aid, a global prescription would suggest, but of course that assumes it offers opportunities worth investing in. In fact, globalization may hurt as well as help (Collier 2007): the previous success of Asia puts Malawi in a tougher spot since it would face strong competition if it were to try to break into world markets, openness will tempt richer Malawians to ship their funds to safer havens abroad, and building human capital may just enable the best and brightest to seek their fortunes elsewhere. None of the brief counterpoints implies that the prescriptions should not be tried, for indeed the multi-drug "treatment" of property rights and education and a stable, responsive government and an open society is likely to help the "patient," but they do convey that administering development medicine is an inherently complex task.

Yet it can be done. While Malawi struggled, Botswana prospered. Indeed, in the last three decades of the twentieth century it grew at world-record pace, even faster than Korea (Leith 2005: 4). One reason was that it began with very little, so any small improvement meant a large rate of growth: at independence in 1966, it had no electricity or telephone system, no sewage or water pipes, only five kilometers of paved roads, and so on (93). With few educated leaders, Botswana had to start its modern development nearly from scratch. It got help from technical experts invited to staff its ministries. More than in most African countries, its leaders largely favored the national over the personal or tribal good. Early on, Botswana devised some institutions that worked well, such as national development plans that drew on its long tribal tradition of making decisions by seeking consensus. It adopted some sensible policies, for example by avoiding a "bloated state-owned enterprise sector" (100). The government also typically did not spend all of the growing income it received, enabling it to build up credit and foreign exchange reserves that helped to absorb any economic shocks (106–7). By comparison with Malawi, it was in a better spot, taking advantage of economic ties with South Africa. Of course, Botswana also got lucky when major mineral reserves, especially diamonds, were discovered there. But Botswana still had to manage its luck, which it did by attracting foreign mining capital (De Beers in particular) in the first place and then by using the proceeds for the population at large.

Botswana's success shows unmistakably that poor countries can improve their lot, and in particular that poor African countries need not be stuck in a poverty trap. If only Malawi had better leaders, better institutions, better policies, better neighbors, and perhaps a nice diamond mine or two, it could do just as well as Botswana. Facetious comparisons aside, how much Malawi can really learn from it remains an open question. After all, Botswana owes its development to "sound" economic policies made possible by "tradition, institutions, and leadership" (Leith 2005: ix), which covers a lot of ground. Add luck and location to the equation, and the secret to Botswana's success appears to be a distinctive combination of factors, not easily copied in Malawi. Nor would Malawi want to copy Botswana in all respects, for that success is not without blemishes: most of its growth was due simply to more money put into infrastructure and education rather than higher productivity as in Asia, in spite of all its growth nearly a quarter of its people remained very poor, and even among African countries it had a high rate of HIV infection. If Botswana were able to continue on its old path, and Malawi could adapt some of the lessons in Botswana's story, it would obviously benefit their people by cutting poverty. But such success would still not alter the global picture of inequality much since with less than 2 million people Botswana is the size of a small Chinese city.

Summary and Conclusion

In the third wave of globalization, the Asian revival began to close gaps with still-growing developed countries while chronic problems in Africa widened them. A smaller part of the world population lives in absolute poverty but the plight of the "bottom billion" remains a stark challenge. Caveats accompany such generalizations: data on key issues are often inadequate, comparisons across countries and over time are hard. Some participation in globalization seems essential for countries to catch up, but how to do it and how to make it pay off will vary from case to case. Korea, or even Botswana, cannot serve as a straightforward model for countries like Malawi.

Yet much depends on what Botswana, Malawi, and their counterparts among developing countries do. As long as poverty is as deep as it is for the "bottom billion" who are worst off in the world, the tyranny of place remains nearly as strong as ever. As long as global inequality is as great as it is, globalization has yet to feel real to many people. As this chapter has shown, globalization is not bound to make the rich richer and the poor poorer. But if it is to lead to a more tangible "world society," it will have to help reduce poverty and inequality far more.

Classic recipes for reducing poverty and inequality prescribe development – economic growth. However, as the next chapter shows, growing global concern about the environment has raised questions about those recipes.

Questions

1   In one view of the capitalist world-system, countries or regions may change places but an overall system of inequality remains in place, and due to the forces in the system some countries will not be able to move up. How do the specific records of Malawi, Botswana, and Korea, or general indications that the "great divergence" has ended, affect this line of argument?
2   Most scholars regard both poverty and inequality as serious problems but some distinguish between the two, on the grounds that global inequality results mostly from the gains made by the "winners" compared to relatively stagnant "losers," and therefore may be a sign of overall increases in human welfare. Is this a valid point? Would inequality still matter as much as it does today if most of humanity achieved at least Korea's standard of living?
3   Two scholars of economic globalization, Robert Hunter Wade and Martin Wolf, have debated whether "globalization works," i.e. whether it reduces both poverty and inequality, with Wolf cheering the proposition and Wade casting doubt on it. How does the chapter help to settle the debate?
4   If world society would commit to eradicating poverty in a few decades, what should be its first steps?

Further Reading

Alice H. Amsden, *The Rise of "the Rest": Challenges to the West from Late-Industrializing Economies* (Oxford University Press, 2001)

Paul Collier, *The Bottom Billion: Why the Poorest Countries Are Failing and What Can Be Done About It* (Oxford University Press, 2007)

William Easterly, *The Elusive Quest for Growth: Economists' Adventures and Misadventures in the Tropics* (MIT Press, 2001)

David Held and Ayse Kaya (eds.), *Global Inequality* (Polity Press, 2007)

Branko Milanovic, *Worlds Apart: Measuring International and Global Inequality* (Princeton University Press, 2005)

Jeffrey Sachs, *The End of Poverty: Economic Possibilities for Our Time* (Penguin, 2005)

12

THE GLOBAL ENVIRON[
SAVING THE PLANE[

- Dams and Development
- Creating the (Global) "Environment"
- The Global Environmental Regime
- From Ozone to Climate
- The "Greening" of World Society?
- Summary and Conclusion

Dams and Development

In 1979, Indian authorities approved more than 3,000 dam projects, including 165 big dams, along the course of the Narmada River, which flows east to west through several Indian states into the Arabian Sea (Khagram 2004: 65). The huge scheme, which would flood about 90,000 acres and displace an estimated 100,000 people (Doyle 2005: 129), was the latest in a series of similar ventures: with more than 800 major dams completed since independence, India had become a leading dam-building country. Its first prime minister, Jawaharlal Nehru, was an enthusiastic supporter who could wax rhapsodic about dams as secular temples serving the good of mankind. He had reason for his enthusiasm, since dams seemed an obvious and practical solution to several problems his country faced: they could generate electricity relatively cheaply, collect water for reliable irrigation, and supply drinking water to parched areas. Dams powered development, and development was what India needed. The World Bank agreed. Over the years, by one estimate, it lent more than $58 billion to more than 600 projects in some 93 countries (Khagram 2004: 7). Not surprisingly, when the Narmada projects were announced, the Bank was prepared to provide support, especially for the big 455-foot-high Sardar Sarovar dam.

In spite of that initial support, however, the dam would not be built for quite some time. One reason was that Indian states wrangled over costs and benefits with each other and with the central government. But beyond the ordinary power struggles something more dramatic happened: the Narmada basin became the object of an environmental struggle as well. That struggle in turn had a global dimension.

...mestic opponents, allied with transnational organizations, challenged the projects by appealing to global norms. Together, they put pressure on international institutions like the World Bank to change course. They did not just take on the dams; many also questioned the model of development the dams embodied. Their efforts turned a seemingly local issue into a global cause. They thus contributed to a larger sea change in world society, described in this chapter, that made "the environment" a global problem and devised new ways of addressing it in the form of a global "regime."

Immediately after the initial approval of the Narmada projects, farmers in the upstream state of Madhya Pradesh whose land was likely to be submerged already raised their voice in protest, and in response officials in that state tried to get better terms from downstream Gujarat, the main beneficiary of the dam, for people who would have to be resettled. In Gujarat, too, many groups were concerned. Through two INGOs, Oxfam and Survival International, they gained access to the World Bank, arguing that the projects should only move forward if they respected the human rights of tribal or indigenous peoples and would guarantee adequate rehabilitation and resettlement for anyone removed from their land (Khagram 2004: 92–5). The World Bank listened, approving a 1985 loan agreement with Indian state governments on the condition that they adopted a detailed resettlement program. Similar concerns resonated within India: its Supreme Court ordered proper treatment of displaced persons, and the Ministry of Environment and Forests worried that Gujarat would not do enough. Under increasing pressure, Gujarat changed its approach, promising far more compensation for people to be ousted from their land.

Some dam critics were willing to help implement the promised reforms. Others, however, took a more radical tack, opposing the dams altogether as an environmental disaster. The tribunal that approved the projects had paid little attention to environmental issues but the Indian government had already begun to adopt some environment-friendly policies, such as a forest conservation effort, that soon came into play in the Narmada controversy when a federal ministry refused to give environmental clearances (Khagram 2004: 107). The World Bank, too, greatly increased its attention to environmental concerns in the 1980s, making environmental arguments a more effective weapon in the arsenal of nongovernmental groups that were pressuring the Bank to change its approach and used the Narmada, in the words of one critic, to "symbolize destructive development" (108). That became a mantra of Indian activists, led by the charismatic Medha Patkar, who added to the transnational pressure and the domestic hurdles by mobilizing villagers across the Narmada region to stop the dam. Formed in 1989, the Narmada Bachao Andolan, or Save the Narmada Movement, drew public attention with rallies, marches, and acts of nonviolent resistance. The World Bank felt the pressure and asked for the first ever independent review of a project it supported, which resulted in a 1992 report expressing great concern about the dams' ecological impact and urging the Bank to step back. After the Bank adopted benchmarks that could not be met, India in fact decided to forego the remaining loans for Sardar Sarovar (130). But dam building continued, spurring the Andolan to protest more intensely – "Save and Drown Squads" threatened to stay in villages to be submerged, Medha Patkar staged a hunger strike – and to file suit in the Indian Supreme Court in 1994. After lengthy proceedings, the court decided in 1997 to put implementation of Sardar Sarovar on hold, in part due to insufficient environmental safeguards in the projects, handing the Andolan a major victory.

As the court case confirmed, in less than two decades the environment had become a major issue in the conflict about the Narmada. The Narmada protesters did not make that happen by themselves. In India, environmental issues were already percolating in policy circles. Outside India, NGOs had become very active in dealing with the environment. Dams and rivers had become a flashpoint in global debate about development, stimulated by new organizations like the International Rivers Network. Even the World Bank's stance was already shifting in the 1980s. The Narmada campaign thus drew strength from budding global environmentalism and amplified it in turn. Though focused on an apparently "domestic" or local project, it nevertheless had the hallmarks of other major environmental campaigns: it involved global civil society, became entwined with the reform of global governance, and pushed forward a shift in global environmental consciousness. As this chapter shows, with regard to more distinctly global environmental problems world society has seen even more distinctly global attempts at redress that point both to new global institutions and to a new ecological awareness. But the Indian story is also a cautionary tale. The Andolan victory proved short-lived when in 2000 and again in 2005 the Indian Supreme Court gave the go-ahead to building Sardar Sarovar at close to its planned height. A domestic institution thus decided the issue in a manner that fit environmentalists' worst fears. I return to the implicit caution in the conclusion.

Creating the (Global) "Environment"

Sardar Sarovar was by no means the first big dam to become controversial. In the US, a fight had erupted in 1900 over plans by the city of San Francisco to build a dam some 150 miles away in the Hetch Hetchy Valley in Yosemite National Park, intended to assure a reliable supply of drinking water. John Muir of the Sierra Club, long-time advocate for Yosemite, took the lead in opposing the project. Though the political struggle turned complicated, Muir and his allies consistently defended the special beauty of the valley against the dastardly plans of ambitious city leaders. While they certainly loved the "wilderness," they also envisioned a different use for the valley, setting it aside for nature tourism (Righter 2005: 6), and if this retrospective view is right, they in effect advocated a different form of development rather than pure preservation. Regardless of their exact motives, another kind of development won out in California, as it did later in India: Congress gave permission to flood the valley in 1913, and the major dam was completed ten years later.

In spite of the outcome, the Hetch Hetchy fight illustrates the state of environmental concern, at least in the US, of about a century ago. At the time of the dam battle, Muir was already an iconic figure thanks to his eloquent defense of nature in the American west. His voice was one of many, going back to the writers Henry David Thoreau and Ralph Waldo Emerson, that had ascribed spiritual meaning to human relationships with nature and therefore insisted on its protection. Even in Muir's day, that was not the only way influential people thought about nature (Guha 2000). San Francisco city leaders, perhaps more closely attuned to majority opinion at the time, held to the old-fashioned idea of nature as resource, to be mastered for the benefit of people. Another strand in proto-environmental thinking, prevalent in forestry circles, advocated a form of scientific conservation of natural habitats as resources deserving of careful respect. But Muir's thinking had contributed more than most to the emerging conservation movement, whose clearest success was America's national park system – Yellowstone was established in 1872, Yosemite in 1890 – which became a model soon followed in other countries. Muir also took the initiative in founding the Sierra Club in 1892, a civic organization long dedicated to conservation. The club swung into action at Hetch Hetchy. Just as the Indian environmental movement might have come of age in the initial Narmada campaign (Kothari, cited in Khagram 2002: 222), the Hetch Hetchy fight is a plausible candidate for marking the "birth of modern environmentalism" in America (Righter 2005).

Of course, saying so requires the benefit of hindsight: at least among a significant minority in the early twentieth century, the environment had become an issue, but "the environment" as a publicly recognized problem, let alone environmental*ism* as a concerted movement to deal with it, did not yet exist. According to standard environmental history, "the environment" and environmental*ism* took off in the US thanks an event that occurred much later: the publication of Rachel Carson's book, *Silent Spring*, in 1962. In vivid prose, Carson evoked the "contamination of man's total environment with substances of incredible potential for harm." Among the "elixirs of death" increasingly used by farmers to kills pests, she singled out DDT, explaining how it first leached into soil and water and then entered the food chain. In New England, she argued, insecticides sprayed on elm trees made their way into worms that then poisoned robins, whose death caused the "silent spring" of her title. The disturbing facts conveyed the broader message that nature was an "intricate web of life whose interwoven strands lead from microbes to man," a "complex, precise and highly integrated system of relationships between living things."

As a marine zoologist, Carson used her scientific credentials to lay out "the facts" and trace the causes of environmental harm. As a writer, she matched reason with passion, conveying the sheer urgency of stopping environmental destruction. As a thinker, she advocated a view of nature as an ecosystem in which humans were inextricably involved. Carson herself died of cancer soon after the publication of her book but her message lived on. In fact, in many ways she provided a model for environmental thinking for a generation to come, by mixing science with a sense of moral responsibility in the belief that appropriate human action, guided by reason, could forestall the grave dangers ahead, if only humans could see themselves as part of the "intricate web." "Like the heart of the movement she galvanized," says one historian, she was "more moderate than radical," inspiring reform rather than transformation of modern industrial uses of nature (Peterson del Mar 2006: 102).

The book became a big success in the US, selling half a million copies in hardback alone. It produced concrete results, in the form of a ban on DDT and federal legislation dealing with other toxic substances in the early 1970s. By stirring the American public's ecological consciousness, it planted the seeds of environmental activism that would flourish in the following decades. Among the beneficiaries were traditional environmental organizations – the National Wildlife Federation had been "just sitting here," in the words of one member, and suddenly faced an influx of new members pushing its size to half a million in 1970, and the Sierra Club similarly enjoyed a nearly sixfold rise in membership between 1959 and 1970 (Peterson del Mar 2006: 105). Carson's book also lit sparks abroad: it was translated into 12 languages and "had a striking impact on the resurgence of environmentalism throughout Europe" (Guha 2000: 73). In short, it ignited a "green fire" (Peterson del Mar 2006: 102).

The standard history may give Carson a bit too much credit, for some fires were already burning and other people had already added fuel when she wrote. In 1956, for example, the venerable Sierra Club and the Wilderness Society had teamed up to block a dam on the Colorado River, a striking reversal of the Hetch Hetchy debacle and a sign of changes in American public sentiment and political priorities. In the early 1960s, the US Congress was already working on laws dealing with clean air, clean water, and solid waste. Other authors had been writing on issues similar to Carson's with less public acclaim, and she relied on the research of colleagues that documented the impact of human activities on nature. The love of nature to which she appealed was reviving in the emerging counterculture of the 1960s. Carson's sparks thus hit timber ready to burn, and in the US the fire spread quickly. In 1970, for example, the Nixon administration created the Environmental Protection Agency. On April 22 of that year, the first Earth Day celebration drew some 20 million people altogether, perhaps the largest demonstration of that era. Only eight years after Carson's book, American environmental sensibility peaked early (Peterson del Mar 2006: 108).

While America was among the environmental leaders at the time, the green fire moved around the globe. New organizations fanned the flames (Wapner 1996). Founded in 1961 with the support of elite patrons like Prince Philip in Britain and Prince Bernhard in the Netherlands, the World Wildlife Fund (WWF) focused its efforts on conserving wildlife in what was then called the Third World, specializing in projects that involved local communities in preventing poaching and other forms of destruction. In 1969, former Sierra Club executive director David Brower founded Friends of the Earth (FOE) to take the cause where the old club did not want to go. Without actively recruiting members or founding offices, FOE spread to more than 50 countries, each with an independent branch simply committed to "conservation,

restoration and rational use of our planet's resources." Without much central coordination FOE affiliates came to play a major role on issues like spurring quicker
action on ozone depletion and stopping the cutting of tropical hardwood forests.
In 1972 Greenpeace emerged out of Canadian protests against US nuclear tests, and
with a bit more central direction than FOE it spread globally as well, gaining renown
with spectacular stunts to interfere with whaling and weapons testing. WWF, later
renamed the Worldwide Fund for Nature (WWFN), grew to be the largest environmental INGO with over 5 million members and 90 country offices; FOE gained
70 national affiliates, some of them, like the Dutch association Milieudefensie with
its nearly 100,000 members and supporters, among the more sizeable NGOs in their
countries; and Greenpeace attracted more than 2.5 million members spread across
41 countries (Chasek et al. 2006: 74). Their strategies differed – WWF took a more
"localist" tack in solving specific problems, Greenpeace at least initially had a more
"globalist" vision of fostering an ecological sensibility among the public (Wapner
1996) – but their campaigns overlapped and they had much in common as strands
in a single movement.

A major UN meeting in Stockholm in 1972 added more fuel to the fire (Lechner
and Boli 2005: 95–7; DeSombre 2006: 22–5; Speth and Haas 2006: 56–61). A preparatory report carried the telling title *Only One Earth* and called for "shared loyalty
to the earth." The very name of the meeting, "Conference on the Human Environment," indicated that "the environment" had definitely arrived as a global concern.
Attendance by 113 states attested to a rising sense of urgency. The Stockholm
Declaration adopted at the meeting asserted the need for a "common outlook"
and "common principles" to preserve the environment, now an "imperative goal
for mankind." Still protective of state sovereignty in exploiting natural resources
and confident in the use of "rational planning" to solve environmental problems,
the declaration nevertheless expressed a new sensibility. Along with another preparatory report it also alluded to an issue that would haunt environmental debate in
the years to come, claiming that underdevelopment in poor countries caused harm
to the environment and that economic development was essential to improve it.
Among the problems discussed in Stockholm was acid rain, a special concern for
Scandinavians, who complained that their pristine lakes were fouled by emissions
originating in far-away places – one of many "transboundary" problems that came
to crowd the global agenda – and the Stockholm discussions cleared the way for
the Convention on Long-Range Transboundary Air Pollution that went into force
in 1983. Similarly, an elaborate action plan adopted in Stockholm – containing no
less than 109 policy recommendations in six areas – called for a conference on trade
in endangered species, which took place soon after and resulted in the 1973 Convention on International Trade in Endangered Species of Wild Fauna and Flora
(CITES).

The meeting also spawned a new institution, the United Nations Environment
Programme (UNEP), formally created by the General Assembly (DeSombre 2006:
9–21). Some large UN member states and developing nations had opposed a big
new independent agency, and even the resolution creating UNEP noted that

"responsibility for action to protect and enhance the environment rests primarily with government and, in the first instance, can be exercised more effectively at the national and regional levels." As a program, UNEP became dependent on voluntary donations, which varied from year to year, leading to chronic financial difficulty. Not surprisingly, it proved challenging for UNEP to live up to its task of monitoring and coordinating and promoting new environmental activity. It has in fact become a clearinghouse for environmental data with its regular Global Environmental Outlooks and its Global Resource Information Database. With occasional success, it has also fostered programs to protect regional seas, such as the Mediterranean. It has also helped to boost negotiations on specific issues, though it often played only a limited role after agreements were reached. Thanks to energetic leadership by its director, it helped plan a major UN meeting in 1992. Perhaps only modestly effective by design, it has nevertheless taken a central place in environmental governance.

In the year of the Stockholm meeting, another book stirred the green fire. Issued by the Club of Rome, *Limits to Growth* (Meadows et al. 1972) resembled *Silent Spring* in some respects. While it lacked eloquent prose, it had a scientific patina of its own, demonstrating ominous trends in humanity's use of resources with numerous statistics and calculations based on computer models. Like Carson, the authors of *Limits* thought of nature as one large ecosystem, and urged immediate action to bring about a "sustainable state of global equilibrium." *Limits* became a bestseller, too. At the same time, though Carson might well have been in sympathy with the Club of Rome, the report marked a departure from her way of thinking and the environmental mainstream at the time. More than Carson, the Club of Rome authors questioned the merits of mere reform. They explicitly challenged the drive toward growth and thought of environmental problems as truly global. Together with other such departures, their report pointed to a new thrust in global environmentalism that would gather strength, as I discuss in a later section.

Ignited in the 1960s, the green fire thus grew in the 1970s and by the 1980s had swept the globe. The metaphor captures the drama and passion in one phase of environmentalism but it is also misleading, since the movement was a creative conflagration. Out of its energies emerged a global environmental "regime," described in the next section. But apart from the details of that regime, environmentalism also represented globalization in action. By the 1980s, more people thought globally. More problems were recognized as intrinsically global. More civil organizations spread globally. More institutions operated globally. From the point of view of one scholar, Roland Robertson, it thus exemplified most strikingly the compression of the globe as a single place along with intense awareness of that compression (Robertson 1992).

In the process, environmentalism as a global force unsettled old ways of doing things. Again using Robertson's terms, it helped crystallize a "global field," in which individuals and states related to both the system of states and humankind itself. As in globalization generally, environmentalism "relativized" individuals' sense of citizenship, for example because more people thought of themselves as world citizens first. Similarly, it "relativized" states' authority because increasingly they had to arrange their affairs in relation to global environmental standards. Conversely, the interests of humanity, conceived in ecological terms, and the prospects of world society as a whole, conceived as occupying one planet, fed into the affairs of ordinary people and countries alike. In effect, environmentalism was a movement that gave form to those complex links. While the links were complex, the global field took very concrete shape in images of the "blue planet," a fragile floating ball seen from outer space thanks to Apollo missions to the moon. The image solidified the core experience of globalization, of all humanity forming one world on one shared planet.

The Global Environmental Regime

By the 1980s, world society had begun to address "the environment" as its common concern. A "regime" took shape, in the form of an array of institutions that applied new policies following similar norms and procedures on the basis of shared assumptions (Vogler 1995: Meyer, Frank et al. 1997). At the heart of the regime was the environmental culture just described, centered on the new ecological awareness that sprouted in the 1960s. Nature had come to matter more in public life, nature was no longer just "out there" for humans to use, and nature required rational care in order to assure human progress. The common model linked moral responsibility to scientific rationality for the sake of environmental protection. Some of its assumptions were in tension; for example, how to balance the new needs of nature and the old human desire for material progress was not immediately clear. In its 1987 report *Our Common Future*, the title yet another sign of the global perspective that had become entirely routine, the World Commission on Environment and Development (WCED 1987) tried to square that particular circle with an artful compromise that popularized a concept others had proposed before: environmental protection should achieve "sustainable development." As the Brundtland Report, so-named for the Norwegian politician who chaired the commission, famously put it, "Humanity has the ability to make development sustainable – to ensure that it meets the needs of the present without compromising the ability of future generations to meet their own needs," a process of change "in which the exploitation of resources, the direction of investments, the orientation of technological development, and institutional change are all in harmony and enhance both current and future potential to meet human needs and aspirations." At least as emphatically as Carson and the Club of Rome, the commission also treated environmental change as inherently global, a problem of the "global commons" to be addressed by the global community (Mol 2001: 54–5).

After 1972, a series of major meetings served as rituals expanding environmental consciousness and the related policy script. Already in the 1970s, UNEP arranged meetings on issues like climate change, soon to become more salient. It laid the groundwork for the summit of summits in 1992 at Rio de Janeiro (Lechner and Boli 2005: 81–4; Speth and Haas 2006: 69–74). With 178 states attending and some 1,400 NGOs accredited, it was perhaps the largest international meeting of any sort to date. Though its nickname, the "Earth Summit," was suitably evocative, its official name, the UN Conference on Environment and Development (UNCED), was in keeping with the central theme of environmental discourse of the preceding years. If nothing else, the meeting helped to turn the sustainable development mantra into a truly global principle. In "Agenda 21," the conference outlined plans of action on a host of issues, from the atmosphere to water to waste. State officials signed conventions that had been prepared beforehand on biological diversity and climate change but failed to reach agreement on forest protection. In spite of other disagreements, the Rio Declaration on Environment and Development expressed a consensus of sorts: it recognized the "integral and interdependent nature" of the earth, "our home," proclaimed the right of human beings to live in harmony with nature, and called for a "global partnership" to protect the "integrity" of the globe's ecosystem. Ten years later in Johannesburg, the World Summit on Sustainable Development took stock of the work of the previous decade, lamenting things left undone but affirming most of the old commitments. Though its own output did not match that of Rio, and as policymaking events both meetings left something to be desired in the eyes of environmentalists (DeSombre 2006: 28–30), as rituals affirming what a segment of world society considered sacred they did their job, thereby supporting the global regime.

Just as Stockholm led to the creation of UNEP, Rio gave birth to the UN Commission on Sustainable Development (CSD) (DeSombre 2006: 32–5). In the UN hierarchy, it has a subordinate position: its 53 member states are elected by another UN commission, the Economic and Social Council (ECOSOC), to which CSD also reports. Like UNEP, it has information-gathering duties, for example to monitor state progress toward reaching goals, but perhaps even more than UNEP it has trouble doing so, for example because developing countries have argued that reporting should be voluntary and not be used for comparisons of environmental performance. Initially bent on addressing the full Agenda 21 laundry list, it has since focused each year on single "themes" – seas and oceans are slated for attention in 2014–15 – but precisely how much it adds to the capacity of relevant parties to work on such themes is less clear. Like many UN bodies, skeptics charge, it is "long on dialogue and speech making but short on stimulating action" (Speth and Haas 2006: 72). Even if "real" effects perhaps do not match the expectations of CSD proponents, as another formal expression of international commitment it adds a building block to the global regime.

CSD opened doors for environmental INGOs in the UN system but UNEP became an even stronger magnet for environmental organizations. Around 2000, its Environmental Liaison Centre in Nairobi, Kenya, directly linked 535 NGOs to UNEP while maintaining relations with 10,000 others (Frank et al. 1999: 84). The global scene had changed beyond recognition. Between 1882 and 1990, 173 dedicated environmental INGOs were founded, most in the late twentieth century

(ibid.). The 1972 and 1992 meetings served as stimulants, encouraging environmentalists to form new groups to attend or to follow up on the meeting, and about
1,400 were present in Rio. While in Muir's time people from only a few Northern
countries participated in the early NGOs, by the 1990s most countries played some
role, and Europe's share of members declined from 77 to 31 percent (86). In all
organizations membership fluctuates, of course, and some popular environmental
(I)NGOs leveled off after an initial spurt, but some did especially well in the late
twentieth century – the WWFN, for example, grew nearly tenfold to over 5 million
people just between 1985 and 1995 (86–7). In the ecology of environmental INGOs,
everybody also became more connected to everybody else, as illustrated by the
International Union for the Conservation of Nature, which in 1965 had ties to three
IGOs and seven other INGOs but increased those links to 69 and 148, respectively,
by 1995 (90). In the wider global civil society and the structure of global governance,
discussed in Chapters 7 and 8, environmentalists had created a habitat of their own.
Within that habitat, some environmental INGOs, like FOE, ranged widely, covering
many issues, while others specialized in dealing with their own "turf."

Some of the work of the global regime was carried out by nation-states. With few
exceptions, such as the early US environmental legislation, their actions followed
the founding of international associations and the adoption of the first treaties; in
other words, while they were obviously involved in shaping the regime, they also
took their cues from it (Meyer, Frank et al. 1997: 625–6). Many developed countries
established environmental ministries in the early 1970s, quickly joined, as mentioned above, by countries like India, and a second spurt followed just prior to the
Rio summit. In many instances, this also entailed more environmental legislation,
and environmental-impact assessment laws, such as the one applied in the Narmada
case, rose from 1 in 1969 to 50 by 1990 (Frank et al. 2000: 98). As the Narmada
example already suggested, the new legal requirements did not necessarily improve
the environment greatly. Yet regardless of their rather variable performance, the
welfare and education states described in Chapter 6 also became environmental
states in short order, as if they were following "blueprints of nation-state environ-
mentalization" (Frank et al. 2000: 96). The green script took hold nearly everywhere. In some countries, Green parties emerged to make that script a hot political
item. The West German Green Party was the first to enjoy electoral success, entering
Parliament in 1983.

Even the brief description of the global environmental regime as an institutional
ecosystem within a larger global setting suggests that its growth has no single cause.
As a system of many parts it draws nutrients from many sources. The very idea of
nature as ecosystem, once presented and elaborated, had a certain power of persuasion. The authority of science, invoked by Carson and the Club of Rome and the
Stockholm Declaration, also helped in backing the new environmental culture. So
did creative entrepreneurs who took advantage of opportunities in civil society to
create vigorous new organizations. From another point of view, Western countries
had grown wealthy enough in the 1960s to be able to afford focusing on environmental problems as a prime "post-material" priority. Once institutionalized,

domestically in ministries and internationally in the UN system, the regime reinforced itself: environmental governance created more environmental governance. The institutionalized green fire became a torch relay, the flames reaching new issues and new places but never really being extinguished.

The global regime in fact consists of particular regimes, niches in a larger system centered on particular problems. Just as global governance generally is polycentric, multilayered and "striped," as Chapter 7 argued, so is environmental governance. Certainly UNEP plays a central role, but each set of issues has attracted its own set of rules, worked out by different sets of interested parties. The next section describes some of these niches to convey their variety and impact. Focusing on ozone depletion, deforestation, and climate change, it asks what all the consciousness raising and organizing really accomplished.

From Ozone to Climate

Throughout the 1970s, FOE worked with other groups to get American states to limit chlorofluorocarbon (CFC) propellants in aerosol sprays, and in the late 1980s it kept its collective eye on the issue, now trying to get cities to recycle CFCs (Wapner 1996: 126–9). In 1989 Greenpeace was still on the case as well, infiltrating a DuPont plant to hang a banner from a tall water tower praising DuPont as the number one ozone destroyer and to block a CFC transport by bolting a box to the plant's railroad tracks (53). By that time, though activists obviously were not satisfied, much had changed. In a relatively short period, scientific discoveries about the harmful impact of widely used chemicals had led to successful negotiation of a convention limiting their use, ushering in "perhaps the strongest and most effective global environmental regime" (Chasek et al. 2006: 114), with an "impressive impact" on state behavior (DeSombre 2006: 116).

In the early 1970s, scientists found that chlorofluorocarbons, man-made chemicals used as coolants, solvents, and propellants, could harm the "layer" of ozone gas in the stratosphere that protects life on earth against ultraviolet radiation from the sun (Vogler 1995: 127–36; Chasek et al. 2006: 106–14; Speth and Haas 2006: 87–96). Their work spurred FOE into action. The US began to limit CFC use with a 1977 ban on their use in spray cans and wanted other states to follow suit. At first, that was not easy. Some CFC producers in Europe still doubted the science. Developing countries feared the cost of restricting them. Given European opposition to strict regulation, as well as uncertainty about the extent of ozone depletion (Vogler 1995: 127), the 1985 Vienna Convention for the Protection of the Ozone Layer had provisions on monitoring but required no reductions. The parties agreed to renegotiate if new evidence emerged. By convenient coincidence, it did. Soon after the signing of the convention, scientists announced that the ozone layer above Antarctica had thinned. The one-two punch of basic chemistry combined with fresh observations, dramatically packaged as the "ozone hole," forced former opponents finally to accept 50 percent reductions in CFC production and use in the 1987 Montreal Protocol on Substances that Deplete the Ozone Layer. The protocol included strict controls and sanctions while providing developing countries with a transitional grace period. In light of further evidence produced by the new regime's Scientific Assessment Panel, which made the problem seem that much more serious, follow-up meetings of the parties strengthened requirements, applied them to a broader range of chemicals, and instituted an implementation fund, the first of its kind, for control measures in developing countries that had somewhat reluctantly joined the convention. However, disputes over another ozone-depleting chemical, methyl bromide, dragged on, with the US now taking a more anti-regulatory stance.

In spite of lingering differences between state parties and fairly weak enforcement provisions in the convention, ozone is a success story. From 1989 to 2003, CFC consumption declined from 1.1 million to 100,000 tons (Chasek et al. 2006: 114). CFC concentrations in the atmosphere have declined as well, and the ozone layer appears to have a good chance of recovery in the twenty-first century. The ozone regime had much going for it. The basic science, though complex, was quite straight-forward, and the regime allowed new information to guide new measures. A major producer country pushed for regulation at the outset, and key players like the DuPont chemical company got on board when they saw profit in CFC substitutes. Technical solutions limited the societal impact of restrictions, making them politically palatable. The cost of subsidizing CFC replacement in developing countries was manageable at about $2 billion overall, and this helped to improve global compliance. No wonder the ozone regime was effective, at least by comparison with others.

Protecting forests turned out to be more challenging (Chasek et al. 2006: 181–90). When the Malaysian FOE affiliate allied with the World Rainforest Movement to support the indigenous rights of the nomadic Penan people of Sarawak (on Borneo) in resisting the clear-cutting of their native forest habitat in the 1980s, and when FOE International joined with the Japan Tropical Forest Action Network to organize foreign boycotts of Malaysian hardwood (Keck and Sikkink 1998: 150–60), the Malaysian government did not take kindly to the intervention. Prime minister Mahathir Mohamad made his sentiments quite clear in 1990 by saying that it was his "policy to bring all jungle dwellers into the mainstream," and his government reiterated the point in the run-up to the Rio Earth Summit by arguing that the "environmentalist activists have no right to stand in the way of the Penans in this process of change and human development [away from forest dwelling]" (cited in Guha 2000: 124). Not surprisingly, Malaysia was part of a "veto coalition" of countries that regarded forests as a sovereign national resource and opposed limits on their exploitation. In the face of such opposition, Rio produced not a treaty but merely a set of "Forest Principles" that failed to treat forests as part of the "global commons" or to restrict trade to "sustainably managed" forest products.

A regime of sorts had already emerged prior to Rio. Forestry had long played a role in Western conservation efforts. After World War II, the Food and Agriculture

Organization (FAO) provided a forum for international discussion, and in 1971 it established a committee on forestry. Negotiations among key producers yielded an International Tropical Timber Agreement in 1983, followed by the establishment in 1986 of the International Tropical Timber Organization (ITTO), intended to promote trade in and management of tropical timber. In spite of the global polarization around the issue, negotiations continued after the relative failure of Rio. Perhaps to assure access to foreign markets for its timber companies, Malaysia began to support a global convention and found common ground with countries like Canada, leading to a round of bargaining in a new Intergovernmental Panel on Forests, established by the CSD (Chasek et al. 2006: 184–5). However, for lack of real enforcement power, or even a method to follow up, the hundred proposals issued by the panel in 1997 had little demonstrable effect on actual policy. At the same time, a new veto coalition, led by Brazil and the US, complicated moves toward a full-fledged treaty. Suspicious of Malaysia's shift, NGOs also turned skeptical. But intense dialogue continued, notably in the United Nations Forum on Forests (UNFF), established by ECOSOC in 2000.

A real agreement remained out of reach. The forest regime had grown, with the ITTO in the 1980s and later the UNFF. Forests received consistent attention, both in official circles and from NGOs. Some steps were taken to apply the principle of sustainable development to forests. With mixed results, the World Bank tried to put such ideas into practice, for example by refusing to support commercial logging in primary tropical forests after 1991, and with greater success it joined the WWF in 1998 to create an Alliance for Forest Conservation and Sustainable Use, which among other things has established more than 190,000 square miles of protected areas (Chasek 2006: 62–3). In spite of such positive steps, no rules with teeth, so to speak, materialized. The main reason is simply that too many interests in too many places fostered opposition. At crucial junctures, major countries could exercise an effective veto on global agreements. Compared to ozone, forests are complex, and while much is known about them, that knowledge is less easy to translate into policy solutions. While policymakers dithered, forests shrank: in spite of the campaign against it, Sarawak logging continued at a rate of millions of cubic meters of hardwood per year (Keck and Sikkink 1998: 158), and in the 1990s alone, Africa lost more than 5 million, South America nearly 4 million, hectares of forest cover (Chasek et al. 2006: 182). Small gains in developed regions only made up for some of the losses.

Still more complex than deforestation is the problem of climate change. One indicator is the lack of early INGO action. Nuclear tests or whale hunting or air pollution or ivory poaching, even ozone depletion, were all easy to visualize, easy to target; by comparison, even for those concerned about the issue, the threat of climate change was big, abstract, and hard to convey – not as "marketable," not as successful a "celebrity issue" (Ungar 1998). By the same token, a climate change regime was still in its "infancy" and climate change itself "an hypothesis" well into the 1990s (Vogler 1995: 137–9). A decade later, as its "discovery" had been "confirmed" (Weart 2003), global warming was at the very center of the

Table 12.1 Land area covered by forest, in percentage of total, 1990–2005

	1990	2000	2005
World	31.3	30.6	30.3
Sub-Saharan Africa	29.2	27.3	26.5
Latin America	50.3	47.5	46.3
South-Eastern Asia	56.3	49.9	46.8
Eastern Asia	16.5	18.1	19.8
Southern Asia	14.0	14.3	14.2
Developed regions	30.4	30.7	30.8

Source: UN 2007MDG

global environmental regime, the "celebrity issue" par excellence widely felt to be the main collective challenge for world society. Climate change quickly rose to the top of the global agenda but it had a running start (Chasek 2006: 115–28; DeSombre 2006: 117–24). Science had known for a long time that when the earth releases heat absorbed from the sun in the form of infrared radiation, certain gases in the atmosphere trap the energy before it can escape into space, creating a "greenhouse effect" that maintains a livable temperature on the planet. More than a century ago, scholars also began to speculate that human beings might increase the earth's temperature by releasing more carbon dioxide into the atmosphere, especially by burning fossil fuels, thus artificially enhancing the natural greenhouse effect. Later, monitoring stations began to document that CO_2 was in fact building up, and the growing concerns about the possible effects led the World Meteorological Organization (WMO) to convene the first World Climate Conference in 1979. Reviewing the evidence up to that point, a subsequent meeting in Villach, Austria, in 1985, organized by UNEP and the WMO, reached consensus on the basic point that global warming was a serious possibility (Chasek 2006: 118). As the hot summer of 1988 raised the public profile of the issue, UNEP and the WMO took the next step in defining it by setting up the Inter-governmental Panel on Climate Change (IPCC), a hybrid organization whose working committees would be composed of scientists but which would reach decisions about its course of action in annual meetings of non-expert government representatives, and charged it with collecting and assessing the best information on all aspects of climate change. Its series of assessment reports, compiled by hundreds of experts, set the benchmark for global thinking on the subject, and its first one in 1990, along with a second World Climate Conference, spurred further negotiations on a possible climate convention. These were even more complex than most, because North and South, large and small emitters, potential victim and beneficiary states all had different stakes. The UN Framework Convention on Climate Change, signed in Rio in 1992, therefore contained rather non-committal commitments to "stabilization" rather than actual reductions of greenhouse gas (GHG) concentrations, to support for developing country transition

(a)   (b)

Plate 12.1a and 12.1b   Photographs of Muir Glacier at Muir Inlet in Glacier Bay National Park and Preserve, Alaska, taken in 1899 and 2003, show retreat of glacier and growth of vegetation attributed to global warming
Sources: 12.1a © G.K.Gilbert/US Geological Survey Photographic Collection
      12.1b © Ronald Karpilo/US Geological Survey Photographic Collection

costs, and, of course, to further study. The problem was defined as real but it was not yet real in its consequences.

Those became slightly more real in protracted negotiations leading to adoption of the Kyoto Protocol in 1997. The protocol set real targets for industrialized countries, requiring them to make their emissions about 5 percent lower on average in 2008–12 than they had been in 1990. It allowed countries to reach those targets in several creative ways, for example by buying carbon "credits" from countries that were likely to stay well under their target or by sponsoring "clean development" projects in developing countries that introduced less carbon-intensive technology. In further discussion about how to implement the protocol, concluded in 2001, parties had to reach compromises on whether those creative methods could be used only in addition to serious domestic changes and on how carbon "sinks" that absorbed CO_2 could be counted as steps toward lowering emissions. After enough countries ratified, the protocol officially went into effect in 2005. That happened without American support: though the US had been closely involved in Kyoto, the US Senate had unanimously opposed joining the treaty if it did not commit developing countries to lower emissions, and in 2001 President George W. Bush formally withdrew from it, citing both the lack of developing country commitments and the likely harm to the American economy. The self-serving argument did point to a real problem, in that China and India had become large GHG producers, without whose participation the actual effect of Kyoto on GHG concentrations would be modest at best. As a step toward a more serious climate change regime, Kyoto represented a breakthrough, but its design also raised questions about more effective schemes that might succeed it.

Those schemes could rely on better knowledge. As the Kyoto Protocol parties geared up to implement its provisions, the IPCC continued to chart the problem itself, drawing on the expanding work of the wider scientific community. By the

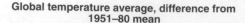

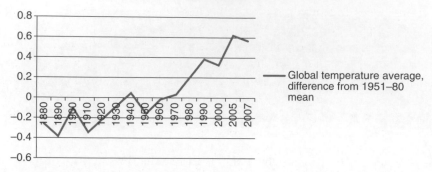

Figure 12.1 Development of average global temperature, 1880–2007, measured as anomaly values in land-ocean index, i.e. difference from 1951–1980 mean
Note: 1. Current estimates of temperature change vary by dataset and analysis, but generally fit this illustrative pattern of a significant rise in the late twentieth century. 2. Temperature line simplifies underlying data by not covering years between dates in graph.
Source: Goddard Institute for Space Studies data series, data.giss.nasa.gov/gistemp/graphs/ GLB_USHCN.2006vs.2005.txt

time of its fourth assessment report, published in 2007 (IPCC 2007), its models of atmospheric warming had become more sophisticated, taking into account many variables ranging from solar activity to cloud formation to ocean circulation. Its data had also improved, with more sources and instruments contributing more observations from more places. About the basic chemistry of warming due to GHG scientists had been quite certain to begin with. Now other patterns also became much clearer: the IPCC estimated that CO_2 in the atmosphere had increased by about a third over pre-industrial levels to more than 380 parts per million, that the earth's surface had warmed by approximately 0.74 degrees Celsius between 1906 and 2005, and that sea level had risen nearly 3 inches in the preceding 40 years. It also projected that the earth would warm further at a more rapid rate, between 1.8 and 4 degrees Celsius in the course of the twenty-first century. It judged the potential consequences very serious, pointing to more extreme weather in some regions, threats to agriculture from drought in others, and exposure to still higher sea levels in low coastal areas. Former US vice president Al Gore gave the cool reporting of these inconvenient truths a hot visual form with his movie *An Inconvenient Truth*. For their efforts, Gore and the IPCC earned the 2007 Nobel Peace Prize. Global warming had become *the* global problem.

Precisely what to do about it was less clear. One reason had to do with basic science: climate models were very complex and not yet fully understood – one expert calls computer climate modeling "perhaps the most complex endeavor ever undertaken by mankind" (Emmanuel 2007: 39) – and the interaction between the many factors that affect warming, along with potential "feedback" effects that can strengthen a trend when it starts, left some uncertainty about the effects of particular GHG reductions on overall temperatures. The long-term trend was not in serious doubt but projections of future temperatures necessarily involved an estimated range, leaving some uncertainty about how much warming would have to be reduced to reach a chosen target. The social effects of climate change were even more difficult to judge and likely to vary across the globe, giving some countries a much greater stake in it than others. By most accounts, Africa would be worst off; in Malawi, for example, higher temperatures and less rain might lead to more droughts, poor harvests, and possible starvation (UN 2007: 93). Russia, on the other hand, might gain valuable land for agriculture.

But even on the assumption that the effects could be reasonably anticipated and treated as a single global issue, the economics of climate change presented difficult choices as well, for example about how to weigh the future value of costly current reforms. In a massive and ominous report to the British government, intended to influence national policy, the economist Nicholas Stern (2007) argued that we should treat the interests of future generations as currently present and the same as our own and therefore urged large, immediate emission reductions, equivalent to imposing a tax of several hundred dollars per ton of carbon. The economist William Nordhaus found such proposals for big early reductions "much more expensive than necessary," in fact "more costly than doing nothing today"; he argued, by contrast, that we should discount the costs to future generations in light of the growth they will have enjoyed ($1,000 of damages in a century would have a present value of $20) and therefore recommended a more modest, but rising and uniform, carbon tax as the most efficient solution (Nordhaus 2008: 10, 201).

Designing any effective environmental regime is hard, and one expert cites the "embarrassingly long list" of factors that might contribute to it, from "political support within the participating nations" to having a "compliance-promoting mechanism" (DiMento, cited in Speth and Haas 2006: 133). Designing a regime for climate change is harder than any other, a daunting task even if would-be designers had more to go on than that "long list." Some of the underlying science is nearly as good as in the case of ozone but its complexity is much greater. Technical innovation is expected to help – and major economies in fact have been "decarbonizing" in the sense of producing more wealth with less fossil energy – but climate requires both more and better technical solutions, to be implemented on an even larger scale. Science and technology can only do so much, since climate change also involves deeper philosophical choices about how to design policy in the first place, as just illustrated with the conundrum of how to take into account the interests of future generations. Because GHG emissions stem from so many uses of fossil fuel, regime rules potentially affect and disrupt a much wider range of activities, making them that much more sensitive. Countries' widely varying stakes in fossil fuel use and in preventing global warming create even more conflicting interests than deforestation – which itself may contribute to warming because clearing land for agricultural use may lead to production of more methane, a GHG. Given the many tough choices

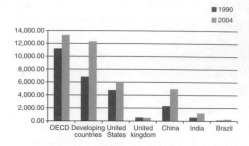

Figure 12.2 Total carbon dioxide emissions, in millions of tons of CO_2, for selected regions and countries, 1990–2004
Source: UN 2007: Table 24

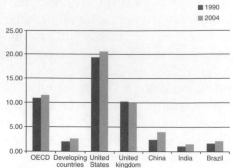

Figure 12.3 Carbon dioxide emissions per capita, in tons of CO_2, for selected regions and countries, 1990–2004
Source: UN 2007: Table 24

inevitably involved in climate policy, the political tangles also promise to be greater than in ozone and forests. Even a "simple" solution like a modest universal carbon tax would face enormous hurdles in a world where carbon emissions kept increasing after 1990, up to an estimated 27 billion tons in 2007, with America accounting for over a fifth of the total at just under 6 billion tons or about 20 tons per person. In many ways, then, climate change is a test of world society, and American society in particular, to devise collective solutions to a shared problem.

As pieces of the climate change regime, the Kyoto Protocol, the IPCC, and Nicholas Stern's review all reflect a common interest in using the tools of science to understand the earth's ecology and in using that knowledge to assess the costs and benefits of different solutions, ultimately to assure continued human progress. If we may call this the mainstream in the global environmental regime, another stream has moved in a different direction, trying to turn world society a deeper shade of green.

The "Greening" of World Society?

At a huge Narmada rally in Harsud in 1989, the *sankap* or resolve taken by protesters was "We want development, not destruction" (Khagram 2002: 222). For that ecological vanguard, development was not a dirty word. At the time, of course, it also figured prominently in global thinking about the environment, exemplified by the work of the Brundtland commission. In the standard model, at the heart of the global regime, it was development that had to be sustainable. But could it be, and if so, should it be? Even as the concept took off, critics thought it was "riddled with contradictions," "merely a mantra" that falsely implies that growth can be made sustainable because human ingenuity can find a way out of an "intractable dilemma" (Lipschutz 2004: 70–1). Such critics have proposed replacing the hubris of sustainable development with a simple belief in "sustainability" as such (Edwards 2005). The "sustainability revolution," in one version of the new paradigm, requires a "recalibration of human intentions to coincide with the way the biophysical world works" so that we may see ourselves as members of an ecological community, as "trustees of all that is past with all that is yet to come – a mystic chain of gratitude, obligation, compassion and hope," and thereby even prove ourselves "worthy of being sustained" (David Orr, in Edwards 2005: xiv–v). The old regime is anthropocentric, focused on what is good for humans; a new one should be biocentric, valuing the integrity of nature for its own sake – real greens believe we must respect nature "regardless of its value to us" and obey its "laws" (Pepper 1996: 11; Edwards 2005: 115–7). A biocentric approach to nature is also distinctly "holistic," centered on a vision of the "Whole Earth" that tells us to rethink how "mankind's world" relates to "nature's earth" (Caldwell, cited in Durant 2004: 29).

As they give sustainability a biocentric twist, critics of the old regime challenge the very notion of growth. Sustainable development is intractable, they argue, because a finite planet provides only finite resources for a finite population: "development forever" is a chimera, limits to growth are inevitable. It follows, at the very least, that "we cannot grow or consume our way out of the crisis" (Lipschutz 2004: 243). We already live in a nearly "full world," ecological economists argue (Daly and Farley 2004), and even if we could extract more resources from nature for a while, our wastes would overwhelm the earth's ecosystem. It therefore makes more sense to move toward a "steady-state economy at optimal scale" that would still allow for improvements in quality of life – defined not just by financial wealth alone – but give up on mindlessly increasing the economy's "throughput." Because growth is ultimately counterproductive, it cannot be equated with progress, and the critical thrust in environmental thinking in effect questions the validity of "progress" itself.

Not just the economics of the old regime has come under fire, so has the science that plays such an important role in it, as exemplified by the massive research effort devoted to climate change. Few environmentalists would dismiss the value of the knowledge it might gather, and traditionally they have invoked science to bolster their cause. But they have also been ambivalent (Yearley 2005: 113–5). Not finding in science a moral basis for the green case (Yearley 2005: 141), environmentalists have often "chosen their values first" and used science mainly for a "seal of approval" (Worster, cited in Pepper 1996: 21). They were rarely deterred by scientific findings that did not fit their agenda, as in the case of early Greenpeace activists who predicted large waves from nuclear tests but did not cease their protests when the waves did not occur. Since science always wants to know more and is liable to change, it has been an "unreliable" and "insufficient" friend for environmentalists (Yearley 2005). But the green critique also goes deeper. Science separates human observers from the environment, elevates a certain kind of knowledge over others, and

supplies the means of environmental destruction (cf. Pepper 1996: 240). The implication is not so much to reject science as to question the authority it has acquired
in the global environmental regime.

The regime not only relies on science but also puts its trust in markets and state
agreements, and it is therefore deeply embedded in several distinctly modern institutions. The regime embodies the spirit of "ecological modernization" (Mol 2001),
in the sense that it has confidence in the innovative ability of those modern institutions, guided by good-faith efforts to reach consensus, to solve the environmental
crisis. Critics are skeptical. Like opponents of neoliberalism such as those mentioned in Chapter 5, with whom they have a strong affinity, they argue that "market-
based solutions to market-generated problems do not eliminate the problem,"
which means that real change requires "asserting the primacy of politics over
markets" (Lipschutz 2004: 233). To make markets work sustainably for the environment would minimally involve "making prices reflect the full environmental costs"
of any product or service (Speth and Haas 2006: 140; cf. Bryner 2004: 94). Rather
than hope for change "from above" through the actions of state representatives,
regime critics also think a "bottom up," locally based transformation holds more
promise than the old state structure (Lipschutz 2004: 243). Even as people work
"from the bottom up," they should be guided by a sense that "the world is my
country" (224), a "strong sense of global citizenship" (Bryner 2004: 97). In practice,
radical environmentalists do not dismiss the gains under the old regime entirely; in
theory, however, they strive for a different way of organizing world society, including a "second attempt" at global environmental governance (Speth and Haas
2006: 125).

The current regime is, of course, one instance of globalization in action – it
connects more people in more ways across larger distances, it gives form to a
deeply felt interdependence. But, as the misgivings about the global regime
already imply, from the critical environmentalist standpoint globalization itself
may be at fault. "Students of globalization," says one scholar, "must take seriously the possibility that the underlying structure of the modern (now globalized) world order – capitalism, the state, industrialism, nationality, rationalism
– as well as the orthodox discourses that sustain them, may be in important
respects irreparably destructive" (Scholte, cited in Mol 2001: 71). In Chapter 2
we have seen more concrete examples: the globalization of sushi has harmed
tuna stocks and flying fish around the globe adds to its environmental cost, and
the globalization of hamburgers has helped to destroy ecosystems and encouraged methane-producing cattle breeding. In fact, environmentalists may question
whether the fossil-fuel dependent infrastructure of globalization is itself sustainable. In their preference for local solutions to global problems – locally rather
than globally sourced food, for example, or "self-sustaining regions and communities" rather than more trade (Pepper 1996: 12) – some show a new defer-
ence for distance.

Contrasting "old" elements of the current environmental regime with "new"
deep-green biocentric thinking simplifies actual global trends: environmentalism

is not neatly divided into two opposing camps but rather contains many "discourses" (Dryzek 2005). Many seemingly new ideas also have old roots, and if Muir or Carson came back, chances are they would sympathize with the more radical strands in contemporary environmentalism. Like some of their predecessors, current "bioenvironmentalists" (Speth and Haas 2006: 138) put their faith in nature as a way to answer ultimate questions about the meaning of life – it has many ingredients to make it the favorite religion of the irreligious (Dunlap 2004). Even if they represent a minority view for now, that has implications for world society. Globalization, in the Robertsonian perspective, unfolds in part through a contest of world images. How groups of people define the global situation has real consequences for the way they live in it. That applies to many groups in civil society discussed in Chapter 8 as well as the religious communities discussed in Chapter 9. But it applies especially to global environmentalism, a branch of which now proposes a worldview very different than the one that sustained much of globalization thus far. It calls into question the old ideas of rational progress and individual well-being, promoted by growing liberal nation-states in an expanding world society. Whereas, to use Robertsonian language again, conventional globalization "relativizes" individual and society in relation to a larger human setting, radical environmentalism "relativizes" human world society itself in the context of the earth as ecosystem. In one sense, this represents the ultimate "deterritorialization," since it makes unmistakably clear that life in one place inextricably depends on events in many other places; paradoxically, it also represents reterritorialization, by affirming our collective dependence on our common planetary space.

That dependence is now widely acknowledged, an integral part of global consciousness. Other parts of the "sustainability paradigm" are more controversial. From traditional standpoints focusing on rational use or pragmatic conservation of nature, striving to sustain ecosystems in a particular state or grant rights to species looks quite anthropocentric, cutting against the natural grain of vast change over millions of years in ecosystems and species. Similarly, traditionalists would regard the effort to "save" a planet hardier than its human inhabitants as mainly a human idea about how humans should live. Especially in the global South, as the conclusion suggests, the idea has not yet been fully accepted.

Summary and Conclusion

From nineteenth-century roots, environmentalism has grown into an influential global movement, inspired by canonical texts and energized by civic groups. A new ecological consciousness has taken institutional form in an elaborate global regime dealing with many specific problems, from ozone to deforestation to climate change. Its ecological results may be mixed at best, but as a social innovation reshaping world society it has already had a major impact. However, the regime is being called into question by cutting-edge environmentalists who challenge its premises and propose more deeply green solutions to problems caused in part by globalization itself.

Though some people in the global South work at that cutting edge, deeper green bioenvironmentalism is still mainly a Northern movement. At the 1972 Stockholm meeting, Indian prime minister Indira Gandhi famously asked, "How can we speak to those who live in villages or slums about keeping the oceans, the rivers and the air clean when their own lives are contaminated at the source?" (cited in Keck and Sikkink 1998: 124). Ever since, as the earlier comments by Mahathir Mohamad attest, leaders in developing countries have treated poverty as a cause of environmental degradation and advocated development as a way to improve the environment of the poor. Even among Southern environmentalists, one sympathizer suggests, environmental issues are first and foremost a matter of human survival; they do not have "the luxury of pursuing non-human welfare issues" (Doyle 2005: 136).

Another dam illustrates the division in world society over environmental protection: against foreign opposition, China pushed forward with the building of the Three Gorges Dam on the Yangtze River, a dam even larger than Sardar Sarovar that would create a reservoir extending nearly 400 miles, displace more than 2 million Chinese, and supply 20 times more power than America's Hoover Dam. An integral part of China's development strategy, Three Gorges stands as a monument to an old-fashioned dream of world mastery. Silting of the river and erosion of its banks indicate that such mastery does not come easily. That the dam may help to produce relatively clean energy, reducing China's annual CO_2 emissions by perhaps 100 million tons, is small comfort to environmentalists. Nor would they expect the dam to make a significant dent in China's output of GHG, already the largest in the world in 2007, even if optimists turn out to be right in thinking that the country has become more committed to environmental protection and given more leeway to environmental organizations (Ho 2006).

The debates about the Narmada and Three Gorges projects are skirmishes in a wider global struggle, the outcome of which is by no means clear. Obviously, the ecological impact matters most, especially in the case of global warming. But the social outcome matters as well. Environmentalism is rarely just about the environment; it always also deals with society. Certainly, the leading edge of the global environmental movement has a distinct vision of world society, one that may well become more influential in spite of the cautions suggested by the Indian and Chinese examples. In the Narmada campaign, as a leading activist there once put it, "[t]he goal has always been to empower people to fight for their own rights; to create a just society; to create a space in that society for justice and environmental responsibility" (Doyle 2005: 131). While such space may still be lacking in countries like China, on this score environmentalists have many allies. A similar vision of justice motivates other critics of globalization, the focus of the next chapter.

Questions

1   The chapter discusses the difficulties in building a regime dealing with three main environmental issues. What would be the distinct challenges in designing one for problems like loss of biodiversity or depletion of ocean fisheries?

2   The Copenhagen Consensus is a project that brings together prominent economists to rank investments in solving world problems by their impact on human well-being, or how we could get the "biggest bang for the buck." In 2008 they ranked "mitigation," immediate active reduction, of GHG emissions low on the list. What could justify that ranking, and is it justified?

3   Many environmentalists tend to be critical of the way globalization has affected the environment. What are their main points? In what ways might globalization also help to cope with environmental problems?

4   Many environmental groups have roots in the 1960s and 1970s. Since then, both the scope of environmental governance and the nature of environmental problems have changed. What new challenges does this entail for environmental INGOs? How can they be most effective in the twenty-first century? If a "second attempt" at global governance comes to pass, what role could they play in it?

Further Reading

Pamela S. Chasek, David L. Downie, and Janet Welsh Brown, *Global Environmental Politics* (Westview Press, 2006)

Elizabeth R. DeSombre, *Global Environmental Institutions* (Routledge, 2006)

Sanjeev Khagram, *Dams and Development: Transnational Struggles for Water and Power* (Cornell University Press, 2004)

William Nordhaus, *A Question of Balance: Weighing the Options on Global Warming Policies* (Yale University Press, 2008)

Philip Shabecoff, *A Fierce Green Fire: The American Environmental Movement* (Island Press, 2003)

Nicholas Stern, *The Economics of Climate Change: The Stern Review* (Cambridge University Press, 2007)

13

GLOBAL JUSTICE: IS ANOTHER WORLD POSSIBLE?

- Globalization Under Fire
- Before Seattle
- After Seattle
- "Another World"
- Is Another World Possible?
- Summary and Conclusion

Globalization Under Fire

For critics of globalization, November 30, 1999, is a memorable date. On the morning of that day, official delegates from around the world had expected to start a ministerial meeting of the World Trade Organization (WTO) in Seattle. Their task was to begin a new round of trade liberalization, especially in investment and services – the grandly named Millennium Round. It was not to be, for uninvited guests had shown up as well. Locking hands in a human chain, protesters blocked access to the meeting place, delaying the opening of the conference. Afterward, they took to the streets of downtown Seattle in a massive demonstration, chanting slogans and waving banners denouncing the WTO, accompanied by the percussion rhythms of groups like the Infernal Noise Brigade (Notes 2003: 204–27). The crowd of 50,000 quickly shut down the city center, and the ensuing chaos caught authorities by surprise. When anarchists clad in black began smashing windows – a McDonald's restaurant was one obvious target – police responded with force, firing tear gas and arresting many demonstrators. Seattle mayor Paul Schell declared a civil emergency, the Washington State governor sent in National Guard units to help clear the streets, and a curfew for the downtown area took effect that evening. With more attention-grabbing demonstrations hampering their meeting in the following days, WTO delegates cut short the conference and went home empty-handed. The protesters, it seemed, had won what soon became known as the "Battle of Seattle."

Broadcast around the world, images of the battle inspired globalization critics everywhere. As neoliberal globalization gathered strength in the closing decades of the twentieth century, people on the left had looked on with dismay. After the end of the Cold War, with communist regimes in decline and old-style socialist politics out of favor, their critical voices had weakened. Even before Seattle, however, some groups had tried to revive the left's fortunes by addressing the evils of globalization. The Battle of Seattle helped to galvanize their disparate efforts into a more coherent cause. As they joined forces, "Seattle" became an iconic moment in the evolution of a global movement. Initially described as the "antiglobalization" movement, it also acquired names such as the "otherglobalization" or "global justice" movement (GJM). The different labels capture a new wave of activism by people on the political left from many countries who viewed "neoliberal" globalization as dangerous and unjust. Through the "sea-change" in their transnational activism (Reitan 2007: 1), by mobilizing more groups from more places in more common efforts, they globalized a way of thinking about globalization. Out of the decades-long "degenerative crisis" of the global left (Santos 2006: 1) and its resulting "desolate landscape" (Mertes 2004: vii), from the "ruins" of the old left that had focused on class struggle guided mainly by a communist vision, a new "landscape" of the global left thus emerged in the early years of the twenty-first century (Sader 2004: 248). Seattle did not create the new landscape from scratch but helped available seeds to grow and also planted new ones. This chapter recounts how it happened and assesses the results.

"Seattle" gave the movement a boost. For one thing, the protests turned the WTO into a symbol of all that ailed globalization. The big issue for many protesters was that under WTO rules countries could not require their trading partners to protect workers and the environment, since that would inhibit "free" trade. This left Third-World workers exposed to exploitation, forced unfair competition on Northern countries, and thus affirmed how the WTO valued trade over human welfare. The WTO had its priorities wrong because it anchored a system that had its priorities wrong. "WTO = capitalism without conscience," as one Seattle slogan put it (Della Porta et al. 2006: 1). The protesters also attacked the WTO as an undemocratic behemoth, an organization run by the powerful for the powerful and beholden to corporate interests. In this respect, too, the WTO simply illustrated the larger problem of an unjust global economic system that did not work for the vast majority of people. By picking the WTO as a suitable target, Seattle gave activists a way to make an abstract critique of neoliberal injustice quite concrete. It also gave them a good idea, namely to stage other protests at the meetings of prominent international organizations, thereby making life difficult for those institutions and attracting attention to the cause. Seattle provided not only a symbolic target but also a media strategy.

The Seattle protesters made a motley crowd. The police should not have been surprised: when earlier in the year a group of activists in Geneva issued a call for demonstrations in Seattle, 1,387 groups signed on (Della Porta et al. 2006), and many of these spent months getting ready. The streets in Seattle displayed the diversity of the budding movement: by contrast with the stark black of the anarchists, 200 environmentalists showed up as turtles, trying to use these symbols of wisdom to prevent violence (2), while union members, the largest contingent among the crowds, dressed more conservatively in nylon jackets. Different groups contributed in different ways, delving into their own repertoire or trying new things (Smith 2002). Key links in the human chain blocking the WTO delegates were Jubilee 2000 activists, the originally Christian group arguing that odious debts of developing countries should be canceled as a matter of global economic justice, mentioned in Chapter 9 (Reitan 2007: 83). They were joined by "green guerillas" from New York City's community gardening groups, just one set of activists for whom Seattle offered the opportunity to link their local grievances to much bigger global issues (Tarrow 2005: 59–60). One force behind the drama of Seattle was the Direct Action Network, a coalition of groups that included radical environmentalists from Earth First! and activists linked to the Zapatista uprising in Mexico, People's Global Action. A more moderate element in the Network was the NGO Global Exchange, which organized a Fair Trade Fair and whose members used their passes to enter the inaugural WTO event, before being arrested for the disruption they caused (Della Porta et al. 2006: 2). Away from the streets, the International Forum on Globalization, comprising the intellectual leadership of several antiglobalization groups, hosted more sedate teach-ins to explain the thrust of their critique of the WTO. Among the more media-savvy protesters was José Bové, a French peasant used to spending more time in protest than tending to his sheep, who came to Seattle to hand out smuggled Roquefort cheese from his region that had been slapped with high import duties as part of WTO-approved sanctions imposed on the European Union due to its ban on hormone-treated beef. From offbeat to conventional, each group of protesters brought their own style, their own particular views to Seattle. They showed the sheer variety of the growing movement.

Though Seattle invigorated a movement, the events of 1999 also contained signs of weakness. In the heat of the battle, reformers and radicals tried to put aside their differences, but they did not agree on what was to be done – for example, whether the WTO was amenable to reform or should be abolished altogether. In spite of agreement on fundamentals, the movement in fact remains split along ideological lines, between those who want to "reshape" and those who want to "roll back" economic globalization (Broad 2002: 5). While the battle gained a "global" aura in the retelling, most participants were from North America, and most among them were union members, brought in by the AFL-CIO, whose main demand for limits on trade agreements could have been mistaken by workers elsewhere for a form of self-serving protectionism rather than an expression of global solidarity. Much as activists would like to see such solidarity grow, it still faces major obstacles. Within the WTO, at any rate, representatives of developing countries looked askance at the demand, one reason the talks ran into trouble; they also complained about undemocratic procedures, another issue that derailed the poorly prepared conference. Though protesters took credit for the meeting's failure, the WTO might have managed to accomplish that all by itself. Even at the height of its energies, the movement's impact was more limited than activists wished. Reflecting on Seattle and the activism it inspired, thus also raises questions about its limitations – questions I will address in the conclusion.

Even if the new activism's political impact in major countries and organizations has remained modest, the very fact of its revival around 2000 is nonetheless significant, for it shows how the "movement" of neoliberal reform in the previous decades triggered a "countermovement" claiming to represent the interests of society at large, how "hegemonic" globalization also provoked "counterhegemonic" dissent about the direction of globalization (Evans 2005; McMichael 2005). The main point of this chapter is simply that we cannot understand globalization without understanding the critical strand within it. From the Robertsonian perspective alluded to in earlier chapters, it supplies a distinct world image that may steer globalization in a particular direction. The critique also encompasses many elements of globalization: it is the work of global civil society (Chapter 8), focused on recent global economic change (Chapter 5), motivated first and foremost by the problem of global inequality (Chapter 11), often proposing new kinds of global governance (Chapter 7). "Antiglobalization" is thus a misnomer: the movement enacts globalization by organizing the interdependence of activists and framing it in terms of a new kind of critical consciousness. In the end, the movement's own dominant vision, which equates globalization with a particular kind of economic model, may be too constricted, mistaking one dimension of one phase of globalization for the whole. Seen from the "generic" vantage point of this book, the GJM contributes to globalization in the broad sense as it criticizes one version of it.

Before Seattle

Before Seattle, there was Chiapas. Again, a single date marks the meaning of the place: January 1, 1994 – a "symbolic founding moment" for "anti-systemic dissent" (Mertes 2004: viii). On that day, the North American Free Trade Agreement (NAFTA) went into effect. On that day, too, several thousand fighters of the Zapatista Army of National Liberation (EZLN) emerged from the jungle to attack towns and ranches in Chiapas, Mexico's southernmost state. Their offensive was brief, and less than two weeks later the Mexican army largely restored control in the area, leaving some territory in EZLN hands before retaking most of it the following year. The EZLN kept a foothold in some independent municipalities but its main leaders, especially Subcomandante Marcos, stayed in hiding. An accord with government negotiators in 1996 seemed to meet many Zapatista demands for land reform and cultural autonomy, but Mexico's president rejected the agreement, producing a long stalemate. Yet while their military prowess left something to be desired and their actual power was always fragile at best, the Zapatistas made a big international splash (Lechner and Boli 2005: 155ff.). Supporters flocked to Chiapas and joined the Zapatistas in *encuentros*, gatherings of solidarity. They spread the word not just in Mexico but also around the world, especially via websites devoted to the cause. Through his speeches and writings, Marcos became a celebrity of the global left, his ski mask a symbol of resistance. Not surprisingly, people inspired by the Zapatistas took a major role in staging the Seattle protests. Distant as they were, there was a direct line from southern Mexico to the northern US.

By 1999, the EZLN had already pioneered many tools of resistance. The Zapatistas had been motivated by local outrage over unfairness in land distribution and oppression in state government but through the words of their canny commander that local cause became linked, via NAFTA, to global injustice. Marcos created a new "frame" for the rebellion by portraying "neoliberalism" as the true cause of indigenous misfortune and the real target of the rebellion. The Zapatistas said "Ya Basta" (enough is enough) to neoliberalism's "oppressive power and machinery of death," offering a slogan that would resonate widely; they envisioned replacing the neoliberal hell with a more "plural, different, inclusive, tolerant" world (Marcos 2001: 118, 123). They made their public debut with violence but quickly shifted to a nonviolent strategy by appealing to global civil society for moral support in bringing pressure to bear on the Mexican government. In the "parched" terrain of the left in the early 1990s, they lit a spark, and the enthusiastic response from activists turned the Zapatistas into a focus of global solidarity (Reitan 2007). In the process, they also fostered a new network of activists, both among those who visited them in Mexico and among more far-flung supporters, thereby seeding protest movements elsewhere (Olesen 2005). They had roots in an unpromisingly poor region of a developing country but used modern technology, both TV coverage and especially the Internet, in addition to old-fashioned newspapers, notably the sympathetic left-leaning *La Jornada*, to get their message out. In fact, the original uprising had been planned as a spectacle designed to get attention, and the press subsequently kept up with the story (Bob 2005: 128–9). By enlarging their frame, building a network, and virtually transmitting their message, they "scaled up" their efforts transnationally, serving as a model for others in later years (Tarrow 2005). Marcos was quite deliberate about the scaling up, telling one gathering of comrades that from Chiapas an echo could go forth "of the local and particular, which reverberates in an echo of . . . the intercontinental and galactic," an echo of the "rebel voice transforming itself and renewing itself in other voices" (Marcos 2001: 122). The echoes found receptive ears: when Marcos and his fellow fighters addressed an audience of more than 100,000 in Mexico City in 2001, Italian activists, nicknamed "white monkeys" for their white overalls, served as security guards, and several "left-wing luminaries," including the inevitable José Bové, added luster to the event (Bob 2005: 117). The Zapatistas had become a favorite cause of the global left.

Bové had made a name for himself by staging a little rebellion of his own. Shortly before traveling to Seattle, he had led comrades from the Confédération Paysanne (CP), a group of activist farmers, in dismantling a new McDonald's restaurant in Millau, a French town near his farm. Staged as a spectacle coordinated with local authorities, it had drawn great media attention. Bové used his unexpected arrest to his advantage, and his pipe and mustache became as familiar as Marcos's mask. Of course, Bové did not simply want to express a culinary preference for Roquefort over hamburger and fries but rather wanted to tar fast food as inherently "bad food" that corrupted local cuisines – the event was intended as a strike "for proper food against *malbouffe*" (Bové 2004: 142). McDonald's also symbolized corporate power in agriculture, as it subjected the value of the land and its workers to the need for profit – the attack was "[for] agricultural workers against multinationals" (ibid.). And of course McDonald's was a cog in a larger global system that not only degraded food and land but also imposed a capitalist straitjacket on everything, a sentiment expressed in Bove's favorite protest slogan, "Our world is not for sale!" (Bové and Dufour 2001), a slogan that would serve as the name of an anti-WTO group organized in Seattle (Reitan 2007: 124). Like Marcos, Bové consciously "scaled up," framing the problems of French sheep farmers in broader terms, using McDonald's to make a transnational point, and seeking support from global civil society. In fact, when he and his partners in crime appeared in court in 2000, Millau could barely handle the large crowds of sympathizers, at least some of whom were from abroad (Notes 2003: 278–85). Sabotaging McDonald's had catapulted the CP into the "vanguard of the anti-neoliberal struggle" (Reitan 2007: 161).

This did not happen by accident. For Bové, it capped a career in activism that started when he took up "resistance farming" as an anti-war student in solidarity with people in the Larzac region opposed to expansion of NATO practice grounds (Bové 2004; Reitan 2007: 159). Uniting in the CP, the farmers' agenda had gradually expanded to protect a way of life against big agribusiness and intensive farming (Bové 2004: 140), making McDonald's an inviting target. The CP also sought ties with similar groups around the world, such as the Movimento dos Sem Terra, the movement of landless peasants in Brazil, with which it co-founded the Via Campesina (Peasant Way), a loose network of farmers and rural organizations that somewhat boldly claims to speak for 400 million people (Reitan 2007: 148). Via Campesina's leaders remind the larger movement that peasants are at special risk in the global market, that large corporations have taken undue control, for example by selling new seeds, and that therefore the inequities of capitalism are especially evident in the countryside. Taking some Roquefort with him, Bové represented Via Campesina in Seattle to demand that food be taken out of trade agreements as a step toward restoring countries' food sovereignty. For this professional protester, it was a small hop from Millau to Seattle.

In 1998 the CP joined another French organization that would take a leading role in the anti-neoliberal struggle. In a 1997 lament against the "tyranny" of the financial markets, Ignacio Ramonet, editor of the influential magazine *Le Monde Diplomatique*, had half-seriously called for a popular association named ATTAC, probably picking the catchy acronym before coming up with the more cumbersome full name: Association pour la Taxation des Transactions financières pour l'Aide aux Citoyennes et Citoyens (Association for the Taxation of Financial Transactions for the Aid of Citizens). The name referred to a suggestion by the American economist James Tobin to impose a small tax on short-term capital movements across borders to prevent them from causing financial havoc. Ramonet's larger idea was that the opposition to neoliberal policies and the rule of the market should get

organized. Among leftist thinkers already concerned with the impact of globalization, the article hit fertile ground. Another journalist, Bernard Cassen, took the
proposal seriously and recruited like-minded organizations and individuals into a
new "action-oriented movement of popular education" – named ATTAC, of course
– that grew to some 30,000 members in over 200 local committees and quickly
inspired imitators abroad, turning ATTAC into a transnational network in its own
right (Cassen 2004: 152–7). Ramonet's lament became the group's new frame: it
favored a new form of civil politics over global markets, and it called for a more
redistributive state as a bulwark against inequality and corporate power – an outlook
one scholar calls "associational statism" (Ancelovici 2002: 433, 451). In this way, it
scaled up the domestic discontent that its leftist member organizations had felt for
some time and that had intensified during a wave of strikes in 1995. Even so, its
actual educational activities took place mostly among the French within France,
and the target of its concrete proposals was still the French state (454). Yet it also
scaled up in another, more concrete way: its role in linking critics and framing their
critique took on a wholly different dimension when, after a conversation with
Brazilian colleagues, Cassen had the bright idea to propose holding a World Social
Forum (WSF) in Porto Alegre, Brazil, as an alternative to the "neoliberal" World
Economic Forum held annually in Davos, Switzerland (Cassen 2004: 161–2). Held
for the first time in 2001, the WSF would prove to be the ideal successor event to
Seattle.

After Seattle

Porto Alegre had several advantages. Brazil's Workers' Party (PT) held power there
and could help to host the forum. Influential progressive groups, such as the landless movement, could supply their energy. And Porto Alegre was in the South, a
suitable site to highlight inequities that came from the North. Staged very soon after
Cassen had his vision, the first WSF made up in exuberance for what it lacked in
organization. Some 10,000 attendees, mostly from Brazil and Europe, held a "March
against Neoliberalism" in the streets of Porto Alegre and met in sessions at a local
Catholic university. Bové was there, of course, eliciting chants of "We are all José
Bové." Though organizers wanted to keep the WSF completely open and democratic, avoiding any impression that they were trying to impose ideas on the participants, the WSF did issue the "Porto Alegre Call for Mobilisation" (WSF 2001a).
The WSF, it said, represented a "great alliance to create a new society" eager to
demonstrate "our total rejection of the neoliberal policies of globalisation" and "the
concentration of wealth, the globalization of poverty and the destruction of our
earth" they caused. The WSF could be "a way to achieve peoples' sovereignty and
a just world." More than 100 labor, peace, environmental, and women's groups
signed on to the Call for Mobilisation, which was heard loud and clear by activists
elsewhere. To provide some direction after the meeting, some Brazilian organizers

Plate 13.1   Protesters marching at the World Social Forum, Porto Alegre, Brazil, January 25, 2001
Source: © Reuters

proposed a "World Social Forum Charter of Principles," which described the forum as an open, plural, nongovernmental meeting place for groups that are "opposed to neoliberalism and to domination of the world by capital" and instead want to build a "planetary society centered on the human person" (WSF 2001b). The WSF itself, the charter suggested, could become a permanent "world process" of seeking alternatives, motivated by the slogan formulated at the first WSF, "Another World Is Possible." The WSF experience proved infectious: more than 50,000 activists showed up the following year, greatly expanding the scope of the meeting and the range of issues it addressed, and making Porto Alegre the global left's favorite destination (Ponniah and Fisher 2003).

The WSF indeed became a "world process" of sorts. Attracting many activists to the same place, it enabled them to talk to and learn from each other. Even in the age of the Internet, meeting face-to-face is important: the "space for encounter" helped in "building toward one global network" (Reitan 2007: 140). The WSF allowed many groups to express many perspectives, and even attempts by a group of attendees calling itself the Social Movement Assembly to pull disparate issues together into a coherent "call" to conclude the forum often produced only the unity of the laundry list (142). Nonetheless, the very fact that those issues were aired at all, in the same place for similar reasons by like-minded people, created a sense of commonality. Issues that otherwise might have been "merely" domestic gained a global aura, and the WSF thus helped turn inter-national activism into a global movement. Of course, the simple act of gathering in a mostly joyous atmosphere, at least as long as attendees could struggle against global capital rather than against rain and mud in their tent camps, also fostered warm feelings of solidarity. Clearly, the World Economic Forum faced some serious ideological competition.

The success of the early meetings was sufficiently inspiring to turn the WSF into an annual event – for a while, meeting in Porto Alegre was just what the movement did – and to spawn many regional forums as well, thus taking the format and content on the road, as it were. The first European Social Forum took place in Florence, Italy, in 2002, an Asian Social Forum was held in Hyderabad, India, in 2003, and a Social Forum of the Americas followed in Quito, Ecuador, in 2004. In that same year, the global forum was staged in Mumbai, India, to broaden its appeal outside Brazil. Some things changed there: Indian issues, such as those of the untouchables and indigenous peoples, took center stage; Indian progressive celebrities, such as the writer Arundhati Roy, played a prominent role; and she and others broadened the agenda by calling on opponents of neoliberalism to support the resistance to the US and its partners in Iraq. But the event also had an air of familiarity: a program that appeared only after the event had begun illustrated logistical challenges; drumming even more insistent than in Seattle energized the crowds; and a People's Forum against Coca-Cola highlighted the ideological thrust of the meeting. As much as it reflected the places where it unfolded, by 2004 the WSF had become a global institution.

If the WSF was mostly about expressing a leftist alternative to the dominant model of globalization, other events attacked the enemy more directly. After Seattle, major meetings of the IMF, the World Bank, the WTO, and the G7 conclave of world leaders became prime targets of activists for several years. Perhaps the most dramatic confrontation occurred in Genoa, Italy, in July 2001, at a meeting of the G8 – the G7 plus Russia. The Genoa Social Forum, a coalition of 800 groups that included ATTAC's Italian branch, the large umbrella organization Rete Lilliput (Lilliput's Network), as well as eco-pacifist and Catholic activists, wanted to use the event to stage a huge protest against neoliberalism. Left-wing parties and unions also planned to get involved. Having learned from similar events since Seattle, the Italian authorities were ready: they created a protected "red zone" around the summit site, tried to prevent militants from reaching the city, and sealed off Genoa's port, airport, and city center (Della Porta et al. 2006: 3). A march for migrants' rights on the first day remained peaceful, but the next day a Black Bloc of radicals began to vandalize buildings, attack other protesters, and challenge police, who responded with water cannons, tear gas, and batons that hit peaceful demonstrators as well (4–5). When a stuck police jeep was attacked by a crowd, an officer fired a gun, killing Carlo Giuliani – the first casualty of the protests, who rapidly became a martyr symbolizing police brutality in the eyes of protesters. At a massive march of more than 200,000 people on July 21, demonstrators in vain tried to prevent Black Bloc disruption and as a result suffered drastic police charges that sent hundreds of people to local hospitals. Though activists had tried to get attention in different ways – their "repertoire" ranged from the Gandhian nonviolent civil disobedience of Rete Lilliput to the more active kind aimed at the red zone by the White Overalls (139) – media attention to the violence overwhelmed their efforts and muffled their message. The Italian police action signaled a political backlash against certain kinds of leftist activism. For the majority of peaceful activists, it raised the question whether they should change strategy, if only to keep the wildfire started in Seattle under control.

Regardless of the recriminations after the fact, Genoa represented yet another step in building a global movement. The G8, like the main international economic organizations, had functioned as a kind of "coral reef," attracting protesters who then created their own ecosystem of dissent (Tarrow 2001: 15, using a term suggested by Ron Jepperson). The ecosystem of the movement might have looked new but it contained old species – in Seattle, the AFL-CIO was crucial, French unions played a big role in ATTAC, Brazil's PT provided key support to the WSF, and the Communist Party of India (Marxist) invigorated the Mumbai forum even though it was held outside its stronghold in Bengal. While Genoa-style intense confrontation proved hard to sustain – and many on the left did not care to try – the series of events that led up to it energized the troops, so to speak. The events themselves recycled ideas and symbols and forms of protest, all easily diffused by attendees and via the Internet. For example, the human chain in Seattle had copied an earlier one used at a G8 meeting in Birmingham, England; "direct action," challenging authorities in the streets, also spread from place to place. Reflecting on what they did, activists turned the series of protests into a narrative of struggle; "Chiapas," "Seattle," "Porto Alegre," and "Genoa" all represented parts of an unfolding story. After years of marginalization, the "left of the left" (Ancelovici 2002: 432) thus got its act together and gained a stronger public voice. Overall, as one scholar sums up, the "mobilizations on global justice issues . . . express a conflict defined as 'global,' allowing new collective identities to emerge; they employ protest repertoires in transnational campaigns innovating on the margins of forms already widespread in the past; and they construct transnational networks" (Della Porta 2007: 17). But as Genoa also hinted, in spite of the appearance of growing solidarity, it was still not clear that the movement really moved as one or could speak with one voice.

"Another World"

In the late nineteenth century, people who felt hurt by the second wave of globalization united in various movements to demand radical change. In the US, for example, farmers struggling with declining prices for food and land formed the Farmers' Alliance in the mid-1870s – a Confédération Paysanne of that era. In Europe, low-paid workers joined forces in the first trade unions and political parties – the German Social Democratic Workers' Party of 1869 was a forerunner of Brazil's PT. Its founders wanted to be part of the International Workingmen's Association, later called the "First International," which promoted revolutionary worker solidarity across borders under the guidance of intellectuals like Karl Marx. The sheer dislocations of global change and the hardships of second-wave capitalism thus triggered a "countermovement" of dissent, a label now adopted by leaders of the GJM. To simplify a very intricate history, that reaction took three forms, all favoring a kind of collectivist solution to the problems caused by liberalizing change – politics over markets, in the contemporary language of ATTAC. Karl Marx, of course, inspired followers by arguing that capitalism was inherently exploitative, bound to sink into crises, and after a revolutionary class struggle would give way to a classless communist society. Initially tempted by the revolutionary path, revisionists in the workers' movement believed instead that exploitation could be offset by redistribution, crises resolved through state regulation, and a new, more equitable society built by reforming the capitalist system. Leaving aside the third, German national socialist form of collectivism, the second wave of globalization shaped what became the "left" in global politics. In their own way, its partisans already thought that "another world is possible." The two main strands, the Marxian revolutionary alternative and the social democratic grand compromise, left their imprint on critiques of globalization in the third wave, even though one prominent WSF participant has complained that in the "blindness" of their practice WSF activists actually show "contempt" for the "rich leftist theoretical tradition" (Santos 2006: 161).

Observed close up, in the streets of Seattle, Porto Alegre, Genoa, or Mumbai, those critiques seem very diverse in style and content, as noted above. Longshoremen or public servants mobilized by the AFL-CIO in Seattle differ from Italian Catholics in the Jubilee debt-forgiveness movement who came to Genoa, and they in turn differ from advocates for peasant interests in Brazil or India. The diversity is also evident in the key documents issued at the main protest events, which may blame a specific organization or a more abstract system, focus on trade or ecology for future action, invoke peace or democracy as guiding values, and so on (Della Porta et al. 2006: Tables 6, 7, 8). Together, activists have articulated an enormous range of issues and demands, from WTO reform and taxes on capital movements, to food sovereignty and protection of indigenous cultures, to ending violence against women or war in the Middle East, to workers' rights or environmental disasters, to poverty or capitalism as such (Della Porta 2007: 16). Some care more about culture, others about economics; some want to go local, others focus on the globe as such; some hold out hope for reform, others reject the current system altogether (Fisher and Ponniah 2003: 8–10). Yet it is easy, perhaps too easy, to overstate the differences. Over time, a "master frame" has evolved among activists (Ayres 2005), a general diagnosis and prescription that most can rally around. Some of its elements would ring familiar to their predecessors of a century before.

According to the common diagnosis, the world is undergoing the second coming of untrammeled markets that dissolve communities, undermine states, and corrupt cultures. Through purposeful policy and historical happenstance, powerful elites backed by strong states and operating through large corporations have been able to rewrite the rules of the world economy for their benefit, stripping the powerless of social protection and deepening already large divisions. A new great power, the US, dominates the world, and new organizations, such as the IMF and the WTO, help to run the *neo*liberal system, but its structure and problems remain the same. Far from delivering great benefits, new technologies such as genetic modification or nuclear power only intensify old problems. As in an earlier era, land and labor become mere commodities to be bought, sold, and exploited for profit, casting aside the needs of workers and harming the environment. But just as the old liberal world faced its demise in the conflagration of the World War I and the Great Depression, the "neoliberal" world will prove equally unstable. Conflicts among great powers, and between labor and capital, spelled its undoing then; tensions between North and South, and the sheer burden imposed on the environment, may unravel the current system again before long. Globalization has created a system that is too divided, too unequal, too damaging, and too unjust to be sustainable. A world that gives no voice to the vast majority of its people is bound to spin out of control.

Like the previous model, neoliberal globalization has tried to convey a sense of inevitability through the notion that "there is no alternative." Its dominant ideology portrays individuals as free to choose in a world society that guarantees basic liberties. But neoliberal globalization in fact imposes a particular world order that leaves little to choose. At the same time, however, it fosters the forces that unmask the false freedom and nurture real alternatives, a "movement of movements" that gives voice to the voiceless. By contrast with the hierarchy inherent in actual globalization, the movement practices equality; by contrast with the lack of real democracy in the real world, it strives for inclusion of many groups. Whereas a century earlier the budding movements of industrial workers and national liberation took a leading role, today women and environmentalists and indigenous groups have become more influential. Together they strive for "global justice" in "another world" – a world that satisfies more people's basic needs, distributes its goods more evenly, and respects all human rights of all people more fully. Through active resistance, states and communities may regain some control over seemingly irreversible globalization, and steer it in a more humane direction. New types of global governance, drastically reformed old institutions or freshly created ones, will complement such collective control. In practice, this also means finding a way to counter America's eminence as an economic and military power, as a step toward a less imperial, more balanced world order. While granting protection to distinct cultures, all of equal value, the other world will be guided by a cosmopolitan spirit that expresses the solidarity of human beings regardless of background. That solidarity must be centered on shared care of the planet, humanity's common home, and thereby will make a new form of globalization more sustainable.

The GJM thus attacks a common target, envisions another world, and tries to embody the virtues of its vision (Lechner and Boli 2005: 157–64). Of course, that only describes its shared frame quite abstractly. Beyond the lofty diagnosis and prescriptions, the old divisions on the left have not disappeared. On one side are people like Walden Bello from the Philippines, founder of Focus on the Global South, frequent participant in social forums, and a radical critic of neoliberalism inspired by the Marxian tradition (Bello 2001, 2002, 2004). In his view, the system is beyond redemption and therefore not worth reforming: it must be rolled back. Specifically, Bello advocates "deglobalization," having people and countries withdraw from the current world system in order to reorganize their affairs, mobilize their own resources, and promote development from within. In a manner reminiscent of radical environmentalist proposals discussed in the previous chapter, this would reorient economies "from the emphasis on production for export to production for the local market" while "de-emphasizing growth and maximizing equity" by making all economic decisions "subject to democratic choice" (Bello 2002: 113). This "re-empowerment of the local and national" also needs another kind of global economic governance, a "pluralistic" rather than a centralized system of institutions, one of which would be devoted to preserving indigenous economies (114–15). It is fruitless to fix the IMF or the WTO, irretrievable cogs in neoliberal globalization – better to "decommission" or "neuter" them (116). Without explicitly invoking the second-wave vision of a classless society, deglobalization thus offers one contemporary version of the old revolutionary ideal. But just as Marx left his prescriptions a bit vague, Bello does not make entirely clear how much poor countries would benefit from focusing on the local market and de-emphasizing growth. Few seem likely to try: communist countries that turned inward, such as North Korea, Cambodia, and China in the 1960s, do not present appealing models, and Latin American countries have long since moved away from import substitution. The Marxian hope for total transformation lingers, but Marx himself might have questioned Bello's lack of faith in technological progress. Even on the more radical end of the spectrum, then, the temper of third-wave transformation is rather different from that of Marx.

On the other side of the spectrum are people like the British political scientist David Held, no doubt less popular among die-hard activists but an important advocate of what he calls "global social democracy" (Held 2004). Perhaps aiming at Bello, he calls the radical antiglobalist position "deeply naïve about the potential for locally based action to resolve . . . the governance agenda generated by the forces of globalization" (162). By contrast with critics like Bello, he disputes the notion that economic globalization is merely an "ideological veil," defends "free trade as an admirable objective for progressives in principle," and even allows for the possibility that corporations can be a force for good (29, 58, 153). Like social democrats of the past, Held has made his peace with markets yet insists that they be politically "tamed" to serve the poor by striving for a global bargain that resembles the "national bargains" that have made many liberal democracies more decent societies. Instead of deglobalization he argues for fairer trade rules that will serve the most vulnerable; instead of calling for decommissioning of international organizations he advocates democratic reform in global governance. Yet he also has much in common with people to his left. For example, his plea for more "global issue networks" to address common problems resembles Bello's call for "pluralistic" governance. Few on the left would take issue with Held's emphasis on "cosmopolitan values," such as equal dignity or sustainability, as a basis for his social democratic program. Precisely how to translate such abstract principles into feasible reform remains a challenge, of course: social democratic countries had developed a national culture and a sense of belonging that enabled different classes to make their "national bargains," but that same feeling of commonality does not yet exist worldwide and therefore the specific tools of social democracy, such as collective bargaining or entitlement programs, would be difficult to realize globally. Social democracy, needless to say, also involves democracy, which raises the thorny problem of how it could flourish globally before all existing countries have themselves become democratic. Even Held's more moderate proposals therefore contain just a bit of wishful thinking.

To some extent, such thinking is inherent in all globalization critiques and in all visions of "another world." Bello and Held mark two ends of the wide spectrum of those critiques. In principle, at least, they represent drastically different ways of dealing with globalization: rolling back versus reshaping, transformation versus reform, deglobalization versus reglobalization. The very contrast has a long tradition on the left. Yet there is ample room in between, and the GJM and its academic sympathizers have been busy filling it with studies, proposals, and web discussion. The enormous outpouring of critical reflection has created a counterculture, as it were, to the dominant culture the critics oppose (Lechner and Boli 2005: ch. 7). Many thousands of people in hundreds of ways insist that, in fact, "there is an alternative." Academics have joined in, turning the study of globalization into "critical globalization studies" (Appelbaum and Robinson 2005) and helping to frame "global resistance" (Amoore 2005). As in the second wave, then, globalization has once again brought forth a form of opposition. Some themes have stayed the same – the objections to neoliberalism would not have surprised anyone on the left in 1900. Other themes are largely new – around 1900 few people worried much about "the environment." History has had an effect on how problems are framed – the record of actually existing communism in the twentieth century means that more recent globalization critics treat it with caution. And of course globalization has affected its ostensible opponents – the counterculture of the second wave was already international, but in the third wave globalization critics have globalized even more. But if the global left is making a comeback, what can it achieve?

Is Another World Possible?

The apparent success of the US and the UK under Ronald Reagan and Margaret Thatcher depressed many people on the left, illustrated in the work of David Harvey discussed in Chapter 5. Even though few had much affection for the old Soviet Union, the end of the Cold war made it worse, if only because the US so clearly came out on top. The world was taking a wrong turn at a time when the left felt sidelined. Hence the left faced a "desolate" landscape and a "degenerative crisis" by the early 1990s. But much has changed since then: a movement emerged that lifted the spirits of people on the left, gave them new energy and a new focus, and amplified their voice in global debates. Exuberant neoliberalism, it turned out, also created opportunities for opposition. Its technologies provided resources to its critics; its global thrust provoked the formulation of a new critical "frame." Combining all those ingredients of social movements in an original way, the growth of the "antiglobalization," now "global justice," movement is an accomplishment in itself. It has left its imprint on the way many people think about globalization, its critique serving as a kind of public prism. In its heyday in the early 2000s, for example, it found ample support in European public opinion (Della Porta 2007). More generally, in global debates globalization now means partly what its opponents make of it. By their very presence, "otherworldly" visions already create "another world" than would have existed without them. That counts as one kind of impact.

The specific impact of the GJM on international institutions is more difficult to gauge. The reason for the difficulty is simple: the three main institutions have changed in many ways over many years, and at best the GJM served as one factor among others pushing them in a different direction. The WTO certainly faced its travails after 1999, but these had more to do with the competing interests of its members and the rising influence of countries like Brazil and India than with the GJM. One big change in the WTO, the inclusion of new members such as China, ran counter to GJM desires; it suggests that, if anything, many countries are still strongly invested in free trade as a vehicle for growth. The IMF and World Bank have moved toward an "augmented Washington consensus," moderating the "tough" liberalization policies they once championed, but that was spurred by reflection on their mistakes and push-back from clients as much as by outside criticism from the GJM. Groups allied with the GJM, such as the women's movement discussed in Chapter 8 and environmentalists discussed in Chapter 12, have greatly affected the way the World Bank might look at development issues or dam-building projects or education policies but whether this counts as an impact of "the" GJM is a matter of judgment. To sum up very briefly, neither reformers nor dismantlers among GJM activists have gotten their way. Judging by the record of institutional reform, "another world" may be possible, but it will be slow going at best.

The movement faces its own challenges as well. For one thing, its energy and global focus are difficult to sustain. In the US, for example, many participants in Seattle, like the New York gardeners, quickly returned to their domestic agenda, a "downward" scale shift from the heights of globally oriented activism as a result of which the American movement went "from a bark to a whimper" (Hadden and Tarrow 2007: 212, 214, 222). American activists typically face a less friendly public than their European colleagues, since Americans overall are "less favorably disposed toward antiglobalization protesters" (224). In the immediate aftermath of the terrorist attack on US targets of September 11, 2001, the GJM had even less opportunity to bring its issues to the fore and domestic criticism of the US was less well received. At the same time, a growing economy with low unemployment and low inflation failed to feed the fears that might have motivated greater interest in the GJM agenda. All that can change, of course, and within the movement, as outside of it, the American experience by no means sets the norm for the world as a whole. It would be an odd inversion of anti-imperialist arguments to infer GJM failure from America's lack of enthusiasm. The point is simply that, as difficult as it is to keep any movement going, sustaining a transnational movement focused on a global cause is that much more challenging. Even for committed activists, "another world" is often far from home.

In more mundane domestic arenas, the US may be an outlier but the GJM record is mixed in any case. Brazilian voters heartened WSF attendees by electing Luiz Inácio Lula da Silva, leader of the PT, president in 2001. The election of Hugo Chávez in Venezuela, a leader even more in sync with the thrust of WSF thinking, and then the like-minded Evo Morales in Bolivia gave another boost to the global left's fortunes. WSF-style activism cannot take direct credit for such victories, but these political developments do help to measure its influence and bolster its support. By the same yardstick, it has not fared as well in other places. After getting involved in the Battle of Seattle with his group Public Citizen, Ralph Nader, the most visible figure among American antiglobalists, ran for president but only attracted 2.9 million votes, possibly affecting the outcome in some key states but trailing the Democratic and Republican candidates. When George W. Bush won re-election four years later with a then-record popular vote of about 62 million, Nader's total declined to slightly more than 400,000. In Mexico, the Zapatistas gained attention as well as support from a segment of the public but this did not translate into political clout. In 2000, for example, Mexican voters elected center-right candidate Vicente Fox of the National Action Party (PAN) and in 2006 the left again lost to another leader of the PAN, Felipe Calderón. In France in 2002, a divided left lost the first round of the first presidential elections after the founding of ATTAC, and the main candidate of the right, Jacques Chirac, emerged victorious. After disclaiming presidential ambitions, José Bové ran in the 2007 elections, garnering 483,000 votes, compared to 19 million for the eventual winner of the right, Nicolas Sarkozy. Finally, the Genoa demonstrations lifted spirits on the left at a time when the right in Italian politics still savored its victory in the national elections held in May of 2001, in which it captured over 40 percent of the vote compared to about 5 percent for the Communist Refoundation Party most in tune with the protesters. Led by Silvio Berlusconi, the right won again in 2008, and this time the smaller left parties most sympathetic to the global justice cause lost their representation in Parliament altogether.

In several developed countries, as these examples show, the GJM and its closest allies have not done well in electoral politics. Not surprisingly, even sympathetic observers conclude that the GJM impact on domestic policy has been similarly modest, hampered even in Europe by an institutionalized left of labor unions and social democratic parties that tends to be skeptical of GJM activists' tactics and proposals (Della Porta et al. 2006: 209–11, 220). Judging by recent history, "another world" is unlikely to emerge from normal politics in most liberal democracies. Spokesmen for the movement have typically responded that their lack of political and policy impact only shows the futility or crisis of representative democracy, a "false" or merely formal system that does not allow the true voice of the people to be heard (Falk 1999; Bello 2004: 69; Santos 2006: 43). Instead, they search for "other forms" of democracy that somehow more directly express the interests of the people (Della Porta 2006 et al.: 196). In doing so, however, they run the risk of equating "democracy" with the content of a particular set of policies rather than the process of majority voting or competitive elections, which can produce the awkward result of claiming democratic virtues for proposals that actual voters reject. Since "another world" will have to arise from the current one, it is difficult to see how the "democratic transformation" of global institutions at the core of leftist globalization critiques (Patomäki and Teivainen 2004) can take place without stronger roots in the democratic politics of liberal nation-states.

For all the fervor at Seattle and Porto Alegre and Genoa, the prospects of "another world" are less clear than they once were. At the risk of straining the historical parallels, the third wave of globalization has not yet reached the point where the second wave crashed. At the end of the second wave of globalization, after all, "another world" seemed on the horizon. Collectivist alternatives to capitalist globalization were gaining strength. Well into the third wave, however, several once-inspiring "other worlds" are no longer plausible: racially tinged national socialism has long been consigned to the dustbin of history, of course, and most versions of single-party authoritarian communism have joined it there. Their failure raises the bar for would-be utopians: especially those who now draw on the socialist tradition, without pursuing the kind of revolution that still beckoned at the end of the second wave, will have to persuade global publics that new utopias avoid the drawbacks of the undemocratic and unsustainable socialisms of the past century – not to mention the inevitable costs of pursuing any "utopia" in the first place. Compared to a century before, third-wave world society may also have created more buffers to global turmoil, at least in the form of more layers of protection for a large minority that now has more to lose, which raises the potential cost of reaching for another world and therefore makes it harder for utopians to gain traction. The double movement of an earlier era has left its mark, certainly on many developed countries, so that many risk-averse world citizens enticed by the vision of "another world" could nevertheless rationally decide that things could be worse – another hurdle for the GJM to overcome.

Summary and Conclusion

Though its political prospects may be uncertain, the global left has revived in the GJM, a concerted transnational effort by groups from different backgrounds united by their opposition to the way "neoliberal" globalization has unfolded. At peak events, as in Seattle in 1999 or subsequent meetings of the WSF in Porto Alegre, it captured public attention, thereby also redirecting ongoing debates about globalization. The movement embodies the hope that "another world is possible," a vision that comes in different forms.

Even if, for the moment, history has ended for nation-states, in the sense that a version of liberal democracy squeezes out any radical notion of doing things differently (Fukuyama 1992), global history has barely started. We are bound to keep debating what the world should look like, what rules should govern it, and how its parts should be tied into a larger whole. Deep conflict on all points is to be expected, especially in periods of economic turmoil. The future of world order is very much open, and the GJM or its offshoots are likely to play a role in it. If it does, it will add further variety to a world society that is already considerably more complex than the GJM-style diagnosis typically acknowledges. As this book has tried to show, world society does not work according to one set of rules or ideology. Global civil society, backbone of the GJM, does not follow the same script as the world economy, and even the world economy is not wholly "neoliberal." Neither global sports nor global law quite fit the rules of other sectors, nor do world religions. Global environmentalism has already brought about major change and is likely to do more. Through the critiques in the GJM, visions of "another world" seep into the actual one.

In all these ways, world society is more interestingly diverse than the image that prevails in its counterculture. The third wave of globalization has put down varied new sediments as the foundation of a new kind of world society. If this book is right, the wave still has some momentum left. In spite of GJM efforts thus far, it remains to be seen whether it will bring liberty and justice for all. But, strictly speaking, the WSF slogan only states the obvious: of course, "another world is possible" – in fact, it is inevitable. Another world is already in the making.

Questions

1 Many participants in what is now commonly called the global justice movement (GJM) were unhappy with its original label, the "antiglobalization" movement. What was wrong with that label?

2 Severe economic and social problems at the end of the second wave of globalization fueled oppositional movements of that time. Does third-wave globalization provide similar fuel? If not, how could conditions change to stir hopes for "another world"?

3 The chapter argues that the GJM faces political hurdles in the electoral politics of most major countries. But could it successfully follow a strategy focusing on global objectives like major changes in the way IGOs work that would try to circumvent those hurdles by gaining global strength in spite of any "local" weakness?

4 Both radical environmentalists, discussed in Chapter 12, and GJM activists are critical of current world society. How do their critiques align? How can they translate into a practical alliance?

Further Reading

Robin Broad (ed.), *Global Backlash: Citizen Initiatives for a Just World Economy* (Rowman & Littlefield, 2002)

Donatella Della Porta, Massimiliano Andretta, Lorenzo Mosca, and Herbert Reiter, *Globalization from Below: Transnational Activists and Protest Networks* (University of Minnesota Press, 2006)

Subcomandante Marcos, *Our Word Is Our Weapon: Selected Writings* (Seven Stories Press, 2001)

Tom Mertes (ed.), *A Movement of Movements: Is Another World Really Possible?* (Verso, 2004)

Ruth Reitan, *Global Activism* (Routledge, 2007)

Boaventura de Sousa Santos, *The Rise of the Global Left: The World Social Forum and Beyond* (Zed, 2006)

GLOSSARY

Civil society, global: the sphere of institutions, organizations, and individuals located between the family, the state, and the market in which people associate voluntarily to advance common interests (Anheier 2004: 22); globally, the "third force" of voluntary associations, especially INGOs, not operating in markets or on behalf of states, advancing a version of the common good (Florini 2000).

Commons, global: areas beyond state jurisdiction, including high seas beyond territorial waters and parts of the earth's atmosphere. (Traditionally, "commons" meant pasture for grazing open to all.)

Comparative advantage: if country A produces goods X and Y more efficiently than country B, both will still benefit from trade if A focuses on what it produces best (i.e., where it has the "comparative advantage") and B produces the other good; also used as label for the economic argument that generalizes the basic principle to explain benefits of trade.

Core-periphery: groups of more productive, capital-owning countries and less productive, labor- or resource-supplying countries; in dependency and world-system theory, regions with distinct roles and exploitative relationship within capitalist system; see world-system.

Cultural imperialism: process by which, or argument to the effect that, the West or the US or corporate actors impose an ideology that serves their interests and reinforces their dominance; specifically, use and role of (commercial) media in this process, as "missionaries of global capitalism" (Herman and McChesney 1997).

FDI, Foreign Direct Investment: investment made to acquire lasting interest (effective ownership) in enterprises operating outside the economy of the investor. (Distinguished from portfolio investment in stocks and bonds.)

Gini coefficient (or index): measure of inequality of income distribution, based on shares of total (national, world) income received by individuals or countries, ranging between 0, for perfectly equal shares, to a maximum of 1 (or 100 for index), with one country or person receiving all income; technically derived from the size of the area between a line representing perfect equality and a curve representing cumulative shares of people or countries from low to 100 percent.

Globalization: process in which spatial constraints on social life diminish, resulting in compression of globe and awareness thereof (Waters 2001; Robertson 1992).

Glocalization: "interpenetration of the global and the local, resulting in unique outcomes in different geographic areas" (Ritzer 2004: 163).

Governance: forms of rule over or management of sectors and problems without direct reliance on sovereign state authority and police power.

Hegemony: dominance of one actor over others, especially if exercised by means other than coercion, e.g., by obtaining willing acquiescence or conformity with rules set by hegemon.

Islamism: political use of Islam with aim of bringing about rule of Islamic law in Islamic state; also labeled (Islamic) fundamentalism.

Market fundamentalism: overly strong faith in market solutions to social and economic problems, pejoratively ascribed to certain economists and policymakers by critics of neoliberalism (see Stiglitz 2002).

Neoliberalism: trend toward, or set of policies to bring about, diminished role of government in economic affairs, through privatization of state-owned companies, reduction in government services, and deregulation and liberalization of markets, especially by lowering barriers to trade and investment (Harvey 2005).

PPP, Purchasing Power Parity: method for converting currencies into common currency by calculating and comparing purchasing power with regard to a basket of selected goods and services, or result thereof applied to a particular currency expressed in "international dollars," used to compare actual purchasing power and living standards in different countries (as alternative to comparisons based on fluctuating market-based exchange rates).

Path dependence: manner in which, or argument to the effect that, choices made at one time restrict options at a later time; specifically refers to long-term influence of institutional legacies.

Regimes: "Sets of implicit or explicit principles, norms, rules and decision-making procedures around which actors' expectations converge in a given area of international relations" (Krasner 1983: 2), including institutions.

Value chain, global: sequence of geographically dispersed steps in production of a good or service, e.g., to supply a final buyer or controlled by lead producer; akin to global commodity chain (Gereffi 2005).

Vatican II: watershed council of Roman Catholic Church leaders, 1962–5, called to modernize Church affairs; abolished Latin mass, produced new teaching on religious liberty and human rights.

World polity: global system of multiple sovereign states operating through common rules, promoted in part by international organizations, in absence of authoritative center (Meyer et al. 1997).

World-system (modern): capitalist world economy originating in sixteenth century, focused on capital accumulation, consisting of single geographical division of labor with multiple states arranged in hierarchy of wealth and power (Wallerstein 1974).

REFERENCES

Ahrne, Göran, and Nils Brunsson. 2006. "Organizing the World." Pp. 74–94 in *Transnational Governance: Institutional Dynamics of Regulation*, edited by Marie-Laure Djelic and Kerstin Sahlin-Andersson. Cambridge: Cambridge University Press.

Alba, Richard, and Victor Nee. 2003. *Remaking the American Mainstream: Assimilation and Contemporary Immigration*. Cambridge, MA: Harvard University Press.

Albrow, Martin. 1997. *The Global Age: State and Society Beyond Modernity*. Stanford, CA: Stanford University Press.

Algar, Hamid. 2001. *Wahhabism: A Critical Essay*. Oneonta, NY: Islamic Publications International.

Allen, John L. 2007. "The Uphill Journey of Catholicism in China." *National Catholic Reporter* 6.

Alvarez, José E. 2007. "Legal Perspectives." Pp. 58–81 in *The Oxford Handbook on the United Nations*, edited by Thomas G. Weiss and Sam Daws. Oxford: Oxford University Press.

Amoore, Louise (Ed.). 2005. *The Global Resistance Reader*. New York: Routledge.

Amsden, Alice H. 2001. *The Rise of "the Rest": Challenges to the West from Late-Industrializing Economies*. Oxford: Oxford University Press.

Ancelovici, Marcos. 2002. "Organizing Against Globalization: The Case of ATTAC in France." *Politics and Society* 30:427–63.

Anderson, Allan H. 2004. "The Contextual Pentecostal Theology of David Yonggi Cho." *Asian Journal of Pentecostal Studies* 7:101–23.

Anderson, Kenneth, and David Rieff. 2005. "'Global Civil Society': A Sceptical View." Pp. 26–39 in *Global Civil Society 2004/5*, edited by Helmut K. Anheier, Mary H. Kaldor, and Marlies Glasius. London: Sage.

Andrews, David L., and George Ritzer. 2007. "The Grobal in the Sporting Glocal." *Global Networks* 7:135–53.

Ang, Ien. 1985. *Watching Dallas*. London: Methuen.

Anheier, Helmut K. 2004. *Civil Society: Measurement, Evaluation, Policy*. London: Earthscan.

Anheier, Helmut K., Marlies Glasius, and Mary H. Kaldor (Eds.). 2001. *Global Civil Society 2001*. Oxford: Oxford University Press.

An-Na'im, Abdullahi Ahmed. 2008. *Islam and the Secular State: Negotiating the Future of Shar'ia.* Cambridge, MA: Harvard University Press.

Appadurai, Arjun. 1996. *Modernity at Large: Cultural Dimensions of Globalization.* Minneapolis, MN: University of Minnesota Press.

Appelbaum, Richard P., and William I. Robinson (Eds.). 2005. *Critical Globalization Studies.* New York: Routledge.

Arjomand, Said Amir. 1988. *The Turban for the Crown: The Islamic Revolution in Iran.* New York: Oxford University Press.

Arjomand, Said Amir. 1993. *The Political Dimensions of Religion.* Albany, NY: State University of New York Press.

Arjomand, Said Amir. 2003. "Islam." Pp. 28–39 in *Global Religions: An Introduction*, edited by Mark Juergensmeyer. Oxford: Oxford University Press.

Arrighi, Giovanni, and Beverly Silver. 1999. *Chaos and Governance in the Modern World System.* Minneapolis, MN: University of Minnesota Press.

Ayres, Jeffrey. 2005. "From 'Anti-Globalization' to the Global Justice Movement: Framing Collective Action against Neoliberalism." Pp. 9–27 in *Transforming Globalization: Challenges and Opportunities in the Post 9/11 Era*, edited by Bruce Podobnik and Thomas Reifer. Leiden: Brill.

Baker, David P., and Gerald K. LeTendre. 2005. *National Differences, Global Similarities: World Culture and the Future of Schooling.* Stanford, CA: Stanford University Press.

Barba Navaretti, Giorgio, and Anthony J. Venables. 2004. *Multinational Firms in the World Economy.* Princeton, NJ: Princeton University Press.

Barker, Chris. 1997. *Global Television: An Introduction.* Oxford: Blackwell.

Barnes, Brooks. 2007. "NBC Faces Trials Bringing 'Law and Order' to France." *Wall Street Journal* (March 1).

Beale, Alison. 2002. "Identifying a Policy Hierarchy: Communication Policy, Media Industries, and Globalization." Pp. 78–89 in *Global Culture: Media, Arts, Policy, and Globalization*, edited by Diana Crane, Nobuko Kawashima, and Ken'ichi Kawasaki. New York: Routledge.

Beckles, Hilary McD. 1998. *The Development of West Indies Cricket*, 2 vols. Kingston: University Press of the West Indies.

Beckles, Hilary McD., and Brian Stoddart (Eds.). 1995. *Liberation Cricket: West Indies Cricket Culture.* Manchester: Manchester University Press.

Bello, Walden. 2001. *The Future in the Balance: Essays on Globalization and Resistance.* Oakland, CA: Food First Books.

Bello, Walden. 2002. *Deglobalization: Ideas for a New World Economy.* London: Zed.

Bello, Walden. 2004. "The Global South." Pp. 49–69 in *A Movement of Movements: Is Another World Really Possible?*, edited by Tom Mertes. London: Verso.

Bellos, Alex. 2002. *Futebol: The Brazilian Way of Life.* London: Bloomsbury.

Benedict XVI, Pope. 2006. "Faith, Reason and the University: Memories and Reflections." Regensburg, lecture, September 12.

Bennett, W. Lance. 2004. "Global Media and Politics: Transnational Communication Regimes and Civic Cultures." *Annual Review of Political Science* 7:125–48.

Bergen, Peter, and Paul Cruickshank. 2008. "The Unraveling: The Jihadist Revolt Against Bin Laden." *New Republic* (June 11).

Berkovitch, Nitza. 1999. *From Motherhood to Citizenship: Women's Rights and International Organizations.* Baltimore, MD: Johns Hopkins University Press.

Berman, Harold J. 1988. "The Law of International Commercial Transactions." *Emory Journal of International Dispute Resolution* 2:235–310.

Berman, Harold J. 1995. "World Law." *Fordham International Law Journal* 18:1617–22.

Berman, Harold J. 2005. "Faith and Law in a Multicultural World." Pp. 69–89 in *Religion in Global Civil Society*, edited by Mark Juergensmeyer. Oxford: Oxford University Press.

Bestor, Theodore C. 2000. "How Sushi Went Global." *Foreign Policy* (November/December):54–63.

Bestor, Theodore C. 2004. *Tsukiji: The Fish Market at the Center of the World*. Berkeley, CA: University of California Press.

Bicket, Douglas. 2005. "Reconsidering Geocultural Contraflow: Intercultural Information Flows through Trends in Global Audiovisual Trade." *Global Media Journal* 4(6) (http://lass.calumet.purdue.edu/cca/gmj/sp05/gmj-sp05-bicket.htm).

Bielby, Denise D., and C. Lee Harrington. 2004. "Managing Culture Matters: Genre, Aesthetic Elements, and the International Market for Exported Television." *Poetics* 32:73–98.

Bignell, Jonathan. 2005. *Big Brother: Reality TV in the Twenty-First Century*. London: Palgrave Macmillan.

Blom, J. C. H., and P. Romijn. 2002. *Srebrenica – a 'Safe' Area: Reconstruction, Background, Consequences and Analyses of the Fall of a Safe Area*. Amsterdam: Netherlands Institute for War Documentation.

Bob, Clifford. 2005. *The Marketing of Rebellion: Insurgents, Media, and International Activism*. Cambridge: Cambridge University Press.

Bokenkotter, Thomas. 1977. *A Concise History of the Catholic Church*. New York: Doubleday.

Boli, John. 1999. "Conclusion: World Authority Structures and Legitimations." Pp. 267–300 in *Constructing World Culture: International Nongovernmental Organizations Since 1875*, edited by John Boli and George M. Thomas. Stanford, CA: Stanford University Press.

Boli, John, and David V. Brewington. 2007. "Religious Organizations." Pp. 205–33 in *Religion, Globalization, and Culture*, edited by Peter Beyer and Lori Bearman. Leiden: Brill.

Boli, John, and George M. Thomas. 1997. "World Culture in the World Polity: A Century of International Non-governmental Organization." *American Sociological Review* 62:171–90.

Bonney, Richard. 2004. *Jihād: From Qur'an to Bin Laden*. New York: Palgrave Macmillan.

Bose, Mihir. 2006. *Bollywood: A History*. Brimscombe Port, UK: Tempus.

Boudewijnse, Barbara, André Droogers, and Frans Kamsteeg (Eds.). 1998. *More Than Opium: An Anthropological Approach to Latin American and Caribbean Pentecostal Praxis*. Lanham, MD: Scarecrow Press.

Bové, José. 2004. "A Farmers' International?" Pp. 137–51 in *A Movement of Movements: Is Another World Really Possible?*, edited by Tom Mertes. London: Verso.

Bové, José, and François Dufour. 2001. *The World Is Not For Sale: Farmers Against Junk Food*. London: Verso.

Boyle, Elizabeth Heger. 2002. *Female Genital Cutting: Cultural Conflict in the Global Community*. Baltimore, MD: Johns Hopkins University Press.

Brady, David, Jason Beckfield, and Martin Seeleib-Kaiser. 2005. "Economic Globalization and the Welfare State in Affluent Democracies, 1975–2001." *American Sociological Review* 70:921–48.

Braithwaite, John, and Peter Drahos. 2000. *Global Business Regulation*. Cambridge: Cambridge University Press.

Brandmüller, Walter. 2005. "Christianity and Islam in History." Pontifical Lateran University, conference lecture, December 13.

Broad, Robin (Ed.). 2002. *Global Backlash: Citizen Initiatives for a Just World Economy*. Lanham, MD: Rowman & Littlefield Publishers.

Brouwer, Steve, Paul Gifford, and Susan D. Rose. 1996. *Exporting the American Gospel: Global Christian Fundamentalism*. New York: Routledge.

Brubaker, Rogers. 1992. *Citizenship and Nationhood in France and Germany*. Cambridge, MA: Harvard University Press.

Brusco, Elizabeth. 1993. "The Reformation of Machismo: Asceticism and Masculinity among Colombian Evangelicals." Pp. 143–58 in *Rethinking Protestantism in Latin America*, edited by Virginia Garrard-Burnett and David Stoll. Philadelphia, PA: Temple University Press.

Bryner, Gary C. 2004. "Global Interdependence." Pp. 69–104 in *Environmental Governance Reconsidered: Challenges, Choices, and Opportunities*, edited by Robert F. Durant, Daniel J. Fiorino, and Rosemary O'Leary. Cambridge, MA: MIT Press.

Bull, Hedley. 1990. "The Importance of Grotius in the Study of International Relations." Pp. 65–93 in *Hugo Grotius and International Relations*, edited by Hedley Bull, Benedict Kingsbury, and Adam Roberts. Oxford: Clarendon Press.

Bull, Hedley. 2000 [1966]. "The Grotian Conception of International Society." Pp. 95–124 in *Hedley Bull on International Society*, edited by Kai Alderson and Andrew Hurrell. New York: St Martin's.

Bump, Micah N., B. Lindsay Lowell, and Silje Pettersen. 2005. "The Growth and Population Characteristics of Immigrants and Minorities in America's New Settlement States." Pp. 19–53 in *Beyond the Gateway: Immigrants in a Changing America*, edited by Elzbieta M. Gozdziak and Susan F. Martin. Lanham, MD: Lexington Books.

Bunch, Charlotte. 2001. "Women's Human Rights: The Challenges of Global Feminism and Diversity." Pp. 129–46 in *Feminist Locations: Global/Local Theory/Practice in the Twenty-First Century*, edited by Marianne DeKoven. New Brunswick, NJ: Rutgers University Press.

Bunch, Charlotte, and Niamh Reilly. 1994. *Demanding Accountability: The Global Campaign and Vienna Tribunal for Women's Human Rights*. New York: UNIFEM.

Burns, Robert A., OP. 2001. *Roman Catholicism after Vatican II*. Washington, DC: Georgetown University Press.

Butcher, Melissa. 2003. *Transnational Television, Cultural Identity and Change: When STAR Came to India*. New Delhi: Sage.

Buzan, Barry. 2004. *From International to World Society? English School Theory and the Structure of Globalisation*. Cambridge: Cambridge University Press.

Calomiris, Charles W. 2005. "Capital Flows, Financial Crises, and Public Policy." Pp. 36–76 in *Globalization: What's New*, edited by Michael M. Weinstein. New York: Columbia University Press.

Carson, Rachel. 1962. *Silent Spring*. Boston: Houghton Mifflin.

Carter, Gary. 2004. "Epilogue – In Front of Our Eyes: Notes on Big Brother." Pp. 250–57 in *Big Brother International: Formats, Critics and Publics*, edited by Ernest Mathijs and Janet Jones. London: Wallflower Press.

Casanova, José. 1997. "Globalizing Catholicism and the Return to a 'Universal' Church." Pp. 121–43 in *Transnational Religion and Fading States*, edited by Susanne Hoeber Rudolph and James Piscatori. Boulder, CO: Westview.

Cassen, Bernard. 2004. "Inventing ATTAC." Pp. 152–74 in *A Movement of Movements: Is Another World Really Possible?*, edited by Tom Mertes. London: Verso.

Castles, Francis G. 1998. *Comparative Public Policy: Patterns of Post-War Transformation.* Cheltenham, UK: Edward Elgar.

Castles, Stephen, and Mark J. Miller. 2003. *The Age of Migration.* New York: Guilford Press.

Chang, Yu-Li. 2007. "The Role of the Nation-State: Evolution of STAR TV in China and India." *Global Media Journal* 6(10) (http://lass.calumet.purdue.edu/cca/gmj/sp07/gmj-sp07-chang.htm).

Chasek, Pamela S., David L. Downie, and Janet Welsh Brown. 2006. *Global Environmental Politics.* Boulder, CO: Westview Press.

Clark, Gregory. 2007. *A Farewell to Alms: A Brief Economic History of the World.* Princeton, NJ: Princeton University Press.

Collier, Paul. 2007. *The Bottom Billion: Why the Poorest Countries Are Failing and What Can Be Done About It.* Oxford: Oxford University Press.

Conroy, Anne C., Malcolm J. Blackie, Alan Whiteside, Justin C. Malewezi, and Jeffrey D. Sachs. 2006. *Poverty, AIDS, and Hunger: Breaking the Poverty Trap in Malawi.* New York: Palgrave Macmillan.

Corten, André, and Ruth Marshall-Fratani. 2001. *Between Babel and Pentecost: Transnational Pentecostalism in Africa and Latin America.* Bloomington, IN: Indiana University Press.

Cox, Harvey. 1995. *Fire from Heaven: The Rise of Pentecostal Spirituality and the Reshaping of Religion in the Twenty-First Century.* Reading, MA: Addison-Wesley.

Craton, Michael, and James Walvin. 1970. *A Jamaican Plantation: The History of Worthy Park 1670–1970.* Toronto: University of Toronto Press.

Crawford, James, and Tom Grant. 2007. "International Court of Justice." Pp. 193–213 in *The Oxford Handbook on the United Nations*, edited by Thomas G. Weiss and Sam Daws. Oxford: Oxford University Press.

Cronon, William. 1991. *Nature's Metropolis: Chicago and the Great West.* New York: W. W. Norton.

Crosby, Alfred W. 1972. *The Columbian Exchange: Biological and Cultural Consequences of 1492.* Westport, CT: Greenwood.

Curtin, Michael. 2007. *Playing to the World's Biggest Audience: The Globalization of Chinese Film and TV.* Berkeley, CA: University of California Press.

Daly, Herman, and Joshua Farley. 2004. *Ecological Economics: Principles and Applications.* Washington, DC: Island Press.

Della Porta, Donatella. 2007. "The Global Justice Movement: An Introduction." Pp. 1–28 in *The Global Justice Movement: Cross-National and Transnational Perspectives*, edited by Donatella Della Porta. Boulder, CO: Paradigm.

Della Porta, Donatella, Massimiliano Andretta, Lorenzo Mosca, and Herbert Reiter. 2006. *Globalization from Below: Transnational Activists and Protest Networks.* Minneapolis, MN: University of Minnesota Press.

DeSombre, Elizabeth R. 2006. *Global Environmental Institutions.* New York: Routledge.

Dollar, David. 2005. "Globalization, Poverty, and Inequality." Pp. 96–128 in *Globalization: What's New*, edited by Michael M. Weinstein. New York: Columbia University Press.

Doyle, Michael W., and Nicholas Sambanis. 2007. "Peacekeeping Operations." Pp. 323–48 in *The Oxford Handbook on the United Nations*, edited by Thomas G. Weiss and Sam Daws. Oxford: Oxford University Press.

Doyle, Timothy. 2005. *Environmental Movements in Minority and Majority Worlds: A Global Perspective*. New Brunswick, NJ: Rutgers University Press.

Drache, Hiram M. 1964. *The Day of the Bonanza: A History of Bonanza Farming in the Red River Valley of the North*. Fargo, ND: North Dakota Institute for Regional Studies.

Drewnowski, Adam. 1999. "Fat and Sugar in the Global Diet: Dietary Diversity in the Nutrition Transition." Pp. 194–206 in *Food in Global History*, edited by Raymond Grew. Boulder, CO: Westview Press.

Droogers, André. 2001. "Globalisation and Pentecostal Success." Pp. 41–61 in *Between Babel and Pentecost: Transnational Pentecostalism in Africa and Latin America*, edited by André Corten and Ruth Marshall-Fratani. Bloomington, IN: Indiana University Press.

Dryzek, John. 2005. *The Politics of the Earth: Environmental Discourses*. Oxford: Oxford University Press.

Dunlap, Thomas R. 2004. *Faith in Nature: Environmentalism as Religious Quest*. Seattle, WA: University of Washington Press.

Durant, Robert F. 2004. "Reconceptualizing Purpose." Pp. 29–34 in *Environmental Governance Reconsidered: Challenges, Choices, and Opportunities*, edited by Robert F. Durant, Daniel J. Fiorino, and Rosemary O'Leary. Cambridge, MA: MIT Press.

Durch, William J., and James A. Schear. 1996. "Faultlines: UN Operations in the Former Yugoslavia." Pp. 193–274 in *UN Peacekeeping, American Politics, and the Uncivil Wars of the 1990s*, edited by William J. Durch. New York: St Martin's Press.

Edwards, Andres R. 2005. *The Sustainability Revolution: Portrait of a Paradigm Shift*. Gabriola Island: New Society Publishers.

Eichengreen, Barry. 1996. *Globalizing Capital: A History of the International Monetary System*. Princeton, NJ: Princeton University Press.

Eisenstadt, S. N. 1999. *Fundamentalism, Sectarianism, and Revolution: The Jacobin Dimension of Modernity*. Cambridge: Cambridge University Press.

Elasmar, Michael G. 2003. "An Alternative Paradigm for Conceptualizing and Labeling the Process of Influence of Imported Television Programs." Pp. 157–79 in *The Impact of International Television: A Paradigm Shift*, edited by Michael G. Elasmar. Mahwah, NJ: Lawrence Erlbaum.

Emmanuel, Kerry. 2007. *What We Know About Climate Change*. Cambridge, MA: MIT Press.

Engel, Charles, and John H. Rogers. 1996. "How Wide Is the Border?" *American Economic Review* 86:1112–25.

Entzinger, Han. 2003. "The Rise and Fall of Multiculturalism: The Case of the Netherlands." Pp. 59–86 in *Toward Assimilation and Citizenship*, edited by Christian Joppke and Ewa Morawska. Houndmills: Palgrave Macmillan.

Entzinger, Han. 2006. "Changing the Rules While the Game Is On: From Multiculturalism to Assimilation in the Netherlands." Pp. 121–44 in *Migration, Citizenship, Ethnos*, edited by Y. Michal Bodemann and Gökçe Urdakul. New York: Palgrave.

Eriksen, Thomas Hylland. 2007. "Steps to an Ecology of Transnational Sports." *Global Networks* 7:154–65.

Esping-Andersen, Gøsta. 1990. *The Three Worlds of Welfare Capitalism*. Princeton, NJ: Princeton University Press.

Esping-Andersen, Gøsta. 1999. *Social Foundations of Postindustrial Economies*. Oxford: Oxford University Press.

Etter, Lauren. 2006. "What Makes a Sport Olympic?" *Wall Street Journal* (February 18–19).

Evans, Peter. 2005. "Counter-Hegemonic Globalization: Transnational Social Movements in the Contemporary Global Political Economy." Pp. 655–70 in *Handbook of Political Sociology*, edited by Thomas Janoski, Robert R. Alford, Alexander M. Hicks, and Mildred Schwartz. Cambridge: Cambridge University Press.

Eyffinger, Arthur. 2005. "Living Up to a Tradition." Pp. 29–45 in *The Hague: Legal Capital of the World*, edited by Peter J. Van Krieken and David McKay. The Hague: Asser Press.

Falk, Richard. 1999. *Predatory Globalization: A Critique*. Malden, MA: Polity Press.

Fallows, James. 2007. "China Makes, the World Takes." Pp. 48–72 in *The Atlantic* (July/August).

Fallows, James. 2008. "The $1.4 Trillion Dollar Question." *The Atlantic Online* (January/February) (www.theatlantic.com/doc/200801/fallows-chinese-dollars).

Favell, Adrian. 2001. *Philosophies of Integration: Immigration and the Idea of Citizenship in France and Britain*. London: Palgrave.

Ferree, Myra Marx. 2006. "Globalization and Feminism: Opportunities and Obstacles for Activism in the Global Arena." Pp. 3–23 in *Global Feminism: Transnational Women's Activism, Organizing, and Human Rights*, edited by Myra Marx Ferree and Aili Mari Tripp. New York: New York University Press.

Findlay, Ronald, and Kevin H. O'Rourke. 2007. *Power and Plenty: Trade, War, and the World Economy in the Second Millennium*. Princeton, NJ: Princeton University Press.

Finnemore, Martha. 1999. "Rules of War and Wars of Rules: The International Red Cross and the Restraint of State Violence." Pp. 149–65 in *Constructing World Culture: International Nongovernmental Organizations since 1875*, edited by John Boli and George M. Thomas. Stanford, CA: Stanford University Press.

Firebaugh, Glenn. 2003. *The New Geography of Global Income Inequality*. Cambridge, MA: Harvard University Press.

Firebaugh, Glenn, and Brian Goesling. 2007. "Globalization and Global Inequalities: Recent Trends." Pp. 549–64 in *The Blackwell Companion to Globalization*, edited by George Ritzer. Malden, MA: Blackwell.

Fisher, William F., and Thomas Ponniah (Eds.). 2003. *Another World is Possible: Popular Alternatives to Globalization at the World Social Forum*. London: Zed.

Fleischhauer, Carl-August. 1995. "Inducing Compliance." Pp. 231–43 in *United Nations Legal Order*, vol. 1, edited by Oscar Schachter and Christopher C. Joyner. Cambridge: Cambridge University Press.

Flew, Terry. 2007. *Understanding Global Media*. Houndmills: Palgrave Macmillan.

Flora, Peter (Ed.). 1986. *Growth to Limits: The Western European Welfare States since World War II*. Berlin: W. de Gruyter.

Florini, Ann M. (Ed.). 2000. *The Third Force: The Rise of Transnational Civil Society*. Tokyo: Japan Center for International Exchange.

Flynn, Dennis O., and Arturo Giráldez. 2006. "Globalization Began in 1571." Pp. 232–47 in *Globalization and Global History*, edited by Barry K. Gills and William R. Thompson. New York: Routledge.

Franda, Marcus. 2006. *The United Nations in the Twenty-First Century: Management and Reform Processes in a Troubled Organization*. Lanham, MD: Rowman and Littlefield.

Frank, David John, Ann Hironaka, John W. Meyer, Evan Schofer, and Nancy Brandon Tuma. 1999. "The Rationalization and Organization of Nature in World Culture." Pp.

81–99 in *Constructing World Culture*, edited by John Boli and George M. Thomas. Stanford, CA: Stanford University Press.

Frank, David John, Ann Hironaka, and Evan Schofer. 2000. "The Nation-State and the Natural Environment over the Twentieth Century." *American Sociological Review* 65:96–116.

Frankel, Jeffrey. 2000. "Globalization of the Economy." Pp. 45–71 in *Governance in a Globalizing World*, edited by Joseph S. Nye Jr. and John D. Donahue. Washington, DC: Brookings Institution Press.

Freeman, Gary P. 2004. "Immigrant Incorporation in Western Democracies." *International Migration Review* 38:945–69.

Freston, Paul. 1997. "Charismatic Evangelicals: Mission and Politics on the Frontiers of Protestant Growth." Pp. 184–204 in *Charismatic Christianity: Sociological Perspectives*, edited by Stephen Hunt, Malcolm Hamilton, and Tony Walter. New York: St Martin's Press.

Frieden, Jeffry A. 2006. *Global Capitalism: Its Fall and Rise in the Twentieth Century*. New York: W. W. Norton.

Friedman, Thomas L. 2007. *The World Is Flat: A Brief History of the Twenty-First Century*. New York: Picador.

Fukuyama, Francis. 1992. *The End of History and the Last Man*. New York: Free Press.

Fuller, Bruce. 1991. *Growing up Modern: The Western State Builds Third World Schools*. New York: Routledge.

Gallagher, Peter. 2005. *The First Ten Years of the WTO 1995–2005*. Cambridge: Cambridge University Press.

Garrett, Geoffrey. 1998. *Partisan Politics in the Global Economy*. Cambridge: Cambridge University Press.

Gelchu, Ahmed, and Daniel Pauly. 2007. "Growth and Distribution of Port-Based Global Fishing Effort within Countries' EEZs from 1970 to 1995." Vancouver: The Fisheries Centre, University of British Columbia.

Gereffi, Gary. 2005. "The Global Economy: Organization, Governance, and Development." Pp. 160–82 in *Handbook of Economic Sociology*, edited by Neil J. Smelser and Richard Swedberg. Princeton, NJ: Princeton University Press.

Gerges, Fawaz A. 2005. *The Far Enemy: Why Jihad Went Global*. New York: Cambridge University Press.

Gifford, Paul. 1987. "Africa Shall Be Saved": An Appraisal of Reinhard Bonnke's Pan-African Crusade." *Journal of Religion in Africa* 17:63–92.

Gifford, Paul. 1994. "Ghana's Charismatic Churches." *Journal of Religion in Africa* 24:241–65.

Gillmeister, Heiner. 1997. *Tennis: A Cultural History*. London: Leicester University Press.

Giry, Stéphanie. 2006. "France and Its Muslims." *Foreign Affairs* 85 (September/October) (http://www.foreignaffairs.org/20060901faessay85508/stephanie-giry/france-and-its muslims.html).

Giulianotti, Richard. 1999. *Football: A Sociology of the Global Game*. Oxford: Polity Press.

Giulianotti, Richard. 2000. "Built by the Two Varelas: The Rise and Fall of Football Culture and National Identity in Uruguay." Pp. 134–54 in *Football Culture: Local Contests, Global Visions*, edited by Gerry P. T. Finn and Richard Giulianotti. London: Frank Cass.

Giulianotti, Richard, and Roland Robertson. 2004. "The Globalization of Football: A Study in the Glocalization of the 'Serious Life'." *British Journal of Sociology* 55:545–68.

Glatzer, Miguel, and Dietrich Rueschemeyer. 2005. "An Introduction to the Problem." Pp. 1–22 in *Globalization and the Future of the Welfare State*, edited by Miguel Glatzer and Dietrich Rueschemeyer. Pittsburgh, PA: University of Pittsburgh Press.

Glendon, Mary Ann. 2001. *A World Made New: Eleanor Roosevelt and the Universal Declaration of Human Rights*. New York: Random House.

Goldblatt, David. 2008. *The Ball Is Round: A Global History of Soccer*. New York: Riverhead Books.

Gong, Gerrit W. 1984. *The Standard of "Civilization" in International Society*. Oxford: Clarendon Press.

Goody, Jack. 1982. *Cooking, Cuisine, and Class: A Study in Comparative Sociology*. Cambridge: Cambridge University Press.

Gould, Mark. 2008. "Islam, the Law, and the Sovereignty of God." *Policy Review* (June/July) (http://www.hoover.org/publications/policyreview/19457189.html).

Govil, Nitin. 2007. "Bollywood and the Frictions of Global Mobility." Pp. 84–98 in *Media on the Move: Global Flow and Contra-Flow*, edited by Daya Kishan Thussu. London: Routledge.

Grew, Raymond. 1999. "Food and Global History." Pp. 1–29 in *Food in Global History*, edited by Raymond Grew. Boulder, CO: Westview Press.

Griffin, Joseph A. 1997 [1930]. "The Sacred Congregation de Propganda Fide: Its Foundation and Historical Antecedents." Pp. 57–95 in *Christianity and Missions, 1450–1800*, edited by J. S. Cummins. Aldershot: Ashgate.

Grimshaw, Patricia. 2001. "Reading the Silences: Suffrage Activists and Race in the Nineteenth Century." Pp. 31–48 in *Women's Rights and Human Rights: International Historical Perspectives*, edited by Patricia Grimshaw, Katie Holmes, and Marilyn Lake. New York: Palgrave.

Grotius, Hugo. 2005 [1625]. *The Rights of War and Peace*, book 1. Indianapolis, IN: Liberty Fund.

Guha, Ramachandra. 2000. *Environmentalism: A Global History*. New York: Longman.

Gunn, Geoffrey C. 2003. *First Globalization: The Eurasian Exchange, 1500–1800*. Lanham, MD: Rowman & Littlefield.

Guthrie, Doug. 2006. *China and Globalization: The Social, Economic and Political Transformation of Chinese Society*. New York: Routledge.

Gutiérrez, Gustavo. 1973. *A Theology of Liberation: History, Politics and Salvation*. Maryknoll, NY: Orbis Books.

Guttmann, Allen. 1984. *The Games Must Go On: Avery Brundage and the Olympic Movement*. New York: Columbia University Press.

Guttmann, Allen. 1994. *Games and Empires: Modern Sports and Cultural Imperialism*. New York: Columbia University Press.

Guttmann, Allen, and L. Thompson. 2001. *Japanese Sports: A History*. Honolulu: University of Hawaii Press.

Hadden, Jennifer, and Sidney G. Tarrow. 2007. "The Global Justice Movement in the United States." Pp. 210–31 in *The Global Justice Movement: Cross-National and Transnational Perspectives*, edited by Donatella Della Porta. Boulder, CO: Paradigm.

Haeri, Shahla. 1993. "Obedience versus Autonomy: Women and Fundamentalism in Iran and Pakistan." Pp. 181–213 in *Fundamentalisms and Society: Reclaiming the Sciences, the Family, and Education*, edited by Martin E. Marty and R. Scott Appleby. Chicago, IL: University of Chicago Press.

Hagan, John. 2003. *Justice in the Balkans: Prosecuting War Crimes in the Hague Tribunal.* Chicago, IL: University of Chicago Press.

Hannum, Horst. 1995. "Human Rights." Pp. 319–48 in *United Nations Legal Order*, vol. 1, edited by Oscar Schachter and Christopher C. Joyner. Cambridge: Cambridge University Press.

Hargreaves, John. 2002. *Freedom for Catalonia? Catalan Nationalism, Spanish Identity and the Barcelona Olympic Games.* Cambridge: Cambridge University Press.

Harindranath, Ramaswami. 2003. "Reviving 'Cultural Imperialism': International Audiences, Global Capitalism, and the Transnational Elite." Pp. 155–68 in *Planet TV: A Global Television Reader*, edited by Lisa Parks and Shanti Kumar. New York: New York University Press.

Harrigan, Jane. 2001. *From Dictatorship to Democracy: Economic Policy in Malawi 1964–2000.* Aldershot, UK: Ashgate.

Harvey, David. 2005. *A Brief History of Neoliberalism.* New York: Oxford University Press.

Havens, Timothy. 2006. *Global Television Marketplace.* London: British Film Institute.

Hayakawa, Noriyo. 2001. "Nationalism, Colonialism and Women: The Case of the World Woman's Christian Temperance Union in Japan." Pp. 16–30 in *Women's Rights and Human Rights: International Historical Perspectives*, edited by Patricia Grimshaw, Katie Holmes, and Marilyn Lake. New York: Palgrave.

Hefner, Robert W. 2000. *Civil Islam: Muslims and Democratization in Indonesia.* Princeton, NJ: Princeton University Press.

Held, David. 2004. *Global Covenant: The Social Democratic Alternative to the Washington Consensus.* Cambridge: Polity Press.

Held, David, Anthony McGrew, David Goldblatt, and Jonathan Perraton. 1999. *Global Transformations: Politics, Economics, and Culture.* Stanford, CA: Stanford University Press.

Helleiner, Eric. 1994. *States and the Reemergence of Global Finance: From Bretton Woods to the 1990s.* Ithaca, NY: Cornell University Press.

Herman, Edward S., and Robert W. McChesney. 1997. *The Global Media: The New Missionaries of Global Capitalism.* London: Cassell.

Hicks, Alexander. 1999. *Social Democracy and Welfare Capitalism: A Century of Income Security Politics.* Ithaca, NY: Cornell University Press.

Hicks, Alexander, and Christopher Zorn. 2005. "Economic Globalization, the Macro Economy, and Reversals of Welfare: Expansion in Affluent Democracies, 1978–94." *International Organization* 59:631–62.

Ho, Peter. 2006. "Sprouts of Environmentalism in China? Government-Organized NGOs and Green Organizations in Disguise." Pp. 135–60 in *Shades of Green: Environmental Activism Around the Globe*, edited by Christof Mauch, Nathan Stolzfus, and Douglas R. Weiner. Lanham, MD: Rowman & Littlefield.

Hobsbawm, E. J. 1975. *The Age of Capital, 1848–1875.* London: Weidenfeld and Nicolson.

Hollenbach, D. 1998. *Justice, Peace and Human Rights: American Catholic Social Ethics in a Pluralistic World.* New York: Crossroads.

Huber, Evelyne. 2005. "Globalization and Social Policy Developments in Latin America." Pp. 75–105 in *Globalization and the Future of the Welfare State*, edited by Miguel Glatzer and Dietrich Rueschemeyer. Pittsburgh, PA: University of Pittsburgh Press.

Huber, Evelyne, and John D. Stephens. 2001. *Development and Crisis of the Welfare State: Parties and Policies in Global Markets.* Chicago, IL: University of Chicago Press.

Hubka, David. 2002. "Globalization of Cultural Production: The Transformation of Children's Animated Television." Pp. 233–55 in *Global Culture: Media, Arts, Policy, Globalization*, edited by Diana Crane, Nobuko Kawashima, and Ken'ichi Kawasaki. New York: Routledge.

Huntington, Samuel P. 2004. *Who Are We? The Challenges to America's National Identity*. New York: Simon & Schuster.

ICJ. 1986. "The Republic of Nicaragua v. The United States of America." The Hague: International Court of Justice.

ICTY. 2008. "ICTY at a Glance." The Hague: Criminal Tribunal for the Former Yugoslavia (www.un.org/icty, retrieved May 2, 2008).

Independent, The. 2007. "Morse: The No. 1 Gentleman Detective." April 27.

IFC. 2006. "Fact Sheet: Emerging Markets at a Glance." Washington, DC: International Finance Corporation.

IMF. 2008. *World Economic Outlook 2008: Housing and the Business Cycle*. Washington, DC: International Monetary Fund.

Inglehart, Ronald, and Pippa Norris. 2003. "The True Clash of Civilizations." *Foreign Policy* (March/April):62–70.

IOM. 2005. *World Migration 2005: Costs and Benefits of International Migration*. Geneva: International Organization for Migration.

IPCC. 2007. *Climate Change 2007 (Fourth Assessment Report, in 4 parts)*. Cambridge: Cambridge University Press and www.ipcc.ch.

Ireland, Rowan. 1991. *Kingdoms Come: Religion and Politics in Brazil*. Pittsburgh, PA: University of Pittsburgh Press.

Issenberg, Sasha. 2007. *The Sushi Economy: Globalization and the Making of a Modern Delicacy*. New York: Gotham Books.

Jacobsson, Bengt, and Kerstin Sahlin-Andersson. 2006. "Dynamics of Soft Regulations." Pp. 247–65 in *Transnational Governance: Institutional Dynamics of Regulation*, edited by Marie-Laure Djelic and Kerstin Sahlin-Andersson. Cambridge: Cambridge University Press.

Jeffery, Renée. 2006. *Hugo Grotius in International Thought*. New York: Palgrave Macmillan.

Jenkins, Philip. 2002. *The Next Christendom: The Coming of Global Christianity*. Oxford: Oxford University Press.

Joppke, Christian. 1999. *Immigration and the Nation-State: The United States, Germany and Great Britain*. Oxford: Oxford University Press.

Joppke, Christian. 2007. "Beyond National Models: Civic Integration Policies for Immigrants in Western Europe." *West European Politics* 30:1–22.

Kasimow, Harold. 1999. "John Paul II and Interreligious Dialogue: An Overview." Pp. 1–23 in *John Paul II and Interreligious Dialogue*, edited by Byron L. Sherwin and Harold Kasimow. Maryknoll, NY: Orbis Books.

Katz, Tamar, and Elihu Liebes. 1990. *The Export of Meaning: Cross-Cultural Readings of Dallas*. New York: Oxford University Press.

Kaufman, Jason, and Orlando Patterson. 2005. "Cross-National Diffusion: The Global Spread of Cricket." *American Sociological Review* 70:82–110.

Kaur, Raminder, and Ajay J. Sinha. 2005. "Bollyworld: An Introduction to Popular Indian Cinema through a Transnational Lens." Pp. 11–32 in *Bollyworld: Popular Indian Cinema through a Transnational Lens*, edited by Raminder Kaur and Ajay J. Sinha. New Delhi: Sage.

Keane, John. 2003. *Global Civil Society?* Cambridge: Cambridge University Press.

Keck, Margaret E., and Kathryn Sikkink. 1998. *Activists beyond Borders: Advocacy Networks in International Politics.* Ithaca, NY: Cornell University Press.

Kellner, Douglas, and Clayton Pierce. 2007. "Media and Globalization." Pp. 383–95 in *The Blackwell Companion to Globalization*, edited by George Ritzer. Malden, MA: Blackwell.

Kelly, William W. 2007. "Is Baseball a Global Sport? America's 'National Pastime' as Global Field and International Sport." *Global Networks* 7:187–201.

Kelsay, John. 2007. *Arguing the Just War in Islam.* Cambridge, MA: Harvard University Press.

Kennedy, Paul. 2006. *The Parliament of Man: The Past, Present, and Future of the United Nations.* New York: Random House.

Kenny, Charles. 2004. "Why Are We Worried About Income? Nearly Everything That Matters Is Converging." *World Development* 33:1–19.

Khagram, Sanjeev. 2002. "Restructuring the Global Politics of Development: The Case of India's Narmada Valley Dams." Pp. 206–30 in *Restructuring World Politics: Transnational Social Movements, Networks, and Norms*, edited by Sanjeev Khagram, James V. Riker, and Kathryn Sikkink. Minneapolis, MN: University of Minnesota Press.

Khagram, Sanjeev. 2004. *Dams and Development: Transnational Struggles for Water and Power.* Ithaca, NY: Cornell University Press.

Khomeini, Ruhollah, and Hamid Algar. 1985. *Islam and Revolution: Writings and Declarations of Imam Khomeini.* London: KPI.

Kingsbury, Benedict, and Adam Roberts. 1990. "Introduction: Grotian Thought in International Relations." Pp. 1–64 in *Hugo Grotius and International Relations*, edited by Hedley Bull, Benedict Kingsbury, and Adam Roberts. Oxford: Clarendon Press.

Kirgis, Frederic L. 1995. "Specialized Law-Making Processes." Pp. 109–68 in *United Nations Legal Order*, vol. 1, edited by Oscar Schachter and Christopher C. Joyner. Cambridge: Cambridge University Press.

Kleijwegt, Margalith. 2005. *Onzichtbare Ouders: De Buurt van Mohammed B.* Zutphen: Plataan.

Klein, Alan M. 2006. *Growing the Game: The Globalization of Major League Baseball.* New Haven, CT: Yale University Press.

Klenow, Peter J., and Andrés Rodríguez-Clare. 2005. "Externalities and Growth." Pp. 817–61 in *Handbook of Economic Growth*, vol. 1A, edited by Philippe Aghion and Steven N. Durlauf. Amsterdam: Elsevier.

Koenig-Archibugi, Mathias. 2002. "Mapping Global Governance." Pp. 46–69 in *Governing Globalization: Power, Authority and Global Governance*, edited by David Held and Anthony McGrew. Cambridge: Polity Press.

Korzeniewicz, Miguel. 1994. "Commodity Chains and Marketing Strategies: Nike and the Global Athletic Footwear Industry." Pp. 247–65 in *Commodity Chains and Global Capitalism*, edited by Gary Gereffi and Miguel Korzeniewicz. Westport, CT: Praeger.

Korzeniewicz, Roberto Patricio, and Timothy Patrick Moran. 2007. "World Inequality in the Twenty-First Century: Patterns and Tendencies." Pp. 565–92 in *The Blackwell Companion to Globalization*, edited by George Ritzer. Malden, MA: Blackwell.

Krasner, Stephen D. (Ed.). 1983. *International Regimes.* Ithaca, NY: Cornell University Press.

Kumar, Shanti. 2006. *Gandhi Meets Primetime: Globalization and Nationalism in Indian Television.* Urbana, IL: University of Illinois Press.

Küng, Hans. 2007. *Islam: Past, Present and Future*. Oxford: Oneworld.

Kurzman, Charles. 2004. *The Unthinkable Revolution in Iran*. Cambridge, MA: Harvard University Press.

Kyle, David. 2000. *Transnational Peasants: Migrations, Networks, and Ethnicity in Andean Ecuador*. Baltimore, MD: Johns Hopkins University Press.

LaFeber, Walter. 2002. *Michael Jordan and the New Global Capitalism*. New York: W. W. Norton.

Lake, Marilyn. 2001. "From Self-Determination via Protection to Equality via Non-Discrimination: Defining Women's Rights at the League of Nations." Pp. 254–71 in *Women's Rights and Human Rights: International Historical Perspectives*, edited by Patricia Grimshaw, Katie Holmes, and Marilyn Lake. New York: Palgrave.

Lechner, Frank J. 2005. "Religious Rejections of Globalization." Pp. 115–33 in *Religion in Global Civil Society*, edited by Mark Juergensmeyer. Oxford: Oxford University Press.

Lechner, Frank J. 2007. "Imagined Communities in the Global Game: Soccer and the Development of Dutch National Identity." *Global Networks* 7:215–29.

Lechner, Frank J. 2008. *The Netherlands: Globalization and National Identity*. New York: Routledge.

Lechner, Frank J., and John Boli. 2005. *World Culture: Origins and Consequences*. Malden, MA: Blackwell.

Lehmann, David. 2002. "Religion and Globalization." Pp. 299–315 in *Religion in the Modern World: Traditions and Transformations*, edited by Linda Woodhead. London: Routledge.

Leifer, Eric M. 1995. *Making the Majors: The Transformation of Team Sports in America*. Cambridge, MA: Harvard University Press.

Leith, J. Clark. 2005. *Why Botswana Prospered*. Montreal: McGill-Queen's University Press.

Levitt, Peggy. 2001. *The Transnational Villagers*. Berkeley, CA: University of California Press.

Levitt, Peggy, and Nina Glick Schiller. 2004. "Conceptualizing Simultaneity: A Transnational Social Field Perspective on Society." *International Migration Review* 38:1002–39.

Lie, John. 1998. *Han Unbound: The Political Economy of South Korea*. Stanford, CA: Stanford University Press.

Lipschutz, Ronnie D. 2004. *Global Environmental Politics: Power, Perspectives, and Practice*. Washington, DC: CQ Press.

Loya, Thomas A., and John Boli. 1999. "Standardization in the World Polity: Technical Rationality over Power." Pp. 169–97 in *Constructing World Culture: International Nongovernmental Organizations since 1875*, edited by John Boli and George M. Thomas. Stanford, CA: Stanford University Press.

Maguire, Joseph. 1999. *Global Sport: Identities, Societies, Civilizations*. Cambridge: Polity Press.

Maguire, Joseph, and Mark Falcous. 2005. "'Making Touchdowns and Hoop Dreams': The NFL and the NBA in England." Pp. 23–40 in *Power and Global Sport: Zones of Prestige, Emulation and Resistance*, edited by Joseph Maguire. London: Routledge.

Maguire, Sean. 2003. "A Religious Revolutionary." Pp. 46–57 in *Pope John Paul II: Reaching out across Borders*, edited by Philip Pullella. Upper Saddle River, NJ: Reuters Prentice Hall.

Malone, David M. 2007. "Security Council." Pp. 117–35 in *The Oxford Handbook on the United Nations*, edited by Thomas G. Weiss and Sam Daws. Oxford: Oxford University Press.

Mangan, J. A. 2001. "Prologue: Imperialism, Sport, Globalization." Pp. 1–4 in *Europe, Sport, World: Shaping Global Societies*, edited by J. A. Mangan. London: Frank Cass.

Mangan, J. A., and Colm Hickey. 2001. "Globalization, the Games Ethic and Imperialism: Further Aspects of the Diffusion of an Ideal." Pp. 105–30 in *Europe, Sport, World: Shaping Global Societies*, edited by J.A. Mangan. London: Frank Cass.

Mann, Michael. 1993. *The Sources of Social Power*, vol. 2: *The Rise of Classes and Nation-States, 1760–1914*. Cambridge: Cambridge University Press.

Manow, Philip. 2001. "Comparative Institutional Advantages of Welfare State Regimes and New Coalitions in Welfare State Reforms." Pp. 146–64 in *The New Politics of the Welfare State*, edited by Paul Pierson. Oxford: Oxford University Press.

Marcos, Subcomandante. 2001. *Our Word Is Our Weapon: Selected Writings*. New York: Seven Stories Press.

Markovits, Andrei S., and Steven L. Hellerman. 2001. *Offside: Soccer and American Exceptionalism*. Princeton, NJ: Princeton University Press.

Markovits, Andrei S., and Steven L. Hellerman. 2003. "Women's Soccer in the United States: Yet Another American Exceptionalism." *Soccer and Society* 14:14–29.

Marks, Robert B. 2002. *The Origins of the Modern World: A Global and Ecological Narrative*. Lanham, MD: Rowman & Littlefield.

Martin, David. 1990. *Tongues of Fire: The Explosion of Protestantism in Latin America*. Oxford: Blackwell.

Martín-Barbero, Jesús. 1995. "Memory and Form in the Latin American Soap Opera." Pp. 276–84 in *To Be Continued . . . : Soap Operas around the World*, edited by Robert C. Allen. London: Routledge.

Massey, Douglas S. 2006. "Patterns and Processes of International Migration in the Twenty-First Century: Lessons for South Africa." Pp. 38–70 in *Africa on the Move: African Migration and Urbanisation in Comparative Perspective*, edited by Marta Tienda, Sally Findley, Stephen Tollman, and Eleanor Preston-Whyte. Johannesburg: Wits University Press.

Massey, Douglas S., Joaquín Arango, Hugo Graeme, Ali Kouaouci, Adela Pellegrino, and J. Edward Taylor. 1998. *Worlds In Motion: Understanding International Migration at the End of the Millennium*. Oxford: Clarendon Press.

Massey, Douglas S., and J. Edward Taylor. 2004a. "Introduction." Pp. 1–12 in *International Migration: Prospects and Policies in a Global Market*, edited by Douglas S. Massey and J. Edward Taylor. Oxford: Oxford University Press.

Massey, Douglas S., and J. Edward Taylor. 2004b. "Back to the Future: Immigration Research, Immigration Policy, and Globalization in the Twenty-First Century." Pp. 373–88 in *International Migration: Prospects and Policies in a Global Market*, edited by Douglas S. Massey and J. Edward Taylor. Oxford: Oxford University Press.

Mathews, Jessica T. 1997. "Power Shift." *Foreign Affairs* 76:50–66.

Mathijs, Ernest, and Janet Jones (Eds.). 2004. *Big Brother International: Formats, Critics and Publics*. London: Wallflower Press.

Maudoodi, Syed Abul Ala. 1991. *West versus Islam*. New Delhi: International Islamic Publishers.

Mayer, Ann Elizabeth. 2007. *Islam and Human Rights: Tradition and Politics*. Boulder, CO: Westview Press.

Mazoyer, Marcel, and Laurence Roudart. 2006. *A History of World Agriculture: From the Neolithic Age to the Current Crisis*. New York: Monthly Review Press.

Mazumdar, Sucheta. 1999. "The Impact of New World Food Crops on the Diet and Economy of China and India, 1600–1900." Pp. 58–78 in *Food in Global History*, edited by Raymond Grew. Boulder, CO: Westview Press.

McGrew, Anthony. 2007. "Globalization in Hard Times: Contention in the Academy and Beyond." Pp. 16–28 in *The Blackwell Companion to Globalization*, edited by George Ritzer. Malden, MA: Blackwell.

McMichael, Philip. 2005. "Globalization." Pp. 587–606 in *The Handbook of Political Sociology: States, Civil Society, and Globalization*, edited by Thomas Janoski, Robert R. Alford, Alexander M. Hicks, and Mildred A. Schwartz. Cambridge: Cambridge University Press.

McMichael, Philip. 2007. "Globalization and the Agrarian World." Pp. 216–38 in *The Blackwell Companion to Globalization*, edited by George Ritzer. Malden, MA: Blackwell.

McNeely, Connie. 1995. *Constructing the Nation-State: International Organization and Prescriptive Action*. Westport, CT: Greenwood Press.

McNeill, William H. 1963. *The Rise of the West: A History of the Human Community*. Chicago, IL: University of Chicago Press.

Meadows, Donella H., Dennis L. Meadows, Jørgen Randers, William W. Behrens, Janine Delaunay. 1972. *Limits to Growth: A Report for the Club of Rome's Project on the Predicament of Mankind*. New York: Universe Books.

Mekata, Motoko. 2000. "Building Partnerships toward a Common Goal: Experiences of the International Campaign to Ban Landmines." Pp. 143–76 in *The Third Force: The Rise of Transnational Civil Society*, edited by Ann M. Florini. Tokyo: Japan Center for International Exchange.

Mertes, Tom (Ed.). 2004. *A Movement of Movements: Is Another World Really Possible?* London: Verso.

Meyer, John W. 2004. "The Nation as Babbitt: How Countries Conform." *Contexts* 3:42–7.

Meyer, John W., John Boli, George M. Thomas, and Francisco O. Ramirez. 1997. "World Society and the Nation-State." *American Journal of Sociology* 103:144–81.

Meyer, John W., David John Frank, Ann Hironaka, Evan Schofer, and Nancy Brandon Tuma. 1997. "The Structuring of a World Environmental Regime, 1870–1990." *International Organization* 51:623–51.

Meyer, John W., Joane Nagel, and Conrad W. Snyder, Jr. 1993. "The Expansion of Mass Education in Botswana: Local and World Society Perspectives." *Comparative Education Review* 37:454–75.

Meyer, John W., Francisco O. Ramirez, Richard Rubinson, and John Boli[-Bennett]. 1977. "The World Educational Revolution, 1950–1970." *Sociology of Education* 50:242–58.

Mhone, Guy C. Z. (Ed.). 1992. *Malawi at the Crossroads: The Post-Colonial Political Economy*. Harare: Sapes Books.

Milanovic, Branko. 2005. *Worlds Apart: Measuring International and Global Inequality*. Princeton, NJ: Princeton University Press.

Miller, Toby, Nitin Govil, John McMurria, Richard Maxwell, and Ting Wang. 2005. *Global Hollywood 2*. London: British Film Institute.

Mintz, Sidney W. 1986. *Sweetness and Power: The Place of Sugar in Modern History*. New York: Penguin.

Missiroli, Antonio. 2002. "European Football Cultures and their Integration: The "Short' Twentieth Century." *Culture, Sport, Society* 5:1–20.

Moghadam, Valentine M. 2005. *Globalizing Women: Transnational Feminist Networks.* Baltimore, MD: Johns Hopkins University Press.

Mol, Arthur P. J. 2001. *Globalization and Environmental Reform: The Ecological Modernization of the Global Economy.* Cambridge, MA: MIT Press.

Moran, Albert. 1998. *Copycat Television: Globalisation, Program Formats and Cultural Identity.* Luton, UK: University of Luton Press.

Morawska, Ewa. 2004. "Exploring Diversity in Immigrant Assimilation and Transnationalism: Poles and Russian Jews in Philadelphia." *International Migration Review* 38:1372–412.

Morgan, Glenn. 2006. "Transnational Actors, Transnational Institutions, Transnational Spaces: The Role of Law Firms in the Internationalization of Competition Regulation." Pp. 139–60 in *Transnational Governance: Institutional Dynamics of Regulation,* edited by Marie-Laure Djelic and Kerstin Sahlin-Andersson. Cambridge: Cambridge University Press.

Mucchielli, Laurent, and Veronique Le Goaziou. 2006. *Quand les Banlieues Brûlent: Retour sur les Émeutes de Novembre 2005.* Paris: La Découverte.

Muravchik, Joshua. 2005. *The Future of the United Nations: Understanding the Past to Chart a Way Forward.* Washington, DC: AEI Press.

Murdock, Graham. 2006. "Cosmopolitans and Conquistadors: Empires, Nations and Networks." Pp. 17–32 in *Communications Media, Globalization and Empire,* edited by Oliver Boyd-Barrett. Eastleigh, UK: John Libbey.

Murray, Bill. 1996. *The World's Game: A History of Soccer.* Urbana, IL: University of Illinois Press.

Nandy, A. 2000. *The Tao of Cricket.* Oxford: Oxford University Press.

Naughton, Barry. 2007. *The Chinese Economy: Transitions and Growth.* Cambridge, MA: MIT Press.

Nordhaus, William. 2008. *A Question of Balance: Weighing the Options on Global Warming Policies.* New Haven, CT: Yale University Press.

Notes from Nowhere. 2003. *We Are Everywhere: The Irresistible Rise of Global Anticapitalism.* London: Verso.

Obstfeld, Maurice, and Alan M. Taylor. 2004. *Global Capital Markets: Integration, Crisis, and Growth.* Cambridge: Cambridge University Press.

OCHA/IRIN. 2005. *Broken Bodies, Broken Dreams: Violence against Women Exposed.* Kenya: OCHA/IRIN [Office for the Coordination of Humanitarian Affairs/Integrated Regional Information Networks].

OECD. 2007a. *International Investment Perspectives: Freedom of Investment in a Changing World.* Paris: OECD.

OECD. 2007b. *Social Expenditure 1980–2003: Interpretative Guide of SOCX.* Paris: OECD.

OECD. 2007c. *Society at a Glance: OECD Social Indicators* (2006 edn.). Paris: OECD.

Offen, Karen. 2001. "Women's Rights or Human Rights? International Feminism between the Wars." Pp. 243–53 in *Women's Rights and Human Rights: International Historical Perspectives,* edited by Patricia Grimshaw, Katie Holmes, and Marilyn Lake. New York: Palgrave.

Ogus, A. I. 1982. "Great Britain." Pp. 150–264 in *The Evolution of Social Insurance 1881–1981,* edited by Peter A. Köhler and Hans F. Zacher. London: Frances Pinter.

Ohnuki-Tierney, Emiko. 1997. "McDonald's in Japan: Changing Manners and Etiquette." Pp. 161–82 in *Golden Arches East: McDonald's in East Asia,* edited by James L. Watson. Stanford, CA: Stanford University Press.

Olesen, Thomas. 2005. *International Zapatismo: The Construction of Solidarity in the Age of Globalization*. London: Zed.

O'Rourke, Kevin H., and Jeffrey G. Williamson. 2002. "When Did Globalization Begin?" *European Review of Economic History* 6:23–50.

Osterhammel, Jürgen, and Niels P. Petterson. 2005. *Globalization: A Short History*. Princeton, NJ: Princeton University Press.

Paterson, Matthew. 2000. *Understanding Global Environmental Politics: Domination, Accumulation, Resistance*. New York: St Martin's.

Patomäki, Heikki, and Teivo Teivainen. 2004. *A Possible World: Democratic Transformation of Global Institutions*. London: Zed.

Pepper, David. 1996. *Modern Environmentalism: An Introduction*. London: Routledge.

Peterson del Mar, David. 2006. *Environmentalism*. Harlow: Pearson Education.

Pew. 2006. *Spirit and Power: A 10-Country Survey of Pentecostals*. Washington, DC: Pew Forum on Religion and Public Life.

Pflanze, Otto. 1990. *Bismarck and the Development of Germany*, vol. 3: *The Period of Fortification, 1880–1898*. Princeton, NJ: Princeton University Press.

Pierson, Paul. 1994. *Dismantling the Welfare State? Reagan, Thatcher, and the Politics of Retrenchment*. Cambridge: Cambridge University Press.

Pilcher, Jeffrey M. 2005. *Food in World History*. New York: Routledge.

Pirie, Iain. 2008. *The Korean Developmental State: From Dirigisme to Neo-Liberalism*. London: Routledge.

Poewe, Karla O. (Ed.). 1994. *Charismatic Christianity as a Global Culture*. Columbia, SC: University of South Carolina Press.

Pogge, Thomas. 2007. "Why Inequality Matters." Pp. 132–47 in *Global Inequality*, edited by David Held and Ayse Kaya. Cambridge: Polity Press.

Pogge, Thomas, and Sanjay G. Reddy. 2005. "How *Not* to Count the Poor [version 6.2]." (www.socialanalysis.org, retrieved 2008).

Polanyi, Karl. 1957. *The Great Transformation: The Political and Economic Origins of Our Time*. Boston: Beacon Press.

Pomeranz, Kenneth. 2000. *The Great Divergence: China, Europe, and the Making of the Modern Economy*. Princeton, NJ: Princeton University Press.

Ponniah, Thomas, and William F. Fisher. 2003. "Overview: Key Questions, Critical Issues." Pp. 23–9 in *Another World Is Possible: Popular Alternatives to Globalization at the World Social Forum*, edited by William F. Fisher and Thomas Ponniah. London: Zed.

Portes, Alejandro, Cristina Escobar, and Alexandria Walton Radford. 2007. "Immigrant Transnational Organizations and Development: A Comparative Study." *International Migration Review* 41:242–81.

PRB. 2007. "2007 World Population Data Sheet." Washington, DC: Population Reference Bureau.

Pritchett, Lance. 1997. "Divergence, Big Time." *Journal of Economic Perspectives* 11:3–18.

Prokopy, Joshua, and Christian Smith. 1999. "Introduction." Pp. 1–16 in *Latin American Religion in Motion*, edited by Christian Smith and Joshua Prokopy. New York: Routledge.

Pullella, Philip (Ed.). 2003. *Pope John Paul II: Reaching out across Borders*. Upper Saddle River, NJ: Reuters Prentice Hall.

Qutb, Sayyid. 1981. *Milestones*. Cedar Rapids, IA: The Mother Mosque Foundation.

Qutb, Sayyid. 2000. *Social Justice in Islam*. Oneonta, NY: Islamic Publications International.

Rahman, Fazlur. 1982. *Islam and Modernity: Transformation of an Intellectual Tradition.* Chicago, IL: University of Chicago Press.

Ramirez, Francisco O., and John Boli. 1987a. "Global Patterns of Educational Institutionalization." Pp. 150–72 in *Institutional Structure: Constituting State, Society, and the Individual,* edited by George M. Thomas. Newbury Park, CA: Sage.

Ramirez, Francisco O., and John Boli. 1987b. "The Political Construction of Mass Schooling: European Origins and Worldwide Institutionalization." *Sociology of Education* 60:2–17.

Rantanen, Terhi. 2005. *The Media and Globalization.* London: Sage.

Reitan, Ruth. 2007. *Global Activism.* London: Routledge.

Richter, Philip. 1997. "The Toronto Blessing: Charismatic Global Warming." Pp. 97–119 in *Charismatic Christianity: Sociological Perspectives,* edited by Stephen Hunt, Malcolm Hamilton, and Tony Walter. New York: St Martin's Press.

Riedel, James, Jing Jin, and Jian Gao. 2007. *How China Grows: Investment, Finance, and Reform.* Princeton, NJ: Princeton University Press.

Rieger, Elmar, and Stephan Leibfried. 2003. *Limits to Globalization: Welfare States and the World Economy.* Cambridge: Polity Press.

Righter, Robert W. 2005. *The Battle over Hetch Hetchy: America's Most Controversial Dam and the Birth of Modern Environmentalism.* Oxford: Oxford University Press.

Rimlinger, Gaston V. 1971. *Welfare Policy and Industrialization in Europe, America, and Russia.* New York: John Wiley.

Ritzer, George. 2004. *The McDonaldization of Society.* Thousand Oaks, CA: Pine Forge Press.

Ritzer, George. 2007. "Introduction." Pp. 1–13 in *The Blackwell Companion to Globalization,* edited by George Ritzer. Malden, MA: Blackwell.

Robertson, Roland. 1992. *Globalization: Social Theory and Global Culture.* London: Sage.

Robertson, Roland. 1995. "Glocalization: Time-Space and Homogeneity-Heterogeneity." Pp. 25–44 in *Global Modernities,* edited by Mike Featherstone, Scott Lash, and Roland Robertson. London: Sage.

Robertson, Robbie. 2003. *The Three Waves of Globalization: A History of a Developing Global Consciousness.* London: Zed.

Roche, Maurice. 2000. *Mega-Events and Modernity: Olympics and Expos in the Growth of Global Culture.* London: Routledge.

Rodrik, Dani. 2006. "Goodbye Washington Consensus, Hello Washington Confusion? A Review of the World Bank's *Economic Growth in the1990s: Learning from a Decade of Reform.*" *Journal of Economic Literature* 44:973–87.

Rosanvallon, Pierre. 2000. *The New Social Question: Rethinking the Welfare State.* Princeton, NJ: Princeton University Press.

Roscoe, Jane. 2004. "Watching Big Brother at Work: A Production Study of Big Brother Australia." Pp. 181–93 in *Big Brother International: Formats, Critics and Publics,* edited by Ernest Mathijs and Janet Jones. London: Wallflower Press.

Rosefsky Wickham, Carrie. 2005. "The Islamist Alternative to Globalization." Pp. 149–69 in *Religion in Global Civil Society,* edited by Mark Juergensmeyer. Oxford: Oxford University Press.

Rosenau, James N. 2000. "Governance in a Globalizing World." Pp. 181–90 in *The Global Transformations Reader: An Introduction to the Globalization Debate,* edited by David Held and Anthony McGrew. Cambridge: Polity Press.

Rosenne, Shabtai. 2005. "The Permanent Court of International Justice and the International Court of Justice." Pp. 181–240 in *The Hague: Legal Capital of the World*, edited by Peter J. Van Krieken and David McKay. The Hague: Asser Press.

Rowe, David. 2003. "Sport and the Repudiation of the Global." *International Review for the Sociology of Sport* 38:281–94.

Roy, Olivier. 2004. *Globalized Islam: The Search for a New Ummah*. New York: Columbia University Press.

Rubin, Barry (Ed.). 2007. *Political Islam: Critical Concepts in Islamic Studies* (3 vols.). New York: Routledge.

Rudolph, Susanne Hoeber. 1997. "Introduction: Religion, States, and Transnational Civil Society." Pp. 1–24 in *Transnational Religion and Fading States*, edited by Susanne Hoeber Rudolph and James Piscatori. Boulder, CO: Westview Press.

Ruggie, John Gerard. 1982. "International Regimes, Transactions, and Change: Embedded Liberalism in the Postwar Economic Order." *International Organization* 36:379–415.

Ruggie, John Gerard. 1993. "Territoriality and Beyond: Problematizing Modernity in International Relations." *International Organization* 47:139–74.

Rumford, Chris. 2007. "More Than a Game: Globalization and the Post-Westernization of World Cricket." *Global Networks* 7:202–14.

Rupp, Leila J. 1997. *Worlds of Women: The Making of an International Women's Movement*. Princeton, NJ: Princeton University Press.

Ryall, David. 2001. "The Catholic Church as a Transnational Actor." Pp. 41–58 in *Non-State Actors in World Politics*, edited by Daphné Josselin and William Wallace. Houndmills, UK: Palgrave.

Sader, Emir. 2004. "Beyond Civil Society: The Left After Porto Alegre." Pp. 248–61 in *A Movement of Movements: Is Another World Really Possible?*, edited by Tom Mertes. London: Verso.

Sala-i-Martin, Xavier. 2002. "The Disturbing 'Rise' of Global Income Inequality." *NBER Working Paper No. 8904*. National Bureau of Economic Research.

Santos, Boaventura de Sousa. 2006. *The Rise of the Global Left: The World Social Forum and Beyond*. London: Zed.

Schachter, Oscar. 1995. "The UN Legal Order: An Overview." Pp. 1–31 in *United Nations Legal Order*, vol. 1, edited by Oscar Schachter and Christopher C. Joyner. Cambridge: Cambridge University Press.

Schiller, Herbert I. 1976. *Communication and Cultural Domination*. New York: International Arts and Sciences Press.

Schiller, Herbert I. 2003 [1991]. "Not Yet the Post-Imperialist Era." Pp. 318–33 in *Media and Cultural Studies: Key Works*, edited by Meenakshi Gigi Durham and Douglas M. Kellner. Malden, MA: Blackwell.

Schofer, Evan, and John W. Meyer. 2005. "The Worldwide Expansion of Higher Education in the Twentieth Century." *American Sociological Review* 70:898–920.

Scholte, Jan Aart. 2005. *Globalization: A Critical Introduction*. New York: St Martin's Press.

Sherwin, Byron L., and Harold Kasimow (Eds.). 1999. *John Paul II and Interreligious Dialogue*. Maryknoll, NY: Orbis.

Shifman, Bette. 2005. "The Permanent Court of Arbitration." Pp. 127–80 in *The Hague: Legal Capital of the World*, edited by Peter J. Van Krieken and David McKay. The Hague: Asser Press.

Sinclair, John, Elizabeth Jacka, and Stuart Cunningham (Eds.). 1996. *New Patterns in Global Television: Peripheral Vision*. Oxford: Oxford University Press.

Sklair, Leslie. 1995. *Sociology of the Global System* (2nd edn.). London: Prentice Hall.

Skocpol, Theda. 1992. *Protecting Soldiers and Mothers: The Political Origins of Social Policy in the United States.* Cambridge, MA: Belknap Press of Harvard University Press.

Slackman, Michael. 2007. "Voices Rise in Egypt to Shield Girls from an Old Tradition." *New York Times* (September 20).

Slaughter, Anne-Marie. 2004. *A New World Order.* Princeton, NJ: Princeton University Press.

Smart, Barry. 2007. "Not Playing Around: Global Capitalism, Modern Sport and Consumer Culture." *Global Networks* 7:113–34.

Smith, Jackie. 2002. "Globalizing Resistance: The Battle of Seattle and the Future of Social Movements." Pp. 207–28 in *Globalization and Resistance: Transnational Dimensions of Social Movements,* edited by Jackie Smith and Hank Johnston. Lanham, MD: Rowman & Littlefield.

Smith, Robert C. 2006. *Mexican New York: Transnational Lives of New Immigrants.* Berkeley, CA: University of California Press.

Snyder, Margaret. 2006. "Unlikely Godmother: The UN and the Global Women's Movement." Pp. 24–50 in *Global Feminism: Transnational Women's Activism, Organizing, and Human Rights,* edited by Myra Marx Ferree and Aili Mari Tripp. New York: New York University Press.

Sobal, Jeffrey. 1999. "Food System Globalization, Eating Transformations, and Nutrition Transitions." Pp. 171–93 in *Food in Global History,* edited by Raymond Grew. Boulder, CO: Westview.

Soysal, Yasemin Nuhoglu. 1994. *Limits of Citizenship: Migrants and Postnational Membership in Europe.* Chicago, IL: University of Chicago Press.

Speth, James Gustave, and Peter M. Haas. 2006. *Global Environmental Governance.* Washington, DC: Island Press.

Stark, Jayson. 2006. "The World Is Shrinking." espn.com (posted March 19).

Stephens, John D. 2005. "Economic Internationalization and Domestic Compensation: Northwestern Europe in Comparative Perspective." Pp. 49–74 in *Globalization and the Future of the Welfare State,* edited by Miguel Glatzer and Dietrich Rueschemeyer. Pittsburgh, PA: University of Pittsburgh Press.

Stern, Nicholas. 2007. *The Economics of Climate Change: The Stern Review.* Cambridge: Cambridge University Press.

Stiglitz, Joseph E. 2002. *Globalization and Its Discontents.* New York: W. W. Norton.

Strange, Susan. 1996. *The Retreat of the State: The Diffusion of Power in the World Economy.* Cambridge: Cambridge University Press.

Streeck, Wolfgang. 1997. "Beneficial Constraints." Pp. 197–219 in *Contemporary Capitalism: The Embeddedness of Institutions,* edited by J. Rogers Hollingsworth and Robert Boyer. Cambridge: Cambridge University Press.

Sugden, John. 2002. "Network Football." Pp. 61–80 in *Power Games: A Critical Sociology of Sport,* edited by John Sugden and Alan Tomlinson. London: Routledge.

Sugden, John, and Alan Tomlinson. 1998. *FIFA and the Contest for World Football: Who Rules the Peoples' Game?* Cambridge: Polity Press.

Sutcliffe, Bob. 2004. "World Inequality and Globalization." *Oxford Review of Economic Policy* 20:15–37.

Swank, Duane. 2001. "Political Institutions and Welfare State Restructuring: The Impact of Institutions on Social Policy Change in Developed Democracies." Pp. 197–237 in *The*

New Politics of the Welfare State, edited by Paul Pierson. Oxford: Oxford University Press.

Swank, Duane. 2002. *Global Capital, Political Institutions, and Policy Change in Developed Welfare States*. Cambridge: Cambridge University Press.

Tarrow, Sidney G. 2001. "Transnational Politics: Contention and Institutions in International Politics." *Annual Review of Political Science* 4:1–20.

Tarrow, Sidney G. 2005. *The New Transnational Activism*. New York: Cambridge University Press.

Thomas, Amos Owen. 2005. *Imagi-Nations and Borderless Television: Media, Culture and Politics across Asia*. New Delhi: Sage.

Thomas, George M. 2001. "Religion in Global Civil Society." *Sociology of Religion* 62:515–33.

Thussu, Daya Kishan. 2007a. "The 'Murdochization' of News? The Case of Star TV in India." *Media, Culture and Society* 29:593–611.

Thussu, Daya Kishan. 2007b. "Mapping Global Media Flow and Contra-Flow." Pp. 1–32 in *Media on the Move: Global Flow and Contra-Flow*, edited by Daya Kishan Thussu. London: Routledge.

Tibi, Bassam. 2002. *The Challenge of Fundamentalism: Political Islam and the New World Disorder*. Berkeley, CA: University of California Press.

Timmons, Heather. 2008. "Bollywood Goes to Hollywood, With Some Tinsel of Its Own." *New York Times* (June 23).

Tomich, Dale W. 1990. *Slavery in the Circuit of Sugar: Martinique and the World Economy, 1830–1848*. Baltimore, MD: Johns Hopkins University Press.

Traub, James. 2006. *The Best Intentions: Kofi Annan and the UN in the Era of American World Power*. New York: Farrar, Straus and Giroux.

Tripp, Aili Mari. 2006. "The Evolution of Transnational Feminisms: Consensus, Conflict, and New Dynamics." Pp. 51–75 in *Global Feminism: Transnational Women's Activism, Organizing, and Human Rights*, edited by Myra Marx Ferree and Aili Mari Tripp. New York: New York University Press.

Tyrrell, Heather. 1999. "Bollywood versus Hollywood: Battle of the Dream Factories." Pp. 260–73 in *Culture and Global Change*, edited by Tracey Skelton and Tim Allen. London: Routledge.

UN. 1999. *The Fall of Srebrenica (Report of the Secretary-General)*. New York: UN General Assembly.

UN. 2006. *Human Development Report 2006*. New York: UN.

UN. 2007. *Human Development Report 2007/2008. Fighting Climate Change: Human Solidarity in a Divided World*. New York: UN.

UN. 2007MDG. *The Millennium Development Goals Report*. New York: UN.

UNESCO. 2005a. "International Flow of Selected Goods and Services, 1994–2003: Defining and Capturing the Flows of Cultural Trade." Montreal: UNESCO Institute for Statistics.

UNESCO. 2005b. *Education Trends in Perspective: Analysis of the World Education Indicators*. Montreal: UNESCO Institute for Statistics.

Ungar, Sheldon. 1998. "Bringing the Issue Back In: Comparing the Marketability of the Ozone Hole and Global Warming." *Social Problems* 45:510–27.

UNICEF. 2008. *The State of the World's Children 2008*. New York: UNICEF.

Van Bottenburg, Maarten. 2001. *Global Games*. Urbana, IL: University of Illinois Press.

Van Cuilenburg, Jan, and Denis McQuail. 2003. "Media Policy Paradigm Shifts: Towards a New Communications Policy Paradigm." *European Journal of Communication* 18:181–207.

Van Krieken, Peter J., and David McKay. 2005. *The Hague: Legal Capital of the World*. The Hague: Asser Press.

Varg, Paul A. 1958. *Missionaries, Chinese, and Diplomats: The American Protestant Missionary Movement in China, 1890–1952*. Princeton, NJ: Princeton University Press.

Vázquez, Manuel A., and Marie Friedmann Marquardt. 2003. *Globalizing the Sacred: Religion across the Americas*. New Brunswick, NJ: Rutgers University Press.

Velho, Otávio. 1997. "Globalization: Object, Perspective, Horizon." Pp. 98–125 in *Cultural Pluralism, Identity, and Globalization*, edited by Luiz E. Soares. Rio de Janeiro: UNESCO.

Vertovec, Steven. 2004. "Migrant Transnationalism and Modes of Transformation." *International Migration Review* 38:970–1001.

Vogler, John. 1995. *The Global Commons: A Regime Analysis*. Chichester, UK: John Wiley.

Voigtländer, Nico, and Hans-Joachim Voth. 2006. "Why England? Demographic Factors, Structural Change and Physical Capital Accumulation during the Industrial Revolution." *Journal of Economic Growth* 11:319–61.

Vreeland, Hamilton, Jr. 1917. *Hugo Grotius: The Father of the Modern Science of International Law*. New York: Oxford University Press.

Wade, Robert H. 2004. "Is Globalization Reducing Poverty and Inequality?" *World Development* 32:567–89.

Waldinger, Roger. 2007. *Between Here and There: How Attached Are Latino Immigrants to Their Native Country?* Washington, DC: Pew Hispanic Center.

Waldinger, Roger, and David Fitzgerald. 2004. "Transnationalism in Question." *American Journal of Sociology* 109:1177–95.

Wallerstein, Immanuel. 1974. *The Modern World-System: Capitalist Agriculture and the Origins of the European World-Economy in the Sixteenth Century*. New York: Academic Press.

Wallerstein, Immanuel. 2004. *World-System Analysis: An Introduction*. Durham, NC: Duke University Press.

Wapner, Paul. 1996. *Environmental Activism and World Civic Politics*. Albany, NY: State University of New York Press.

Waters, Malcolm. 2001. *Globalization*. New York: Routledge.

Watson, James L. 1997a. "McDonald's in Hong Kong: Consumerism, Dietary Change, and the Rise of a Children's Culture." Pp. 77–109 in *Golden Arches East: McDonald's in East Asia*, edited by James L. Watson. Stanford, CA: Stanford University Press.

Watson, James L. 1997b. "Introduction: Transnationalism, Localization, and Fast Foods in East Asia." Pp. 1–38 in *Golden Arches East: McDonald's in East Asia*, edited by James L. Watson. Stanford, CA: Stanford University Press.

WCED [World Commission on Environment and Development]. 1987. *Our Common Future*. Oxford: Oxford University Press.

Weart, Spencer R. 2003. *The Discovery of Global Warming*. Cambridge, MA: Harvard University Press.

Weigel, George. 1992. *The Final Revolution: The Resistance Church and the Collapse of Communism*. New York: Oxford University Press.

Westney, D. Eleanor. 1987. *Imitation and Innovation: The Transfer of Western Organizational Patterns to Meiji Japan*. Cambridge, MA: Harvard University Press.

Willetts, Peter (Ed.). 1996. "*The Conscience of the World*": *The Influence of Non-Governmental Organisations in the UN System*. Washington, DC: Brookings Institution.

Williams, Carol J. 2008. "Roots of Haiti's Food Crisis Run Deep." *Los Angeles Times* (May 13).

Williamson, John (Ed.). 1990. *Latin American Adjustment: How Much Has It Happened?* Washington, DC: Institute for International Economics.

Wilson, Chris. 2001. "On the Scale of Global Demographic Convergence 1950–2000." *Population and Development Review* 27:155–71.

Winner, David. 2001. *Brilliant Orange: The Neurotic Genius of Dutch Football*. London: Bloomsbury.

Wittenberg, Dick. 2007. "Wie een Fiets Heeft, Is de Rijkste Man." *NRC Handelsblad* (April 23).

World Bank. 2007GDF. *Global Development Finance 2007*. Washington, DC: World Bank.

World Bank. 2007GEP. *Global Economic Prospects: Managing the Next Wave of Globalization*. Washington, DC: World Bank.

World Bank. 2007GMR. *Global Monitoring Report 2007*. Washington, DC: World Bank.

World Bank. 2007WDI. *World Development Indicators 2007*. Washington, DC: World Bank.

World Bank. 2008a. *International Comparison Program : Tables of Final Results*. Washington, DC: World Bank.

World Bank. 2008b. *World Development Indicators 2008*. Washington, DC: World Bank.

Wright, Lawrence. 2008. "The Rebellion Within: An Al Qaeda Mastermind Questions Terrorism." *New Yorker* (June 2).

WSF. 2001a. "Porto Alegre Call for Mobilisation." Porto Alegre: World Social Forum.

WSF. 2001b. "World Social Forum Charter of Principles." São Paolo: World Social Forum.

Wu, Jinglian. 2005. *Understanding and Interpreting Chinese Economic Reform*. Mason, OH: Thomson/South-Western.

Yan, Yunxiang. 1997. "McDonald's in Beijing: The Localization of Americana." Pp. 39–76 in *Golden Arches East: McDonald's in East Asia*, edited by James L. Watson. Stanford, CA: Stanford University Press.

Yearley, Steven. 2005. *Cultures of Environmentalism: Empirical Studies in Environmental Sociology*. New York: Palgrave Macmillan.

Zlotnik, Hania. 2004. "Population Growth and International Migration." Pp. 15–34 in *International Migration: Prospects and Policies in a Global Market*, edited by Douglas S. Massey and J. Edward Taylor. Oxford: Oxford University Press.

Zlotnik, Hania. 2006. "The Dimensions of Migration in Africa." Pp. 15–37 in *Africa on the Move: African Migration and Urbanisation in Comparative Perspective*, edited by Marta Tienda, Sally Findley, Stephen Tollman, and Eleanor Preston-Whyte. Johannesburg: Wits University Press.

Zöllner, Detlev. 1982. "Germany." Pp. 1–92 in *The Evolution of Social Insurance 1881–1981*, edited by Peter A. Köhler and Hans F. Zacher. London: Frances Pinter.

INDEX